Public Space Unbound

Through an exploration of emancipation in capitalist urbanization, this book argues *the political* is enacted through the everyday practices of publics producing space. This suggests democracy is a spatial practice *rather than* an abstract professional field organized by institutions, politicians and movements.

Public Space Unbound brings together a cross-disciplinary group of scholars to examine spaces, conditions and circumstances in which emancipatory practices impact the everyday life of citizens. We ask: How do emancipatory mo(ve)ments relate with public space under 'post-political conditions'? In a time when democracy, solidarity and utopias are in crisis, we argue that productive emancipatory claims already exist in the lived space of everyday life rather than in the expectation of urban revolution and future progress.

Sabine Knierbein is Associate Professor for Urban Culture and Public Space and the Director of the Interdisciplinary Centre for Urban Culture and Public Space, Faculty of Architecture and Planning, TU Wien, Austria. Her research foci are theory of urbanization, critique of everyday life, planning theory and civic innovation. She is the editor of *Public Space and the Challenges of Urban Transformation in Europe* (2014), *Public Space and Relational Perspectives* (2015) and *City Unsilenced* (2017).

Tihomir Viderman is an architect and planner, currently affiliated with the Interdisciplinary Centre for Urban Culture and Public Space of TU Wien, Austria. For a number of years, he has been engaged in interdisciplinary research and teaching, focusing on culturally inclusive and locally embedded approaches. He is particularly interested in how the expression of cultural difference is modulated by professionals in lived space.

Routledge Research in Planning and Urban Design

Routledge Research in Planning and Urban Design is a series of academic monographs for scholars working in these disciplines and the overlaps between them. Building on Routledge's history of academic rigour and cutting-edge research, the series contributes to the rapidly expanding literature in all areas of planning and urban design.

www.routledge.com/Routledge-Research-in-Planning-and-Urban-Design/book-series/RRPUD

Public Space Unbound

Urban Emancipation and the
Post-Political Condition

**Edited by Sabine Knierbein
and Tihomir Viderman**

Routledge
Taylor & Francis Group

NEW YORK AND LONDON

First published 2018
by Routledge
711 Third Avenue, New York, NY 10017

and by Routledge
2 Park Square, Milton Park, Abingdon, Oxon, OX14 4RN

Routledge is an imprint of the Taylor & Francis Group, an informa business

© 2018 Sabine Knierbein and Tihomir Viderman

The right of Sabine Knierbein and Tihomir Viderman to be identified as the authors of the editorial material, and of the authors for their individual chapters, has been asserted in accordance with sections 77 and 78 of the Copyright, Designs and Patents Act 1988.

Library of Congress Cataloging-in-Publication Data
Names: Knierbein, Sabine, 1977– editor. | Viderman, Tihomir, editor.
Title: Public space unbound : urban emancipation and the post-political condition / edited by Sabine Knierbein and Tihomir Viderman.
Description: New York : Routledge, 2018. | Series: Routledge research in planning and urban design | Includes bibliographical references and index.
Identifiers: LCCN 2017050369 (print) | LCCN 2017050667 (ebook) | ISBN 9781315449203 (ebook) | ISBN 9781138213098 (hardback : alk. paper)
Subjects: LCSH: Public spaces—Social aspects. | Public spaces—Political aspects. | Architecture and society.
Classification: LCC HT185 (ebook) | LCC HT185 .P835 2018 (print) | DDC 720.1/03—dc23
LC record available at https://lccn.loc.gov/2017050369

ISBN: 978-1-138-21309-8 (hbk)
ISBN: 978-1-315-44920-3 (ebk)

Typeset in Sabon
by Apex CoVantage, LLC

MIX
Paper from
responsible sources
FSC   FSC™ C013985

Printed in the United Kingdom
by Henry Ling Limited

Contents

Figures

Tables

Contributors

Serjara Aleman is a PhD candidate in Anthropology at the University of Lausanne, Switzerland, and grantee of the Swiss National Science Foundation. In her thesis, she explores the emancipatory potential of urban art for women in Lima, Peru.

Evangelia Athanassiou is Associate Professor in Urban Planning and the Environment at the School of Architecture, Aristotle University of Thessaloniki, Greece. She studied in Thessaloniki, York and Edinburgh. Current research interests include critical approaches to urban sustainability, formal policies and citizen-led initiatives regarding public space, with special reference to Greece.

Charis Christodoulou has worked as a professional architect and urban designer consulting with local authorities for almost 20 years. She is Assistant Professor at the School of Architecture, Aristotle University of Thessaloniki, Greece. Her research focuses on landscapes of sprawl, public space, urban processes and the socio-spatial transformations of Greek cities.

Barbara Dellwo is a PhD candidate in Social Sciences at the University of Lausanne, Switzerland. Her research is part of the project '(In)visible Islam in the City' (directed by Monika Salzbrunn and funded by the Swiss National Science Foundation) and concerns transnational elites of Muslim background in the Lake Geneva area.

Gabriella Esposito De Vita, PhD in Regional Sciences and Urban Planning, is a senior researcher at the National Research Council (CNR-Italy). She coordinates projects on policy design for urban regeneration and cultural heritage valorization. She has taught urban planning since 1998 and received the qualification of Associate Professor in 2014.

Lukas Franta is a doctorate candidate at TU Wien, Austria, at the Centre of Sociology at the Department of Spatial Planning. His research focuses on the relation of contentious politics and urban space in the post-democratic city with special attention to governance of resistance in European cities.

Angelika Gabauer is a political scientist whose primary focus is the field of political theory and its interface with urban studies. She currently works at the Interdisciplinary Centre for Urban Culture and Public Space at

TU Wien, Austria. Her interests include research on democracy, social movements, (urban) space and planning theory.

Alexander Hamedinger is Associate Professor at TU Wien, Austria; he is head of the Centre of Sociology at the Department of Spatial Planning. His research foci are urban and regional governance, social inequality and space, urban sociology, planning theory and sustainable urban development.

Jeffrey Hou is Professor of Landscape Architecture and Adjunct Professor of Urban Design and Planning at the University of Washington, Seattle, USA. His work focuses on community design, civic engagement and public space and democracy, with an emphasis on the engagement of marginalized social groups in planning, design and placemaking.

Matina Kapsali is a PhD candidate in Urban Planning at the Aristotle University of Thessaloniki, Greece. Her research interests include urban commoning, democratic politics, urban governance, participatory urbanism and housing. She holds an MSc in Global Urban Development and Planning (University of Manchester, UK) and a PG Diploma in Architecture (AUTh).

Maria Karagianni is a PhD candidate in Urban Planning at the Aristotle University of Thessaloniki, Greece. Her research interests include urban environmental politics, the urban commons, public space and housing. She holds an MSc in Global Urban Development and Planning (University of Manchester, UK) and a PG Diploma in Architecture (AUTh).

Sabine Knierbein is Associate Professor for Urban Culture and Public Space and the Director of the Interdisciplinary Centre for Urban Culture and Public Space, Faculty of Architecture and Planning, TU Wien, Austria. Her research foci are theory of urbanization, critique of everyday life, planning theory, and civic and open innovation.

Kanerva Kuokkanen is a political scientist and a postdoctoral researcher at the Swedish School of Social Science, University of Helsinki, Finland. She has written her PhD thesis on urban participatory projects. Her main fields of interest are citizen participation, policy analysis, governance and the 'projectification' of public policies.

Christine Mady is Assistant Professor in Urban Planning, Urban Design and Architecture at Ramez Chagoury Faculty of Architecture, Arts and Design at the Notre Dame University–Louaize, Lebanon. Her research interests include public space and social integration, temporary urban uses, heritage landscapes and planning for social infrastructure.

Stijn Oosterlynck is Associate Professor in Urban Sociology at the University of Antwerp, Belgium. He is the chair of the Centre for Inequality, Poverty, Social Exclusion and the City (OASeS) and the Antwerp Urban Studies Institute. His research focuses on the political sociology of urban development and planning.

Emilia Palonen is Senior Lecturer in Political Science at the University of Helsinki, Finland, with a PhD in Ideology and Discourse Analysis, Essex. An expert on populism and urban symbolic politics, she explores forms of democracy and representation practically and theoretically. Since 2013, she conducts action research on local participatory planning processes.

Stefania Ragozino is a PhD researcher with the National Research Council of Italy, IRISS Institute (Naples). She is interested in public spaces and operational tools for urban regeneration. She is active member of the AESOP Thematic Group Public Space and Urban Culture working in Self-Organized Management Network for the Public Relations.

Paula Rosa, PhD, is Professor of Sociology at Faculty of Social Sciences of the University of Buenos Aires, Argentina, a lecturer at the National University of San Martín, Argentina, and a research associate at the National Council for Scientific and Technical Research (CONICET) since 2013.

Monika Salzbrunn, PhD, is Professor of Religion, Migration and Diaspora Studies at the University of Lausanne, Switzerland. She holds an ERC grant on ARTIVISM, Art and Activism and is the principal investigator of several projects, notably '(In)visible Islam in the City: Material and Immaterial Expressions' (Swiss National Science Foundation).

Rob Shields's work spans architecture, planning and urban sociology. He is an award-winning author and co-editor, including 'Places on the Margin', 'City-Regions in Prospect' and 'Spatial Questions'. He directs participatory research on infrastructure, innovation and place at the City Region Studies Centre at University of Alberta, Canada. See www.ualberta.ca/~rshields.

Gilbert Siame is a lecturer and researcher in the Department of Geography and Environmental Studies at the University of Zambia, where he also directs the Centre for Urban Research and Planning. He holds master's and PhD degrees from the University of Cape Town, South Africa.

Amila Širbegović is an architect in Vienna, where she works, teaches and researches at the intersection of urban planning, migration and production of space with a focus on transdisciplinary approaches. As part of her work for the Viennese Office for City Renewal, she develops and initiates community participatory projects.

Elisabet Van Wymeersch is a PhD candidate in Urban Development and Spatial planning at the University of Antwerp, Belgium, Faculty of Design Sciences. Her research is concerned with the transformative potential of urban planning conflicts.

Andrea Varriale is a PhD researcher at the Bauhaus University of Weimar, Germany. His research analyzes occupations, social movements and politics in contemporary Naples. He has been teaching in urban studies in Weimar

(2013–2016) and since 2016 works as an assistant in Human Geography at the Europa-Universität Flensburg.

Tihomir Viderman is an architect and planner. For a number of years, he has been engaged in research and teaching, focusing on culturally inclusive and locally embedded approaches to working with lived urban space. He is particularly interested in how the expression of cultural difference is modulated by professionals.

Regina Vidosa is a PhD candidate at the Centre for Urban and Regional Studies (CEUR-CONICET) and a lecturer in Political Economy at the University of Buenos Aires, Argentina. She is pursuing a dual PhD degree in Urban Regional Studies, a cooperation between the National University of Cordoba, Argentina and the Bauhaus-Universität Weimar, Germany.

Vanessa Watson is Professor of City Planning at the University of Cape Town, South Africa, where she is also a Fellow. She holds degrees, including a PhD, from South African universities and the Architectural Association of London and is on the Executive Committee of the African Centre for Cities.

Japhy Wilson is a lecturer in International Political Economy at the University of Manchester, UK. His research explores the entanglement of ideology and materiality in the transformation of social reality under conditions of global capitalism. He has published widely in the fields of human geography, political economy, critical theory and development studies.

Burcu Yigit Turan is Assistant Professor at the Swedish University of Agricultural Sciences, Sweden, Department of Urban and Rural Development, Division of Landscape Architecture in Uppsala. Her recent works have focused on cultural landscapes of planetary urbanism and emancipatory planning and design practices in critical cultural and ecological contexts.

Acknowledgments

The starting point for this book was a summer school titled *Designing places of emancipation? Aiming to understand and change the social world through participation, action and research in public space* led jointly by Sabine Knierbein, Tihomir Viderman and colleagues in Vienna in 2014. The weeklong exchange brought together 60 scholars and students from Austria, Belgium, Bulgaria, Canada, Croatia, France, Germany, Israel, Italy, Japan, Poland, Russia, Slovenia, Turkey, Serbia, Switzerland and the United States in Vienna's 21st district, Floridsdorf. Conceived as an international and cross-disciplinary research and teaching programme, the summer school explored and reflected upon contemporary emancipatory practices in cities around the world. The event was structured around five themes: (1) Beyond participatory discourse and process; (2) Between emancipatory practices and everyday life; (3) The material, the mental and the lived space; (4) Cultural practices creating alternative values and (5) Between everyday life and scientific insights. Based on experiential approaches to reinterpret and question the notion of emancipation in the design and planning fields, the event provided an opportunity for extensive discussions on the emancipatory potential of collective urban actions. This context revealed possibilities for discussing the post-political and its discontents through recent approaches in planning theory and political theory; such an approach would allow for the exploration of issues and possibilities for contemporary urban emancipation and public space.

This book is also part of an ongoing pedagogical experiment at the Interdisciplinary Centre for Urban Culture and Public Space (http://skuor. tuwien.ac.at) at the Department of Spatial Planning, Faculty of Architecture and Planning, TU Wien (Austria). Directed by Sabine Knierbein, the centre is an interdepartmental institution, funded by the City of Vienna (2008–2018) to undertake innovative curriculum developments in planning and architecture schools and to broaden the skills of future professionals in the field. This exceptional initiative came about between 2008 and 2018 as Vienna's governmental and university institutions entered into a partnership out of recognition of the need to reinforce the link between planning and architectural education, social needs, cultural demands and related policy fields.

The financial support of the Vienna City Administration has enabled the founding of Visiting Professorships and inauguration of a series of international and transdisciplinary explorations, in the forms of educational training (summer schools, graduate and post-graduate teaching modules, participatory action research) and public events (lectures, symposia and conferences). Each year has been dedicated to a specific theme, and the activities have been co-designed with the annually invited international visiting professors. The themes and invited scholars include civil society, culture and conflict (Thomas Sieverts and Chiara Tornaghi, 2009); state, politics and planning (Ali Madanipour and Aglaée Degros, 2010); markets, economy and innovation (Sophie Watson and Tore Dobberstein, 2011); resources, aesthetics and materiality (Maria Kaika, 2012); knowledge, education and difference (Jeffrey Hou, 2013); ways of life, everyday life and insights (Rob Shields and Elke Krasny, 2014); past(s), urban peace and the welfare state (Nikolai Roskamm, 2015); present(s), urban solidarity and European crises (Sybille Frank, 2016); and future(s), urban equity and the global agenda (Ed Wall, 2017).

We would like to thank all our colleagues and friends for the rigorous discussions on public space and urban emancipation that challenge the 'post-political' conditions. In particular, we would like to thank participants of educational activities at TU Wien and various sessions of the Association for European Schools of Planning (AESOP) Thematic Group on Public Spaces and Urban Cultures, particularly the 'Unstable Geographies—Dislocated Publics' Meetings in Porto, Beirut, Vienna, Ljubljana and Lisbon (2015–2017). The thinking behind this volume has also benefitted from discussion at a number of events, including the AESOP Young Academic Conference in Munich 2017, the Unsettled Conference 2017 at TU Wien and the AESOP Annual Conference 2017 in Lisbon, Portugal.

A number of individuals and organizations have made the publication of this book possible. Specifically, the City of Vienna Visiting Professorship Programme where the summer school project has been integrated as research-led teaching endeavour made possible by the generous support of the Administrative Group for Urban Development, Traffic and Transport, Climate Protection, Energy and Public Participation, City of Vienna, and by the Faculty of Architecture and Planning and the related Department of Spatial Planning, at TU Wien. The Vienna Science and Technology Funds (WWTF) provided a major portion of the budget to host the summer school as part of the funding programme 'Public Spaces in Transition 2013'. The summer school additionally benefitted from material support by different institutions at TU Wien: the Vice Rectorate for Research and the Vice Rectorate for Academic Affairs and the Department for Spatial Planning. It has been designated a pioneering project of the 'Urban Future Lab' based at the Faculty of Architecture and Planning of the same university.

The summer school project included the realization of transdisciplinary field research in which local NGOs (non-governmental organizations), NPOs (not-for-profit organizations), activists and residents have been involved as much as the international students, keynote speakers and members of the Thematic Group for Public Spaces and Urban Cultures of the Association of European Schools of Planning (AESOP TG PSUC). We are also grateful for several colleagues that have worked with us in various educational activities contributing to this work: Emanuela Semlitsch, Theresa Schütz, Angelika Gabauer, Anna Vukan, Rudolf Scheuvens and Nina Mayerhofer, as well as a number of individuals from local associations and institutions in Vienna who also contributed to the programme. We also wish to thank the keynote speakers of the summer school Jeffrey Hou (University of Washington, Seattle, USA), Rob Shields (University of Edmonton, Canada), Burcu Yigit Turan (Swedish University of Agricultural Sciences, Uppsala), Anton Lederer (Rotor Graz, Austria), and Anja Steglich and Angela Million (TU Berlin, Germany).

We owe sincere acknowledgements to the European mentors at the summer school: Marianita Palumbo and Olivier Boucheron (France), Gabriella Esposito De Vita (Italy), Branimir Rajčič, Dafne Berc, Bojan Mucko and Iva Marčetić (Croatia), as well as the local activists and NGOs in Vienna: Gemeinsame Landwirtschaft Wilde Rauke (Pete Belcher), IGL Marchfeld (Helmut Bauer, Lukas MrozGoals), CIT Collective (Iver Ohm), Laboratoire Dérive (Elke Rauth) and Spacelab Umwelt (Monika Rinner).

We also wish to thank the anonymous reviewers and the colleagues that have provided comments to earlier versions of our chapters, in particular to Elina Kränzle for chapter 1. Elisabet Van Wymeersch and Stijn Oosterlynck acknowledge that chapter 3 benefitted from a presentation at the AESOP symposium 'Moving beyond conflict in planning: towards a critical consensus politics?' at the Centre for Urban Research at RMIT University in Barcelona, 16–17 June 2016. Their research is funded by a Dehousse bursary, granted by the University of Antwerp. Gabriella Esposito De Vita wishes to thank the interviewees for their generous availability and valuable insights for her work in chapter 4. Special thanks to the Pol.I.S. Foundation (Integrated policies for security for the innocent victims of crime and confiscated assets) and to the NPO L'Orsa maggiore for hosting author's fieldwork. Relating to chapter 6, Jeffrey Hou would like to express his sincere thanks to Kang-Oh Lee of Seoul Green Trust for providing the detailed information on the case of Mullae rooftop garden, and to Minsoo Doo for translation. The authors of chapter 7 would like to thank the Swedish School of Social Science at the University of Helsinki, the Finnish Cultural Foundation and the research project ProDem funded by the Academy of Finland for providing funding for research on the Citizen Channel project, and the people of Maunula for active engagement in the planning of the new library, civic education unit and youth centre. They are grateful for the trust invested in them to represent and moderate. Officials from the City of Helsinki are acknowledged for deep cooperation, city decision-makers for funding the multifunction public building, and the many people who have been actively supporting, encouraging and taking part in the public work. Additional thanks go to University of Helsinki and to authors' families for supporting their research in 2012–2016. For chapter 8, Monika Salzbrunn, Barbara Dellwo and Serjara Aleman thank the Swiss National Science Foundation for financing the project '(In)visible Islam in the city: material and immaterial expressions of Muslim practices within urban spaces in Switzerland', and express their acknowledgment to the organizers and participants of "La Grande Table" in Morges for sharing their experiences with them. The author of chapter 12 acknowledges Ian Banerjee for the English translation of the chapter's first draft. Concerning chapter 13, Christine Mady would like to thank NAHNOO for their time spent in interviews, in responding to various questions regarding Horsh Beirut, and for providing her with visual material from their archives. Chapter 14 was developed within the research scheme 'Place-based strategies and policies for local development' coordinated by the Italian National Research Council, IRISS Institute. Its authors are grateful to all interviewees for their time.

Finally, we wish to thank Andrew Prindle and Sally Parker for language review and indexing work. Sabine Knierbein would like to thank Tihomir Viderman for formally editing the book. Without their competent editorial work this book would not have come to fruition.

The summer school project has been documented online: http://skuor. tuwien.ac.at/en/veranstaltungen/sommer-school/summerschool.

As urban emancipation could not have happened without the visible and invisible actions of numerous activists and engaged publics in different corners of the world, this book is dedicated to their struggles, resourcefulness and determination.

Introduction

1 Space, Emancipation and Post-Political Urbanization

Sabine Knierbein and Tihomir Viderman

Aims of This Book

Debates over emancipation have not always been explicitly included in the planning and design discourses. Yet, emancipatory thinking has increasingly been providing valuable impetus to both urban research and practice ever since linkages between emancipation and the city have been affirmed in the philosophical foundations of social sciences (Marx 1844; Weber 1978 [1924]). Throughout the 20th century, a series of emancipatory struggles and attending scientific debates realized the liberatory potential of urban spaces as grounds for opportunity and possibility, cosmopolitanism and freedom from a multitude of political, cultural, social and economic constraints (Lees 2004). Emancipatory movements have involved almost all social identity constructs and social structures, including labour, gender, ethnicity, ecology, peace, freedom and justice. In recent years, emancipatory struggles have predominantly taken place as a critique of different local forms of (neo)liberalization. Struggles for rights and equality have shaped not only institutional politics at various scales, but also the symbolic order of our cities. In particular, Lefebvre's (1968) claim for the "right to the city" has found global resonance with professionals, cultural producers and activists over the past few decades who engage in planning and designing urban spaces. Lefebvre's claim has been broadly adopted as a leitmotif of theoretical and practical endeavours against dispossession, displacement and exclusion.

Urban studies situate emancipatory mo(ve)ments in the history of capitalist urbanization. Urban movements, predominantly understood as constituted around a collective political idea(l), have been studied to understand how certain symbolic and social orders have emerged, and how insurgent publics have influenced trajectories of urbanization. However, emancipation seems to preserve its ambiguous meaning for a broad portion of the social and political scientific communities, as well as the design and planning disciplines. Much of the contemporary debate in political theory tends to refrain from spatializing emancipatory praxis, while attempts at transferring political thought to the fields of urban studies and planning theory (Roskamm

2017; Metzger et al. 2014), with the exception of Swyngedouw (2015), tend to circumvent explicitly dealing with emancipation.

This book consolidates a variety of approaches to emancipation in relation to capitalist urbanization. Thereby, we seek to:

(1) *carve out an unambiguous working definition* for *emancipation on its own terms* that is attentive to both its radical political meaning and experiences of planning and design professionals;
(2) *advance an understanding* of the conceptual role *of emancipation as an interface between* different *key concepts in urban theory*;
(3) *identify spatial relations and affective geographies* of emancipatory mo(ve)ments, processes and practices within *capitalist urbanization*.

Emancipation, if systematically reviewed, is often not used on its own terms, but rather serves as a mechanism, means or bridge aligning with other concepts relevant for urban theory:

- forms of innovative *self-organization* and *self-management*;
- struggles *for equality and equity* and *against structural patterns of inequality*;
- articulations to *renew democracy* through *utopian praxis and action*;
- *attempts to overcome gridlocked ways of thinking* when conceiving relations between space, society and urbanization;
- calls for *liberation from oppressive constraints*, pointing to the fact that power relations are immanent in all types of social relations.

This book sets out to sketch a way forward in understanding the need for critique and revision of emancipation through empirical, conceptual and methodological approaches.

Whose Emancipation?

Karl Marx (1844) distinguished between *political emancipation* and *social or human emancipation*.[1] *Political emancipation* primarily concerns the relation between the individual and the state: the pursuit of equal access to political decision-making in a modern state against the conditions of oppressive social relations. It is achieved when everyone is treated equally under the law of the state. In political emancipation, the "state is the intermediary between [hu]man and a [hu]man's freedom . . . to whom [a hu]man transfers all [their] non-divinity and all [their] *human unconstraint*" (*Ibid.*, original emphasis). This process has further been reinforced by the introduction of state bureaucracy. Emancipated individuals adhere to the rule of law, which in return protects their individual freedoms, offering individuals to "do everything which does not harm others" (*Ibid.*). Marx admits that "in the existing world order", i.e. capitalism, "political emancipation is . . . a big step forward" (*Ibid.*). Yet, he also expresses the idea that "real practical emancipation" might go beyond a reduced version of political emancipation towards full social emancipation (*Ibid.*). Criticism was directed against bourgeois aspects of the emancipatory project, which separate political and social power(s). The wider social striving for emancipation came to a halt when many people had been granted rights to vote, even though the material living conditions of all members of the society had not changed for better. For Marx, social emancipation can only be accomplished through individual de-alienation. This is achieved when "man re-absorbs in himself the abstract citizen" and turns again into "a *species-being* in his everyday life" (*Ibid.*, original emphasis). Thereby, people recognize and organize their "'own powers' as social powers" including the separation between social powers and themselves, a separation previously resulting from political emancipation (cf. *Ibid.*). In this sense, (social) emancipation cannot be prescribed to another person, but starts from within a person, collective, group, public, milieu or class.

Marx's argument has been taken up in more recent thought when claiming the need for emancipation in processes of global urbanization. Here, social emancipation is a guarantor for political emancipation, whereas political emancipation does not automatically provide social emancipation (cf. Merrifield 2006: 114). Differentiations between political and social emancipation can be transferred to current debates in planning theory that make similar distinctions. As Purcell (2009) outlines, present liberal democracies have been based on an unsolved tension between *political equality* and *social inequality*. These have been explained by frequent shortcomings of liberal democracies to overstress freedom and underemphasize equality (Mouffe 2000, Gabauer, this volume).[2] In this sense, emancipatory struggle is unavailing for social suffering associated with lived experiences of exclusion, marginalization or inequality (Bourdieu 1984).

Cities as Liberating Ground?

Overcoming aporias and pitfalls related to unfulfilled utopian promises of social equality requires to address shifting relations and responsibilities between cities and nation states to conceptualize new, innovative and prototypical forms of urban citizenship in post-migrational societies (Blockland et al. 2012; Yildiz and Hill 2015). This perspective radically challenges the idea of national citizenship and nation-oriented legal status. Thereby it seeks to reconnect social emancipation with revised ideas about political emancipation. This corresponds with Lees's (cf. 2004: 5) emphasis on the initial concept of *civitas*[3] which significantly related the body of people to the city rather than their place, settlement type or institutional status.

A close link between the city, citizenship and emancipation, however, might bear the risk of essentializing and territorialising emancipatory praxis as bound to *urban* space. Taking on Weber's analysis of the Northern European city of the Middle Ages as place of emancipation, Siebel (2004) relates to the sociopolitical dimension of emancipation when coining the cities as birth-places of the *Wirtschaftsbürger* (capitalist bourgeois), the *citoyens* who have freed themselves from feudalist rule and politically emancipate themselves to perform in the self-organization of towns and cities as free citizens ('City air liberates!'). Siebel (cf. 2004: 11ff) designates the ideal-type European city as the breeding ground for Western modernity and emancipation from which rationalism, capitalism and bureaucracy have developed. For him, "Euro-pean urban history is emancipation history" (*Ibid.*: 13),[4] a history showing that urban dwellers can liberate themselves from political, economic and social constraints. While Siebel's account has been criticized for its inher-ent Eurocentric, paternalist and implicit colonialist underpinnings, he uses emancipation to carve out an ideal-type of the city as a utopian project. This goes along with what Lees (2004: 6) identifies as the double-edged quality of urban emancipation meandering between the real and the ideal city. Simi-larly, Amin and Thrift (2004: 231–232) are cautious about attempts that establish a relation between cities and emancipation over strictly territorial dimensions:

> The common thread . . . is the interpretation of the political through the city: the urban is the formative arena of both the 'major' politics of grand schemes and protest movements and the 'minor' politics of every-day struggle and discontent.
>
> (*Ibid.*: 231–232)

The authors have strong doubts regarding:

> how far the contemporary city even remotely resembles this understand-ing of a politics ventured by and through the urban. . . . The political can no longer (if it ever could) be collapsed into a simple notion of the territorial. . . . What then remains of the urban in the politics of emancipation?
>
> (*Ibid.*)

Emancipation and Urbanization

This book does not situate emancipation in the static space of the ideal(ized) city. On the contrary, it takes on the challenge of revisiting the relation between *emancipation and urbanization* as dynamic and mutually inter-twined processes producing space. Spaces in which traces of urbanization occur are not reducible to prototypical cities or urban spaces. Neverthe-less, the density in which urbanization processes unfold may better cor-relate with where social centralities prevail, that is, in cities. According to Lefebvre (2003 [1970]), urbanization processes are key vehicles that spatially catalyze growth, competition and alienation. Simultaneously, they are characterized by continuous attempts of urban societies to self-organize through acts of resistance as part of their endeavour towards human emancipation and meaningful lives (*Ibid.*). Also, critics of the destructive and fragmenting features of urbanization have repeatedly uttered warnings: Ceceña (2008: 12), for instance, indicates the sheer need and relevance of contemporary liberating moments since

> capitalism has arrived at a level of ecological and social destruction, at a level of humanitarian disaster from which—to paraphrase Rosa Luxemburg— we need to opt between emancipation or catastrophe, between emancipation or the eradication of the species . . . The struggle is for life.
> (Ceceña 2008: 12, see also Wilson, this volume)

Global processes of urbanization accrete locally in manifold ways, (contributing to) instituting a specific, contingent social order, which in turn is continuously contested by insurgent publics agonistically engaging in struggles for political possibilities along plural identity lines (Swyngedouw 2015). Such places of political struggle are scrutinized as a terrain "in which two heterogeneous processes collide: that one of government in an almost Foucauldian sense of governmentality [the police] and that one of emancipation [the political]" (Marchart 2010, cited in Mullis and Schipper 2013: 79).

In this book, we understand social emancipation as those practices and discourses, doings and sayings, actions and ideations that contribute to the uneven struggle against social inequality and all those efforts to establish social *and* political equality under capitalist urbanization. An ambiguous relation between the order of institutional *politics* and the radical dimension of *the political* is inherent to this struggle. We therefore refer to *egalitarian politics* as those continuous endeavours of institutional politics and of political insurgencies that seek to overcome the shortcomings of liberal democracies' overstressing freedom and underemphasizing equality (Mouffe 2000, see Gabauer, this volume).[5]

Emancipation as Colonizing Force

The concept of emancipation and the pervasive influence of Western modernity have both fallen into crisis (Laclau 2007 [1996]). Despite the partly liberating character of cities, particularly for the bourgeoisie, the extensive entanglement between Western modernity (and modernization through spatial reforms), ideas of order, progress and emancipation became the main anchor points for the moral foundation of the tyrannical expansion of modernity under the banner of liberal democracies. This process of spatial colonialization was first directed outwards towards the most vulnerable and the colonies and, as Lefebvre (2014) argues, eventually shifts its focus internally, i.e. to the inner peripheries (e.g. the *banlieue*) of Western cities. Decades later, Bayat (2010: 30, own insertion) showed "how the fundamental ideals and expectations [of the Western world]—freedom, development, democracy, . . . emancipation—. . . reflect the genuine desire for autonomy and emancipation, and at the same time serve as discursive tools for imperialistic domination". Emancipatory modernist thought, seen through the lens of those who suffer(ed) from colonization, is hence nothing but a Trojan horse of Western imperial capitalism. This finding might propel a complete rejection of working with the concept of emancipation (Laclau 2007 [1996], see Watson and Siame, this volume).

While De Sousa Santos (2006: 14) agrees that modern(ist) means to achieve emancipation are in fact anachronistic colonizing forces, he insists that the original aims of emancipation are still, if not even more, globally relevant. In his view, a tension between the everyday *experience* of people and their *expectations* is central to the understanding of emancipatory potential (cf. *Ibid.*: 13–14). Throughout modernity, capitalism has maintained the narrative that social improvement is possible for (nearly) everyone based on the rights resulting from capitalistic political emancipation (*Ibid.*). Despite the maintained discrepancy between political equality and social inequality, during the 20th century the modern emancipatory project preserved social peace and order by coupling emancipatory struggle with social regulation, effectively working to regulate tensions arising from discrepancies between the regulatory forces and emancipatory drivers of urbanization. Regulation did not eliminate disjunctures between political equality and social inequality, leaving the struggle for social emancipation incomplete.

The early 21st century witnessed a break away from these fragile regulatory routines, as for a great deal of the world population, the *expectations* have become less positive than the current *experience* (*Ibid.*, own emphasis): This is because the balance between regulation and emancipation has been distorted towards regulation, which meant control and order, whereas emancipatory action was delineated as chaotic, and thus to be regulated and ordered (*Ibid.*). Real emancipatory potential has shrunk (*Ibid.*: 14). This shrinkage takes place through processes which Guerrero Antequera (2008: 269ff) coins as *neoliberal democratic disciplining* as the

> democracy . . . projects something very different from the emancipatory praxis that created it. . . . The actual democracy which presents itself like our truth, is nothing but the interruption of the unfolding acts of democratization, of the liberating practices that escaped and put the controls and codifications of previous forms of oppression in crisis
>
> (*Ibid.*: 276).[6]

Against this structural background, we think that there is an urgent need—through a focus on emancipation—to shift attention again on the innovative and centrifugal powers of the critique of everyday life (Lefebvre 2014). We address emancipation in relation with Lefebvre's production of space as inherently characterized not only by control, domination and colonization, but first and foremost by insurgencies from everyday life and acts of resistance in the lived space of urbanized areas. We stress the self-activating affects, passions and powers that stem from ordinary life as the very precondition of emancipatory praxis embedded in local space and a specific sociohistorical context. We work with an understanding of politics as a practice, rather than a political field—such an understanding emphasizes "the temporalization of politics into an activity" (Marchart 2007: 54). We thereby seek to reinforce a conceptualization of emancipatory politics as "all-encompassing permanent dimension of all social life" (*Ibid*.: 55).

Emancipation, Planning and Post-Political Governance

A plurality of planning and design responses have attempted to address unequal patterns of space production. These approaches to the making of cities have mostly broken with elitist boundaries of professionally closed disciplines in favour of more emancipatory (i.e. inclusive, participatory, integrative) approaches to urban development attentive to the incremental production of social space (Crawford 2008). They build on, but are not restricted to, relational perspectives for revealing empowering relations and dependencies among people and their everyday space (Tornaghi and Knierbein 2015), playful practices as a means of appropriating space (Franck and Stevens 2006), the agency of urban communities to make change (Hou 2010), insurgent citizenship (Holston 2008) or insurgent planning (Miraftab 2009). In praxis, however, places of emancipation prove to be extremely difficult to enact for the benefit of society, particularly for marginalized groups and individuals. Emancipatory notions such as 'liberating change', 'inclusive development' and 'social transformation' might fail to deliver on the promise of genuine social emancipation.

Against this background of critical revision of emancipation as a key facet of capitalist urbanization, critics have pointed to existing paradoxes at the beginning of the new millennium that cannot be simply grasped by improving emancipatory planning or design techniques. The problem lies deeper. Only a decade after Lees's (2004) well-cited book on emancipation and post-modern thought was published, emancipation has become a new buzzword also in the institutionalized realms of spatial governance and planning that contribute to further expanding modes of capitalist urbanization, thus creating new types of profound ambivalences. Wilson and Swyngedouw (2015) have analyzed that in recent decades, politics have been reduced to a broad consensus among actors in power from all societal spheres seeking to ground the capitalist free market and the liberal state as social foundations. Swyngedouw (2007) has labelled this consensual mode of governance as *post-political condition* characterized by patterns of depoliticization; the disappearance of the political; an erosion of democracy; the weakening of the public sphere and a politics of violent disavowal. This transition has, in turn, inevitably entailed silences and absences of vulnerable groups and individuals who have fallen behind on embracing the competitive practices of the free market. Although Wilson and Swyngedouw (2015) scarcely engage in the topic of emancipation, their account provides an in-depth understanding of the systemic configurations that prevent the emergence of truly political moments, which might challenge the established order and institute new social foundations. In their understanding, "technocratic mechanisms and consensual procedures that operate within an unquestioned framework of representative democracy, free market economics and cosmopolitan liberalism" (*Ibid.*: 6) subsume political antagonisms and discontents to social administration "managed by experts and legitimated through participatory processes in which the scope of possible outcomes is narrowly defined in advance" (*Ibid.*: 6). This in turn desecrates the capacity of people to act as a disruptive political collective. The *people* are supplanted by the *population*—the aggregated object of opinion polls, surveillance and bio-political optimization (*Ibid.*). Citizens become consumers and elections are framed as just another choice in which individuals privately select their preferred managers of the conditions of economic necessity (*Ibid*).

Swyngedouw's and Wilson's observations resonate with a field of political theory, which has been introduced into scholarly realms of spatial analysis and studies of urbanization relatively recently: debates on post-political aspects of urbanization, philosophically rooted in post-foundational thought (Marchart 2007). This line of thought engages with the matters of the grounding of society, its 'fundamentals', interrogating if and how universal principles of equality and freedom are institutionalized following the moments of liberation. In recent decades, these debates have been popularized in urban studies and planning theory, owing particularly to Hillier's (2003) work on agonistic planning.

Emancipation and Post-Foundational Thought

One of the core arguments of post-foundational thought is that the political re-enactment of equality can only emerge because of the inevitable contradictions of a social order which presupposes equality but simultaneously disavows it (cf. Rancière 2010: 9). A dual notion of foundation is central to post-foundational thought: This duality assumes that while grounding society in a solid foundation is impossible—it is possible to form 'contingent foundations' that operate as a plurality of competing foundational attempts "[seeking] to ground society without ever being entirely able to do so" (Marchart 2007: 7). The impossibility of founding a social order, as in structuralism, thus "serves as a condition of possibility of always only gradual, multiple and relatively autonomous acts of grounding" (*Ibid.*: 155). Such a positioning allows for conceptualizing of human emancipation beyond possibilities offered by (early) modernism (Laclau 2007 [1996]). Laclau (*Ibid.*: 1f) emphasizes that a dimension of ground is inherent in any emancipatory project: "If the act of emancipation is truly radical, if it is really going to leave behind everything preceding it, it has to take place at the level of the 'ground' of the social" (*Ibid.*). Laclau clarifies any ambivalence by stating, "if there is no ground, if the revolutionary act leaves a residue which is beyond the transforming abilities of the emancipatory praxis, the very idea of a radical transformation would become contradictory" (*Ibid.*).

From such a perspective, emancipation crumbles in logical terrain (*Ibid.*). While acknowledging that these doubts do not cast emancipation as socially irrelevant, Laclau suggests a complete replacement of emancipation with concepts of freedom or liberation, while arguing that there is a possibility of "new discourses of liberation" which go beyond emancipation and "are constructed by movements taking place within the system of alternatives generated by the latter" (*Ibid.*: 13). However, without expanding his notion of liberation (which would offer a connection to debates seeking to decolonize emancipation), Laclau marks the "end of emancipation" as the "beginning of freedom", while asserting that the idea of freedom is ambiguous (*Ibid.*: 18). While Laclau's argument on logical inconsistencies may enrich the debate of this book, we reject deconstruction for the purpose of pursuing a hermeneutic endeavour, and try to work through existing empirical contradictions, ambivalences and aporias of urban emancipation, alongside a focus on emancipatory encounters, affects and passions.

The Marxist emancipatory project of utopian nature is—among others—at the heart of post-foundational critique (Laclau 2007 [1996]; Rancière 2010): Rancière, for instance, distances himself from "the latent religiosity of yesterday's modernist concept of future revolutionary event" (Corcoran 2010: 21). Rancière is rather provoked by endeavours to implement emancipation, which

> will always overturn into a form of societal management by 'enlightened' experts. The ground can then only ever be ripe for forms of disappointment that interpret the dream of emancipation as the root cause of the injustices perpetrated by those same experts.
>
> (*Ibid.*: 3)

This finding shows that there is an urgent need to revisit and reactivate the concept of emancipation. Rancière's (2010: 177) political subjects, for instance, are continually driven by endeavours to ground an unconditional equality as 'lived and effective' and not simply 'represented' within/by a particular set of institutions and power relations that are grounding a social order on contingent and incomplete foundations.

Two strands of debate in need of revision concerning emancipation can be identified from these readings: (1) the *temporal dimension* of emancipation concerns the tradition of modernist approaches which reduce emancipation to the joys of reaching future progress and utopian ideals; and (2) the *spatial dimension* of emancipation where space is reduced to a static, bounded and non-differential abstract commodity, in which the pluralist and agonistic manifestation of social and political difference seems impossible. Rancière (2008) fuses the temporal and spatial dimensions of emancipation into a single space-time notion arguing that "the paradoxical relation between the 'apart' and the 'together' is also a paradoxical relation between the present and the future". Rancière (2009: 42) considers this tension in relation to the 'harmonious fabric of community' which fixes everyone to their 'occupation' (place) and their 'capacity to feel, say and do appropriate to their occupation' (time). In view of this, social emancipation emerges as a breaking of "this fit between an 'occupation' and a 'capacity', which entailed an incapacity to conquer a different space and a different time" (*Ibid.*). An analogy can be drawn between this conceptualization and a space-time dialectics that lies at the heart of theories of urbanization (cf. Lefebvre 1991 [1974]), allowing us to situate universal demands of emancipatory struggles socio-historically in local space understood as lived space.

Emancipatory Reconstructions: Emancipation, Lived Space and Everyday Life

We consider the critique of lived space and thus of the changing everyday life under capitalism a largely uncharted realm which carries a great potential for contributing to a needed pluralization of emancipatory thoughts. The key interest of this book is, therefore, to unravel the multifaceted relations between Lefebvre's (2014) *Critique of Everyday Life*, lived space and emancipation in a twofold way; by investigating (1) mo(ve)ments of political insurgencies and (2) everyday urban praxis, both understood as meaningful and intertwined means of co-producing social and political urban transformation. This book aims to track down emancipatory praxis and emancipatory thought by establishing linkages between compatible perspectives on the politics of difference and everyday life. This approach allows us to move between emancipatory thinking of unorthodox Marxist positions and emancipatory de- and reconstructions of post-Marxist thinkers in political theory.

Thus far, we have scrutinized how emancipatory struggles can unfold in different spaces and at different times. The question then is, why are emancipations predominantly scrutinized as emerging in various forms of articulated political insurgences and spaces of social movements? Does this immanent Eurocentric focus on social urban movements (Bayat 2010) as a main vehicle for a (modernist utopian version of) social transformation mainly distract scholarly attention from the everyday unsettling of routines and its genuinely emancipatory character? Amin and Thrift (2004: 233) have related emancipation to the politics of the lived city, involving politics of embodiment and politics of turf. They acknowledge a faltering, but vocal potentiality of cities performing the "constant hum of the everyday and prosaic web of practices" presupposing the "existence of the politics of the minor register full of small gains and losses, which never quite add up" (*Ibid.*). Thereby, they recognize that emancipatory politics evolve out of the numerous forms of ordinary urban sociality (*Ibid.*: 234).

This book draws on a critique of everyday emancipations to establish crossovers between Lefebvre's (2014) *Critique of Everyday Life* and Gramsci's (1999 [1971]) notion of 'everyone is a philosopher.' This approach configures spaces of everyday life as realms for emancipatory praxis, and philosophy as realm for emancipatory thought. Exploring affective geographies of everyday life through an analysis of lived space and by producing philosophy about and from everyday life recognizes everyday settings as realms for emancipatory struggles that cut across all scales of spatial analysis to dynamize the balance between the particular and the universal.

> It is in spaces of the public that the discovery of both power and demos is made, and it is in the contestation of public space that democracy lives. Emancipation must accordingly be understood as an awakening, a (re)discovery of power that is deeply rooted in processes of mobilization and transformation.
>
> (Springer 2010, 554, referring to Kothari 2005)

Springer expands emancipation further as not just a mere subject-object relation in which emancipators (for instance, activists, loners and scholars) relate to those in need of emancipation (those disposed, disenfranchised and marginalized) (cf. *Ibid.*). Studying lived space thus means studying active emancipations, keeping in mind Rancière's (2009: 19) understanding of emancipation as "the blurring of the boundary between those who act and those who look; between individuals and members of a collective body" (*Ibid.*). Lived experiences of emancipation are, therefore, in the focus of our research. This encompasses (1) the tracing of *everyday, practical, critical* and *active emancipations* through an inquiry of lived space. It also (2) involves a continuous critical reflection on the positionality of professionals in emancipatory struggles, with regard to both *emancipatory capacity to know* and *emancipatory power to act*. Swyngedouw and Wilson (2015: 309) consider this approach an opportunity to rethink the relationship between "our critical theories" and "egalitarian-emancipatory" struggles, with the focus on the political subject who, through such a struggle, "aims to take control again of life and its conditions of possibility". As Guerrero Antequera (2008: 279) has emphasized, these struggles can be nourished by a liberating imaginary of social transformation that does not work in a utopian or an eschatological manner, but promotes a concrete path of emancipatory praxis which simultaneously transforms people, circumstances and conditions. This book is therefore organized in four sections: (Part I) *Everyday emancipation*; (Part II) *Practical emancipation*; (Part III) *Critical emancipation*, and (Part IV) *Active emancipation*.

Structure of the Book

Part I—Everyday Emancipation. Beyond Utopia,
Law and Institutions

This book section (Part I) deals with emancipation as practiced from everyday life. In chapter 2, Japhy Wilson presents *concrete utopian dimensions* of places of planetary urbanization where capitalism is urbanizing nature. His case study is the *Manta-Manaus Project*, a *transport corridor* stretching from Ecuador to Brazilian Amazonia. Wilson analyzes this grand infrastructure project by reconnecting two topoi omnipresent in urban theory, utopia and emancipation, by asking: Is planetary urbanization devoid of utopian elements, i.e. of emancipatory hope? Elisabet van Wymeersch and Stijn Oosterlynck, the authors of chapter 3, call for a more relational approach to what has been coined as *political difference* in the debate on the post-political, thereby addressing the distinction between policing practices which create order in society and practices that disrupt this order by claiming an equal right to speak. They ask how the field of tension between the particular and the universal can be navigated, thus fostering unconditioned equality through *equal rights to speak*. In chapter 4, Gabriella Esposito De Vita outlines how emancipatory cooperation between public, private and civic stakeholders unfolds in planning contexts distorted by organized crime in Mafia-controlled territories. By analyzing lands and properties confiscated from criminal organizations, sociocultural means for spatially weakening Mafia influence through emancipatory forms of writing public law are presented. Can government and insurgent publics form emancipatory coalitions for redemocratization against the Mafia via place-based processes of urban regeneration? Rob Shields, in chapter 5, differentiates between *emancipation-from*, *emancipation-to* and *co-emancipation* when interpreting Lyotard's critique of emancipation as metanarrative. In search of what it is that affects us, Shields promotes a design focus on the *ethics of everyday encounters* relating to urban commons. Can an understanding of emancipation overcome the prioritization of law favouring an ethics of the moment, the encounter on the street or an ethos of improvisation?

Part II—Practical Emancipation. On Places,
Projects and Events

The relation between emancipation and spatial praxis is explored in Part II with an emphasis on concrete paths and tools of emancipation. In chapter 6, Jeffrey Hou explores connections between street vending, dancing and music in East Asian cities and their potential emancipatory character in producing more long-lasting and *substantive changes* in planning and politics. If emancipation requires the formation of consciousness in fighting injustice and *strategic actions* to engage in resistance to induce *structural change*, how can *everyday insurgencies* contribute to more long-lasting agency addressing conditions of urban inequality and injustice? Kanerva Kuokkanen and Emilia Palonen, the authors of chapter 7, analyze participatory projects in Helsinki, Finland. By focusing on *urban governance projects*, they tackle a key dimension of mundane urban institutional praxis involving partnerships, expert NGOs and participatory models that are fiercely criticized by post-foundational thinkers. Does post-foundational thought downplay the potential impact of neighbourhood activism, thus tending to overlook differences in participatory forms of action beyond protest? In chapter 8, Monika Salzbrunn, Barbara Dellwo and Serjara Aleman present the multicultural festival *La Grande Table* in Morges, Switzerland. By analyzing convivial practices by different ethnic, religious and national groups, oscillations between integration and patriarchism, exoticism and folklore are identified. Can urban events, even if they are orchestrated by a top-down hegemony, be considered as potential spaces for emancipation? In chapter 9, Amila Širbegović develops an empowering methodological repertoire marking a change of migration research from victimizing or criminalizing migrants towards post-migrational discourse of self-empowered, emancipated migrants. How can researchers get involved in areas characterized by migration and participate in spaces of everyday culture, thereby aiming at questioning and critically transforming the role of planners?

Part III—Critical Emancipation. On Romanticisms, Agonism and Liberation

Authors in Part III use emancipation as a way to critique spatial planning and design, aiming at better engagement with emerging groups and publics. Vanessa Watson and Gilbert Siame analyze *spatial co-production* in Kampala (Uganda) in chapter 10 to show how communities use both conflict and engagement to negotiate urban upgrading of their material living conditions through self-enumeration, mapping, learning exchanges and savings groups. The authors wonder if emancipatory transformation can be achieved in Kampala without broader challenges to coloniality: Is *emancipation* the project of the (previous) colonizers, while *liberation* is the project of those (formerly) colonized? In chapter 11, Burcu Yigit Turan emphasizes the emancipatory potential of urban design praxis, while criticizing the fragmented *landscape complexes* produced by neoliberal policies. She points to the growing entanglement of authoritarian, anti-secular, neoliberal and neoconservative politics as key catalysts for uneven development. By focusing on the NGO 'ÇEKÜL' in Istanbul's Yeldeğirmeni neighbourhood, she asks: How do different urban designers position themselves in relation to oppressive conditions emerging from neoliberal urbanism? By reviewing planning theory through the prism of political science, in chapter 12, Angelika Gabauer reviews the emancipatory ideals underlying *communicative planning* while delineating how approaches seeking to build on rational consensus and to employ discursive conflict avoidance make emancipatory planning impossible *a priori*. Can the concept of emancipation be addressed more radically to theoretically explore how and if emancipatory planning might be enabled? Christine Mady analyzes urban transformation in Lebanon in chapter 13, which is continuing to witness post-war instabilities, yet shows efforts to reinstate inclusive public spaces within a society characterized by politico-sectarian divides. The NGO 'NAHNOO' has reopened the city's largest urban park, Horsh Beirut, after four decades of closure. Does this project serve as a pilot for shaping public space in unstable contexts, particularly because it involves an emancipatory approach to overcome linkages of traumatic postmemory narratives?

Part IV—Active Emancipation. On Influence, Recovery and Hybrid Ownership

The last section (Part IV) explores emancipation as an activity of urban life in light of more structural constraints. In chapter 14, Stefania Ragozino and Andrea Varriale analyze a large project of post-industrial renewal in Bagnoli, Italy, where several movements initially formed coalitions with the city government against the national government. The authors use three categories to analyze emancipatory processes: *cognitive*, *communicative* and *practiced emancipation*; thereby asking not just if, but how emancipation can be understood as a transition of subaltern, marginalized and deprived people to acquire knowledge, articulate positions and exert influence. Regina Vidosa and Paula Rosa inquire in chapter 15 how the activity of one of the main metallurgical factories (IMPA) in Buenos Aires, Argentina, has been recovered by a *workers' cooperative* through modes of emancipatory self-organization. *Factory recoveries* through occupation tactics work as embodied emancipatory practices in which political action gains visibility by showing what has been excluded from the established order. This case shows how *emancipatory self-organization* contributes to the recalibration of productive spatial relations. Understanding the role of public space as counter space in processes of neoliberal urbanization, the authors of chapter 16, Lukas Franta and Alexander Hamedinger illuminate *practices of commoning* against the background of post-democracy. Commons are interpreted as relational processes to produce, maintain, distribute and/or consume urban resources in an emancipatory way. Does commoning satisfy basic needs beyond the state and the market or is it undergoing co-optation as a key vehicle of hegemonic governance arrangements? In chapter 17, Evangelia Athanassiou, Charis Christodoulou, Matina Kapsali and Maria Karagianni reflect on the relation between *ownership and emancipation* in Thessaloniki, Greece, where new modes of developing, managing and using public space emerged as by-product of the crisis. The chapter seeks to unveil aims, permanence and relations of ownership hybridization processes: Do these changes in 'ownership' promote democratic change and emancipation, or do they form an intrinsic part of neoliberal governance under conditions of austerity?

Notes

1. Marx (1844) works out this differentiation in an article that has been controversially discussed regarding potential anti-Semitic bias. While we agree on the general need to further expand this controversy and position ourselves against all forms of discrimination and prosecution, including anti-Semitism, we understand Marx's thoughts on emancipation in the context of our book as a precursor for this later-developed theory of historical materialism that has greatly affected urban theory.
2. An expansion of this argument can be found in Knierbein and Hou (2017).
3. The connotations of '*citivas*' as included in *cité* (French), *ciudad* (Spanish), city (English) and *cidade* (Portuguese) refer to the body of people assembling rather than to the settlement type, institutional configuration or mode of regulation. Yet, although the saying '*Stadtluft macht frei!*' ('City air liberates!') is cited in many international contributions on emancipation (including Lees 2004; Goonewardena 2011) it is particularly the German-language use of '*Stadt*' (similar with '*stad*' as in Swedish or Dutch) that more clearly points to the settlement form than to the body of citizens, and thus, to a stronger rootedness in connotations relating to settlement types, institutional configurations and modes of regulation. *Stadt* derives from *Statt* which means 'place, site, dwelling, domicile' and has been used since the 12th century, whereas the distinction between spelling *Stadt* and *Statt* was introduced later in the 16th century.
4. All translations from German, Spanish and Portuguese have been provided by the authors.
5. The authors recognize current debates in the US and UK regarding equality vs. equity. We opt to use equality here as it relates to the German *Gleichheit* and the French *egalité* which Mouffe's and Gabauer's work relies on.
6. Guerrero Antequera (2008) presents the case of post-dictatorship Chile and brilliantly analyses how neoliberal governmentality rendered emancipatory practices non-democratic, which actually led to the erosion and overcoming of the Chilean dictatorship, and thus, to liberation.

References

Amin, A. and Thrift, N. (2004) The 'Emancipatory' City? In L. Lees (ed.) *The Emancipatory City? Paradoxes and Possibilities*. London: Sage Publications, pp. 231–235.

Bayat, A. (2010) *Life as Politics: How Ordinary People Change the Middle East*. Redwood City: Stanford University Press.

Blockland, T., Hentschel, C., Holm, A., Lebuhn, H. and Margalit, T. (2012) Urban Citizenship and the Right to the City: The Fragmentation of Claims. *International Journal of Urban and Regional Research* 36(4), pp. 655–664.

Bourdieu, P. (1984) *Distinction: A Social Critique of the Judgement of Taste* (Translated by R. Nice). London: Routledge & Kegan Paul.

Ceceña, A.E. (ed.) (2008) *De los saberes de la emancipación y de la dominación*. Buenos Aires: Clacso Libros.

Corcoran, J. (2010) Editor's Introduction. In J. Rancière (2010) *Dissensus: On Politics and Aesthetics* (Edited and translated by S. Corcoran). London and New York: Continuum, pp. 1–24.

Crawford, M. (2008) Introduction. In J. Chase, M. Crawford and J. Kaliski (eds.) *Everyday Urbanism, Expanded Version*. New York: Monacelli Press.

De Sousa Santos, B. (2006) *Renovar la teoría crítica y reinventar la emancipación social*. Buenos Aires: Clacso Libros.

Franck, K.A. and Stevens, Q. (eds.) (2006) *Loose Space: Possibility and Diversity in Urban Life*. Abingdon, Oxon: Routledge.

Goonewardena, K. (2011) Critical Urbanism: Space, Design, Revolution. In T. Banerjee and A. Loukaitou-Sideris (eds.) *Companion to Urban Design*. New York and London: Routledge, pp. 97–108.

Gramsci, A. (1999 [1971]) *Selections from the Prison Notebooks* (Edited and translated by Q. Hoare and G. Nowell Smith). London: Elec Book.

Guerrero Antequera, M. (2008) Tras el exceso de la sociedad: emancipación y disciplinamiento en el Chile actual. In A.E. Ceceña (ed.) *De los saberes de la emancipación y de la dominación*. Buenos Aires: Clacso Libros, pp. 261–282.

Hillier, J. (2003) Agon'izing over Consensus: Why Habermasian Ideals Cannot Be 'Real'. *Planning Theory* 2(1), pp. 37–59.

Holston, J. (2008) *Insurgent Citizenship: Disjunctions of Democracy and Modernity in Brazil*. Princeton: Princeton University Press.

Hou, J. (ed.) (2010) *Insurgent Public Space: Guerrilla Urbanism and the Remaking of Contemporary Cities*. Abingdon, Oxon: Routledge.

Knierbein, S. and Hou, J. (2017) City Unsilenced: Spatial Grounds of Radical Democratization. In J. Hou and S. Knierbein (eds.) *City Unsilenced: Urban Resistance and Public Space in the Age of Shrinking Democracy*. New York and London: Routledge, pp. 231–241.

Kothari, R. (2005) *Rethinking Democracy*. New Delhi: Orient Longman.

Laclau, E. (2007 [1996]) *Emancipation(s)*. London and New York: Verso.

Lees, L. (ed.) (2004) *The Emancipatory City? Paradoxes and Possibilities*. London: Sage Publications.

Lefebvre, H. (1968) *Le droit a la ville*. Paris: Éditions Anthropos.

Lefebvre, H. (1991 [1974]) *The Production of Space*. Oxford: Basil Blackwell.

Lefebvre, H. (2003 [1970]) *The Urban Revolution*. Minneapolis: University of Minnesota Press.

Lefebvre, H. (2014 [1947]) *The Critique of Everyday Life: The One Volume Edition*. London and New York: Verso.

Marchart, O. (2007) *Post-Foundational Political Thought: Political Difference in Nancy, Lefort, Badiou and Laclau*. Edinburgh: Edinburgh University Press.

Marchart, O. (2010) *Die politische Differenz. Zum Denken des Politischen bei Nancy, Lefort, Badiou, Laclau und Agamben*. Berlin: Suhrkamp Verlag.

Marx, K. (1844) *On the Jewish Question* [Online]. Available at: www.marxists.org/archive/marx/works/1844/jewish-question/ [Accessed 11 August 2017].

Merrifield, A. (2006) *Henri Lefebvre: A Critical Introduction*. New York and London: Routledge.

Metzger, J., Allmendinger, P. and Oosterlynck, S. (eds.) (2014) *Planning against the Political: Democratic Deficits in European Territorial Governance*. New York and London: Routledge.

Miraftab, F. (2009) Insurgent Planning: Situating Radical Planning in the Global South. *Planning Theory* 8(1), pp. 32–50.

Mouffe, C. (2000) *The Democratic Paradox*. London and New York: Verso.

Mullis, D. and Schipper, S. (2013: 79) Die postdemokratische Stadt zwischen Politisierung und Kontinuität. Oder ist die Stadt jemals demokratisch gewesen? *Sub/Urban Zeitschrift für Kritische Stadtforschung* 2(1), pp. 79–100.

Purcell, M. (2009) Resisting Neoliberalization: Communicative Planning or Counter-Hegemonic Movements? *Planning Theory* 8(2), pp. 140–165.

Rancière, J. (2008) Aesthetic Separation, Aesthetic Community: Scenes from the Aesthetic Regime of Art. *Art & Research: Journal of Ideas, Contexts and Methods* 2(1) [Online]. Available at: www.artandresearch.org.uk/v2n1/pdfs/ranciere.pdf [Accessed 2 September 2017].

Rancière, J. (2009) *The Emancipated Spectator*. London: Verso.

Rancière, J. (2010) *Dissensus: On Politics and Aesthetics* (Edited and translated by S. Corcoran). London and New York: Continuum.

Roskamm, N. (2017) Annäherungen an das Außen. Laclau, die Stadt und der Raum. In O. Marchart (ed.) *Ordnungen des Politischen. Einsätze und Wirkungen der Hegemonietheorie Ernesto Laclaus*. Wiesbaden: Springer, pp. 145–167.

Siebel, W. (2004) *Die Europäische Stadt*. Frankfurt am Main: Suhrkamp.

Springer, S. (2010) Public Space as Emancipation: Meditations on Anarchism, Radical Democracy, Neoliberalism and Violence. *Antipode* 43(2), pp. 525–562.

Swyngedouw, E. (2007) The Post-Political City. In BAVO (eds.) *Urban Politics Now Reflect Series: Urban Politics Now: Re-Imagining Democracy in the Neoliberal City*. Rotterdam: Netherland Architecture Institute (NAI) Publishers.

Swyngedouw, E. (2015) Insurgent Architects, Radical Cities and the Promise of the Political. In J. Wilson and E. Swyngedouw (eds.) *The Post-Political and Its Discontents*. Edinburgh: Edinburgh University Press, pp. 171–188.

Swyngedouw, E. and Wilson, J. (2015) There Is No Alternative. In J. Wilson and E. Swyngedouw (eds.) *The Post-Political and Its Discontents*. Edinburgh: Edinburgh University Press, pp. 299–312.

Tornaghi, C. and Knierbein, S. (eds.) (2015) *Public Space and Relational Perspectives: New Challenges for Architecture and Planning*. London and New York: Routledge.

Weber, M. (1978 [1924]) *Economy and Society: An Outline of Interpretive Sociology* (Edited by G. Roth and C. Wittich). Berkeley: University of California Press; Ch. XVI: The City.

Wilson, J. and Swyngedouw, E. (eds.) (2015) *The Post-Political and Its Discontents*. Edinburgh: Edinburgh University Press.

Yildiz, E. and Hill, M. (2015) *Nach der Migration. Postmigrantische Perspektiven jenseits der Parallelgesellschaft*. Bielefeld: Transcript.

Part I

Everyday Emancipation. Beyond Utopia, Law and Institutions

2 Amazon Unbound

Utopian Dialectics of Planetary Urbanization

Japhy Wilson

To hope till hope creates
From its own wreck the thing it contemplates.
Percy Bysshe Shelley, Prometheus Unbound

What is the nature of utopia under conditions of planetary urbanization? In recent years, an emergent literature has begun to theorize the latest wave of capitalist development as a process of 'extended' or 'planetary' urbanization, which is collapsing traditional morphological divisions between urban/rural and city/countryside into a churning morass of 'implosion-explosion', through which capital *implodes* into ever greater agglomerations, while simultaneously *exploding* the urban fabric into the farthest reaches of planetary space (see for example Arboleda 2015; Brenner 2013a; Brenner and Schmid 2015; Kanai 2014; Monte-Mor 2013). The dominant strands of this literature have tended to represent this process as the outcome of abstract economic mechanisms and "large-scale planning strategies" (Brenner 2013b: 20). As such, planetary urbanization would appear to be devoid of utopian elements.

This chapter argues that planetary urbanization is in fact replete with utopian dimensions, which I frame in terms of a dialectic of utopian fantasies that function to conceal and facilitate the apocalyptic dynamics of implosion-explosion, and Real utopias constructed out of urgent necessity at the moment of direct confrontation with these dynamics. These ideas are developed through the case of the Manta-Manaus multimodal transport corridor, and its implementation in Ecuador. Launched in 2007, the corridor runs from the Pacific coast of Ecuador, to the Atlantic coast of Brazil, via the booming industrial city of Manaus in the Brazilian Amazon. It is part of the Initiative for the Regional Integration of South American Infrastructure (IIRSA), a US$158 billion infrastructure project that aims to transform the entire continent in the image of transnational capital (Sanahuja 2012). IIRSA has been identified by Neil Brenner (cf. 2013c: 184) as a paradigmatic example of planetary urbanization in practice and would appear to be a purely functional project of economic globalization. Yet my field research on Manta-Manaus has shown it to be infused with a multitude of utopian dreams and desires.

Through an exploration of these dimensions of the Manta-Manaus corridor, I argue that planetary urbanization is a far more hope-filled process than it may at first appear, while suggesting that a Real utopia can only arise at the point at which all such hopes have been wrecked.

Utopian Fantasies, Real Utopias

Planetary urbanization is animated by the implacable logic of capital, which relentlessly compels the production of territorial infrastructures that drive towards "the annihilation of space by time" (Marx, quoted in Harvey 2001: 244). In his study of the emergence of globalization, *In the World Interior of Capital*, Peter Sloterdijk (2013: 23) has noted the profound existential consequences of this endless obliteration of spatial distance and stability, embodied in an unconscious knowledge that we "can no longer rely on anything except the indifference of homogenous infinite space". Our subjugation to the liquid and volatile space-time of capital is disavowed by a variety of accelerationist fantasies, chief among which is "the neoliberal . . . zero gravity utopia, where flows push towards light speeds" (Featherstone 2010: 128). The etymology of utopia is "no place" (Pinder 2002: 237), and the fantasy space of neoliberal capitalism takes this literally, "despatializing the real globe, replacing the curved earth with an almost extensionless point" and revelling in "the cult of explosion" (Sloterdijk 2013: 13).

  The explosive rage of planetary urbanization is profoundly entangled with an equally powerful drive towards implosion, which is manifested both in the massification of existing agglomerations and in the rapid urbanization of capital in previously peripheral hinterlands (Brenner and Schmid 2015). This chaotic process of implosion is both expressed and concealed by the fetish object of 'the city', which David Wachsmuth (2014: 356) has claimed "is an ideological representation of urbanization processes rather than a moment in them". But ideologies themselves can of course be productive of the realities that they misrepresent. The history of capitalism is replete with utopian fantasies of perfectly ordered cities that do not merely remain 'on paper', but are endowed with the social power to transform reality in their image. As Ross Adams has noted, these utopian schemes are typically underpinned by a "collective fear of some palpable sort, whether it be fear of revolution (Le Corbusier in the 1920s) . . . or our new fear: ecological collapse ('green architecture')" (Adams 2010: 2). In the latter case, Adams argues, the ideological function of the contemporary 'eco-city' is transparently evident: "it is merely a phantasmatic screen, prohibiting us from confronting the true terrors of ecological catastrophe, while at once imploring us to silently identify this terror with the collapse of liberal capitalism itself" (Adams 2010: 7).

  Planetary urbanization is thus infused with utopian fantasies of implosion and explosion that contribute to the long tradition of "obscure utopias" identified by Fredric Jameson, including "liberal reforms and commercial pipedreams, the deceptive yet tempting swindles of the here and now, where Utopia serves as the mere lure and bait for ideology" (Jameson 2005: 3). But, as we will see, this process also generates the conditions for the emergence of events that fleetingly traverse these fantasies through the urgent construction of possible worlds. As Isabell Lorey has argued, such events constitute the actualization of a "presentist democracy", which "follows no teleological logic" (Lorey 2014: 59, 52). On the contrary, they are premised upon a radical renunciation of the phantasmatic promise of an emancipatory future. The planetary completion of global capitalism may be experienced as the closure of all such emancipatory possibilities. But Žižek argues that it is precisely this 'loss of hope' that opens the possibility of a 'Real utopia', beyond the utopian fantasies of perfect urban order and light-speed circulation:

> We have a third utopia, which is . . . precisely the Real—the Real core of utopia . . . A truly radical utopia is not an exercise in free imagination . . . It's something you do out of an inner urge. You have to invent something new when you cannot do it otherwise. True utopia . . . is not a matter of the future. It's something to be immediately enacted when there is no other way. Utopia in this sense simply means: 'Do what appears within the given symbolic coordinates as impossible. Take the risk, change the very coordinates' . . . The point is not about planning utopias. The point is about practicing them. And the point is not 'Should we do it, or should we just persist in the existing order?' The point is much more radical. It's a matter of survival. The future will be utopia, or there will be none.
>
> (Žižek 2003)

Utopian fantasies function to reproduce the established coordinates of reality. A Real utopia, by contrast, can only be constructed in the context of the disintegration of all such fantasies, in which the political subject

> undergoes a 'loss of reality' and starts to perceive reality as an 'unreal' nightmarish universe with no firm ontological foundation; this nightmarish universe is . . . that which remains of reality after reality is deprived of its support in fantasy.
>
> (Žižek 1999: 57)

This understanding of a Real utopia bears no relation to the real utopias celebrated by Erik Olin Wright, for whom 'real' designates everyday reality, and who defines a real utopia as one that operates within the possibilities determined by this reality (Olin Wright 2010). For Žižek, by contrast, a Real utopia is 'real' with a capital 'R', and refers to the Lacanian dimensions of the Real excluded from lived reality by the horizon of possibility established by fantasy (Bosteels 2011: 184–188). The remainder of this chapter explores the utopian fantasies of planetary urbanization in practice, and the 'nightmarish universe' that remains after planetary urbanization has been deprived of its phantasmatic support, in order to illustrate my claim that the 'loss of hope' embodied in "the traumatic passage [through] this 'night of the world'" (Žižek 1999: 38) is a necessary moment in the creation of a Real utopia.

Utopian Fantasies of Manta-Manaus

As Jameson (1989: 44, 49) has emphasized, the utopia of "postmodern hyperspace . . . is not merely a cultural ideology or fantasy but has genuine historical (and socioeconomic) reality". This reality is embodied in the vast material landscapes that underpin the accelerated circulation of capital on a global scale. One such landscape is currently being produced under the aegis of the Initiative for the Regional Integration of South American Infrastructure. Launched in 2000, IIRSA seeks to reorient the energy, transportation and communications infrastructures of the continent towards transnational circuits of capital through the construction and modernization of ports, airports, bridges, tunnels, roads, railways, hydroelectric dams and electricity networks (COSIPLAN 2013). As such, IIRSA embodies the explosive dynamic of planetary urbanization through which "landscapes are being comprehensively produced, engineered, or redesigned through a surge of infrastructure investments . . . intended to support the accelerated growth and expansion of agglomerations around the world" (Brenner 2013b: 20).

Among the most emblematic of the IIRSA projects is the Manta-Manaus multimodal transport corridor (Wilson and Bayón 2015a). The Manta-Manaus corridor begins from the planned deep water port of Manta, on the Pacific coast of Ecuador, crosses the Ecuadorian Andes via over 800 km of new and modernized highways, transfers to river at the new intermodal port of Providencia on the River Napo in the Ecuadorian Amazon, and then heads downriver for over 3,000 km via Manaus to the Atlantic port of Belen. Plans for Manta-Manaus justify it in terms of "less time, less cost", in comparison to alternative global trade routes (Ministerio de Relaciones Exteriores 2010), and predict that the project will transform Ecuador into "the key node of . . . commercial exchange between the Amazon basin and the Pacific rim" (Autoridad Portuaria de Manta 2006).

Manta-Manaus thus embodies the commitment to competitive acceleration characteristic of planetary urbanization. But as David Harvey (2013: 48) has noted, "Speed-up, turnover time, and the like, when driven onwards by the coercive laws of competition, alter the temporal frame not only of the circulation of capital but also of daily life". These processes can provoke resistances from those who dwell in the spaces that they transform, but are often embraced by marginalized communities hoping for inclusion in the postmodern hyperspace of globalized consumer capitalism (Dalakoglou and Harvey 2012). For the majority of the excluded and impoverished population of the Ecuadorian Amazon, the Manta-Manaus corridor has not been resisted as a threat to their established ways of life, but has been infused with utopian fantasies of market integration and geographical freedom. One inhabitant of Providencia, where the new intermodal port is being constructed, described having been "impressed" and "inspired" by a promotor of Manta-Manaus who had visited the community with a laptop computer on which he had shown them a video with animated images of "great ships" arriving there by river. His aunt then awoke him late at night, telling him that she had just had a "spectacular" dream about Manta-Manaus and insisting that they purchase land along the riverbank (Local landowner, personal interview, 11 February 2015, Shushufindi, Ecuador). The leader of the Siekopai, an indigenous nationality based near Providencia, also told us that he hoped that the corridor would generate economic opportunities, which his community would be able to "take advantage of by creating companies". Manta-Manaus, he declared, was "the dream of the Siekopai nation" (Elias Piaguaje, leader of the Siekopai nation, personal interview, 10 February 2015, San Pablo, Ecuador). Capital's furious abolition of all spatial limits thus comes to be draped in the futurescapes of an emancipatory modernity and dusted with "the glitter of progress, the lure of profit, the promise of circulation, movement and a better life" (Harvey and Knox 2012: 534).

The explosion of infrastructure networks across South America is dialectically related to the implosion of capital in other parts of the world, functioning to channel the natural resources of the continent into the unprecedented industrial revolution currently under way in East Asia (Veltmeyer and Petras 2014). At the same time, the production of new infrastructures and the opening of new spaces of accumulation is catalyzing the rapid agglomeration of capital into the newly constructed hubs and nodes of this emergent network. Providencia, as the intermodal port of the Manta-Manaus corridor, is one of these new sites of implosion. Before the arrival of Manta-Manaus, Providencia was an isolated indigenous community, which could only be accessed by river. In 2013, a new highway was completed, cutting through 46 kilometres of Amazonian rainforest to the village, where a container port is now being constructed (see Figure 2.1).

The economic strategy for the new port city is being designed in collaboration with Greg Lindsay, author of a seminal text of neoliberal urbanism entitled *Aerotropolis: The Way We'll Live Next* (Kasarda and Lindsay 2011). Lindsay celebrates "the aerotropolis as globalization made flesh" in the form of new world cities like Dubai constructed around airports. In an era of "frictionless competition" in which "humans aren't bound by distance, but by time", Lindsay claims that "it's possible to imagine a world capital in a place that was once an absolute backwater" (Lindsay 2006). As Will Self (2011) has noted, *Aerotropolis* is

> a classic example of the Fin de Siècle scientific romance in its utopian guise. It aims, like its predecessors, to resolve the contradictions and divisions of the present by thrusting its readers . . . into a future typified by plenty, social accord, and clean, green cities linked together by clean, green jets.

The urban plan for Providencia is entitled *Divining Providencia: Building a Biocultural Capital for the Amazon* (cityLAB 2013). It reproduces Lindsay's utopian fantasy of planetary urbanization as a harmonious and contradiction-free process, with international airspace replaced by the vast fluvial network of the Amazon, along which sustainably produced and ethically

Figure 2.1 Official port under construction in Providencia
Source: Manuel Bayón, 2015

sourced products will be shipped from Colombia, Peru, Bolivia and Brazil (cityLAB 2013: 57), with Providencia serving as the "material, scientific, and commercial repository for the biodiversity of the entire basin" (cityLAB 2013: 48). Providencia will be

> a new type of trade zone, one that combines the global presence and exposure of free trade zones with . . . the more buyer-producer model of Fair Trade . . . establishing a synergy between IIRSA, which will ferry resources there from throughout the Amazon, and the knowledge and artisanal skills of local indigenous peoples capable of transforming it into unique cultural products of human use and value.
>
> (cityLAB 2013: 87, 149)

Divining Providencia thus embodies the fantasy space of the contemporary eco-city as "the liberal answer to ecological catastrophe: an enclosed, self-contained economic free zone" (Adams 2010: 7). The implosive forces of planetary urbanization are simultaneously celebrated and concealed by a "utopia of spatial form" (Harvey 2000) that promises a harmonious and sustainable form of capitalist development without addressing the fundamental social antagonism that underpins it, corresponding precisely to

Žižek's (1989: 23) definition of utopian fantasy as "a belief in the possibility of a universality without its symptom".

Welcome to the Desert of a Real Utopia

The utopian fantasies of Manta-Manaus and *Divining Providencia* embody the apparently opposed ideologies of technological progress and ecological romanticism, which as Žižek (1997: 13) has noted, ultimately function together as "two complimentary gestures . . . obfuscating the underlying deadlock". This deadlock has been reasserted, however, by the material dynamics of planetary urbanization, through which the economic infrastructures of Manta-Manaus have been appropriated by the oil industry (Wilson and Bayón 2015b). In 2013, the Ecuadorian government announced the exploitation of Block 43, a rich oil field that is partly located within the highly biodiverse Yasuni National Park. Block 43 occupies a vast extension of territory adjacent to Peru and is accessed via the River Napo on the route of Manta-Manaus. With the completion of the new highway in the same year, Providencia became the closest port to Yasuni accessible by road and has since been rapidly transformed into the de facto oil port for Block 43. Oil services companies have bought up land along the river bank to build a series of private ports, and a wave of land speculation has driven up prices and intensified the deforestation of the area (see Figure 2.2).

Figure 2.2 One of several private oil ports in Providencia
Source: Manuel Bayón, 2015

The accelerating pile-up of oil capital in Providencia has shattered the dreams of market integration and geographical freedom that Manta-Manaus had once inspired in the poor and marginalized inhabitants of the region. The leader of the Siekopai who had described Manta-Manaus as 'the dream of the Siekopai nation' explained that "There is no room for the [indigenous] nationalities, or the *colonos* [mestizo colonizers], or anyone, we are just the observers of big deals between big interests . . . We have nothing. We are in a total desert" (Elias Piaguaje, leader of the Siekopai nation, personal interview, 10 February 2015, San Pablo, Ecuador). Despite having invested over US$50 million in the highway and the port, the government has not installed water or sanitation in Providencia, and the community has had to connect their own electricity lines from the mainline that feeds the oil ports. In the words of another local leader, "They take all the black gold from here and leave us with nothing" (Castillo 2015).

Providencia has thus been rapidly transformed from an isolated indigenous community into an epicentre of planetary urbanization, where the implosive agglomeration of capital threatens to collapse all social structures into a space of absolute disintegration. Yet these forces of material destruction have simultaneously opened the possibility of a Real utopia. In 2010, when they first began to receive warnings and threats of expropriation, the Kichwa population of Providencia decided to organize to defend themselves against this eventuality, forming an association called 'Sumak Ñambi', which roughly translates as 'Gorgeous Road', conveying the utopian hopes that at that time were still embodied in the highway. Since then, the community has been confronted with further threats of dispossession, and the completion of the highway has been followed by the building of the official port and the multiple private oil ports; the arrival and departure of huge diesel-spilling barges shifting materials down to Block 43; and the construction of a stone-crushing factory in the middle of the village.

The few remaining thatched wooden houses of Sumak Ñambi have been engulfed within this churning, roaring space of frenzied agglomeration.[1] In March 2015, the president of Sumak Ñambi, Nelson Castillo, called an assembly and addressed the association. Shouting over the growling engines, blaring reverse sirens and crashing rockslides of a constant line of trucks loading gravel onto barges bound for Block 43, Castillo insisted on the urgent necessity of immediate action:

> Look at the machinery they bring here every day, the pollution, the impacts that we suffer without compensation . . . We are peaceful, gullible people, waiting for the goodwill of someone who might one day decide to help us, when instead we should be demanding our rights . . . We are going to keep being dispossessed little by little, as is already happening . . . It is time for us to wake up and live in unity!
>
> (Castillo 2015)

The association decided that the most effective way to defend their claim to their land would not be to seek to salvage the despoiled fragments of the rural space that remained to them, but rather to assert their right to the city, by creating their own urban project on the land they still possessed. Unable to afford to contract an urban planner to design their new space, they instead invited a local topographer to draw up a plan in return for membership of their association and a plot of land in the new town. The resulting plan locates the town in ten hectares of rainforest along the riverbank to the east of the official port. Five quadrangular blocks are divided into a total of 60 lots, each of which has space for a house and a large garden. The plan also includes a plaza, a cemetery, a basketball court, a guesthouse, a space for tourist projects and a communal meetinghouse.

For an impoverished community faced with imminent dispossession, the realization of such an ambitious plan was seemingly impossible. But soon after Castillo's speech to the assembly, an opportunity unexpectedly presented itself, when a shipping and haulage company attempted to purchase the riverside land of the community, with the aim of opening yet another private port. Rather than refusing the offer on the basis of the non-alienability of their land, Sumak Ñambi made a counter-proposal: in exchange for the lease of a space for the port at the far eastern end of their land, the company would cut and surface the roads for their town. Within two months, the roads had been sliced through the jungle, with the felled trees providing the wood for the construction of the houses (see Figure 2.3). Every weekend Sumak Ñambi gathered in *minga* (collective community labour), and the town began to take form. In Castillo's words, "We were happy and content to be realizing our project" (Nelson Castillo, personal interview, 20 June 2015, Providencia).

The case of Sumak Ñambi demonstrates that a Real utopia is not an exercise in "free imagination" but an act "of the utmost urgency" (Žižek 2011), which retroactively creates the conditions of its own possibility by changing "the very parameters of what is considered 'possible' in the existing configuration" (Žižek 1999: 237). There is nothing overtly utopian about Sumak Ñambi's humble town. It reproduces the conventional spatial form of oil towns across the region and has been hacked from the jungle with the same ferocity as the private and official ports. It expresses no political ideology and contains no ambition to either transcend or subtract itself from the dynamics of planetary urbanization. Yet it conceals a Real utopian kernel—the desperate decision of a historically marginalized community to assert its equal right to the very process of planetary urbanization that threatens its destruction. As Alain Badiou has argued, "A change of the world is real when an inexistent of the world starts to exist in the same world with maximum intensity" (quoted in Swyngedouw 2014: 171). As such, the construction of Sumak Ñambi's simple settlement within the maelstrom of planetary urbanization was not only an authentically utopian act. It was also a political event in Jacques Rancière's sense of the term, occurring at the very point at which such an event appeared impossible. According to Rancière (1999: 27), politics exists

Figure 2.3 Freshly cut streets of Sumak Ñambi
Source: Manuel Bayón, 2015

when "those who have no right to be counted . . . make themselves of some account, setting up a community by the very fact of placing . . . the contradiction of two worlds in a single world." By materializing their utopia amid a world that had no place for them, Sumak Ñambi brought this contradiction 'of two worlds in a single world' to the surface of social reality, confronting the utopian fantasies of Manta-Manaus and *Divining Providencia* with a "return of the repressed" (Žižek 1989: 55).

The response of "professional urbanism" (Merrifield 2015) was swift and uncompromising. As soon as they had been informed of the situation, in June 2015, the municipal government imposed a legal order that halted construction and prevented any further development of the site.[2] The municipality was now working with other levels of government on the implementation of *Divining Providencia*, and Sumak Ñambi's new town was being constructed on land that had been designated as an industrial zone for the eco-products of the Amazon. The absurdity of this situation, of course, was that Providencia had become a de facto oil port, and *Divining Providencia* already lay in ruins. The Real utopia of Sumak Ñambi was therefore being cancelled out by a utopian fantasy that would never be realized. As Žižek (2015a) has noted: "If you're caught in another's dream, you're fucked".

Conclusion

Global capitalism has collided with the limits of planetary space and is now surging back upon itself in a tidal wave of creative destruction that implodes into seething agglomerations and explodes into tangled highways and wastelands of resource extraction. In the examples of Manta-Manaus and *Divining Providencia*, we have seen how the traumatic dynamics of implosion-explosion are both sublimated and facilitated by utopian fantasies. The implacable drive of capital towards the annihilation of space by time has been represented by the promotors of Manta-Manaus as a postmodern hyperspace of smooth accelerated circuits, and infused with the desires of poor and marginalized populations for full participation in an imagined world of market integration and geographical freedom. Meanwhile the equally relentless pressure of agglomeration has been framed by *Divining Providencia* as a domain of perfect socio-spatial order, in which sustainably sourced eco-products will be serenely shipped from the entire Amazon Basin to Providencia, where they will be fashioned into environmentally friendly commodities by the healthy, happy inhabitants of the new eco-city. These twin fantasies of explosion and implosion function to mutually "obfuscate the absolute synchronicity of the antagonism in question" (Žižek 1997: 14). In practice, however, both fantasies have been shattered by the material forces of this synchronicity. The monolithic imperative of endless accumulation has driven the expansion of the Ecuadorian oil frontier and appropriated the economic infrastructure of Manta-Manaus, while the rapid agglomeration of oil capital in Providencia has triggered a chaotic process of accumulation by dispossession that has overwhelmed *Divining Providencia*'s vision of a rationally ordered city.

In contrast to these utopian fantasies of implosion-explosion, Sumak Ñambi constitutes a Real utopia, located at an epicentre of planetary urbanization, where the seductions of hope are extinguished and the creation of possible worlds becomes an urgent necessity. This utopia has no transcendent political ideology, and following its initial gains it was quickly obstructed by the immeasurably greater social forces of state and capital. Yet it is Real, to the extent that it began from the destruction of all utopian fantasies and from the stark realization that all hope had been lost. This realization forced the community into action, catalyzing the production of a possible world under conditions of seemingly objective impossibility, and constituting what Žižek has described as a Real political act, "which occurs *ex nihilo*, without any phantasmatic support" (Žižek 1999: 460). There is a lesson here for the rest of us, seduced by the utopian fantasies that sustain our own unsustainable worlds. In the words of the Invisible Committee (2009: 23), which capture the spirit of a Real utopianism: "From whichever angle you approach it, the present offers no way out. This is not the least of its virtues."

This conclusion may appear distressingly nihilistic to those accustomed to more comforting utopias. But as Žižek has argued, "the courage of hopelessness" is precisely what is required if we are to confront and act upon "the deadlock of our predicament" (Žižek 2015b: 248). Once an act of this kind has been undertaken, the dialectics of utopia are set in motion and can move in unexpected ways. By the time the Real utopia of Sumak Ñambi was shut down by government bureaucrats and spatial planners in June 2015, a collapse of the international oil price had driven the Ecuadorian economy into recession, and the construction of the great port of Manta-Manaus was abandoned a few months later. When I last visited Providencia, in June 2016, the half-completed official port was overgrown with weeds, the political and financial support for *Divining Providencia* had evaporated, and the company that had planned to build a port in Sumak Ñambi's territory had gone bankrupt. Yet the streets and houses of Sumak Ñambi were quietly flourishing (see Figure 2.4). A dialectical inversion had occurred. Amidst the ruined fantasies of state and capital, Sumak Ñambi now stood as a fragile testament to the possibility that utopian horizons are opened, not by dreaming of better worlds, but by confronting the destruction of all such dreams. To quote Žižek once again: "The true utopia is when the situation is so without issue, without a way to resolve it within the coordinates of the possible, that out of the pure urge of survival you have to invent a new space" (Žižek 2011). The lesson of Sumak Ñambi is that, by forcing this space into existence, the future can be reclaimed as an open field of struggle.

Figure 2.4 Sumak Ñambi
Source: Japhy Wilson, June 2016

Notes

1. This account of Sumak Ñambi is based on participant observation undertaken during several visits to Providencia in 2015, as part of the National Centre of Strategies for the Right to Territory (CENEDET), a research centre directed by the human geographer David Harvey, which was collaborating with Sumak Ñambi on their urban strategy. For details of the CENEDET experiment, see Wilson (2017).
2. This was explained during interviews with the heads of planning of the prefectural and municipal governments (both interviews conducted on 18 June 2015, in Lago Agrio and Shushufindi respectively).

References

Adams, R. (2010) Longing for a Greener Present: Neoliberalism and the Eco-City. *Radical Philosophy* 163, pp. 2–7.

Arboleda, M. (2015) Spaces of Extraction, Metropolitan Explosions: Planetary Urbanization and the Commodity Boom in Latin America. *International Journal of Urban and Regional Research* 40(1), pp. 96–112.

Autoridad Portuaria de Manta (2006) *Eje Multimodal Pacífico-Atlántico Ecuador-Brasil* (promotional PowerPoint presentation) [Online]. Available at: www.bankinformationcenter.org/en/Document.100332.pdf [Accessed 18 February 2017].

Bosteels, B. (2011) *The Actuality of Communism*. New York: Verso.

Brenner, N. (2013a) *Implosions/Explosions: Towards a Study of Planetary Urbanization*. Berlin: Jovis Verlag.

Brenner, N. (2013b) Introduction: Urban Theory without an Outside. In N. Brenner (ed.) *Implosions/Explosions: Towards a Study of Planetary Urbanization*. Berlin: Jovis Verlag, pp. 14–35.

Brenner, N. (2013c) Theses on Urbanization. In N. Brenner (ed.) *Implosions/Explosions: Towards a Study of Planetary Urbanization*. Berlin: Jovis Verlag, pp. 181–202.

Brenner, N. and Schmid, C. (2015) Towards a New Epistemology of the Urban? *City* 19(2–3), pp. 151–182.

Castillo, N. (2015) *Speech Delivered at an Assembly of Sumak Ñambi*, 29 March, Providencia.

cityLAB (2013) *Divining Providencia: Building a Bio-Cultural Capital for the Amazon*. Berkeley: UCLA [unpublished draft manuscript].

COSIPLAN (2013) *Cartera de Proyectos* [Online]. Available at: www.iirsa.org/Document/Detail?Id=3716 [Accessed 11 December 2014].

Dalakoglou, D. and Harvey, P. (2012) Roads and Anthropology: Ethnographic Perspective on Space, Time and (Im)mobility. *Mobilities* 7(4), pp. 459–465.

Featherstone, M. (2010) Event Horizon: Utopia-Dystopia in Bauman's Thought. In M. Tester and M. Davies (eds.) *Bauman's Challenge: Sociological Issues for the 21st Century*. Basingstoke: Palgrave Macmillan, pp. 127–147.

Harvey, D. (2000) *Spaces of Hope*. Edinburgh: Edinburgh University Press.

Harvey, D. (2001) *Spaces of Capital*. Edinburgh: Edinburgh University Press.

Harvey, D. (2013) *A Companion to Marx's Capital*, Volume 2. London: Verso.

Harvey, P. and Knox, H. (2012) The Enchantments of Infrastructure. *Mobilities* 7(4), pp. 521–536.

Invisible Committee (2009) *The Coming Insurrection*. New York: Semiotext(e).

Jameson, F. (1989) *Post-Modernism, or, the Cultural Logic of Late Capitalism.* Durham: Duke University Press.

Jameson, F. (2005) *Archaeologies of the Future: The Desire Called Utopia and Other Science Fictions.* New York: Verso.

Kanai, J.M. (2014) On the Peripheries of Planetary Urbanization: Globalizing Manaus and Its Expanding Impact. *Environment and Planning D: Society and Space* 32(6), pp. 1071–1087.

Kasarda, J.D. and Lindsay, G. (2011) *Aerotropolis: The Way We'll Live Next.* London: Allen Lane.

Lindsay, G. (2006) Rise of the Aerotropolis. *Fast Company,* 1 July 2006. Available at: www.fastcompany.com/57081/rise-aerotropolis [Accessed 1 August 2015].

Lorey, I. (2014) The 2011 Occupy Movements: Rancière and the Crisis of Democracy. *Theory, Culture and Society* 31(7–8), pp. 43–65.

Merrifield, A. (2015) Amateur Urbanism. *City* 19(5), pp. 753–762.

Ministerio de Relaciones Exteriores del Ecuador (2010) *Manta-Manaos: Eje Multimodal Bi-Oceánico.* Quito: Ministerio de Relaciones Exteriores del Ecuador [Internal government document, supplied by interviewee].

Monte-Mor, R. (2013) Extended Urbanization and Settlement Patterns in Brazil: An Environmental Approach. In N. Brenner (ed.) *Implosions/Explosions: Towards a Study of Planetary Urbanization.* Berlin: Jovis Verlag, pp. 109–120.

Olin Wright, E. (2010) *Envisioning Real Utopias.* New York: Verso.

Pinder, D. (2002) In Defence of Utopian Urbanism: Imagining Cities after the 'End of Utopia'. *Geografiska Annaler* 84B, pp. 229–241.

Rancière, J. (1999) *Disagreement: Politics and Philosophy.* Minneapolis: University of Minnesota Press.

Sanahuja, J.A. (2012) Post-Neoliberal Regionalism in South America: The Case of UNASUR. *EUI Working Papers.* San Domenico di Fiesole: European University Institute [Online]. Available at: http://cadmus.eui.eu/bitstream/handle/1814/20394/RSCAS_2012_05.pdf?sequence=1 [Accessed 18 February 2017].

Self, W. (2011) The Frowniest Spot on Earth. *London Review of Books* 33(9), pp. 10–11.

Sloterdijk, P. (2013) *In the World Interior of Capital.* Cambridge: Polity.

Swyngedouw, E. (2014) Insurgent Architects, Radical Cities, and the Promise of the Political. In J. Wilson and E. Swyngedouw (eds.) *The Post-Political and Its Discontents: Spaces of Depoliticisation, Spectres of Radical Politics.* Edinburgh: Edinburgh University Press, pp. 169–188.

Veltmeyer, H. and Petras, J. (2014) *The New Extractivism: A Post-Neoliberal Development Model or Imperialism of the Twenty-First Century?* London: Zed.

Wachsmuth, D. (2014) City as Ideology. In N. Brenner (ed.) *Implosions/Explosions: Towards a Study of Planetary Urbanization.* Berlin: Jovis Verlag, pp. 353–371.

Wilson, J. (2017) Perplexing Entanglements with a Post-Neoliberal State. *Journal of Latin American Geography* 16(1), pp. 177–184.

Wilson, J. and Bayón, M. (2015a) Concrete Jungle: The Planetary Urbanization of the Ecuadorian Amazon. *Human Geography* 8(3), pp. 1–23.

Wilson, J. and Bayón, M. (2015b) Manta-Manaus: Interoceanic Fantasies and the Real of Planetary Urbanization. *CENEDET Working Paper #4* [Online]. Available at: https://cenedet.files.wordpress.com/2015/11/cenedet-wp4.pdf [Accessed 18 February 2017].

Žižek, S. (1989) *The Sublime Object of Ideology.* London: Verso.

Žižek, S. (1997) *The Plague of Fantasies*. London: Verso.

Žižek, S. (1999) *The Ticklish Subject: The Absent Centre of Political Ontology*. London: Verso.

Žižek, S. (2003) *The Reality of the Virtual (interview)* [Video file]. Available at: www.youtube.com/watch?v=LuG8ElyirC0 [Accessed 16 December 2016].

Žižek, S. (2011) Slavoj Žižek on Utopia. *Maquinas del Fuego*, 16 August. Available at: http://maquinasdefuego.blogspot.com/2011/08/slavoj-zizek-on-utopia.html [Accessed 1 August 2015].

Žižek, S. (2015a) Greece: The Courage of Hopelessness. *New Statesman*, 20 July. Available at: www.newstatesman.com/world-affairs/2015/07/slavoj-i-ek-greece-courage-hopelessness [Accessed 1 August 2015].

Žižek, S. (2015b) *Trouble in Paradise: From the End of History to the End of Capitalism*. London: Penguin (paperback edition).

3 Applying a Relational Approach to Political Difference

Strategies of Particularization and Universalization in Contesting Urban Development

Elisabet Van Wymeersch and Stijn Oosterlynck

Introduction

Over the last decade, many scholars have analyzed the depoliticization of territorial governance, a phenomenon often referred to as 'post-politics' (Mouffe 2005; Žižek 1999). They argue that with the global acceptance of neoliberal capitalism and the entrepreneurial state as the only legitimate organizational foundations of contemporary society, the antagonisms emerging from the divisions that run through society are suppressed (Swyngedouw 2009). Working from a post-foundational approach to politics (Marchart 2007), these contributions make a sharp distinction between the specific practices and institutions through which socio-spatial order is created on the one hand, and the antagonisms and disagreements that are constitutive to every society on the other. While there are different ways of naming the two sides of this distinction (cf. Wilson and Swyngedouw 2014), we work with Rancière's notions of *'the police'* referring to all practices which create order in a society by distributing places, names and functions (Nash 1996), and *'politics'* to indicate that this distribution can always be disrupted by those who are unaccounted for in the established order (Rancière 2007).

In this chapter, it is argued that research inspired by this perspective predominantly aims either at describing particular instances of spatial politics as suffering from the 'post-political condition' (MacLeod 2013; Swyngedouw 2009; Allmendinger and Haughton 2012; Raco 2015) or at searching for instances of the 'purely political' in all kind of resistance movements (Badiou and Elliott 2012; Douzinas 2013; Bassett 2014). In contrast to approaches privileging one or the other side of this *political difference*, we adopt a more relational approach, searching for political dynamics in the interaction between ongoing attempts of depoliticization and properly political practices (e.g. Chambers 2011; Van Puymbroeck and Oosterlynck 2014; Uitermark and Nicholls 2013; Legacy 2016; Gualini 2015). The proposed relational approach holds on to this binary distinction on the ontological level to stress the absence of an essential ground of any social order, thus keeping open the very possibility of politics. Still, our claim is that politics is not about the annihilation of the police, but that the police inevitably calls into being instances of politics, and that politics works through rather than destroys the police order, hence a relational perspective.

To show the added value of a relational approach to the political difference, this chapter uses a Belgian case of contested urban development—the struggle for '*t Landhuis* in Ghent. In this case, a group of citizens challenged the Ghent City Council and its intention to erect a training complex for their first division soccer team 'A.A. Gent' on the terrain that they had kept occupied for some time. We analyze the political dynamics in this case with particular attention to how both politics and the police have manifested themselves and how the interaction between the two unfolded. To make the rather abstract language in these debates on the political difference more operational, we focus on the frames used by the main actors during the conflict. More specifically, we organize our analysis of these frames around notions of universalization and particularization as used by Rancière, in which the first stands for claims grounded in universal categories such as equality or humanity, while the latter refers to demands reflecting specific interests or positions (Nash 1996).

In what follows, we first introduce post-foundational political thought and explain why the political difference should be approached in a relational way, highlighting what this entails for our understanding of emancipation. Subsequently, this theoretical framework is used to analyze the case of '*t Landhuis* in Ghent. Our analysis focuses on how the main actors frame their demands and thus sheds light on the emancipatory nature of the political dynamics in this case of contestation. We conclude this chapter by stressing how emancipation as subjectivization implies navigating the field of tension between subject positions and acting as a stand-in for a universalizing message of equality.

Post-Foundationalism and the Relational Approach to the Political Difference

For post-foundational political thinkers, mainstream political thinking is too much focused on ordering, managing and governing the social, ignoring the impossibility of a fully ordered society. They argue that any social order must deal with the absence of an essential and definitive foundation, which implies that the social will always be fundamentally split along many different lines (Marchart 2007). For the post-foundational theorist Rancière, the *police order* is what emerges to conceal this absent ground. The police attempts to ground a specific kind of order and pacify its divisions. It is a symbolic order and consists of all the practices that distribute places, names and functions in society, designating everyone into their 'proper' place in a seemingly natural order of things (Dikeç 2002).

However, post-foundational thinkers also argue that this order can only ever be contingent (Wilson and Swyngedouw 2014), as it is always open to disruption by those highlighting the inevitable injustices implied in grounding an order. Called *politics* by Rancière, this activity manifests in antagonistic practices (Marchart 2007). As social and political analysis is too often concerned with the mechanisms of creating order and tends to identify democracy with the institutions ordering political activities, post-foundationalists are foregrounding this *political difference*, developing a different perspective on democracy (Marchart 2007).

We work with Jacques Rancière's interpretation of this political difference because of the way in which he (1) grounds democratic politics in the notion of equality and calls it emancipation; (2) sees equality not as a goal to be attained, but as a presupposition that disturbs the social order and fuels the coming into being of a new political subject and (3) describes this process of subjectivization/emancipation in terms of the universalization of particular conflicts. As explained earlier, we argue for a relational approach of this political difference, as politics and police presuppose each other and neither has any meaning without the other. In this chapter, we aim to give substance to this relational approach by focusing on the interrelation and co-evolving dynamics between universalizing and particularizing framing.

Emancipation as the Promise of Equality: A Rancièrean Approach to Political Difference

To Rancière (2004), politics is not merely about conflict. Antagonism only carries emancipatory potential when the notion of equality is at stake. For him, emancipation emerges because democracy's promise of unconditional equality is inevitably broken. Since every order is based on 'a distribution of names, places and functions', it necessarily institutionalizes inequalities. Emancipation is then the process through which this unequal (police) order is confronted with the democratic promise of equality. It is

> the verification of the equality of any speaking being with any other speaking being. It is always enacted in the name of a category denied either the principle or the consequences of that equality: workers, women, people of color, or other.
>
> (Rancière 1992: 60)

Thus, when a wrong is being declared, a new political subject comes into being by dis-identifying itself from the place, name and function given to it in the social order. This is what Rancière calls political subjectivization, i.e. "the production through a series of actions of a body and a capacity for enunciation not previously identifiable within a given field of experience, whose identification is thus part of the reconfiguration of the field of experience" (Rancière 1999: 35). Hence, there is no privileged political subject pre-existing the occurrence of politics as this subject only comes into being when and if claiming equality (Chambers 2013: 16–17).

According to Rancière, this coming into being of new political subjects "rests on the capacity to universalize particular conflicts as general instances of dissensus" (Panagia and Rancière 2000: 125). Emancipation then is about a "struggle [of people] to free themselves from the place assigned to them, to assert themselves as bearers of a project that could be universally shared" (Rancière 2014 [2008]: 178). It is only when a demand transcends a particularizing framing and starts functioning as a stand-in for a universalizing message of equality, that we can say that a conflict is properly political. Although always initiated by *a part*, i.e. someone with a specific name, place and function, it is the process of dis-identification from the symbolic order by claiming universality in the name of equality that triggers a process of politicization.

While politicization and depoliticization are two sides of the same coin, attempts at particularization have the effect of depoliticizing a conflict by keeping it within a certain fixed partitioning of social space, identities, interests and positions. As Baeten (2009: 248) puts it, through depoliticizing processes

> particular demands (for example the demand for more schools) are kept particular (the demand for more schools) in an attempt to avoid them acquiring a wider, universal status (demand for universal state provision of high-quality public services) that could make them enter the sphere of the political.

By holding a conflict in a particularizing frame of demands and interests, it can be given a place within the existing police, hence not forming a direct threat to this order (Oosterlynck and Swyngedouw 2010).

It should be stressed that particularizing and universalizing framings can take various forms and are inextricably linked to one another, and several ways of framing often occur at the same moment. Universalizing framing cannot exist without a particular conflict, and often particular interests are also at stake when universalizing frames are used in a conflict. Additionally, it must be highlighted that attempts at the universalization of demands inevitably fold back in forms of particularization. However, we do argue that the use of universalizing claims changes the very nature of conflicts, enlarges the basis of struggle, is necessary to open the debate of what is negotiable and what is not, and makes it more difficult to incorporate these claims into the existing order of things.[1] The performativity of forms of politics grounded in this understanding of emancipation as political subjectivization can then be gauged from the extent through which the police order is transformed in the process. The importance of universalization for emancipation, and its interrelation with a particular context and particularizing frames, will form the focus of the empirical analysis in the remainder of this chapter.

The Struggle at Ghent's Landhuis: A Relational Approach

In order to explore the merits of a relational approach to political difference, we utilize this approach to assess the political dynamics in the struggle for *'t Landhuis* in Ghent, a mid-sized Belgian city. *'t Landhuis*, literally translated as 'The Manor', is a former organic farm located at the outskirts of the city.

Figure 3.1 Logo vzw De Warmoezeniers
Source: Elisabet Van Wymeersch, 2015

This domain—housing a central building, a herring smokehouse, outbuildings and some organic farmland—was abandoned in 2009 and squatted in the spring of 2010. The initiating group of occupants were searching for a place to start their own open, urban farming initiative. For about one and a half years, they lived and worked there with the consent of the private owner, who did not mind them occupying the land since he was planning to sell the land to the City of Ghent and had no further intentions to do something with it. During that time, they held sessions on urban gardening, organized vegan peoples' kitchens and allowed neighbours to have their own allotments in the organic garden. By 2015, about 50 people were involved at *'t Landhuis*, of whom about 40 were gardeners who used only the allotments and a dozen who also used the residential building. However, since the purchase of the plot of land by the City of Ghent in the winter of 2011, the continuation of this 'autonomous ecological centre' has been threatened by expulsion and demolition, as the city council intended to erect a training complex for the city's first division soccer team (Van Pee 2012).

In what follows, we examine how this conflict has unfolded since 2011 and the effects on the city as a space that may nurture ecological commons.[2] To reconstruct the conflict, we collected data from newspaper articles reporting on *'t Landhuis*, policy documents and reports of internal meetings of the association 'De Warmoezeniers', meetings between

Figure 3.2 Allotments at *'t Landhuis*
Source: Elisabet Van Wymeersch, 2016

occupants and employees of the City of Ghent, meetings between different departments of the City of Ghent and a meeting between the members of the 'Municipal Committee for Spatial Planning' (GECORO). Furthermore, we interviewed several actors involved in the conflict. On the basis of this empirical material, we identified three phases in the conflict: (1) a first phase in which a non-negotiation policy was applied towards the occupants, (2) a second phase in which the city council started negotiating with them and reached an agreement on the maintenance of the allotments, and finally (3) the revival of the conflict due to the occupants affirming the right to housing.

Squatting *'t Landhuis*: No Voice in 'Property-Holding Democracy'

In the first phase of the conflict, the city council refused to negotiate with the occupants. Even though they used the land and invested their time and resources, the occupants' voices were ignored by aldermen at the time, who identified the occupants as squatters with no legal ownership. The alderman used the policing effects of property rights in the existing social order to reduce the occupants' voices to noise. In December 2011, the parcel at the 'Warmoezeniersweg' was purchased by the City of Ghent and it soon enough became clear that Christophe Peeters, the alderman at the time, would not tolerate squatting. Between 2007 and 2012, Christophe Peeters was alderman of Finance, Facility Management and Sports in a city council that consisted of members of the socialist (SP.a-Spirit) and the liberal (VLD) party. His approach towards squatting stemmed from a long-lasting anti-squatting stance within the Flemish liberal party, of which this alderman is a member. According to this party, it is unacceptable that ownership would not be universally respected.

Furthermore, alderman Peeters already had other plans with the land on which *'t Landhuis* has its activities. He promised the city's first division soccer team that they could use the site to erect an extra training complex (Van Pee 2012). The alderman's vision of ownership in general and his particular intentions with the *Landhuis* terrain specifically explain why he did not perceive the occupants as negotiating partners. Lacking an ownership claim or official political function, they were seen as having no right to co-determine the future of this plot of land. In this context, it came as no surprise when Alderman Peeters ordered the occupants to leave the terrain.

In February 2012, the occupants reacted to this threat of expulsion by starting a petition, titled "wasteland & anti-squat for the socio-ecological project 't Landhuis?!" (vzw De Warmoezeniers 2012). In this petition, they accused the city council of undermining its own sustainable image by closing its eyes to a valuable social-ecological project. Furthermore, the occupants laid down a complaint with the city's ombudsperson, appealing to the value of their project for the city and defending that more than ever, it is crucial to handle our planet in a sustainable way. . . . It would be a shame to put a socio-ecological project in full development on hold, and make the residents/concierges homeless, while there is no worthy alternative scenario laying on the table.

(dienst Ombudsvrouw Stad Gent 2012: 68–69)[3]

In both actions, universalizing framing can be recognized. Although there is no doubt that particular interests were also playing a role in occupying the site, the occupants framed their claims in terms of an equal right to co-determine its (and by extension the city's) socioecological future. By doing so, they disrupted the police order, which requires you to identify as a landowner to be recognized and heard as a negotiation partner. The occupants challenged this 'distribution of names, places and functions' along the lines of property owners and non-property owners, and contested their identification as 'squatters', as they felt it institutionalizes inequalities in discussing the city's socioecological future. It is important, however, to acknowledge that the order of 'property holding democracy' is itself the result of a previous moment of disruption in name of equality, as property law was created to protect citizens against the arbitrariness of political rulers (see John Locke).[4] As this claim to equal rights to property was institutionalized and became part of the existing order, it inevitably created its own inequalities between property and non-property owners. It is against this new inequality, which wrongs everyone's equal right to determine the future of the city as an ecological common, that the occupants in the case of *'t Landhuis* react.[5]

From Noise to Voice

Although official plans were still to evict the occupants, the expulsion date was delayed until August 2012 due to a personal intervention by the mayor. This intervention should be seen in the light of the contentious context in which this struggle was going on: not everyone working in and for the municipality shared the opinion of Alderman Peeters. The ombudsperson, for example, who is a neutral mediator employed by the city council to conciliate in such conflicts, believed tenants should also be heard in discussions on the future use of the land. She suggested the occupiers present themselves as the 'caretakers' rather than squatters of the building and urged the alderman to let them stay in the building under the custody of an anti-squat company provided they were willing to pay rent. The ombudsperson's intervention opened more space for negotiation, but only on the condition that the occupants would take the more 'acceptable' position of tenants and caretakers of the building, a position that could be easier accommodated for in the existing order of property-holding democracy.

Tensions between *Landhuis* adherents and opponents became aggravated in January 2013 when the Green party joined the Socialists and Liberal party in the city council. The occupants of *'t Landhuis* emphasized that their project is in line with the official governing program of both the Greens and the Socialists and spoke to the ambition of the new socialist alderman for Urban Development, Housing and Public Green, Tom Balthazar, to expand garden allotments in the city (Balthazar 2014). Because of the enhanced sensitivity to ecological concerns of the newly established city council and favourable publicity of *'t Landhuis* in a local newspaper, by May 2013 the city council officially changed its approach towards the conflict and announced that it wanted to maintain a share of the allotments at *'t Landhuis*. This action was a first rapprochement towards the occupants, acknowledging their voice as legitimate stakeholders in the discussion. While previously there could be no legally binding conversation with the occupants because they were identified as squatters, they were now invited to share their vision of the situation. By speaking as equals and demanding the right to have a say on the socio-ecological future of the city, the occupants managed to challenge the police order, obtaining a right to speak on certain topics that they previously were not heard and making the preservation of the allotments negotiable.

However, the negotiation on the allotments came with the condition that the occupants would formally organize themselves into an official association, unifying occupants and gardeners. This pushed them into a more particularized subject position. Though not everyone involved at *'t Landhuis* completely agreed with this move, in February 2014 the occupants created

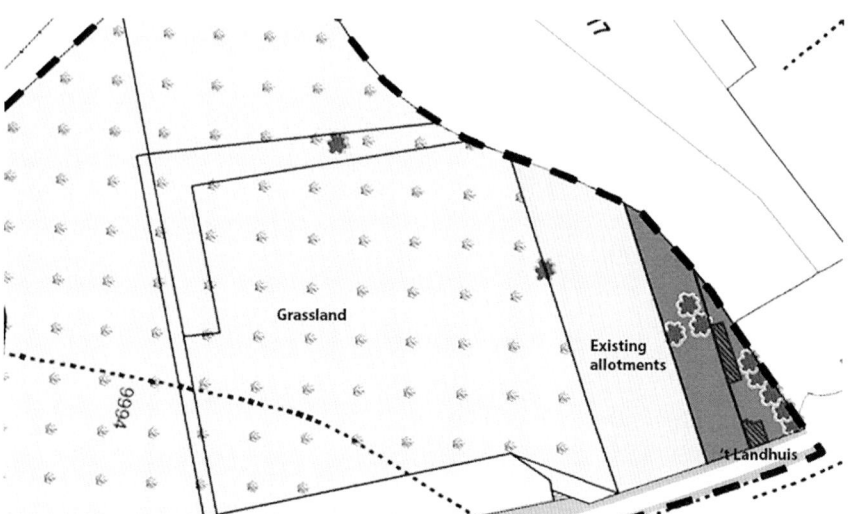

Figure 3.3 Map of the current situation at *'t Landhuis*

Source: Excerpt from *Gemeentelijk Ruimtelijk Uitvoeringsplan nr-160 Groenas 4—Bovenschelde; Figure 'Feitelijke toestand'* [Municipal Spatial Implementation Plan No-160 Green axis 4—Upper Scheldt; Figure 'Current condition']. Adapted by Elisabet Van Wymeersch from Stad Gent (2015)

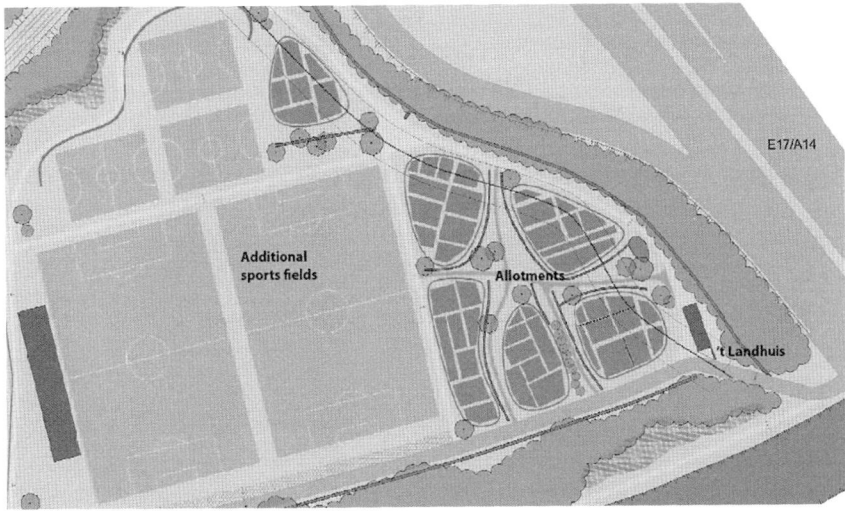

Figure 3.4 Proposed plan by the City of Ghent to maintain and expand the allotments at *'t Landhuis*. On this plan, the residential building is erased

Source: Excerpt from *Ruimtelijk uitvoeringsplan Groenas 4—Bovenschelde Concept-RUP. Infomoment 9 januari; Figure 'Mogelijke invulling van het gebied met sportvelden, parking, verlegde Warmoezeniersweg en uitgebouwde groenas'* [Spatial implementation plan Green axis 4—Upper Scheldt Concept. Info moment 9 January. Figure 'Possible completion of the area with sports fields, parking, displaced road and expanded green axis']. Adapted by Elisabet Van Wymeersch from Stad Gent (2014: 14)

the association 'De Warmoezeniers', whose name is a reference to the street where the allotments are located. After a few months of negotiation, the city council and the association came close to reaching a conclusive solution. It was agreed the occupants' residential building could be demolished. The allotments, on the other hand, could partially stay and be reorganized by the association. In this way, the occupants could safeguard the land for cultivation by neighbours and govern it as ecological commons through the association. At the same time, their involvement in negotiations and subsequently in the management of the land pushed them to see their position and activities in more particularized terms.

The Conflict Repoliticized: The Right to Housing as New Universalizing Strategy

In August 2014, a newly founded neighbourhood committee on cultural heritage[6] intervened in the conflict and started pushing for enhanced maintenance and preservation of the central building, arguing the unique structure should be preserved for cultural heritage. Because of renewed interest in the building, the occupants in the association decided to keep fighting for the preservation of the building as well (vzw De Warmoezeniers 2015). This change of mind should be seen in the light of another discussion regarding the statutes of 'de Warmoezeniers' that was going on between the occupants and the gardeners in the association. In the goals written down in the Articles of Incorporation, it is stated that "the association aims at [p]romoting sustainable agriculture and nutrition, sustainable organic lifestyles, animal welfare, short-chain initiatives and food sovereignty"; "showing solidarity without borders, and resisting oppression and social or environmental abuse, while focusing on communities and farmers in the South"; and "contributing to a positive role for squatting in society" (vzw De Warmoezeniers 2014b: 1).

The city council was unwilling to accommodate the reference to the positive role of squatting, as it shied away from confronting the potential contradictions between its promise to mobilize citizens for an alternative socioecological future and the unequal speaking rights in property-holding democracies. While the primary interest for most gardeners was in maintaining the allotments, others—mostly residents of the building—kept framing their interest in *'t Landhuis* in more overarching universal concerns. In the

Figure 3.5 Residential building at *'t Landhuis*. In the initial agreement between the occupants and the city council, it was agreed on that this building could be demolished and the allotments stay

Source: Elisabet Van Wymeersch, 2015

summer of 2014, this dispute was won by the residents, helping to resist the confinement of their struggle to *'t Landhuis* alone. On the association's general assembly in August 2014, members who did not agree with this more principled approach decided to leave the association (vzw De Warmoezeniers 2014a). Since then, the official point of view of 'de Warmoezeniers' towards the city can be described as follows: no demolition of the building, no eviction of the residents, more space for grassroots initiatives and the recognition of squatting as a valuable answer to the high vacancy rate.

In January 2015, the city eventually withdrew its demolition permit. While this shift can be partly explained by the fact that the city council encountered strong opposition against the expropriation of the adjacent plots, the permanent opposition of 'de Warmoezeniers' and their adherents—framing their claims on universalizing sociopolitical and ecological grounds, which resonated with the stated ambitions of the new city council, also contributed to the shift. One instrument of opposition leading to the withdrawal of the demolition permit was a second petition started by 'de Warmoezeniers', in which they denounced the intentions of the city to tear down the building, referring to both the socioecological value of the initiative, the current affordable housing shortage and the right to housing (vzw De Warmoezeniers 2015).

Regarding the socioecological value of the project, 'de Warmoezeniers' got support from the 'Municipal Advisory Committee for Spatial Planning' of Ghent (GECORO):

> Where does the city want to go? Does she not see the potentials of this growing social and societal relevant initiative, which perfectly complements various thrusts of this year's policy agreement? Given the city's choice for climate neutrality, a green and social policy, co-creation and co-production, it is the GECORO's belief that this should also be reflected in her vision on the future and the choice made by the City for this site.
>
> (De Kezel 2015: 4–5)

After the withdrawal of the demolition permit, a new spatial implementation plan for the area was implemented in which the building was included, but remains located in a recreation zone and should therefore not be permanently inhabited. However, at the time of finishing this chapter, the occupants are still living and organizing activities on a regular basis in *'t Landhuis*.

This case shows how the transformative dynamics of the conflict are driven by attempts of the occupants to position themselves and their demands around *'t Landhuis* as stand-ins for a universalizing message on each and everyone's right to decide on the socioecological future of the city, as well as the right to housing. In a context where the city council had explicitly committed itself to the co-production of a 'socioecological city', they could resist attempts at policing their 'place, name and function' and continue to disrupt the existing order, which increased the collective capacity of citizens to co-determine the city's socioecological future. This acting as a stand-in for a universalizing message is, however, always a precarious exercise, as some members who preferred to focus exclusively on gardening left the association, putting its capacity to mobilize at risk.

Conclusion

In this chapter, we argued for a relational approach to the political difference between politics and the police, which is advanced as a crucial analytical distinction to understand the emancipatory potential of unfolding political dynamics in post-foundationalist political thought. To analyze how new political subjects are co-constituted on a relational field shaped by the logics of politics and policing, we applied Rancière's notions of universalization and particularization and the invocation of equality as a universalizing strategy to a case study on the struggle for ecological commons around *'t Landhuis* in Ghent.

To Rancière, emancipation emerges as the verification of the equality of any speaking being with any other speaking being. He argues that this happens when people contest the distributed name, place and/or function that is given to them and thus become new political subjects. This becoming of new political subjects takes place on a field of tension between a particularization and universalization. In this case, we have shown how the occupiers of *'t Landhuis* acted as properly democratic political subjects by claiming their equal right to have a say on the future of the city, hence contesting the order of 'property holding democracy'. However, during this conflict, as the occupants could use openings in the police order, they were drawn into negotiations, which pushed them to take on a more particular subject position. This is clarified by how the occupants turned into a legally sanctioned formal organization to negotiate the saving of the garden allotments and their governance as ecological commons. From this particular subject position, it was easier to incorporate certain claims in the existing order of things rather than universalizing claims like the rights to housing and the democratic governance of the whole urban environment as ecological commons. In an attempt to put rights to housing more centrally in the political conversation, the occupants took on a more principled position, which led to some of the gardeners leaving the association. This shows how emancipation requires the navigation of a difficult field of tension between particularization and universalization.

Notes

1. We are grateful to Enrico Gualini for drawing our attention to this issue.
2. We define ecological commons as a system in which specific resources are not owned privately but are held in common by a defined community of commoners. In the case of ecological commons, the resources referred to are concerned with the environment.

3. The expropriation of the adjacent plots was fairly rough and it would take time before the training complexes could ever be erected.
4. John Locke, dealing with property rights in 17th-century England, contested the idea that all people are naturally subject to the monarch and as such cannot make claims to property. As a response, Locke developed his liberal theory of limited government in which he argues that all men have certain equal rights, such as the right to life, liberty and property and consequently provided a theory in which safety and security for the growing merchant class of that period was secured. Thus, Locke's theory of limited government intends to provide a check against any power that would violate the individual rights or property (see Chambers 2013).
5. We are grateful to Pascal Debruyne for drawing our attention to this issue.
6. This committee was founded in March 2014 and aimed at collecting and preserving (information on) cultural heritage in the district 'de Ottergemse Dries', the district in which *'t Landhuis* is located.

Further Reading

Gualini, E. (2015) *Planning and Conflict: Critical Perspectives on Contentious Urban Developments*. New York: Routledge. [Conflict in urban development as a potential resource for transformation in local policy].

Legacy, C. (2016) Transforming Transport Planning in the Postpolitical Era. *Urban Studies* 54(14), pp. 3108–3124.

Uitermark, J. and Nicholls, W. (2013) From Politicization to Policing: The Rise and Decline of New Social Movements in Amsterdam and Paris. *Antipode* 46(4), pp. 970–991. [Relational approach to processes of politicization and policing].

References

Allmendinger, P. and Haughton, G. (2012) Post-Political Spatial Planning in England: A Crisis of Consensus? *Transactions of the Institute of British Geographers* 37(1), pp. 89–103.

Badiou, A. and Elliott, G. (2012) *The Rebirth of History: Times of Riots and Uprisings*. London: Verso Books.

Baeten, G. (2009) Regenerating the South Bank: Reworking Community and the Emergence of Post-Political Regeneration. In R. Imrie, L. Lees and M. Raco (eds.) *Regenerating London: Governance, Sustainability, and Community in a Global City*. Abingdon: Routledge, pp. 237–253.

Balthazar, T. (2014) *Beleidsnota Openbaar groen. 40 acties voor meer en mooier groen in Gent 2014–2018*. Gent: Stad Gent.

Bassett, K. (2014) Rancière, Politics, and the Occupy Movement. *Environment and Planning D: Society and Space* 32(5), pp. 886–901.

Chambers, S.A. (2011) Jacques Rancière and the Problem of Pure Politics. *European Journal of Political Theory* 10(3), pp. 303–326.

Chambers, S.A. (2013) *The Lessons of Rancière*. New York: Oxford University Press.

De Kezel, R. (2015) *Sloopvergunning Landhuis -Warmoezeniersweg- mogelijke functionele en sociale invullingen GECORO -advies 015*. Gent: GECORO Gent.

Dienst Ombudsvrouw Stad Gent (2012) *Jaarverslag 2012. Overzicht van alle klachten*. Gent: Stad Gent.

Dikeç, M. (2002) Police, Politics, and the Right to the City. *Geo Journal* 58, pp. 91–98.

Douzinas, C. (2013) *Philosophy and Resistance in the Crisis: Greece and the Future of Europe*. Cambridge: Polity Press.

Gualini, E. (2015) *Planning and Conflict: Critical Perspectives on Contentious Urban Developments*. New York: Routledge.

Legacy, C. (2016) Transforming Transport Planning in the Postpolitical Era. *Urban Studies* 53(14), pp. 3108–3124.

Macleod, G. (2013) New Urbanism/Smart Growth in the Scottish Highlands: Mobile Policies and Post-Politics in Local Development Planning. *Urban Studies* 50(11), pp. 2196–2221.

Marchart, O. (2007) *Post-Foundational Political Thought: Political Difference in Nancy, Lefort, Badiou and Laclau*. Edinburgh: Edinburgh University Press.

Mouffe, C. (2005) *On the Political*. Abingdon: Routledge.

Nash, K. (1996) Post-Democracy, Politics and Philosophy: An Interview with Jacques Rancière. *Angelaki: Journal of the Theoretical Humanities* 1(3), pp. 171–178.

Oosterlynck, S. and Swyngedouw, E. (2010) Noise Reduction: The Postpolitical Quandary of Night Flights at Brussels Airport. *Environment and Planning A* 42(7), pp. 1577–1594.

Panagia, D. and Rancière, J. (2000) Dissenting Words: A Conversation with Jacques Rancière. *Diacritics* 30(2), pp. 113–126.

Raco, M. (2015) Conflict Management, Democratic Demands, and the Post-Politics of Privatisation. In J. Metzger, P. Allmendinger and S. Oosterlynck (eds.) *Planning against the Political: Democratic Deficits in European Territorial Governance*. New York: Routledge, pp. 153–169.

Rancière, J. (1992) Politics, Identification, and Subjectivization. *October* 61, pp. 58–64.

Rancière, J. (1999) *Disagreement: Politics and Philosophy*. Minneapolis: University of Minnesota Press.

Rancière, J. (2004) Introducing Disagreement. *Angelaki: Journal of the Theoretical Humanities* 9(3), pp. 3–9.

Rancière, J. (2007) *Misadventures of Universality*. Paper presented at the Symposium on Philosophy of the Second Moscow Biennale of Contemporary Art, Moscow.

Rancière, J. (2014 [2008]) The Pleasure of Political Metamorphosis. In T. Déri (ed.) *Moments Politiques: Interventions 1977–2009*. New York and Oakland: Seven Stories Press, pp. 171–181.

Stad Gent (2014) *Ruimtelijk uitvoeringsplan Groenas 4—Bovenschelde Concept-RUP. Infomoment 9 januari*. Gent: Stad Gent, Dienst Stedenbouw en Ruimtelijke Planning.

Stad Gent (2015) *Gemeentelijk Ruimtelijk Uitvoeringsplan nr -160 Groenas 4—Bovenschelde*. Gent: Stad Gent, Dienst Stedenbouw en Ruimtelijke Planning.

Swyngedouw, E. (2009) The Antinomies of the Postpolitical City: In Search of a Democratic Politics of Environmental Production. *International Journal of Urban and Regional Research* 33(3), pp. 601–620.

Uitermark, J. and Nicholls, W. (2013) From Politicization to Policing: The Rise and Decline of New Social Movements in Amsterdam and Paris. *Antipode* 46(4), pp. 970–991.

Van Pee, M. (2012) Volkstuintjes ruimen plaats voor voetbalvelden. *De Standaard*, 27 February 2012, p. 15.

Van Puymbroeck, N. and Oosterlynck, S. (2014) Opening Up the Post-Political Condition: Multi-Culturalism and the Matrix of Depoliticisation, Spectres of Radical Politics. In J. Wilson and E. Swyngedouw (eds.) *The Post-Political and Its Discontents: Spaces of Depoliticisation, Spectres of Radical Politics*. Edinburgh: Edinburgh University Press, pp. 86–108.

vzw De Warmoezeniers (2012) 1e Ontruimingsdreiging voor braak en anti-kraak. *Autonome Ecologische Volxstuin 't landhuis* [Online]. Available at: https://tlandhuis.wordpress.com/braak-anti-kraak/2015 [Accessed 1 June 2015].

vzw De Warmoezeniers (2014a) Algemene vergadering De Warmoezeniers 24 August 2014. Minutes of the association's meeting. Gent.

vzw De Warmoezeniers (2014b) *Oprichtingsstatuten* [Online]. Gent. Available at: https://data.be/nl/doc/staatsblad/akte/2014/02/26/De-Warmoezeniers-14302033_20140226_0546849376 [Accessed 10 January 2017].

vzw De Warmoezeniers (2015) *Petitie 2* [Online]. Gent: vzw De Warmoezeniers. Available at: https://tlandhuis.wordpress.com/petitie-2/ [Accessed 10 January 2017].

Wilson, J. and Swyngedouw, E. (2014) *The Post-Political and Its Discontents: Spaces of Depoliticization, Spectres of Radical Politics*. Edinburgh: Edinburgh University Press.

Žižek, S. (1999) *The Ticklish Subject: The Absent Centre of Political Ontology*. London: Verso.

4 How to Reclaim Mafia-Controlled Territory?

An Emancipatory Experience in Southern Italy

Gabriella Esposito De Vita

Discussing the Foreground

The prevailing conceptual binary between governments as hegemonic powers and an insurgent public does not hold for contexts where organized crime controls the territory. Similarly, the usual narrative of the 'retreat of the political' does not adequately describe the complex scenario of actors and forces (Lacoue-Labarthe and Nancy 1997). Mafia-like organizations add a third element to the prevailing conceptual binary, due to its illegal counter-hegemonic local government. Mafia-like organizations operate both in isolation from and intermingled with official governments (Monnier 1998). Although the structure of the Mafia has changed, its centuries-long history of controlling territory and operating as a parallel government survives in some parts of southern Italy. This monopolistic structure has been exported outside Italy, changing its modus operandi in each new territory (Marselli 2009; Sterling 1994).

This chapter aims to better understand how emancipatory cooperation between stakeholders from public, private and voluntary sectors are built in situations where planning and policy are implemented under the distorting influence of organized crime. Could government and insurgent publics form coalitions for redemocratization against the common Mafia *enemy* via place-based regeneration processes? Could this reaction to Mafia control and hegemony be considered an emancipatory process? By exploring these questions, the article seeks to enrich our understanding of the territorial power of organized crime and to point out how its influence on the 'dark side of institutional planning', understood as catering to the interests of the Mafia rather than collective ones (Yiftachel 1998; Saija and Gravagno 2009; Falcone and Padovani 1991), can be weakened. While this is a very specific question, the empirical discussion is embedded within the larger theoretical debate on emancipatory planning, which "needs to focus on conflict and power relations and needs communicative, people-centred, practices" (Albrechts 2003: 905). Unfortunately, instead of participation increasing the power of underprivileged people, it frequently represents an alibi for perverted forms of democracy, particularly the manipulation of consensus and repression

(Mouffe 2000; Forester 1989; Lees 2004; Kunzmann 2016). In this framework, the democratic control of territories being challenged by Mafia-type organizations offers the opportunity to reflect on these power imbalances. The capability of organized crime to control territories has been frequently identified as a hidden parallel government imprisoning territory and citizens (Romano 1969 [1918]). Organized crime exercises control at a variety of levels: "we can consider, on the one hand, the Mafia as an organisation of territorial control and, on the other hand, the Mafia as an organisation of illegal activities" (Scaglione 2016: 60). At a local level, they act as a militia to control and influence a place. Their political and economic control extends to the national level through infiltrating major governing bodies. Their reach even extends globally by operating in international financial markets (Arlacchi 1986). Their socio-spatial expressions therefore range from armed forces controlling the streets to international business and financial organizations. Organized crime can thus be seen as another predatory elite acting for the "erosion of democracy and weakening of the public sphere" (Wilson and Swyngedouw 2015: 5) at both global and local scales.

In urban areas challenged by Mafia-type criminal organizations, such as Camorra in Naples, N'drangheta in Calabria and Mafia in Sicily, planning processes need to deal with the pervasive presence of criminal clans in economic activities and daily life of inhabitants, especially in the most deprived areas (Saija and Gravagno 2009). In this context, social inequalities are linked with the presence of criminal organizations as well as with 'Mafia-supporting systems' (Barbagallo 2010). These systems comprise a complex web of intermingled illegal interests, borderline informal businesses, fears and threats, often creating a pervasively antisocial culture (Barbagallo 2010; Sanfilippo 2005). The atmosphere created by the presence of dominant criminal organizations can lead to some citizens identifying with the devious attitudes and behavioural patterns of the exponents of Mafia clans (Sciarrone and Storti 2014). The general strategy adopted by the Italian government to minimize these consequences addresses "economic and cultural development through a collaborative approach, in which people from different backgrounds exchange knowledge, frame problems, create understanding and perform action on an equal basis" (Saija and Gravagno 2009: 507).

Contesting hegemonies in neoliberal, free market economies often require sustained social organization to reinstitute more democratic means of control and debate. In Sicily and Naples, criminal powers have achieved hegemonic influence over governmental decisions. Novel approaches, developed by anti-Mafia activists and communities, must work to counter the level and depth of Mafia control through policy design and planning to support bottom-up emancipatory initiatives. The consequences of uneven exercise of power by organized crime require that participatory approaches, everyday practices, civil society economics and bottom-up activist planning be studied through action-research perspectives (Chekland and Holwell 1997;

Cahill 2007; Tornaghi 2015). This research approach allows for conceptual integration of both spontaneous and state-sanctioned initiatives in policy design approaches, a complex task. "Working within a research environment with a history dense of memories, habits, expectations, fears, and defensive mechanism requires particular skills and mobilizes issues of research responsibility, values and ethics" (Tornaghi 2015: 35). Such challenges are particularly pertinent to contexts pervaded by a 'Camorra way of life'. It could be an opportunity to investigate how community-led initiatives and social enterprises could be a reaction to the territorial control of organized crime or other forms of totalitarianism (Allulli 2010; Atkinson 2003).

The chapter presents the results of an action-based case study undertaken in an urban area challenged by criminal organizations, the Camorra system in southern Italy. Communities in this kind of area are threatened by both illegal activities perpetrated by Camorra clans and by the weakness of social welfare facilities and services. The Camorra emerged in Campania in the 17th century as a fraternal order working in a counter-hegemonic way by supporting common people during political struggles. Since the 19th century, this hidden phenomenon increased its illegal activities, progressively evolving into a system active in all typologies of criminal trafficking (Barbagallo 2010; Esposito De Vita 2014: 178–180), with highly adaptive patterns of operation allowing for its inconspicuous infiltration into the business and financial system (Brancaccio 2009). The organizational models of the prominent Camorra clans have been compared to the typical entrepreneurial structure in the contemporary economic system: the system network (Direzione Nazionale Antimafia 2016).

The present study analyzes how a previously Mafia-owned property has been used by the Ministry of Justice following its confiscation. The effects of this seize-to-reuse process has been studied in the metropolitan area of Naples[1] where the process of political, economic and spatial decriminalization rely on rebuilding public perception of areas infamously seen as 'crime zones'. The study specifically investigates whether reuse resulted in enhanced quality and accessibility of public spaces and services. The study further investigates whether the repossession of property led to the expulsion of crime from the local economic system and to the emancipation of local communities.

The study of reuse is the La Gloriette Multipurpose Centre. The Centre was the home of Michele Zaza, a once prominent boss of Neapolitan Camorra but is now managed by a not-for-profit organization (NPO) run entirely by women. The villa features a sumptuous, heavy, and provocative architecture, typical of the Camorra subculture. Its interior includes a stone mosaic depicting violent scenes and criminal symbols and a terrace overlooking the Gulf of Naples, surrounded by the Mount Vesuvius and the island of Capri (Figure 4.1). The building, gardens and small nearby rural areas are part of Zaza's properties confiscated in Naples, Rome and Milan.

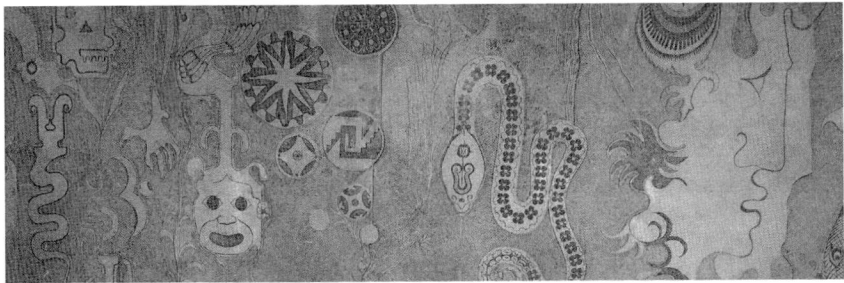

Figure 4.1   La Gloriette Multipurpose Centre. Clockwise: mosaic as ambivalent remi-
niscence of celebrating Camorra symbols, the terrace facing Vesuvius and
one of the NPO's working groups

Source: Gabriella Esposito De Vita, 2016

How Can Activist Planning and Civil Society Initiatives Create Capacity to Deal With Organized Crime?

The dominant approach in Italy is a double-pronged attempt that seeks to both prevent crimes through judicial and police actions and strengthen communities by increasing their capacity to react to organized crime in everyday life. Confronting the growing financialization of criminal power and its influence on cultural codes and on political and economic circles has become more publicly visible, and the civic reuse of former Camorra properties confiscated by the Ministry of Justice resulted in the most prominent and visible approach.

Law 646/1982 passed in 1982. It was the first major law addressing the seizure of Mafia properties as means for preventing further crime, corruption or escape. After the Mafia massacres in the early 90s, Law Decree 399/1994 enabled the authorities to seize all assets for which the convicted are unable to prove the legal origin. Law 109/1996 was introduced to facilitate the reuse of confiscated properties, which were growing in both number and size. A new legal entity was created to deal with the management of the seizure and confiscation of Mafia assets (Law 50/2010): the National Agency for the Administration and Allocation of Anti-mafia Confiscated Assets (ANBSC).

Recently, Law 228/2012 introduced tax benefits and expedited approval for those undertaking a reuse project.

The procedure typically begins with the court's temporary seizure of assets to impede the abilities of alleged criminals to access resources and interfere with an ongoing investigation. If the judicial process results in a conviction, the financial assets are confiscated by the judiciary branch and then moved to a special fund of the Ministry of Justice, the Unified Fund for Justice (FUG). Once the final transfer is complete, all assets can be liquidated and the property can be redeveloped for public services or social initiatives (Table 4.1). Land and buildings can be directly managed by central and local governments, providing services such as schools, public offices, police stations and healthcare facilities. Other properties can be dedicated to social and cultural initiatives managed by not-for-profit organizations (NPOs). A competitive call for projects allow the municipalities in which those properties are located to assign these seized assets to NPOs based on their proposals (ANBSC 2012). The selection criteria include the NPO's curriculum and the typology and quality of the project. NPOs must prove that they have never had any contact with each known affiliate of Mafia groups and that they promote legal behaviours within their community. The selection of the proposal is based on the depth of the NPO's connection to the territory, the necessity for and the ability to provide the services, as well as the public engagement (ANBSC 2012). Although the main goal of the legislation was to diminish the economic power of the Mafiosi and their influence on the territory (Caneppele and Calderoni 2014), additional effects pertaining to social innovation were registered during research.

While property is frequently used by crime organizations for money laundering and corruption, this research demonstrates that it also plays an important role in building the reputation of the clans and strengthening their local roots. The huge variety of properties represent the spatial presence and significance of a given Camorra clan (Figure 4.2). Sometimes properties are 'officially' part of the Camorra patrimony and their existence and meaning is widely known; in other cases, only affiliates and local residents are able to recognize them. Properties include villas and apartments with architectural features inspired by movie characters, opulent and kitsch decorations, rich materials and accessories such as columned patios, swimming pools and sport facilities. This category of building serves to celebrate the role of the criminal within the Camorra hierarchy. Military power is demonstrated by gated, armoured headquarters consisting of residential blocks and other buildings transformed for drug trafficking and other illegal businesses. Communities become part of the support system of clans by offering housing in controlled real estate blocks, helping with surveillance and other forms of complicity. These co-opted, militarized structures are often built by companies managed by clan members operating outside urban planning rules and without requisite permissions. Productive districts also play a role: Factories and farms managed by clans exert unfair competition against other productive activities, influencing the supply chain by intimidation.

Table 4.1 Scheme of the main types of confiscated assets with a focus on immovable assets

Typology	Description	Management models
Financial assets and movable properties	Gold deposit, bank deposit, bonds, stocks, jewellery, art collections and, in general, movable capital assets. Motor vehicles, boats and movable goods not included in company assets.	Destined to the Unified Fund for Justice (FUG). Proceeds from the sale of these goods are assigned to the management of other confiscated goods.
Immovable capital assets	Land and buildings, apartments, villas, farms.	Prevalently allocated as follows: • Maintained as property of the State, for public purposes "purpose of justice, public order and civil protection"; • Maintained as property of the State to be used by the National Agency for the Administration of Anti-mafia Confiscated Assets (ANBSC), for economic purposes; • Transferred to the municipality where the building lies, for social and institutional purposes; the municipality can choose to use it directly or donate it temporarily to a non-profit organization for social uses. • Properties confiscated for drug crimes, generally, are assigned to associations and rehabilitation centres for drug-addictions.
Company goods	Construction, agricultural and food industries, hotels and hospitality structures, restaurants and pizza houses, night clubs and commercial centres. It also includes manufactory plants and machineries.	Offered for sale or reallocation on the market, particularly for companies and businesses.

Note: Based on Reggio's (2013) report produced on behalf of the NGO *Libera—Associazioni Nomi e Numeri contro le mafie* ['Free'—Associations, Names, and Numbers of Mafia] involved in promoting initiatives for reaction to the Mafia-supporting systems

Source: Gabriella Esposito De Vita, 2017

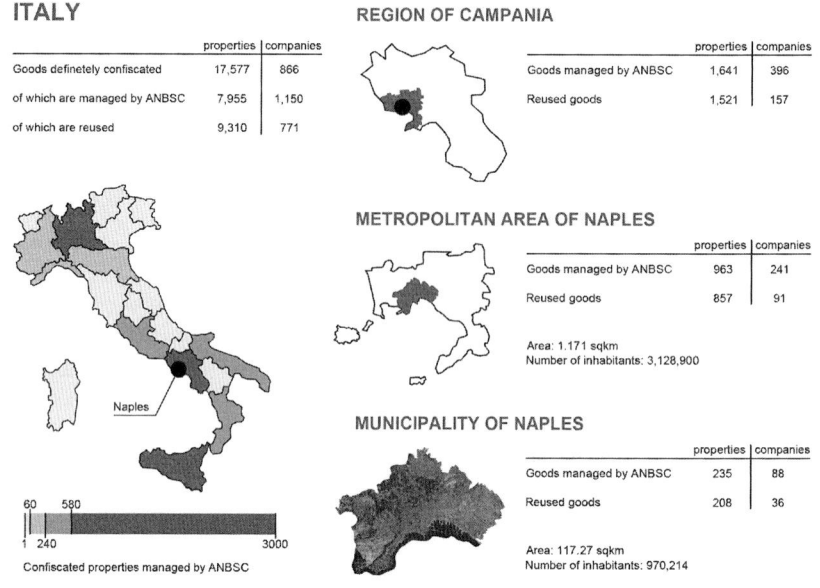

Figure 4.2 Confiscation of Mafia's goods and properties in the metropolitan area of
Naples in relation to the Italian and regional context

Note: Based on data available within the ANBSC public repository www.benisequestraticonfiscati.
it/ [Accessed 11/01/2017], integrated by the fieldwork

Source: Gabriella Esposito De Vita, 2017

The reuse of these buildings could contribute to the reduction of organized
crime's influence in these territories. These initiatives also cover some aspects
of social welfare by delegating specific matters to self-organized actors. Frequently, reuse projects developed by NPOs for providing social services seek
to cover the needs of fragile groups: women under threat, young people with
disadvantaged families, children involved in illicit activities or migrants forced
into informal or illegal labour. The current austerity approaches and the need
for encouraging self-organized initiatives for job creation and local development seem to be influencing decisions to offer the seized Camorra assets to
civil society groups involved in not-for-profit social and cultural initiatives. In
this scenario, local authorities maintain the role of facilitators of the bottom-
up initiatives, by providing control and protection against potential Camorra
threats and infiltrations, and enable the local civil society to build up the
needed capacity to effectively promote place-based initiatives. Civil society
and institutions provide mutually enforced control; this is particularly important as public authorities might be infused by Camorra clans and civil interest
groups could be 'manipulated' by strong hidden players. This kind of initiative
contributes to the production of social capital and activates self-confidence
regarding rights and duties of residents by helping people realize alternative

generative processes of civil democracy that do not rely on being controlled by the local criminal clans. This chapter further addresses the shortcomings and opportunities of this process, contributing to understanding how these experiences, developed within the security law, could be implemented in the local development and urban planning system in Italy and abroad.

Conceptualizing Community as a Place-Based Modus Operandi Against Organized Crime

The capability of the anti-Mafia policy within the context of Campania is strained, limiting the impact of planning disciplines due to Mafia infiltration, market pressures, nepotism and private interests within the public realm, an ineffective bureaucracy and a need for controlling illegal activities. To further contextualize the need for emancipation, the opportunities for empowerment, as well as the possible risk of organized crime infiltrating such projects, the following offers a brief introduction to the idea of community in southern Italy.

Social and urban studies definitions of community in southern Italy consistently describe the concept of community as a place-based social network in which families, neighbours and workers interact, cutting across different social classes and including newcomers and immigrants (Allum 1975; Di Gennaro 1992; Da Molin 1990; Macry 1988; Esposito De Vita et al. 2016). This family and/or place-based network could be considered inclusive and conducive to mutual support and human relationships. Conversely, its permeability, which opens it up to influence from Mafia-type systems and to attending nepotistic dispositions and general mistrust of the public realm, casts a less optimistic shadow (Levi 1996; Sales 1993; Romano 1918).

The main challenges to the community's social space are related to the economic system threatened by crime syndicates, the abandonment and decay of built cultural heritage, the high unemployment rate, as well as the lack of accessible public places and services (Fusco Girard 2012). In such a context, planning disciplines and policymaking struggle to produce effective plans and policies, often resulting in a stalemate which encourages illicit and/or borderline practices. These challenges are countered by opportunities and resources, such as the UNESCO-listed cultural heritage, the well-known landscape resources, as well as the resilience of people in reacting to crises by building adaptive networks based on mutually supportive relationships.

The Camorra has a century's worth of experience infiltrating various groups and consolidating hegemonic influence. While recent community-based organizations allow for resilient approaches to emancipation, these new structures continue to be at risk of infiltration by local networks of criminal organizations, e.g. the Camorra. Social deprivation, unemployment and urban decay are credited with fuelling the rise of recruitment of young affiliates (*affiliati*) for Camorra and other organized criminal syndicates. Conditions of the local community can variably justify the clans' influence over a place, and it can motivate resistance to the Camorra. The opportunities provided by this variability is certainly clear to Camorra. Historically, criminal organizations expanded their support base by creating opportunities and events for increasing the sense of belonging to the district and, by extension, to the leaders of the Camorra clan. This attitude is changing, thanks to the reaction of the civil society, supported by initiatives at regional, urban and district levels.

The taxonomy of confiscated properties in Campania to be reused has been built by collecting data on typology, the stakeholders (promoter-manager) involved, the activities hosted, the original funding scheme and the operational budget, from the national census of the ANBSC and local authorities' databases. Regarding the funding schemes, 50% of surveyed initiatives won financial support. This funding was usually used to cover the refurbishment of lands and buildings.

The majority of initiatives in Campania are located within the municipality of Naples, due to the combination of easy accessibility, high land values, high population (~1 million), strong networks of activists, as well as pressing needs for social services, accessible public spaces and job creation (Figure 4.3). Job-creation initiatives focus on proposing alternative

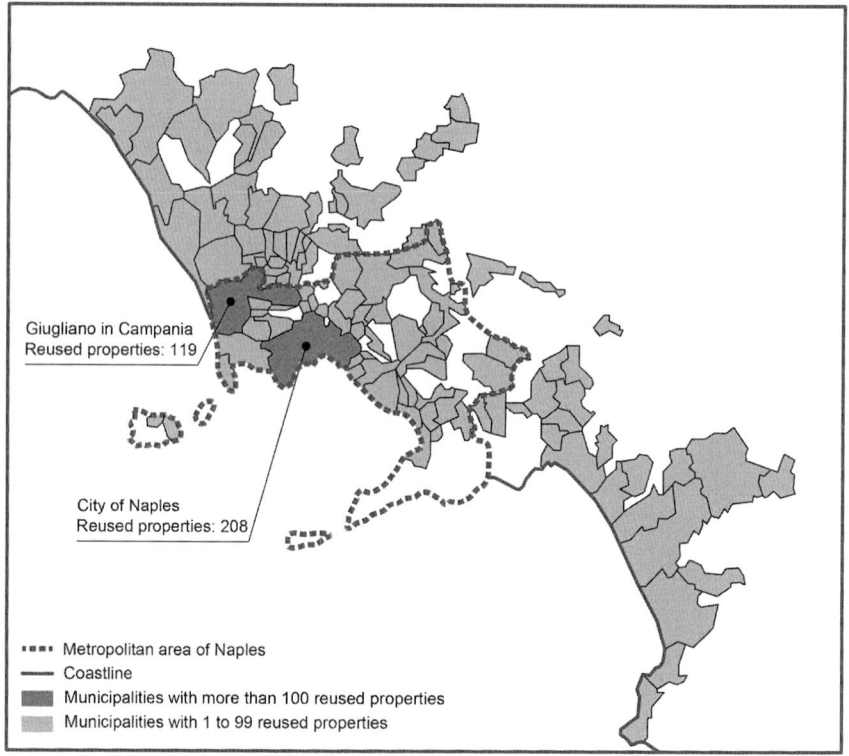

Figure 4.3 Density of properties confiscated ex Law 575/65 and destined to be reused in the metropolitan area of Naples

Note: Data from 30 September 2015, available within the ANBSC public repository, www.benisequestraticonfiscati.it/ [Accessed 11 January 2017], integrated by the fieldwork

Source: Gabriella Esposito De Vita, 2017

models of life compared to those of the Camorra clan and work to thwart the recruitment strategies of criminals. All initiatives are managed by well-rooted associations with a number of volunteers and a strong capacity of networking and community engagement, as in the Multipurpose Community Centre La Gloriette.

First Findings and Focus on a Successful Experience: La Gloriette and its Network

La Gloriette aims to build pathways of autonomy for 'fragile' young subjects involved in a social inclusion programme (www.gloriette.it). More broadly, the project seeks to promote a culture of legal justice through virtuous reuse of prominent confiscated properties. The centre is in an opulent and dense district of Naples, called Posillipo.

The Centre has been activated thanks to a funding project of the *con il Sud* Foundation for valorizing and promoting self-sustainability of confiscated properties in 2010 and is now financing its activities with small contributions from the healthcare system, donations and self-promotion initiatives. The NPO that manages the project is the social enterprise Orsa Maggiore, created in 1995 by a group of women for dealing with social, educational and health problems as well as gender issues. The NPO operates a sort of 'urban piazza' out of the former fortified villa, encouraging young people with disabilities and their families to work together for self-reliance and independence. This initiative is now completely self-funded, thanks to the indefatigable efforts of its members and to their network of communities, volunteers and charity organizations funding the events. The amenities of the building/property helpfully aid the hosting of cultural events and other charitable experiences for fundraising.

Creating emancipation in such contexts means undoing the traditional relationship between people and the Camorra system, where the criminal hegemony has been accepted passively. The 'fuzzy' system of cross-pollinations, where people, Camorra clans, institutions and business intermingle, needs to be challenged not only by controlling criminal activities but also by encouraging responses to the pervasive power of clans (Barbagallo 2010; Fijnaut and Paoli 2004; Sales 1993). This initiative produced an emancipatory reaction to the Camorra subculture through reuse of a 'hyper-private' Camorra property and its integration into counter-hegemonic planning processes.

Transitioning away from Mafia control often involves sustained challenges. People involved with the Zaza clan issued threats and attempted to forcibly occupy an agricultural area next to the buildings where La Gloriette hosts farm-therapy activities. Following the seizure, Zaza's clan tried to acquire the property via figureheads (*prestanome*), members of civil society who are also willing executors of the clans' orders. After these attempts failed, criminals damaged and vandalized the building. The refurbishment of the property slowed due to the necessity to amend the building regulation violations by Zaza during the original criminal occupation as well as to the threats and intimidations by members of the Camorra. Despite these obstacles, the centre plays an important role in demonstrating possibilities for life without a Camorra hegemony over social life. Field research suggests that the social support for the Camorra family has been declining, and different social groups have gained confidence that the reproduction of seemingly stable undemocratic systems such as Camorra can be altered.

The initiative of La Gloriette embodies the major findings of broader field-work in the metropolitan area of Naples. These small-size, well-planned initiatives, developed by applying for funding from different sources and enhanced by a growing networking capacity, are typically the most successful experiences in terms of impact on the social awareness and the communities' engagement, as well as of the cultural reaction against organized crime. By providing a social space for self-organizing insurgencies by sharing dreams and risks, this is a step forward in the direction of de-privatized and de-criminalized uses of these assets. The transformation of Gloriette serves as a demonstrative catalyst for returning Mafia-controlled spaces back to civil society. The transformation demonstrates that returning places of Mafia control can not only mitigate violence but also provide a common good for collective use to the most vulnerable groups, and that their emancipation is a form of broader (self)empowerment.

Such a well-rooted initiative involves multiple parties with dynamic effects. The collaboration of stakeholders and the help of funding opportunities allow for a new social ecosystem to emerge, in which complementary activities and job creation opportunities and services define the social reuse of confiscated assets as a strategy for emancipating communities challenged by organized crime. The strategy, based on enthusiasm and ethical effort of local non-profit associations, could achieve long-term results if based on well-rooted initiatives and place-based and cooperative approaches. Nevertheless, to encourage emancipatory initiatives in challenged territories, a more comprehensive policy is needed.

Experiences of Social Reuse of Confiscated Assets: Possible Emancipatory Processes Within Imprisoned Territories

Organized crime rearticulates ambitions and hopes and drains resources from individuals and groups to capture influence and control of a territory in Campania. In response, civil society works to foster human relationships and initiatives for accessible and emancipatory purposes. The large number of confiscated properties lies at the centre of this process, in that it helps accumulate people, ideas, places and resources for promoting an emancipatory process developed by challenged communities.

The mentioned cases of civil society economy as antidotes to the criminal economy seem to have significant emancipatory potentials. The confiscation of criminal assets has a twofold role: it affects the economic and symbolic power of crime bosses and it undermines the widespread support they enjoy. Reuse mitigates Camorra influence on a territory, particularly by reducing its capacity to recruit young 'soldiers'. By investigating national and urban policies in the field, we have discovered that the opening of those gated properties to the people and providing services and opportunities for redemption can stimulate other virtuous processes, with possible impacts on the entire urban system (Bee and Pachi 2014).

These reuse processes indicate that policy thinking requires careful consideration of the appropriate way for supporting the enhancement, duration and snowball effect of institutional and governance responses (Pugalis and Bentley 2014; Bobbio 2004). Moreover, such responses should consist of collaborative forms of decision-making, involving diverse stakeholder groups (Gilbert 2014). In reflecting on how to integrate these approaches in an emancipatory planning process, we need to consider a revision in terms of agonistic perspectives on institutional planning and decision-making, which in Italy is very close to and influenced by official and hidden hegemonies.

It could be useful to understand, conceptualize and codify these complex relationships between institutional and criminal attacks on the public interest. Some key words and phrases—such as guerrilla urbanism (Hou 2010), insurgent (Miraftab 2009; Friedmann 2011), radical (Grabow and Heskin 1973) and activist planning (Sager 2016)—summarize a counter-hegemonic approach to planning (Purcell 2009) aimed at challenging the frequently hidden private or public interests of hegemonic groups in urban redevelopment strategies. To address this topic from a different perspective, the chapter focused on places where both political clientelism (Hopkin 2006) and organized crime activities affect the planning practices, producing obstacles to bottom-up initiatives that are more aligned with community needs (Esposito De Vita 2014). The positive impact of the analyzed practices could be maximized with institutional policies based on the empowerment of civil society within participatory governance including the reuse initiatives (Fischer 2006).

The study of an imprisoned territory revealed tensions between institutionalized top-down control and the struggle to remove crime-imposed constraints. In such contexts, an action-research approach can ethically support self-reliant emancipatory processes against multi-level organized crime control. The embedded role of the researcher aiding in the reshaping of places and encouraging novel, democratic networks within criminally controlled territories has revealed the 'collaborative potential for emancipation' and challenged established regimes of power.

Note

1. The research started under the umbrella of the project BESECURE (Best Practices Enhancers for Security in Urban Regions; www.besecure-project.eu), funded by the European Union Seventh Framework Programme (7FP). The focus was to identify best practices for preventing and controlling security in urban areas, to be implemented in an early-warning system structured as a Decision Support

System. The screening of Italian policies and practices regarding organized crime has been conducted by the unit of the National Research Council of Italy (IRISS-CNR), composed of Gabriella Esposito De Vita (coordinator), Stefania Ragozino, Stefania Oppido, Gaia Daldanise and Antonio Acierno (urban planning) and Alberto De Vita and Fabrizio Rippa (criminal law). Starting from the results of BESECURE, the research group developed the focus on the reuse of confiscated assets in Campania within the framework of the *Project Place-based Regeneration Strategies and Participatory Processes*, funded by the CNR (2016–2018).

References

Albrechts, L. (2003) Planning and Power: Towards an Emancipatory Planning Approach. *Environment and Planning C: Politics and Space* 21(6), pp. 905–924.

Allulli, M. (2010) *Le Politiche Urbane in Italia. Tra adattamento e frammentazione*. Roma: Cittalia.

Allum, P. (1975) *Potere e società a Napoli nel dopoguerra*. Torino: Einaudi.

ANBSC (2012) *Relazione annuale dell'Agenzia Nazionale per l'amministrazione e la destinazione dei beni sequestrati e confiscati alla criminalità organizzata: Reggio Calabria ANBSC* [Online]. Available at: www.benisequestraticonfiscati.it/Joomla/images/pdf/relazioni/2012_relazione_annuale_anbsc.pdf [Accessed 11 December 2014].

Arlacchi, P. (1986) *Mafia Business: The Mafia Ethic and the Spirit of Capitalism*. London: Verso.

Atkinson, R. (2003) Addressing Urban Social Exclusion through Community Involvement in Urban Regeneration. In R. Imrie and M. Raco (eds.) *Urban Renaissance? New Labour, Community and Urban Policy*. Bristol: Policy Press, pp. 101–119.

Barbagallo, F. (2010) *Storia della Camorra*. Bari-Roma: Editori Laterza.

Bee, C. and Pachi, D. (2014) Active Citizenship in the UK: Assessing Institutional Political Strategies and Mechanisms of Civic Engagement. *Journal of Civil Society* 10(1), pp. 100–117.

Bobbio, L. (2004) *A più voci. Amministrazioni pubbliche, imprese, associazioni e cittadini nei processi decisionali inclusivi*. Napoli: Edizioni Scientifiche.

Brancaccio, L. (2009) Guerre di Camorra: i clan napoletani tra faide e scissioni. In G. Gribaudi (ed.) *Traffici criminali. Camorra mafie e reti internazionali dell'illegalità*. Torino: Bollati-Boringhieri, pp. 65–89.

Cahill, C. (2007) Repositioning Ethical Commitments: Participatory Action Research as a Relational Praxis of Social Change. *ACME: An International Journal for Critical Geographies* 6(3), pp. 360–373.

Caneppele, S. and Calderoni, F. (eds.) (2014) *Organized Crime, Corruption and Crime Prevention: Essays in Honour of Ernesto U. Savona*. Berlin: Springer.

Chekland, P. and Holwell, S. (1997) Action Research: Its Nature and Validity. *Systemic Practice and Action Research* 11(1), pp. 9–21.

Da Molin, G. (1990) *La famiglia nel passato. Strutture familiari nel Regno di Napoli in età moderna*. Bari: Cacucci.

Di Gennaro, G. (1992) *Oltre il familismo. Vecchi e nuovi limiti alla sviluppo del Mezzogiorno, in AAVV Dopo il familismo cosa?* Milano: Franco Angeli.

Direzione Nazionale Antimafia (2016) *Relazione Annuale* [Online]. Available at: www.avvisopubblico.it/home/wp-content/uploads/2016/03/RELAZIONE-DNA-2015.pdf [Accessed 3 January 2016].

Esposito De Vita, G. (2014) Segregative Power of Violence in Belfast and Naples: Exploring the Role of Public Spaces Reconnecting Divided Societies. In A. Madanipour, S. Knierbein and A. Degros (eds.) *Public Space and the Challenges of Urban Transformation in Europe*. London: Routledge, pp. 169–182.

Esposito De Vita, G., Trillo, C. and Martinez-Perez, A. (2016) Community Planning and Urban Design in Contested Places: Some Insights from Belfast. *Journal of Urban Design* 21(3), pp. 320–334.

Falcone, G. and Padovani, M. (1991) *Cose di Cosa Nostra*. Torino: Einaudi.

Fijnaut, C. and Paoli, L. (eds.) (2004) *Organized Crime in Europe: Concepts, Patterns and Control Policies in the European Union and Beyond*. Dordrecht: Springer.

Fischer, F. (2006) Participatory Governance as Deliberative Empowerment the Cultural Politics of Discursive Space. *The American Review of Public Administration* 36(1), pp. 19–40.

Forester, J. (1989) *Planning in the Face of Power*. Berkeley, CA: University of California Press.

Friedmann, J. (2011) *Insurgencies: Essays in Planning Theory*. London and New York: Routledge.

Fusco Girard, L. (2012) Per uno sviluppo umano sostenibile nel Mezzogiorno: Come gestire la transizione verso una nuova base economica urbana. In SVIMEZ *Nord e Sud a 150 Anni dall'Unità d'Italia*. Roma: SVIMEZ, pp. 759–779.

Gilbert, J. (2014) *Common Ground: Democracy and Collectivity in an Age of Individualism*. London: Pluto Press.

Grabow, S. and Heskin, A.D. (1973) Foundations for a Radical Concept in Planning. *Journal of the American Planning Association* 39(2), pp. 106–114.

Hopkin, J. (2006) *Conceptualizing Political Clientelism: Political Exchange and Democratic Theory*. 2006 Annual Meeting of the American Political Science Association, Philadelphia, 31 August–3 September.

Hou, J. (2010) *Insurgent Public Space: Guerrilla Urbanism and the Remaking of Contemporary Cities*. New York: Routledge.

Kunzmann, K.R. (2016) Crisis and Urban Planning? A Commentary. *European Planning Studies* 24(7), pp. 1313–1318.

Lacoue-Labarthe, P. and Nancy, J.-L. (1997) *Retreating the Political*. London: Routledge.

Law 646/1982. *Disposizioni in materia di misure di prevenzione di carattere patrimoniale ed istituzione di una commissione parlamentare sul fenomeno della mafia.*

Law 109/1996. *Disposizioni in materia di gestione e destinazione di beni sequestrati o confiscati.*

Law 50/2010. *Conversione in legge, con modificazioni, del decreto-legge 4 febbraio 2010, n. 4, recante istituzione dell'Agenzia nazionale per l'amministrazione e la destinazione dei beni sequestrati e confiscati alla criminalità organizzata.*

Law 228/2012. *Disposizioni per la formazione del bilancio annuale e pluriennale dello Stato.*

Law Decree 399/1994. *Disposizioni urgenti in materia di confisca di valori ingiustificati.*

Lees, L. (ed.) (2004) *The Emancipatory City? Paradoxes and Possibilities*. London: Sage Publications.

Levi, M. (1996) Social and Unsocial Capital: A Review Essay of Robert Putnam's Making Democracy Work. *Politics & Society* 24(1), pp. 45–55.

Macry, P. (1988) *Ottocento: Famiglia, elités e patrimoni a Napoli*. Torino: Einaudi.

Marselli, C. (2009) *Inside Criminal Network*. New York: Springer.

Miraftab, F. (2009) Insurgent Planning: Situating Radical Planning in the Global South. *Planning Theory* 8(1), pp. 32–50.

Monnier, M. (1998 [1862]) *La Camorra. Notizie storiche documentate*. Lecce: Argo.

Mouffe, C. (2000) *The Democratic Paradox*. London and New York: Verso.

Pugalis, L. and Bentley, G. (2014) Place-Based Development Strategies: Possibilities, Dilemmas and Ongoing Debates. *Local Economy* 29(4–5), pp. 561–572.

Purcell, M. (2009) Resisting Neoliberalization: Communicative Planning or Counter-Hegemonic Movements? *Planning Theory* 8(2), pp. 140–165.

Reggio, M. (2013) *Dal bene confiscato al bene comune. Quaderni della Fondazione*. Roma: Ecra.

Romano, S. (1969 [1918]) *Lo stato moderno e la sua crisi. Saggi di diritto costituzionale*. Milano: Giuffrè.

Sager, T. (2016) Activist Planning: A Response to the Woes of Neo-Liberalism? *European Planning Studies* 24(7), pp. 1262–1280.

Saija, L. and Gravagno, F. (2009) Can Participatory Action Research Deal with the Mafia? A Lesson from the Field. *Planning Theory and Practice* 10(4), pp. 499–518.

Sales, I. (1993) *La Camorra le camorre*. Roma: Editori Riuniti.

Sanfilippo, V. (2005) *Nonviolenza e mafia. Idee ed esperienze per un superamento del sistema mafioso*. Trapani: Di Girolamo.

Scaglione, A. (2016) Cosa Nostra and Camorra: Illegal Activities and Organisational Structures. *Global Crime* 17(1), pp. 60–78.

Sciarrone, R. and Storti, L. (2014) The Territorial Expansion of Mafia-Type Organized Crime: The Case of the Italian Mafia in Germany. *Crime, Law and Social Change* 61(1), pp. 37–60.

Sterling, C. (1994) *Crime without Frontiers: The Worldwide Expansion of Organized Crime and the Pax Mafiosa*. London: Little Brown.

Tornaghi, C. (2015) The Relational Ontology of Public Space and Action-Oriented Pedagogy in Action: Dilemmas of Professional Ethics and Social Justice. In C. Tornaghi and S. Knierbein (eds.) *Public Space and Relational Perspectives: New Challenged for Architecture and Planning*. London: Routledge, pp. 17–41.

Wilson, J. and Swyngedouw, E. (eds.) (2015) *The Post-Political and Its Discontents*. Edinburgh: Edinburgh University Press.

Yiftachel, O. (1998) Planning and Social Control: Exploring the Dark Side. *Journal of Planning Literature* 12(4), pp. 395–406.

5   Improvising an Urban Commons of the Streets

Emancipation-From, Emancipation-To and Co-Emancipation

Rob Shields

Planners have long sought to create cities that contribute to emancipation and the 'good life' for citizens. For example, they have ordained the use of places and areas to reconcile contending land uses, conjoining some uses and separating activities that interfere with each other. However, this often results in a situation in which architects and planners attempt to prescribe and program behaviour. The same criticisms of planning practices have been made as Koolhaas makes of work spaces: "At the moment of its greatest emancipation, humankind is subjected to the most dictatorial scripts" (2004: 168).

This chapter explores the possibility or impossibility of emancipation in the city, beginning from a critique of revolutionary promises of emancipation made by Jean Francois Lyotard, the ethical philosopher of the *Postmodern Condition* (1980). This chapter argues that emancipatory spaces are sites of collective possibility. They must support a performative set of social relations that support forms of 'emancipation-to' achieve goals, rather than simply 'emancipation-from' a particular regime that may be replaced by another order. These collective practices are summarized here by the term 'co-emancipation'.

Historical Promises of Emancipation and the City

Modern revolutions have repeated promises of emancipation and a new beginning to justify their actions. Modernist planners and architects have contributed to this narrative and echoed its themes with promises that rational planning and design would create cities that facilitated emancipation. This is, however, an old argument formulated since Constantine, when the 4th-century union of Christian eschatologies of promised redemption joined with pagan civic religion, ideals of law and sovereignty in the city to create the ideal of the Divine City (Lyotard and Gruber 1999: 80).

The Divine City becomes a utopian destination, a teleological culmination of history and personal life stories centred on redemption, bliss or communion. However, the ideal, emancipated city always had its *chora* (beyond the city walls) of outsiders who were excluded or marginalized. Diana Bocarejo, in a study of how the discourse of spaces of emancipation worked against Indigenous populations in Colombia, cites the intertwined relationship of this ideology of the city as the place of civilization and enlightenment with the creation of aboriginal reserves in rural hinterlands for the unemancipated (see James 2013: 273). This oppressive colonial practice tends to cast Indigenous peoples as out of place in cities, particularly within capitals. "The language and the specific tools of governance of national minorities in many multicultural legal regimes are based upon strict spatialisations of difference" (Bocarejo 2012: 667). This spatial strategy is similar to the British imperial policy of corralling native populations in separated, less desirable reserves and Bantustans. Developed first in Canada and applied in Australia and South Africa, this spatial and territorial strategy had the effect of reducing indigenous groups to child-like dependency on the state while the terms of everyday life and cultural practice were 'whitened' and redefined in a manner that amounted to a form of cultural genocide (Truth and Reconciliation Commission of Canada 2015, Vol.1: 10–11).

Spatial strategies for pluralism and multiculturalism-through-division are often part of liberal attempts to preclude the possibility of conflict (Mouffe 2000: 20), in this case by removing the population to a margin (Shields 1991) where resistance is more difficult. Harvey notes that this aligns with a consideration of places as embodying cultures with the result that a fetishism of place "freeze[s] existing geographical structures of places and norms forever creating a 'dysfunctional' and 'oppressive' political effect" (2001: 285). This cautions us that geography and space are tied as much to promises of emancipation as to subjugation and internment and that forms and ideologies of emancipation may mask subjugation by producing margins, whether *chora* or reserves.

Emancipation-From

Political emancipation has historically designated a state of equal participation, self-determination or freedom from slavery, as in the Emancipation Movement of the 1830s in the northeastern American states (see Harrington 2006: 43). It is also frequently referred to today as a condition that, despite its urgency, has lost its social referents – such as women, slaves and the working class – and also its associations with progressive political projects. Emancipation, at least in English, suggests 'emancipation from' an oppression. It is a successive amelioration over time. Urban public spaces celebrating emancipation-from are common: victory squares such as Moscow's Red Square, monuments to revolution such as Paris's Place de la Concorde and public spaces that commemorate political achievements normalizing limited, selective emancipation as ideal for controlling majorities.

However, in a world where power is defined less by direct domination and more by implicit forms of subjectification, self-discipline, insidious self-motivation techniques and other ideologies of individual responsibility and productivity, emancipation-from becomes hard to define concretely (cf. Foucault 1982). Both emancipated practices and the sources of subjugation or control are harder to define, making escape from ideological entrapment increasingly difficult to achieve or even justify to broader publics who may believe they benefit from existing hierarchies, even when they are oppressed and exploited by them. For example, in contrast to the domination of a feudal lord, many of us now live in a world of continuous indebtedness: to mobile phone subscriptions, mortgage and automobile payments, purchases on credit cards and so on (Lazzarato 2012). Social life is more tightly coordinated via social and locative media; individuals are more 'closely coupled' in both organic and mechanical forms of solidarity and interdependence. Emancipation-from starts to appear to require dropping out, an antisocial and pathological project of self-isolation.

Whether in the theatre of history or the pathos of everyday life, emancipation is elusive.

> Such terms often imply a normative framework largely inherited from certain forms of critical theory and philosophical conceptions of the autonomous person, in which the task of analysis is to identify forms of domination that act as obstacles to the emancipation or fulfilment of human beings.
>
> (Dean 2009: 46)

Dean follows Lyotard and Foucault in criticizing "the assumption that human subjects and the liberty they exercise stand outside relations of power and forms of domination" (Dean 2009: 46). That is, the idea that emancipation is equivalent to an escape from power relations or normative judgements. For Jean-François Lyotard, emancipation is always under the sign of a negative infantilization and the Law—similar to a child's attempt to escape control. This is at the root of a paradox in which emancipation is ensnared. In his 1992 essay 'Mainmise' ('grip'), Lyotard writes:

> *Manceps* is the person who takes hold, in the sense of possession or appropriation. And *mancipium* refers to this gesture of taking hold . . . we are held by the grasp of others since childhood, yet our childhood does not cease to exercise its *mancipium* even when we imagine ourselves to be emancipated.
>
> (1993: 148, italics added)

But for Lyotard, childhood does not refer to 'an age deprived of reason' (1993: 149). Instead, childhood is that condition of 'being affected' or controlled at a time when we do not have the means—linguistic and representational—to name, identify, reproduce and recognize what it is that is affecting us. "By childhood," he says,

> I mean the fact that we are born before we are born to ourselves. And thus we are born of others, but also born to others, delivered into the hands of others without any defences. We are subjected to their *mancipium*, which they themselves do not comprehend. For they are themselves children in their turn, whether fathers or mothers. They do not attain emancipation from their childhood, either from their childhood wound or from the call that has issued from it.
>
> (1993: 149)

Childhood remains as a traumatic experience however happy or ignorant we are to its effects. How can we escape, 'the condition of being affected at a time when we do not have the means'? "Emancipation can never release us from the precedence of the Law; we will never be able to take the event in hand, or grasp the differend as one might solve a problem in engineering" (Curtis 2013: 142). The Law is not a reference to laws but to the symbolic, the metanarrative and social order of classification and authority that predates and frames the Subject, not only as a citizen but also as an individual with a coherent life story in relation to their social and environmental setting. The Law is thus not only a figure of power but of discipline and ethical interaction with the Other. For Lyotard this struggle is endemic to the social condition; for others, it is focused by social division. For example, feminist critics point out that the Law is a quintessentially masculine figure of the Enlightenment, a European construction with anyone else constructed as Other (Benhabib 1984; Grebowicz 2007), an outsider to this political project. Lyotard's point is that 'emancipation-from' is not only utopian but a phantasy that undermines ethical interaction in everyday life where we must face the question of power directly and at every turn. This is because 'emancipation-from' control subtends not only abstract, discursive political rights and practices of freedom but begs the question of how to achieve a more fulfilling, affective self-liberation from the symbolic order of society.

Affect, understood in the Spinozian sense as a melodic line of our feeling of empowerment and disempowerment in relation to our surroundings and situation, is a contextual sentiment related to spatialization and to the temporal moment. Even if emancipation were to release us from political domination, is it possible to imagine forms of emancipation that release us from the precedence of the Law? Is it possible to overcome fear and disempowerment as affects that are embedded in a negative ethos of the moment, of the encounter on the street, the situation of micro-powers, competition and discipline? Lefebvre cites Marx: "Political emancipation is not the complete, contradiction-free mode of human emancipation. . . one can be enslaved in a free State" (Marx 1843–4, Vol.3: 151–152, quoted in Lefebvre 2009

[1964]: 74). Xenophobia and discrimination are central challenges to the formal politics of and rights to emancipation-from.

There are additional concerns with the emphasis on emancipation as a political project. Domenach (1962: x) has asked, "can we conceive of a revolution in the world, an emancipation, that is not, in some fashion or another, linked to some European core"? This raises the postcolonial question of whether emancipation itself needs to be emancipated from the tyranny of a single definition, a single way of being and doing emancipation. For example, what women in India desire as emancipation reflects the deep differences between their situation and that of industrial workers in Europe. At this transnational scale, spaces of emancipation begin to look like universalizing metanarratives. Recent continental feminism is also critical of the politics of freedom and agency and embraces a politics of responsibility instead (Ramazanoglu 1998: 77; Grebowicz 2007). Braidotti (2013), for example, argues for diversity in ways that echo many of Lyotard's interests in 'small narratives' against hegemonic grand narratives.

Stiegler (1998) has argued that emancipation must include the production of a new citizen-subject with a new set of social and environmental relations. He argues that individual consciousness and subjectivity is socially constituted through governmental 'technics', notably the media. These currently favour an unemancipated Subject with an unquestioning, industrialized consciousness. It therefore makes little sense to expect emancipation through resistance by these subjects, particularly through counter-hegemonic reception of media practices and hijacking of meanings. Nor can emancipation-from be achieved solely via a change in spatialization that does not also produce emancipated Subjects and relations. "Emancipation would never be from a dominant ideology disseminated by the media"—and to this we can add technocratic planning practices—"but on the contrary, could only ever be the effect of a new configuration of the subjective and technical syntheses" (Hansen 2006: para.5).

For Jacques Rancière, emancipation is a communicative process of equality of intelligence in all forms as opposed to rote instruction and ignorance. It is thus rooted not in the circulation of information but in critical analyses (Jacotot, cited in Rancière 2009). In important ways, this position echoes Habermas's advocacy of a public sphere of communicative rationality (Habermas 1985), for communication is predicated on a shared basis of competency and horizon of expectation that constructs the 'public sphere' as a framework or space of subsequent political representations. Of course, feminist, race and postcolonial critics would add, this requires admission to these spaces and that all participants' voices are recognized and respected (Fraser 2001); that they find their voices and understand their interests.

Against this active mode, Rancière diagnoses the turn-of-the-millennium years as a 'post-political' situation that he refers to in French as '*la police*' (literally 'police' but also 'policy' and imposition of policy). In this, both centre-right and centre-left parties agree that there is no alternative to neoliberal globalization. This forecloses discussion. Consensus replaces antagonism. Rather than offering choice or true alternatives, leaders resign themselves to administration. Debates around policy efficiency replaces '*le politique*', true political debate that is necessarily antagonistic (Rancière 2004). Thus, politics needs to be not about common affairs or matters of concern (Rancière 2004: 3–9), but about the representation and definition of those shared affairs: not how they are administered but what is included and perceptible as the common, the social. Politics is thus defined by its concern with the definition of the commons. This position foregrounds the spatial dimensions and assumptions that are made in Rancière's proposal. Rancière tends to abstract the commons and emancipation. He discusses the importance of contesting shared definitions of the sensible, but there is less appreciation of its routine manipulation in everyday life to achieve effects of propriety and normalization, framing activities in such a way that some elements go unnoticed (as demonstrated by Goffman 1974; Garfinkel 1986; see also Pringle 2002).

The commons has a long history as common grazing land and collective consumption as a non-market-based form of property. In its key definitions, a commons is non-commodified and inclusive (Ostrom et al. 1999), giving each person an ad hoc stake in common resources at particular ecological scales (Ostrom 1990). However, in cities, commons were closely related to or shared space with actual markets that were adjacent. The urban commons thus complemented monetized and other forms of economic exchange (Bertho 2013). Narotzky (2013) emphasizes that commons can be 'gated' and limited to the exclusive use of a community and regulated to prevent overuse. However, it is classically understood as a right not to be excluded from a common property (Blackmar 2006). Others emphasize the interdependence of people who depend on the resources of a commons. They do not have the option of opting out in favour of private amenities. Thus they share an interest in developing public structures for governing common resources and evening out inequalities in access and overuse that lead to a 'tragedy of the commons' (Hardin 1968). These interests and struggles frame the lives of citizens generally and city inhabitants specifically, despite the difficulty in understanding underlying causes of inequalities (Auyero and Swistun 2009). In effect, one might say that collectives hold in common some form of a commons. For example, Susser and Tonnelat (2013) identify three 'urban commons' as a right to the city: urban everyday life, encounters and the creative life of the city.

> The first urban commons revolves around issues of production, consumption, and use of public services and public goods reframed as a common means for a decent everyday life. The second urban commons comprises the public spaces of mobility and encounter collectively used and claimed by citizens, such as streets, subways, cafés, public gardens, and even the World Wide Web. Next, we contend that the city can also offer a third type of urban commons under the form of collective visions

within which each individual may find a place. This is illustrated by the work of artists in mobilizing communities, and redefining the conditions of perception of their social and spatial environment. This "redistribution of the sensible" (Rancière 2000) makes up the last ingredient of the right to the city, creativity.

(Susser and Tonnelat 2013: 108)

These commons transcend planning and design professions' definitions of urban public space in material and physical terms (Whyte 1998; Hannerz 1980). Contemporary notions of the commons add digital and social media (Arora 2015; Low and Smith 2006) to city parks and squares, transportation, the public street and semi-public sites such as malls and cafés. They do this by including practices, representations and imagined spaces of representation as dimensions of social space or the process by which social life is spatialized and emplaced. Using this Lefebvrean tripartite scheme, rather than simply the representation of the commons as a type of object—a material site or an intangible sensibility—the commons is probed as a set of relationships and practices, and as an ideal but real framework that organizes disparate elements together into a paradigmatic logic of relations and ways-of-doing. The commons is a social spatialization and cultural topology of collective choice (Shields 2013).

The challenge of the commons lies in the question of inclusion and exclusion, of 'commoning' as a practice. This is not only a matter of practical action but of representations that in turn establish preconceptions and spaces of representation about *what* is shared in common, *how* and by *whom*? Often crucial aspects of the commons are discovered only once they are in short supply. For example, overgrazing illustrates the importance of grazing land to communities. A lack of safe play spaces for children in new suburbs draws attention to the lack of communal spaces and the risks built into the urban design that lead to an exclusion of children and their activities. Discovering that aspects of the commons are lacking includes not only frustrated practices but changes to representations of the commons and to public political discussion. This commons-as-absence can lead to the creation and extension of actually existing commons. Lefebvre (1991) highlights this emancipatory potential in the experience of lack or alienation in everyday life that can to yield moments of dis-alienation.

Following Taussig (1998; Simone 2001), the commons emerges from social practices of 'staging' which bring attention to some elements and constituencies while excluding others (Sandıkcı 2013). Only certain elements are favoured by methods and technologies of representation. This results in a limited range of possible elements 'coming to the stage' while others are repressed and taken for granted because they are overlooked, remaining 'off stage' or 'backstage'. These aspects pass by unnoticed, even though they are 'right under our eyes'. Staging explains the reason why aspects of the commons may be rediscovered or only noticed once they have been privatized and removed from collective consumption. In Lefebvrean terms, staging could be understood as a representation of space or of a situation that takes on physical form (a stage set) and that then becomes a living space of representations. It moves from abstract concepts and representations to be realized and actualized as material and virtual.

Emancipation-To

The commons is fundamentally a relation between the individual and the social or collective. That is, a relation between my use, my activity, my water use and something that is open. Writers have tended to think of the commons as theoretically unlimited, whether grazing land or the hydrological cycle. It is an allowance-to rather than a freedom-from. Rather than an asset, thing or space, a *relational* approach can be found across understandings of the commons that span physical and virtual spaces. For example, Latour contrasts the modernist dream of emancipation from the conditions of nature through technology, arguing that its opposite, a respectful 'attachment', is ecologically necessary to counterbalance modernity as emancipation (Latour 2008). This engagement implicitly invokes the shift from 'emancipation-from' (conditions of nature) toward the intentional stance of 'emancipation-to'.

Such a shift also suggests a new temporality that differs from the 'promissory notes' of the historical time of revolutions and eschatology with which we began this essay, to the temporality of the 'small form' of everyday life as performative and the improvisation suggested by Lyotard. That is, emancipation-from looks backward. It is reactive. By contrast, emancipation-to is proactive. It stresses a future-oriented present of relations whose qualities are known only through their effects or outcomes that are anticipated, not already achieved. It is in process, in play. As such, it is open-ended and embraces a multiplicity of forms of actual moments of emancipation.

Play, Street-Aesthesis and Emancipation

In concrete terms, is it possible to trace where and how emancipation-to can be actualized within the city? The commons as relation offers a clue of how one might find emancipation in the improvisations of urban living as a 'small form' rather than in the redemptive promises of 'grand form'. Improvisation as play offers one possible modality for further developing the social relations of the commons. Situating improvisation requires an attention to its affective markers of carefree happiness as well as patterns of physical activity or forms of engagement with the urban environment (see Back and Keith 2004; Galanakis 2016). Returning to the significance of Lefebvre's stress on everyday life as experience and practice: "In the face of the instrumentalist paradigm of urbanism, this creative urban practice is necessarily made possible by being grounded . . . in 'experience'" (Fraser 2015: 220). One example is various 'pop-up' events, exhibitions, activities and facilities promoted by cities (a good example is the seasonal reorganization of streets including changing road lanes, parking, installing temporary fountains, seating and providing animation in Montreal).

Lefebvre had earlier attempted to shift emancipation from the institutional question of the status of slaves and citizens prosecuted through state revolution, to a revolutionary dis-alienation in everyday life pursued through a right to the city and other spatial strategies.

> To *inhabit* finds again its place over habitat. The quality which is promoted presents and represents as *playful* . . . Already, to city people the urban centre is movement, the unpredictable, the possible and encounters. For them, it is either 'spontaneous theatre' or nothing.
>
> (original emphasis; Lefebvre 1996: 172)

For example, in childhood and childishness, Lyotard sees a lively improvisation and play, innovation and openness that is itself an emancipatory form of knowing and living. How might we envision a design praxis indebted to the poetics of improvisation which shifts the conversation from a politics of emancipation—still within the grip of repressed laws—to an ethos of improvisation that addresses the problem in the contexts of everyday life?

In *Spaces of Hope*, David Harvey echoes Lefebvre's position: the idea of imaginative spatial play to achieve specific social and moral goals can be converted into "the idea of potentially endlessly open experimentation with the possibilities of spatial forms" (2000: 182). In support of Lefebvre, Benjamin Fraser explores the work of the Argentinian Ruiz Martin Delgado, who in turn recalls the Canadian Jane Jacobs's metaphor of interaction in major urban centres as a 'sidewalk ballet' (Jacobs 1961). Jacobs and Delgado Ruiz use the metaphor of dance to account for difference and multiplicity in the representation of urban spaces and activities (Delgado Ruiz 2007: 135–136, 245, cited in Fraser 2015: 220):

> the street is "the country of those with no country" (1999: 209) . . . It is in the street where every moment sees the production of "The integration of incompatibles, where the most effective exercises of reflecting about one's own identity can be carried out, where the notion of political commitment as a consequence of the possibilities of action makes sense and where social mobilization allows one to know the potential of the currents of sympathy and solidarity among strangers".
>
> (Delgado Ruiz 1999: 208, cited in and
> translated by Fraser 2015: 220)

Delgado Ruiz's performative 'integration of incompatibles' (the dance of difference) takes place through performative relations. The street is a potential *chora* within the city, which is thus both a site of continual policing, repression and control but also the site where spatial innovation can be negotiated and where struggles for emancipation take place through ongoing activity. The sidewalk ballet and the rhythm of everyday street-life offers a case of struggles over situational ethics. That is, the street is a negotiated space and mode of interaction and affect: it is an *ethos*. This can anchor a relational form of everyday common experience (*aesthesis*), of 'getting along' and 'getting by', that underpins civility and anonymous interaction in cities (Simmel 2002; Maffesoli 1991). Such an '*ethos-aesthesis*' or 'ethical aesthetics' is the opposite of a rule-based, formalistic *Ästhetik* (Baumgarten 1758). This street-aesthesis is both a spatial practice and a framing space of representations. It is opposed to a representation or a discourse that seeks to legislate and enforce a norm around which people and social action is aligned. In his ethical works, Lyotard (1988; 1992) advocates an ethics that "establishes a commonality, that creates a common space for the small discourses, the particular games, the individual subjects themselves, to flourish. Lyotard's conceptions of justice and injustice establish the conditions for just gaming, prohibiting exclusion and preventing totalization" (Nuyen 1998: 41; Lyotard and Thebaud 1985). However, Lyotard's requirement to avoid metanarratives and law-like rules that become oppressive in their turn means that once-and-for-all emancipation is an empty gesture. Instead, a situational ethics is required in which emancipation is continuously re-created.

Street-aesthesis and sidewalk ballets are exactly the performative interpretations that Lyotard advocates to negotiate the expectations of others, from the trivial to the most consequential of habits or 'rules of thumb'. As such, these everyday interactions (ethics) and shared experiences (*aestheses*) are always balancing the dialectic of emancipation-from and emancipation-to. Street-aesthesis shifts emancipation itself from being an all-or-nothing utopian status into a *relational process of interaction* in which duties and freedoms are blurred. This is to say, emancipation is asserted performatively at the same time as the care of the Other is solicited and the fellow-feeling of care and respect for the Other is offered as a basic civility. This social *co-emancipation* may only be a matter of negotiating on what side one passes oncoming individuals on a narrow sidewalk, or the acknowledgement, affirming recognition or respectful disregard and remit for anonymity granted to Others. It is only in this sort of pulsing, live interaction that Delgado Ruiz's 'currents of sympathy and solidarity among strangers' could ever be felt.

Planning for Co-Emancipation

Whether as experiment or play, emancipatory urban spaces need to afford the possibility of 'sidewalk ballets' and other interactions whose endings are not determined and more improvised than scripted. This means a type of 'free-zoning' that is not prescriptive but requires a planning practice that allows active engagement in negotiating uses on a daily basis, adjusting to others, whether in conflict or 'getting along'. What is perhaps most absent in contemporary city building and public spaces are sites that are like this form of urban commons. That is, areas need to have a capacity to host large groups while refraining from attempting to channel or script them.

At the same time, Ostrom and others found that successful commons have defined limits and structuring elements. They are characterized as having clearly defined boundaries, a congruence between local conditions and the demands of users, collective choice, monitoring and graduated sanctions against abuse, and they accommodate nested uses (Ostrom 1990). A planning and design approach that explores the potential of urban commons and street-aesthesis needs to be developed as a professional project on co-emancipation. What are the parameters defining an urban commons?

References

Arora, P. (2015) Usurping Public Leisure Space for Protest Social Activism in the Digital and Material Commons. *Space and Culture* 18(1), pp. 55–68.

Auyero, J. and Swistun, D.A. (2009) *Flammable: Environmental Suffering in an Argentine Shantytown*. New York: Oxford University Press.

Back, L. and Keith, M. (2004) Impurity and the Emancipatory City: Young People, Community Safety and Racial Danger. In L. Lees (ed.) *The Emancipatory City? Paradoxes and Possibilities*. London: Sage Publications, pp. 57–71.

Baumgarten, A.G. (1758) *Aesthetica*. Frankfurt: Kleyb.

Benhabib, S. (1984) Epistemologies of Postmodernism: A Rejoinder to Jean-François Lyotard. *New German Critique* 33, pp. 103–126.

Bertho, A. (2013) Urban Commons and Urban Struggles. *Focaal* 66, pp. 128–129.

Blackmar, E. (2006) Appropriating 'the Commons': The Tragedy of Property Right Discourse. In S. Low and N. Smith (eds.) *The Politics of Public Space*. New York: Routledge, pp. 49–80.

Bocarejo, D. (2012) Emancipation or Enclosement? The Spatialization of Difference and Urban Ethnic Contestation in Colombia. *Antipode* 44(3), pp. 663–683.

Braidotti, R. (2013) *The Posthuman*. Cambridge: Polity.

Curtis, N. (2013) The Politics of Creation: Lyotard, Castoriadis and Malraux. In H. Bickis and R. Shields (eds.) *Rereading Jean-François Lyotard*. London: Ashgate, pp. 205–225.

Dean, M. (2009) *Governmentality: Power and Rule in Modern Society*. London: Sage Publications.

Delgado Ruiz, M. (1999) *El animal público*. Barcelona: Anagrama.

Delgado Ruiz, M. (2007) *Sociedades movedizas: pasos hacia una antropología de las calles* [Mobile Societies]. Barcelona: Anagrama.

Domenach, J.-M. (1962) Les damnés de la terre. *Esprit, New Series* 305(4), pp. 634–645.

Foucault, M. (1982) The Subject and Power. In H. Dreyfus and P. Rabinow (eds.) *Michel Foucault: Beyond Structuralism and Hermeneutics*. Chicago: University of Chicago Press, pp. 208–226 [Online]. Available at: https://foucault.info/doc/documents/foucault-power-en-html

Fraser, B. (2015) *Toward an Urban Cultural Studies: Henri Lefebvre and the Humanities*. New York: Springer.

Fraser, N. (2001) Recognition without Ethics. *Theory, Culture and Society* 18(2–3), pp. 21–42.

Galanakis, M. (2016) Public Spaces for Youth? The Case of the Jane-Finch Neighborhood in Toronto. *Space and Culture* 19(3), pp. 208–223.

Garfinkel, H. (1986) *Ethnomethodological Studies of Work*. London: Routledge.

Goffman, E. (1974) *Frame Analysis*. Cambridge, MA: Harvard University Press.

Grebowicz, M. (ed.) (2007) *Gender after Lyotard*. Albany: State University of New York Press.

Habermas, J. (1985) *The Theory of Communicative Action*. Boston: Beacon Press.

Hannerz, U. (1980) *Exploring the City: Inquiries toward an Urban Anthropology*. New York: Columbia University Press.

Hansen, M. (2006) Realtime Synthesis and the Différance of the Body: Technocultural Studies in the Wake of Deconstruction. *Culture Machine* 6(1).

Hardin, G. (1968) The Tragedy of the Commons. *Science* 162(3859), pp. 1243–1248.

Harrington, A. (2006) Social Theory and Theology. In G. Delanty (ed.) *The Handbook of Contemporary European Social Theory*. Abingdon: Routledge, pp. 37–50.

Harvey, D. (2000) *Spaces of Hope*. Berkeley: University of California Press.

Harvey, D. (2001) *Millennial Capitalism and the Culture of Neoliberalism*. Durham: Duke University Press.

Jacobs, J. (1961) *The Death and Life of the Great American Cities*. New York: Random House.

James, S.W. (2013) Rights to the Diverse City Challenges to Indigenous Participation in Urban Planning and Heritage Preservation in Sydney, Australia. *Space and Culture* 16(3), pp. 274–287.

Koolhaas, R. (with Office for Metropolitan Architecture) (2004) *Content*. Cologne: Taschen.

Latour, B. (2008) 'It's Development, Stupid!' or How to Modernize Modernization? In J. Proctor (ed.) *Post-Environmentalism*. Cambridge, MA: MIT Press.

Lazzarato, M. (2012) *The Making of the Indebted Man*. Cambridge: Semiotext(e)/ The MIT Press.

Lefebvre, H. (1991) *The Critique of Everyday Life*, Volume 1 (Translated by J. Moore). London: Verso.

Lefebvre, H. (1996) *Writings on Cities* (Translated and edited by E. Kofman and E. Lebas). Oxford: Blackwell.

Lefebvre, H. (2009) The Withering Away of the State: The Sources of Marxist-Leninist State Theory. In N. Brenner and S. Elden (eds.) *Henri Lefebvre: State, Space, World: Selected Essays*. Minneapolis: Minnesota University Press, pp. 69–94.

Low, S. and Smith, N. (eds.) (2006) *The Politics of Public Space*. New York: Routledge.

Lyotard, J.-F. (1980) *The Post-Modern Condition: A Report on Knowledge* (Translated by G. Bennington). Minneapolis: University of Minnesota Press.

Lyotard, J.-F. (1988) *The Differend: Phrases in Dispute* (Translated by G. Van Den Abbeele). Minneapolis: University of Minnesota Press.

Lyotard, J.-F. (1992) Mainmise. *Philosophy Today* 36(4), pp. 419–427.

Lyotard, J.-F. (1993) *Political Writings* (Translated by B. Readings and K. P. Geiman). Minneapolis: University of Minnesota Press.

Lyotard, J.-F. and Gruber, E. (1999) *The Hyphen. Between Judaism and Christianity* (Translated by P.-A. Brault and M. Naas). Amherst, NY: Prometheus Books.

Lyotard, J.-F. and Thebaud, J.-L. (1985) *Just Gaming* (Translated by W. Godzich). Minneapolis: University of Minnesota Press.

Maffesoli, M. (1991) The Ethic of Aesthetics. *Theory, Culture and Society* 8(1), pp. 7–20.

Marx, K. (1975 [1843–4]) On the Jewish Question. In K. Marx and F. Engels *Marx and Engels: Collected Works*, Volume 3. London: Lawrence & Wishart, pp. 146–174.

Mouffe, C. (2000) *The Democratic Paradox*. London: Verso.

Narotzky, S. (2013) What Kind of Commons Are the Urban Commons? *Focaal* 66, pp. 122–124.

Nuyen, A.T. (1998) The Politics of Emancipation: From Self to Society. *Human Studies* 21(1), pp. 27–43.

Ostrom, E. (1990) *Governing the Commons: The Evolution of Institutions for Collective Action*. Cambridge: Cambridge University Press.

Ostrom, E., Burger, J., Field, C.B., Norgaard, R.B. and Policansky, D. (1999) Revisiting the Commons: Local Lessons, Global Challenges. *Science* 284(5412), pp. 278–282.

Pringle, T. (2002) The Space of Stage Magic. *Space and Culture* 6(2), pp. 333–345.

Ramazanoglu, C. (1998) Saying Goodbye to Emancipation? In C. Rojek and B.S. Turner (eds.) *The Politics of Jean-François Lyotard: Justice and Political Theory*. New York and London: Routledge, pp. 63–83.

Rancière, J. (2000) *Le partage du sensible: Esthétique et politique*. Paris: La Fabrique editions.

Rancière, J. (2004) Introducing Disagreement. *Angelaki: Journal of the Theoretical Humanities* 9(3), pp. 3–9.

Rancière, J. (2009) *The Emancipated Spectator* (Translated by G. Elliott). London: Verso.

Sandıkcı, Ö. (2015) Strolling through Istanbul's Beyoğlu In-Between Difference and Containment. *Space and Culture* 18(2), pp. 198–211.

Shields, R. (1991) *Places on the Margin: Alternative Geographies of Modernity*. London: Routledge Chapman Hall.

Shields, R. (2003) *The Virtual*. London: Routledge.

Shields, R. (2004) Visualicity. *Visual Culture in Britain* 5(1), pp. 23–36.

Shields, R. (2013) *Spatial Questions: Social Spatialisations and Cultural Topologies*. London: Sage Publications.

Simmel, G. (2002 [1903]) The Metropolis and Mental Life. In G. Bridge and S. Watson (eds.) *The Blackwell City Reader*. Malden, MA: Blackwell, pp. 11–19.

Simone, A. (2001) *On the 'Worlding' of Cities in Africa*. Paper presented at the Annual Meeting of the American Association of Geographers, New York, 27 February–3 March.

Stiegler, B. (1998) *Technics and Time 1: The Fault of Epimetheus* (Translated by R. Beardsworth and G. Collins). Stanford: Stanford University Press.

Susser, I. and Tonnelat, S. (2013) Transformative Cities: The Three Urban Commons. *Focaal* 66, pp. 105–132.

Taussig, M.T. (1998) Viscerality, Faith and Skepticism: Another Theory of Magic. In N. Dirks (ed.) *In Near Ruins: Cultural Theory at the End of the Century*. Minneapolis: University of Minnesota Press, pp. 221–256.

Truth and Reconciliation Commission of Canada (2015) *Canada's Residential Schools: Reconciliation*, Volume 1. Ottawa: Government of Canada.

Whyte, W.H. (1998) *City: Rediscovering the Center*. New York: Doubleday.

Part II

Practical Emancipation. On Places, Projects and Events

6 Rupturing, Accreting and Bridging

Everyday Insurgencies and Emancipatory City-Making in East Asia

Jeffrey Hou

Beneath the glittering skylines that have become symbols of economic growth and globalization in East Asia, the region's urban landscapes are also a domain of informal and seemingly messy everyday activities. Marginalized and often outlawed, many of these activities nevertheless play an important role in the uncompromising dynamism of these cities. In Taipei, for instance, the city's night markets with sprawling street vendors are as iconic as the more recent landmarks that include Taipei 101, formerly the world's tallest building. In Tokyo, with live music banned from Yoyogi Park, near the site of the 1964 Tokyo Olympic Games, young musicians continue to gather and perform on the sidewalks outside the park, creating one of the liveliest spectacles in the city. Every morning in Shanghai, ordinary citizens and passers-by once transformed the highly commercial Nanjing East Road into a site of everyday leisure and recreation by dancing at the department store entrances before the stores are opened.

In the shadow of institutional regulation, activities and events like these constitute a form of everyday insurgencies against the predominant control of urban spaces by the state. In the context of growing corporatization of urban spaces in cities around the world, including in East Asia, these instances of insurgent placemaking represent hopes for resistance and alternatives. They demonstrate the agency of citizens and communities to engage in acts of defiance against corporate-state control. They reveal cracks in the system in which everyday cultural practices can continue to flourish. They suggest the potential of city as a "site for emancipation" (Lees 2004; Amin and Thrift 2004). Beyond non-compliance, tactical circumvention and momentary escapes, however, can actions like these contribute to more substantive changes in planning practices and the political system? How can instances of everyday insurgencies contribute to the actualization and practice of emancipatory city-making in East Asia?

This chapter examines recent cases in Hong Kong, Seoul and Taipei in an attempt to explore linkages between everyday counter-hegemonic spatial practices and their emancipatory potential in producing transformative outcomes. As a preview, it looks at how acts of everyday insurgency can provide an important foundation for organized, collective actions. Specifically,

Figure 6.1 Department stores' entrances on Nanjing East Road in Shanghai were transformed into a dance hall before the stores were opened

Source: Jeffrey Hou, 2007

it examines how contention, resistance and agonistic acts can in turn invite, catalyze and escalate into strategic actions, and how such actions take place through the agency of individual and organized actors. By concluding with a framework of *rupturing*, *accreting* and *bridging*, I focus my observations on the different stages of such processes and how they are interconnected. In this chapter, the elevation from everyday insurgencies to organized actions and transformative outcomes suggest a form of emancipatory practices, as subaltern and ordinary actors become engaged citizens with capacity and intention to join and influence the political process of urban governance. These linkages, I believe, hold the key in understanding the mechanism and significance of everyday insurgencies and their emancipatory, transformative potential.

Beyond Everyday Insurgencies in East Asia?

The discourse of insurgency and insurgent planning has been instrumental in foregrounding an important discussion in planning that highlights the role and practices of subaltern groups in resisting the predominant form of urban governance. In his critique of the limited notion of formal citizenship, Holston (1998) introduces the concept of insurgent citizenship to characterize the claims of subaltern society members such as the homeless, migrants and other marginalized social groups. With insurgent citizenship and insurgent urbanism as its spatial mode, Holston (1998) calls for a rethinking of the social in planning, as rooted in the heterogeneity of lived experience, contrary to the formalized, reductionist state institution. Other planning scholars have since used the term insurgency to conceptualize spatial and social practices of marginalized groups against or outside the official planning regime. Miraftab (2009), for example, describes insurgent planning as a set of counter-hegemonic practices by marginalized groups and as a counterpoint to the normative practice of citizen participation in neoliberal governance. In *Insurgent Public Space* (Hou 2010), I focus on the characteristics and transformative potential of placemaking activities that occur outside or at the border of the regulatory domain. These insurgent acts produce an alternative public realm in contrast to the increasingly regulated, controlled and often-privatized public spaces produced through formal planning processes.

An important aspect of the discourse on insurgency is the focus on the everyday and entanglement with the formal institutions. Holston (1998: 47) suggests that insurgent forms can be found in both organized grassroots mobilization and everyday practices which, "in different ways, empower, parody, derail, or subvert state agendas." This focus on everyday forms of insurgency echoes the earlier work by James C. Scott (1989) that highlights the political significance of the everyday form of resistance by subordinate groups, particularly rural peasants. On the other hand, Perera (2009) describes how insurgent acts are often entangled with formalized systems, rendering the absolute distinction in spatial terms often futile or impossible. Douglass and Daniere (2009: 1) further note that where civic space is not readily provided by the state, "people mobilize to create them through their own effort, as well as with and against the state".

The power to derail and subvert state agenda through acts of everyday insurgencies begs an important question concerning the capacity and potential of everyday insurgencies in producing more substantive changes in urban governance. In other words, how can everyday insurgencies lead to strategic, transformative actions against hegemonic forces of urban governance? More precisely, how can we begin to examine the linkages between everyday, tactical acts of citizens on one hand, and strategic, collective and organized actions on the other? Dikeç (2001) and Albrechts (2003) respectively argue that emancipation requires the formation of consciousness in the struggle against injustice as well as intentional, strategic actions to engage in resistance and produce structural changes. How do everyday insurgencies contribute to intentional struggles for structural changes to address conditions of inequality and injustice in the built environment? How can everyday acts of insurgency contribute to the emancipatory making of cities?

These questions are particularly relevant to cities in East Asia where informal and unsanctioned everyday acts still constitute a significant aspect of the urban experience. Yet, they continue to be marginalized and suppressed by established political and social orders (Hou and Manish 2016). In the following, three recent cases in Hong Kong, Seoul and Taipei are selected for exploring these questions. My observations are based on a combination of field visits from 2009 to 2016, discussion with locals and a review of materials from both popular media and scholarly sources.

Case One: Public Space Gathering in Hong Kong

Since the 1980s, as one of few public open spaces in the city, Statue Square in Central became the site for weekend gathering in Hong Kong by thousands of Filipina domestic workers on Sundays. Over the years, the gathering has sprawled into nearby streets, sidewalks, sky bridges and other unintended spaces including, most prominently, the ground-level lobby of the headquarters of Hong Kong Shanghai Bank (HSBC) designed by Sir Norman Foster. Catering to the influx of foreign domestic workers, new businesses have emerged in the area, particularly those in the nearby Worldwide Plaza, a multistorey indoor commercial centre in an office tower. On weekends, the commercial centre is crowded with workers sending remittance, buying clothing

Figure 6.2 Thousands of Filipina workers converge in Central, Hong Kong, every weekend and transform it into a vibrant, carnivalesque space

Source: Jeffrey Hou, 2009

and supplies and sharing meals with friends. Today, the weekly gathering is one of the most celebrated places for foreign workers in Hong Kong. With events such as the annual Sinulog Festival organized by the League of Overseas Visayan Association, it becomes a place where Filipino/a identity is celebrated.

The case of the weekend gathering of Filipina workers was well documented by scholars, including Nicole Constable (1997); Lisa Law (2002); and Daisy Tam (2016). In her article in 2002, Law describes how gatherings of the workers have created an overlay of ethnic enclave within the heart of finance and commerce in the city. According to Law (2002), the activities surprised Hong Kong Land, the property management firm that initially proposed the closure of Chater Road to attract customers to the deserted financial district during the weekend, not expecting that the area would become a magnet for thousands of Filipina workers. Aside from a social gathering among guest workers, the weekly assemblies have made visible the presence of Filipina workers in Hong Kong society and provided opportunities for political and labour organizing (Law 2002). Over the years, the gathering has served as sites for demonstrations on issues including the protection of maternity leave for domestic workers and minimum wages.

The gathering of Filipina workers at Statue Square is not the only case in which public space has become a focus of attention in Hong Kong. Since 2008, local activists in Hong Kong have challenged the management of privately owned public spaces in many of the city's commercial properties. One of the most prominent incidents took place on the plaza of Times Square in Causeway Bay, a high-rise retail/office complex with a nine-storey mall opened in 1994. In exchange for additional floor area, 3,010 square meters of the ground floor was set aside by the developer for public access in an agreement with the government (Lee 2008). However, the ground-floor space has been leased by the private management for commercial and promotional events and even a Starbucks store. Users of the plaza complained about being harassed by private security guards for gathering and lingering in the space (Lee 2008). In an attempt to call attention to the non-compliance, activists staged performances on the plaza. An event titled Hijacking the Public Sphere was organized by In-Media, an independent advocacy group, as part of a larger festival called CHiE!, or Culture Seizes Politics (Lau 2012). Through social media, the event organizer invited participation of ordinary citizens and even a group of city councillors from an opposition political party. The growing public scrutiny on the government's oversight of these properties eventually forced the Hong Kong government to respond by investigating the conditions of all 150-plus sites of privately owned public space throughout the city, and released a complete list of these sites to the public, affirming citizens' access to these spaces. The proprietor of Time Square was also forced to allow visitors to linger and gather and to ease security measures in the plaza. In-Media's actions, with the help of volunteers and participating citizens, have resulted in a significant change in holding the government and private interests accountable.

Case Two: Citizen Gardening in Seoul

Located in the western part of Seoul, Mullae-dong is a neighbourhood known for a history of industrial activities. At one point, the area hosted around 1,000 steel factories and service centres for automobiles (KBS n.d.). Even after major manufacturing facilities had left the area, the neighbourhood continued to be dotted by suppliers and metal fabrication shops, with noises of machinery from the shops running in the background. Over the years, Mullae-dong has become surrounded by high-rise residential towers, not unlike most other neighbourhoods in the sprawling city. Despite their proximity, however, apartment towers' residents rarely interacted with workers in the industrial part of the neighbourhood or even with each other. In 2010, the dynamic began to change as a small group of residents interested in urban gardening began to cross the physical and social division. Unable to find a suitable site within the residential complex for gardening, residents ended up using the rooftop of a nearby building in the industrial part of the neighbourhood. With help from Seoul Green Trust, a non-profit organization, the group received plant materials and some training in gardening techniques. In addition to box gardening, the group engaged in activities such as urban beekeeping, outdoor cooking, rainwater harvesting workshops and organizing a farmers' market.

As other residents in the neighbourhood became aware of the gardening activities, they began to join. They came not only to grow vegetables, but also to meet and interact with each other. In one example, a single father had recently moved with his daughter into the neighbourhood. Wanting to connect with neighbours and to have his daughter connect with other children, he began to join the gardening activities along with his daughter. The father has since become a core member of the group and contributes regularly in the gardening and social activities. Today, the rooftop garden is a lush, elevated oasis in the midst of an urban jungle, surrounded by nondescript factory buildings and residential towers. Each day, neighbours from the nearby apartments gather here to tend their gardens and chat with one another. The garden has apparently been relocated once already, because the previous owner had other plans for the property. The continued function of the garden after its relocation indicated the resilience of the group.

Started as a leisure activity among neighbours, the Mullae rooftop garden has since spawned other activities in the neighbourhood. For example, participants who designed and helped manage the garden began to organize a Mullae Community Garden tour and opened a book café. Another participant who did the carpentry work for the garden's participation in the Seoul Urban Agriculture Fair has since been holding rainwater harvesting workshops and was following his dream to become a rainwater harvesting and reuse specialist. Similarly, another gardener realized her interest in cooking through an outdoor cooking activity hosted by the garden in 2012. She opened a restaurant called 'Cushy's Rest Stop' in 2013 and plans to contribute to the Farm to Table movement as well as Food Mile Zero movement in

Figure 6.3 Mullae rooftop garden—a lush oasis that brings residents in the neighbourhood together

Source: Jeffrey Hou, 2012

the area. A young man who was in charge of keeping worms and producing worm castings was inspired by the ecologic cycle of organic matter and started a social business with a few other friends. With these examples, the garden has been envisioned as a platform for job creation in the neighbourhood aside from a social space.

The rooftop garden in Mullae is just one of the many community/urban gardening initiatives that Seoul Green Trust is supporting. Established in 2003 by a group of urban forest advocates, the Trust's mission has been to make Seoul greener and healthier through the participation and support from the citizens (Yang and Lee 2008). With a 20-year campaign to create a total of 33 million square meters of new green space in the city, the Trust was instrumental in the creation of Seoul Forest Park—one-third the size of Central Park in New York City (Yang and Lee 2008). In recent years, witnessing the declining municipal resources, the Trust has shifted its strategy to expand green spaces in the city by supporting grassroots efforts in community gardening. Most recently, the Trust was behind the creation of a large urban farm on Nodeul Island, an islet in the middle of the Han River that was once slated as the site of a proposed Opera House. In 2012, with Seoul Green Trust working behind the scenes, the Seoul Metropolitan Government announced the establishment of a public farm as an effort to promote urban agriculture in the city (*The Korea Times* 2012).

Case Three: Night Market Conflicts in Taipei

In Taipei, as in many other cities in Asia, night markets have long been a part of the everyday cityscape. They offer inexpensive food, merchandise and entertainment as well as economic opportunities for a significant segment of the urban population. Vendors of different forms and shapes transform streets, plazas and residual spaces under bridges and freeways into bustling urban places. However, as an activity that exists outside the bounds of institutional planning, night markets can become a thorny issue for the city authority who finds itself caught between the need for regulatory enforcement and the inability to control what have been long-standing cultural practices. While night markets are popular for visitors, they can also become a nuisance for neighbours who face problems of traffic, congestion, noise and trash.

One such conflict between market vendors and neighbouring residents erupted at the Shida Night Market in 2011. Located adjacent to the National Taiwan Normal University, the Shida (a short name of the university pronounced in Mandarin) Night Market has existed in various forms since the 1960s but primarily as a place that serves nearby college students. Over the years, cafés, restaurants, bars and even live music venues have sprouted in the neighbourhood, including its network of narrow alleys. Around 2008, several local merchants began an effort to rebrand the area as 'South Village' to capitalize on the bohemian character of the area. Through promotion on television programmes, the market soon became a mecca for visitors, particularly young people. In 2010, the area was identified by the City and the Tourism Bureau of the Ministry of Communication as a key tourist spot (Huang 2012). The growing reputation soon attracted not only local shoppers but also international visitors, including Mainland Chinese tourists who arrived in large tour buses. In just two years, the number of businesses grew from approximately 200 to over 700 (Huang 2012), as property owners took advantage of the opportunity by subdividing and renting their ground-floor spaces for the ever-increasing number of businesses. Soon, not only had the ground floors of residential buildings been transformed into retail spaces, the entrances and staircases of many of these four- to five-storey apartment buildings were occupied by vendors as well.

On any given evening, the area was flooded by shoppers, causing congestion in the narrow alleys. With the growing business demand, the commercial rent in the area skyrocketed, and new clothing and accessory stores with larger profit margins soon displaced older, family-owned restaurants and shops. Angered by the sudden increase of vendors and the diminished quality of life along with concerns for fire hazards, some residents began to organize and form self-help organizations. They took to the street and filed complaints with the city. Given the market's reputation, the conflict was soon reported in the media, and the city government was suddenly under pressure to act. Known for his heavy-handed approach, Mayor Lung-pin Hau ordered his staff to enforce regulation on businesses in the area by fining and shutting down illegal businesses. As it turned out, the city's planning ordinance prohibits the operation of restaurants, retail stores and service-related businesses in alleys less than six meters wide, a law that few people were aware of (Chung 2012).

Caught by surprise with the city's swift action after decades of leniency, many businesses were angered and got organized as well. They protested against the city government for its lack of clear and consistent policy and the unfair treatment, given that the businesses were barely the only ones in the city that violated the law. In February 2012, nearly 400 stores jointly launched a silent protest by shutting off their store lights for 30 minutes on a Saturday evening, usually the busiest night during the week (Chung 2012). The merchants tied yellow ribbons to their storefronts, merchandise and mannequins in protest. In the meantime, unable to cope with fines and constant harassment by law enforcement officers, some businesses did begin to close, leaving behind vacant storefronts. But other businesses stayed and started to self-regulate by organizing neighbourhood cleanups and removing store signs in the alley to allow fire trucks to come through in the event of emergency (*The China Post* 2012). Today, the area continues to be visited by students and shoppers. As media attention faded away, business as usual seems to have returned, albeit somewhat subdued and scaled back.

Figure 6.4 The tamed Shida Night after vendors engaged in self-regulation by removing the extruding signage from the street right of way

Source: Jeffrey Hou, 2012

The Shida incident is a complex one with intersecting yet competing interests and politics. On one hand, it highlights not only the city's inconsistent law enforcement but also the inability of its antiquated planning ordinance in dealing with the informal and long-standing cultural practices of its citizens. On the other hand, the incident brings attention to the act of 'self-organizing' on the part of both businesses and residents to strike a practical, though perhaps imperfect, equilibrium in a contested urban terrain. In an interesting twist, protest by residents and self-regulation by businesses seem to have protected the market from its newfound persona as an oversized and over-commercialized tourist mecca. The market, in fact, has since regained a more everyday appeal as just another neighbourhood night market in the middle of the city.

Linking Everyday Insurgencies to Strategic, Organized Actions

What can weekend gatherings of foreign workers, rooftop community gardens and night market conflicts tell us about linkages between everyday insurgencies and intentional, organized actions? Below I use the stages of rupturing, accreting and bridging to characterize what I perceive as the common threads.

Rupturing

The three cases in Hong Kong, Seoul and Taipei bring to light the ability of everyday insurgency—acts of individuals and small groups to create ruptures in the hegemonic urban order. In Hong Kong, the gathering of Filipina workers in Central disrupts the typical use of streets, sidewalks and plaza in the city's financial district and highlights the presence of guest workers in the Hong Kong society. The guerrilla acts of activists and citizens at Time Square brought media and public attention to the dubious status of public space managed by private interests. In Seoul, the rooftop gardening activities by residents in Mullae created opportunities for interactions among residents that have been inhibited by the spatial and social structure of the society. They helped bridge the communities that have been segregated by their occupational and class differences. The public farm on Nodeul Island demonstrates possibilities that could be unleashed in other urban sites in Seoul and challenge how urban spaces are programmed and developed. In Taipei, business activities in Shida and many other night markets already involve constant negotiation beyond or at the border of regulatory domain. Together, in these three cases, the everyday acts of individuals, businesses, vendors, shoppers, guest workers and urban gardeners serve to uncover the underlying tensions and contradictions as well as possibilities in the contemporary East Asian city. They created disruptions or openings in the institutional and spatial structure of the city and set the stage for potentially transformative actions.

Accreting

To various extents, while all three cases here demonstrate how the start-ing point of significant events or actions may often seem modest and even insignificant, these everyday insurgent acts have the ability to aggregate, multiply, reproduce and eventually become a force to be reckoned with. In Hong Kong, the weekend gathering in Central started as an opportunity for workers to meet, share a meal, reconnect with friends and do some errands. These individual and small collective acts have since blossomed into regular, albeit temporary, occupation of the square, streets, sidewalks, sky bridges, building lobbies and indoor malls by thousands of workers, weekend after weekend, that in their sheer size and visibility provided the opportunities for political mobilizing. In Seoul, starting with a handful of sites, by 2015 there were 875 pocket gardens, 160 rooftop gardens and 75 community gardens (Seoul Metropolitan Government 2015), and the local government has set a goal to become a world capital of urban agriculture. In Taipei, although the controversy surrounding the Shida Night Market only erupted in 2011, the night market has been thriving for decades, communities and networks of individuals and businesses have been established, and the identity of place has cemented over time. The large number of stalls, businesses and visitors has reinforced the market's identity and existence despite its questionable regulatory status. Collectively, the formation and sheer scale of the market challenged the city's zoning ordinance and rendered it practically unenforce-able. On the other hand, the growing size of the market in recent years also set the stage for opposition by neighbours, perhaps the silent majority here, and the subsequent confrontations.

Bridging

From the above cases, it is also evident that activists, non-profits and indi-viduals like community organizers have played an important role in facilitat-ing organized actions that have helped transform everyday acts of individuals and small groups into forces of political and practical significance. These acts of bridging provide a critical linkage between everyday insurgencies and organized, collective and emancipatory actions. In Hong Kong, non-governmental labour organizations have been instrumental in organizing and advocating for the rights of foreign guest workers. Independent groups such as In-Media have played an important role in raising awareness to the issue and orchestrating specific actions to protect access to public space. In Seoul, Seoul Green Trust provided the initial support for the Mullae roof-top garden and helped negotiate with city government to transform the site on Nodeul Island to a public farm. The Trust's connection to the city and planning institutions enabled it to serve as an important bridge between grassroots volunteer networks and institutional support. In the case of Shida Night Market in Taipei, key individuals representing the businesses and the neighbouring residents each played an important role in organizing their respective constituents, staging protests, communicating to the media and forcing the city authority to respond. In all the cases, without these individual and organizational actors, the organized actions could not have been carried out and the collective power of everyday insurgency would not have materialized.

Emancipatory Potentials (and Limits) of Everyday Insurgencies

From the discussion above, it is clear that everyday acts of insurgency can lead to intentional, organized actions, and potentially political and institutional changes in urban governance. Specifically, everyday insurgency can create critical openings and highlight conditions of contradiction and injustice in the way urban spaces and activities are institutionally and spatially arranged. As individual and collective actions aggregate and scale up, they make visible the issues at hand and provide a fertile ground for mobilization and interventions with the involvement of additional actors. The transition from one stage to the next requires the agency and facilitation of individual and organized actors with specific skills, knowledge and capacity, and sometimes a window of political opportunity, as in the case of the stalled Opera House project on Nodeul Island, as well as the media report of night market conflict in Taipei. Without the involvement of these actors and timing of events, the everyday insurgency may remain as an ephemeral and latent phenomenon whose transformative potential stays unrealized. In other words, if the power of the everyday insurgencies is not harnessed through intentional and organized actions, their emancipatory potential can remain dormant.

It is also important to note that while potentially significant in their ability to destabilize the hegemonic hierarchy in the political and institutional systems, everyday insurgencies may not be inherently positive or benevolent. For example, as much as they challenge the hegemony and occasional contradictions in institutional urban governance, internal contradictions can also exist within insurgent actions and communities. In his study of cases in Asia, Douglass (2008: 29) notes that civil society can also form exclusive spaces, and is "not necessarily engaged in inclusive or tolerant behavior". In a study of an informal market in Kaohsiung, Taiwan, Hsu (2013) reports on a power hierarchy that exists among vendors, particularly between the established ones and the newcomers. In the case of Filipina gathering in Central, Hong Kong, the spaces are actually highly territorialized with groups segregated by origins in their homeland. In addition, more established groups tend to occupy more privileged locations in the area. In Shida Night Market in Taipei, as rent in the market skyrocketed, long-time shop owners have been pushed out of prime spaces along the streets into the alleys, where they faced regulatory enforcement by the city. Similar to the residents, they were also victims in this continued saga of conflicts. These additional examples suggest that insurgent acts in themselves do not necessarily result in broader transformative outcomes.

Nevertheless, the three cases here do suggest that everyday insurgencies, however imperfect or conflict-laden, can create conditions for critical reflection and potential transformation. In its unsettling tendency, everyday insurgencies challenge the perceived stability and limited agency under the predominant paradigm of urban planning and governance that favours rules and controls over engagement, collaboration and negotiation. As the more nuanced understanding here also suggests, everyday insurgencies and their organized outcomes will likely always be an unfinished project. Just as it challenges the formalized system of urban governance, everyday insurgencies also need to be critically examined in terms of their own pitfalls, conflicts and contradictions. As Perera (2009: 54) argues, "the occupation of space, which goes beyond a mere behavioral response to the context, is simultaneously a form of adaptation, questioning, resistance, and transformation." It is in this manner that a critical reflection on the practice of everyday insurgencies, as presented in this chapter, can contribute to the practices of emancipatory city-making.

References

Albrechts, L. (2003) Planning and Power: Towards an Emancipatory Planning Approach. *Environment and Planning C: Government and Policy* 21(6), pp. 905–924.

Amin, A. and Thrift, N. (2004) The 'Emancipatory' City? In L. Lees (ed.) *The Emancipatory City? Paradoxes and Possibilities*. London: Sage Publications, pp. 231–235.

The China Post (2012) Shida Night Market Removes Signs to Prevent Closure. *The China Post*, 10 February [Online]. Available at: www.chinapost.com.tw/taiwan/local/taipei/2012/02/10/331171/Shida-Night.htm [Accessed 19 October 2012].

Chung, J. (2012) Shida Area Shuts Off Lights in Protest. *Taipei Times*, 26 February [Online]. Available at: www.taipeitimes.com/News/front/print/2012/02/26/2003526389 [Accessed 19 October 2012].

Constable, N. (1997) *Maid to Order in Hong Kong: Stories of Filipina Workers*. Ithaca, NY: Cornell University Press.

Dikeç, M. (2001) Justice and Spatial Imagination. *Environment and Planning A* 33(10), pp. 1785–1805.

Douglass, M. (2008) Civil Society for Itself and in the Public Sphere: Comparative Research on Globalization, Cities and Civic Space in Pacific Asia. In M. Douglass, K.C. Ho and O.G. Ling (eds.) *Globalization, the City and Civil Society in Pacific Asia: The Social Production of Civic Spaces*. London and New York: Routledge, pp. 27–49.

Douglass, M. and Daniere, A. (2009) Urbanization and Civic Space in Asia. In A. Daniere and M. Douglass (eds.) *The Politics of Civic Space in Asia: Building Urban Communities*. London and New York: Routledge, pp. 1–18.

Holston, J. (1998) Spaces of Insurgent Citizenship. In L. Sandercock (ed.) *Making the Invisible Visible: A Multicultural Planning History*. Berkeley: University of California Press, pp. 37–56.

Hou, J. (ed.) (2010) *Insurgent Public Space: Guerrilla Urbanism and the Remaking of Contemporary Cities*. London and New York: Routledge.

Hou, J. and Manish, C. (2016) Untangling the Messy Asian City. In J. Hou and C. Manish (eds.) *Messy Urbanism: Understanding the 'Other' Cities of Asia*. Hong Kong: University of Hong Kong Press, pp. 1–21.

Hsu, C.W. (2013) Planned Space and Unplanned Business: Three Stories from New Kujiang, Kaohsiung. In J. Hou (ed.) *City Remaking*. [反造城市：台灣非典型都市規劃術]. Taipei: Rive Gauche, pp. 92–108. (In Chinese).

Huang, C.Y. (2012) Who Killed Shida Night Market? [誰殺了師大夜市！]. *China Times Magazine*, 22 February [Online]. Available at: http://mag.chinatimes.com/print.aspx?artid=12680 [Accessed 19 October 2012]. (In Chinese).

KBS (n.d.) *Art Revitalizes the City via Seoul Art Space-MULLAE* [Online]. Available at: http://world.kbs.co.kr/english/archive/culturenlife_realfield.htm?no=1946&current_page= [Accessed 20 October 2012].

The Korea Times (2012) Seoul to Build Public Hobby Farm on Han River Island. *The Korea Times*, 7 February [Online]. Available at: www.koreatimes.co.kr/www/news/include/print.asp?newsidx=104302 [Accessed 19 October 2012].

Lau, L. (2012) Hijacking the Public Sphere: Performance, Politics, and the Everyday Citizen at Hong Kong Time Square. *Polymath: An Interdisciplinary Arts and Science Journal* 2(3), pp. 35–54.

Law, L. (2002) Defying Disappearance: Cosmopolitan Public Spaces in Hong Kong. *Urban Studies* 39(9), pp. 1625–1645.

Lee, D. (2008) Pushy Times Square Guards Raise Hackles. *The Standard*, 5 March [Online]. Available at: www.thestandard.com.hk/news_print.asp?art_id=62525&sid=17904294 [Accessed 19 October 2012].

Lees, L. (2004) The Emancipatory City: Urban (Re)visions. In L. Lees (ed.) *The Emancipatory City? Paradoxes and Possibilities*. London: Sage Publications, pp. 23–39.

Miraftab, F. (2009) Insurgent Planning: Situating Radical Planning in the Global South. *Planning Theory* 8(1), pp. 32–50.

Perera, N. (2009) People's Spaces: Familiarization, Subject Formation and Emergent Spaces in Colombo. *Planning Theory* 8(1), pp. 51–75.

Scott, J.C. (1989) Everyday Form of Resistance. In F.D. Colburn (ed.) *Everyday Forms of Peasant Resistance*. Armonk, NY and London: M.E. Sharpe, pp. 3–33.

Seoul Metropolitan Government (2015) *Urban Agriculture Master Plan of Seoul*, 2nd ed. (PowerPoint slides).

Tam, D. (2016) Little Manila: The Other Central of Hong Kong. In M. Chalana and J. Hou (eds.) *Messy Urbanism: Understanding the 'Other' Cities of Asia*. Hong Kong: University of Hong Kong Press.

Yang, B.-E. and Lee, K.-O. (2008) *Green Dream, Green City Working with People: The Story of Seoul Green Trust*. 2008 International Urban Parks Conference, Pittsburgh, Pennsylvania, 21–23 September.

7 Post-Political Development and Emancipation

Urban Participatory Projects in Helsinki

Kanerva Kuokkanen and Emilia Palonen

Introduction

There has been a growing interest in public administration and research to create participatory procedures and partnerships in policy-making and planning. The political science literature on governance emphasizes the role of multi-actor networks and the development of participatory and deliberative procedures related to them (Papadopoulos and Warin 2007), while the collaborative planning approach has underlined citizen involvement and consensus in the planning process (Healey 2006).

Literature on the post-political character of these processes has risen as a counter-reaction to the more optimistic views (e.g. Wilson and Swyngedouw 2014a; Paddison 2009). It criticizes consensual forms of participation, seeing them as expert-drawn and giving little space for dissent, political change and the politicization of issues beyond a narrowly predefined framework, while highlighting the potential of insurgent grassroots-level activism as a source of emancipation and change (Wilson and Swyngedouw 2014a; cf. Griggs et al. 2014).

Many participatory and deliberative initiatives are based on fixed-term projects funded by public authorities and implemented by various actors, including NGOs and residents. These projects are based on the simultaneous development of new forms of action and mobilizing citizens and NGOs. They can nevertheless strengthen actors who already possess resources or, alternatively, lead to symbolic and post-political forms of participation (Pinson 2009).

This study addresses these themes through the analysis of two projects in the Helsinki Metropolitan Area. The first one, Citizen Channel, developed a 'toolbox' of participation for the neighbouring municipalities of Helsinki, Espoo, Vantaa and Kauniainen in 2005–2007. The second project is the participatory planning process and the development of a governance model for the Maunula House, a multifunctional municipal building where the Maunula Democracy Project took part in the framework of Democracy Pilots in Helsinki in 2013–2016. The analysis of Citizen Channel is based on qualitative interviews with municipal officials, project administration and the participating residents, while the Maunula case draws on action research, where a researcher actively participates in the process, combining hands-on work in the Maunula Democracy Project and insights from radical democratic theory.[1]

Our claim is that the post-political framework, although describing current participatory governance arrangements rather accurately, downplays neighbourhood activism and does not take into account differences in local participatory projects not based on protest. The research questions connecting both case studies are the following: Can short-term projects affect long-term development? How can traditional decision-making hierarchies, particularly top-down or bottom-up between officials and grassroots organizing, be contested in these projects? Is there a broader shift in the roles and responsibilities of municipal officials and grassroots-level actors? What are the implications for the literatures on post-political development and emancipation? First, we will look at the existing literature on governance, planning, projects and participation, and the counter-reaction of the literature on the post-political development to them. Second, we will present the Finnish context and two case studies from the Helsinki Region, Citizen Channel and Maunula Democracy Project, respectively. Finally, we will relate our findings to research on post-political participation and emancipation.

Governance, Planning, Projects and Participation—and the Post-Political Turn

Since the 1990s, both political science and planning literatures have been concerned with multi-actor and participatory forms of policy-making and planning. In political science, governance (often used with a prefix such as 'collaborative' or 'participatory') refers to networks and partnerships between public authorities, market actors and civil society. In contrast to earlier New Public Management based on marketization, it also emphasizes the role of NGOs and citizens and the development of participatory and deliberative processes (Papadopoulos and Warin 2007; Sørensen 2005). In planning literature, there is an interrelated body of research on collaborative planning (e.g. Healey 2006), based on the Habermasian idea of communicative rationality emphasizing dialogue, consensus and citizen involvement.

Several scholars have pointed to existing deficits in governance arrangements, underlining their weak links to representative institutions and their tendency to favour better-off groups (Papadopoulos and Warin 2007; Sørensen 2005). Communicative rationality and deliberation have been challenged by scholars who see that issues of power also exist behind consensual decisions and emphasize the necessity of dissent in political action (Flyvbjerg 1998; Mouffe 1993; Hillier 2003).

The literature on post-political development, in particular, criticizes governance and participatory and deliberative arrangements where the framework is set by public authorities and there is little room for citizen influence and the politicization of issues beyond a predefined framework (Paddison 2009; Wilson and Swyngedouw 2014a). This literature draws on the writings of Chantal Mouffe, Jacques Rancière and Slavoj Žižek, among others. Here, the concept of post-political refers to the substitution of contestation and agonistic engagement by consensual and technocratic procedures that do not question the political and economic status quo (Wilson and Swynge-douw 2014b: 6). Wilson and Swyngedouw state, "political contradictions are reduced to policy problems to be managed by experts and legitimated through participatory processes in which the scope of possible outcomes is narrowly defined in advance" (*Ibid.*: 6). The post-political framework, in its turn, has been criticized of not taking into account differences and the potential present in some of these participatory processes, seeing the only form of emancipation in protest movements (Larner 2014). Simultaneously, there is a literature that aims to combine the perspectives of consensus and conflict in planning theory (Lebuhn 2017; cf. Purcell 2009). We would like to challenge these dichotomies in the current literature through our case studies.

In practice, governance and participatory arrangements are often project-based (Jensen et al. 2007; Pinson 2009). Projects in cities cover not only building, but the development of administrative and participatory models and the empowerment of residents in 'worse-off' neighbourhoods (Pinson 2009). In the managerial project literature, a 'project' is defined as unique and temporarily limited (Packendorff 1995). However, individual projects coexist, follow and replace one another and together form a long-term social and organizational structure (Boltanski and Chiapello 1999: 158). Pinson (2009) sees that this 'metaproject' includes horizons, principles and policy discourses forming a framework for individual projects.

In line with the governance logic, projects include networks, partnerships, stakeholder involvement, the combination of expert and lay knowledge, and ideas of 'active citizenship' (Pinson 2009; Jensen et al. 2007; Boltanski and Chiapello 1999). Actors implementing publicly financed urban projects include NGOs, research and cultural institutes, consultants and development companies, among others (Nonjon 2012; Pinson 2009). There is a profes-sionalization of paid project staff (Kovách and Kučerová 2006), and the development of participation has become a specific field of expertise (Nonjon 2012). In his analysis of European urban projects, Pinson (2009) sees that although these projects have participatory and deliberative elements, they tend to be elitist and exclude the working class, marginalized groups, the critics of current urban policy and municipal representative institutions—in conformity with the post-political thesis. However, in parallel with pub-licly funded projects, grassroots-level citizen movements have also adopted a project-style form of action: short-term, issue-based activity rather than long-term association-based work. In their study of Dutch neighbourhood activists, van de Wijdeven and Hendriks (2009) draw the picture of neigh-bourhood 'project conductors', not involved in formal politics nor estab-lished governance networks but interested in concrete neighbourhood issues.

The Context of the Study: Finland and Helsinki

Finland is characterized by a unitary state, broad municipal responsibilities and a weak regional level undergoing ongoing political reforms. The Finnish political system has been labelled as 'consensual', referring to collaboration

between associations and officials, a low level of social conflicts and a propor-
tional system of representation (Sjöblom 2011: 243–245). However, a severe
economic depression in the 1990s, followed by high levels of unemployment,
uneven economic development and New Public Management–oriented political reforms, led to a decline in electoral turnout and confidence in politics (cf.
Borg 2013). Since then, public authorities have shown interest in the development of both electoral democracy and direct citizen participation, related to
political reforms at the local level. These issues are also present in the Helsinki
Region, consisting of the Finnish capital and its neighbouring municipalities.

In Helsinki, neighbourhood-level participation has primarily occurred
through self-organized neighbourhood associations representing residents:
they are invited to comment on municipal issues, particularly urban planning.
The umbrella organization, Helsinki Neighborhoods Association Helka,
consists of the 78 district associations. Crucially, Helka is an NGO that
has acquired a status of a semi-official intermediary organization between
the city (top) and the citizens (grassroots) and an expert organization in
questions of resident participation. Its projects gain funding from diverse
public sources. Recently, there has been a proliferation of network-based
local activism in Helsinki not tied to existing neighbourhood associations or
publicly financed projects, characterized by a do-it-yourself spirit and new
forms of community-oriented thinking (Hernberg 2012; Tulikukka 2012).
These may also use resources offered by the municipality (see Table 7.1 for
our two cases contextualized in Helsinki).

Table 7.1 Central organizations and actors in participation in Helsinki

Helsinki
• Municipal institutions: city council and board, mayor, committees and boards, departments
• Fixed-term development programmes conducted by the municipality, often including other organizations (e.g. Uusimaa region, neighbouring municipalities) [Urban Programme for the Helsinki Metropolitan Area; Welfare City programme]
• Projects funded by these programmes, involving municipal administration, local NGOs, residents, companies, etc. [Citizen Channel; KEVEIN]
• Projects and consultations (initiated by the city council) organized by the municipality [Maunula Democracy Project]
• Helsinki Neighborhoods Association Helka: umbrella organization of neighbourhood associations, conducts projects and has contacts to municipal administration, neighbourhoods and residents, institutionalized consultant role [Citizen Channel; KEVEIN]
• Neighbourhood associations: members of Helka in each district
• Residents: use various forms of influence and participation (local associations, projects, loose resident groups, activism, municipal elections, feedback to municipal administration etc.) [Maunula Democracy Project's background]

Source: Kanerva Kuokkanen and Emilia Palonen, 2017

Citizen Channel: NGO-Led Development of Participatory Tools

One of the first participatory projects planned and conducted by Helsinki Neighborhoods Association Helka—together with street-level municipal officials and local NGOs represented in the project administration—was the Citizen Channel project, implemented in 2005–2007. It was funded by the Urban Programme for the Helsinki Metropolitan Area, a metropolitan development programme steered by the municipality of Helsinki, three neighbouring municipalities, the state and inter-municipal organizations. The initial purpose of the project—to develop a common model of interaction between the citizens and the administration for the four central municipalities of Helsinki Metropolitan Area—was soon redefined as a more general development of a 'toolbox' of participatory tools. The pilot areas of the project were neighbourhoods that crossed administrative municipal borders. Tools tested in these areas included neighbourhood-level discussion forums; meetings between residents and municipal officials; internet sites and forums; networks of core neighbourhood actors; workshops with schoolchildren; neighbourhood SWOT analysis (strengths, weaknesses, opportunities and threats) and participatory GIS (geographical information systems). A distinct part of the project developed guidelines for client feedback in municipal services. The final 'toolbox' published by the Citizen Channel project included a description of these central tools.

In interviews among the actors of the Urban Programme and Citizen Channel, Helka was presented as a professional organization in project management, municipal collaboration and neighbourhood participation. Parallels can be drawn to the French literature on 'professionals in participation' in urban policies (Nonjon 2012), combining academic knowledge and 'hands-on' experience from neighbourhoods. Still, the Citizen Channel project administration talked about the development of participation as a 'dream' and 'passion', seeing themselves as 'peers' in neighbourhood projects and representing an alternative working logic to municipal administration, thus combining a professional and a more idealistic role (cf. Tranvik and Selle 2008). During the project, Helka had collaboration both with the administration of the four municipalities involved and with neighbourhood associations and their activists.

While some activities organized by Citizen Channel involved a greater number of residents in the pilot areas, the central participants of the project were activists of neighbourhood associations who had a long history in their neighbourhoods. The official aim of Citizen Channel was to create a model or, later, a toolbox of participation, whereas the participating residents emphasized actual local issues. It was a deliberate choice by project administration to let the residents concentrate on these issues, while the project staff was working on the toolbox of participation using the experiences from the resident events as material. There was some discussion on the topic among project administrators. However, most of them did not question this approach, as they believed that the development of participatory tools would not interest the residents. They hoped that the toolbox of participation would be used in a later phase in municipalities—either in a metropolitan setting or in other contexts—and would give new opportunities for resident involvement.

After project funding ended, the project administration wished that residents could continue to work with the local issues identified during the project. As the initiative for the project came from project administration and not from the residents themselves, the latter had difficulties continuing activities without the project staff organizing them. For the participating residents, the project did not lead to new forms of emancipation or empowerment: they were already active in their neighbourhood before the project; the main benefits they derived from Citizen Channel were the creation of new contacts and networks.

Despite the hopes of the project administration, the municipalities involved did not use the Citizen Channel toolbox after the initial project ended. This caused some discussion among project administrators about the outsourcing of issues from municipal administration to NGOs. From a critical perspective, this meant legitimizing rather than transforming existing policies, as project results were not used in the municipal administration. From a more pragmatic point of view, delegating duties in the field of participation was logical because of Helka's and other NGOs' contacts at the grassroots level and their knowledge of everyday life in the neighbourhoods. After Citizen Channel, Helka and other members of the project administration got involved in new projects on resident participation. Some of the interviewees saw this as a form of creating continuity in the project world (cf. Pinson 2009) and strengthened citizen involvement both inside and outside municipal administration in the long term.

During the ten years since Citizen Channel, Helka has further strengthened its role as a general reference point for local groups and a larger field of participatory projects. Participation has also been taken more seriously by the municipality with a simultaneous rise in resident activism (Tulikukka 2012; Hernberg 2012). Our next case, the Maunula Democracy Project, shows how another participatory project is born without intermediary organizations—although during the course of the project, the project itself requires the status of an intermediary organization and finally, Helka also gets involved.

The Maunula Democracy Project: Active Residents and Interrelated Projects

The Maunula Democracy Project (MDP) started in 2012 as a response to the call for applications for Democracy Pilots by the mayor of Helsinki, aimed to develop new forms of participation and democracy in neighbourhoods or in specific fields like youth work (Sjöblom 2014). Maunula had a long tradition of active local development: various projects have been implemented in the area during the last decades, including those run by Helka. Collaborative culture had been strong in the neighbourhood in the 1980s and 1990s, with street-level bureaucrats collaborating with residents. They fought for a cultural centre since 1986, but the plans made through cooperation with the city did not get financing in the recession of the 1990s, nor in the early 2000s (Staffans 2004). The neighbourhood is currently a socioeconomically mixed area with under-funded cultural facilities, despite an engaged population of primarily middle-class and pensioners.

With the call for Democracy Pilots, demands from earlier decades to build a cultural centre became interrelated with the development of local democracy and participation, central to the Democracy Pilot framework. In 2012, active locals, local councillors and local civil society organizations, including the neighbourhood association Maunula-seura (member of Helka), organized a meeting inviting local associations and interested individuals. Their proposal was accepted as one of eleven Democracy Pilots. It included a demand for democracy spaces—first, the opening of local community centre's street-level offices to citizen-led activity (which will be not dealt with in this analysis) and, second, the participatory planning of the multifunctional building Maunula House—as well as participatory budgeting (which was adopted as a tool for the Maunula House's eventual programme planning). It soon became clear that achieving either of the goals could not be done within the year assigned for the pilots; hence, that project would not have a fixed time frame.

In the first widely announced meeting in 2013, with over 70 participants, the locals decided to "get under the bureaucrats' skin" (Palonen 2017) in the planning of the Maunula House and chose their spokespersons for this. The city reopened the plan for this multifunctional building housing three municipal functions: a library, a youth centre and a civic adult education unit. The MDP's first task was to involve residents throughout the planning process of Maunula House in equal terms with the three municipal departments instead of a traditional planning process which is divided into separate planning and citizen consultation phases. Rather than applying an existing deliberative framework or participatory toolbox (such as the one from Citizen Channel), the MDP started to work on its own approach to participatory planning and co-governance. This was not the case with all Democracy Pilots; in another Helsinki neighbourhood, the municipality forced the pilot to test the citizen jury model, meaning that the many ideas from the public were not discussed and people felt excluded, confirming the problems of post-politics (see Sjöblom 2014).

In Maunula, the citizen spokesperson(s) attended most meetings of the officials alongside the three departments. They insisted that the architects of the Maunula House and landscape architects would first meet with the locals and then test their plans twice with them. Local meetings and larger citizen-led workshops constituted the framework. The open calls sought to engage new groups, schools, renters' associations and immigrants, widening the scope so that meetings always had some regulars and some newcomers. The meetings were led by locals, with officials from municipal departments often present. Rather than seeking consensus, different voices and ideas were gathered, tried out in the plan and articulated into demands for planners. Partnership discourse was a tactic tool to maintain strong discussion among citizen groups and municipal officials.

Little funding was earmarked for the pilots, and when the Democracy Pilot officially ended, the activists of the MDP continued their project by themselves. The MDP refused to be a mere fixed-term project, as it drew on the tradition of neighbourhood activism in Maunula and aimed to establish more enduring results than the assigned one-year-long pilot allowed for, including resident involvement in the planning process and a model of local co-governance for the Maunula House based on resident representation, participatory budgeting and inter-departmental cooperation. Many of the principles came from the planning phase, such as large meetings for voicing and articulating demands and selecting resident representatives to a council and steering group.

While some of the MDP actives started the project with demands for inclusion, this potential conflict was tamed by a positive response from municipal officials. The inclusion of locals lessened conflict between the three municipal departments involved. The process was largely based on consent, although the citizen perspective was sometimes in contradiction with the officials' view. An easily accessible meeting space and a café that could also be run by local groups was the most important demand that the spokespersons hung on to during the first meetings. The second part of the project addressed local democracy in the governance of the House. Conflicts emerged later when the feasibility of these central demands were questioned.

Crucially, the character and model of the MDP developed through conflict. When municipal officials working with issues of participation got involved, they assumed that an existing model of participatory budgeting could be directly adopted in Maunula instead of being adapted through the local co-governance model in development. Their view on participation emphasizing general and transferable participatory tools differed from that of the MPD, which had taken the position of intermediary organization representing the residents. Most importantly, in the MDP, the notion of representation was not tied to representing predefined groups but on articulating demands (cf. Laclau 1996; Disch 2011). These demands were based on the meetings held with the residents, so they could not be overlooked as just another suggestion from the abstract masses.

The MDP had functioned without external funding since the ending of the Democracy Pilots at the end of 2014. However, in summer 2016, they decided to take part in a four-month KEVEIN project (a Finnish acronym for 'From Developer Networks to Innovation Platform') run by Helka and funded by the municipality of Helsinki and the surrounding Uusimaa region through a specific Welfare City programme. The KEVEIN framework appeared to be an attractive way to register the achievements of their initial project for the central MDP actors. After deciding the KEVEIN project would continue the activities of the MDP in practice, they opted to treat it as a supporting side-project while continuing with their own project. The MDP actors hoped that the KEVEIN project would foster citizen-led ethos in other contexts, with the risk that Helka's semi-official role in participation could alienate some active locals not accustomed to Helka's way of working. KEVEIN funding ensured utilizing the newest Maunula Model, but at the same time Maunula was subsumed into KEVEIN's discourse, which emphasized local innovations and innovativeness.

The co-governance model for the Maunula House was revealed and adopted in a meeting in August 2016. This meeting confirmed that during the process even the participating officials' perspectives on local democracy and representation changed. In September 2016, the Maunula Model was presented at an official process on developing participation in Helsinki. In contrast to other models discussed in that event, it was the only concrete proposal stressing the combination of horizontal local engagement with vertical representational processes. The impact of the project, the models of citizen-centred participatory planning and the co-governance model of Maunula House—or the functioning House itself—remains to be seen, but participants on both sides felt it sought to challenge the limits it had been assigned from the above (cf. Wilson and Swyngedouw 2014a). In the opening ceremony of the Maunula House on 4 February 2017, the vice-mayor stated that the participatory model developed in Maunula is one of the most important pilots as the city reforms its participation framework in 2017.

Participatory Projects—Post-Political or Emancipatory?

To summarize, our cases show two distinct ways to organize participatory projects (see Table 7.1). In Citizen Channel, the emphasis was on participatory tools. While the intention was for Helka to coordinate between municipal administration and neighbourhood associations, the role of the project staff became over-pronounced while the residents' role remained limited. This was caused by the decision of the project administration to separate the roles of residents addressing concrete issues from the development of a more abstract participatory toolbox by the project administration. The results of the project were undermined by the fact that the toolbox of participation was not adopted by the municipalities involved. Some interviewees saw the project as a way to legitimize rather than change current policies. However, the more optimistic interviewees saw the project as part of a trajectory that could change administrative and societal culture towards a more participatory one in the long term.

The Maunula Democracy Project, carried out almost a decade later, managed to avoid the pitfalls of Citizen Channel because the initiative came from the residents, there was a clear connection between the developed models and the building of the Maunula House, and municipal officials were open to the residents' propositions. The MDP operated as an open platform but had representatives collaborating with municipal officials simultaneously. During the process, it became an intermediary organization between the residents and the municipality. Considered as the citizens' representative, the MDP invited locals to provide ideas, develop them into demands in open meetings and amplify them through chosen spokespersons alongside the officials. Although the MDP was based on partnership logic, the intention was to gather voices and ideas rather than reach a consensus. The conflicts that emerged were seen as demanding but also useful for the process generally as they widened the bureaucrats' and citizens' perspectives. The MDP created two models, one on participatory planning and the other one on the co-governance of the Maunula House. Participation in the Helka-run innovation platform project was seen as a possible way to enable articulation and exportation of that model and make it more durable than the pilot year or the four years of the MDP. Table 7.2 summarizes the key features of our two cases.

In this research, we asked first whether short-term projects could affect long-term development. Our answer is yes, they can, but not automatically: Despite the problems of Citizen Channel and the fact that the toolbox was not widely adopted, Helka's projects created frameworks for a new ethos of participation in the City of Helsinki. Because of the momentum and enthusiasm at different levels of Helsinki, MDP's initiative was successful and set a model for the whole city. Second, we inquired how the dichotomies between top-down and bottom-up and between officials and grassroots could be contested in these projects, and whether they implied a broader shift in the roles and responsibilities of municipal officials and grassroots-level actors. The two cases show differing processes between municipal officials, city-level NGOs like Helka and organized neighbourhood actors as citizen representatives or spokespeople. Projects, often following one another, enable the interaction between them.

Furthermore, we asked about the implications for the literature on post-political development and emancipation. The cases are not examples of protests or radical social movements presented as alternatives to post-political development (Wilson and Swyngedouw 2014a), but include elements that are often presented as post-political: partnerships, NGOs specializing in participation, participatory models and incremental neighbourhood-level transformation. Tasks from municipalities are outsourced to NGOs and resident actors, using them as developers of pilots and models that may later be used by the municipal administration, but may also establish more permanent co-governance structures.

NGOs and residents equally grab onto opportunities provided by municipalities and publicly funded projects. While in Citizen Channel, the role of participatory models and the influence of NGO-led professional project

Table 7.2 The central elements of Citizen Channel and Maunula Democracy Project

Project	Citizen Channel	Maunula Democracy Project
Central actor	Helsinki Neighborhoods Association Helka (umbrella organization for neighbourhood associations in Helsinki)	Maunula residents and associations call for open meeting to form the spokespeople for MDP, an open platform
Involved actors	Helsinki and three neighbouring municipalities (upper- and street-level bureaucrats); local NGOs represented in the project administration; neighbourhood association activists (and other residents)	Helsinki and its departments involved in Maunula House (key functions: library, youth centre, civic adult education); municipal officials with participation duties (2014–); Helka (through KEVEIN project 2016–); residents, local groups, neighbourhood association
Funding	Project funding through Urban Programme for the Helsinki Metropolitan Area	Minor financing through Mayor's Democracy Pilots and the Helka-run KEVEIN project (financed by the Welfare City programme of Helsinki and the Uusimaa Region)
Idea of participation	Division between local issues (task of the residents) and participatory tools (task of project administration)	Open platform and spokespersons collaborate with officials; articulating demands together, not representing pre-given groups
Consensus and conflict	Consensus rather than conflict; some discussion about the priorities of the project; project administration disappointed by the fact that municipalities did not use the toolbox	Consensus on working together for a new model; ability to voice multiple, contrasting demands and disagreements on common platforms locally or at officials' meetings; central contents of the project emerged through conflict
Results	A 'toolbox' of participation	The citizen-led participatory planning process and a model of co-governance for Maunula House
Long-term effect	The toolbox developed in the project not used by the municipalities; themes continue in later projects by Helka and other actors	The co-governance model in use in Maunula House; MDP inspires participation and local democracy development in Helsinki; potential long-term results

Source: Kanerva Kuokkanen and Emilia Palonen, 2017

administration were over-pronounced when compared to the residents' role; during the last decade Helka acted as an enabling structure in resident-led projects rather than the central actor. More grass-rooted actors may emerge, organize and engage with the city over time as the MDP shows. Here, we share the criticism of Larner (2014) about the literature on post-politics ignoring differences and context in neighbourhood projects and in emerging forms of local activism.

Our case studies question the usual perspectives of the post-political in two ways. First, they challenge the dichotomy between top-down and bottom-up by showing the role of Helka and the MDP as intermediary organizations in participatory projects. Second, the case of MDP showed that participation might include different levels of engagement: citizens both generate horizontal ties and engage in vertical representational processes when generating positions and voicing demands. This contrasts with Deleuze and Guattari (1983)–inspired contributions emphasizing horizontality. Even Purcell's (2009: 159) discussion of Laclau and Mouffe does not stress the crucially joined role of verticality (articulating demands) and horizontality ('chains of equivalence' between groups) in their theory. For example, when the future of participatory models were discussed in September 2016 in an open workshop organized by the City of Helsinki, the Maunula Model was the only concrete proposal stressing horizontality, local engagement and debate, seeing the participating residents as an open-ended and diverse group with multiple conflicting views to be articulated into demands rather than a demographically defined representative body. Still, the status of the project as a positive example of cooperation between locals and city officials across participating departments may have a profound impact on participation in Helsinki.

The articulation of demands is a crucial part of politics from the post-political perspective of Ernesto Laclau (2005, 1996): It requires maintaining both horizontal ties and generating empty and floating signifiers (e.g. projects, demands, spokespersons) that can be referred to and may represent various and heterogeneous demands. In this process, ideas are transformed into demands. For Laclau and Mouffe (1985), politics is not only about conflict and political frontiers but also about the way in which heterogeneous demands can be articulated into a common struggle or cause (Gilbert 2014). It is particularly important in this process that 'empty signifiers' work as sufficient representatives able to traverse widely across diverse, incomplete and contingent groups and demands (Laclau 1996). This demand-gathering activity, articulation process and long-term effects of projects in developing new participatory frameworks are understudied. Yet, they seem to open new possibilities for resident involvement and co-governance instead of juxtaposing consensual and conflictual forms of participation typical of post-politics.

Note

1. The empirical data relating to Citizen Channel has been collected, analyzed and interpreted in a previous scientific publication (Kuokkanen 2016). The Maunula House case has been researched by the second author of this article, political theorist Emilia Palonen, as participant action researcher.

References

Boltanski, L. and Chiapello, È. (1999) *Le nouvel esprit du capitalism*. NRF Essais, Paris: Gallimard.

Borg, S. (ed.) (2013) *Demokratiaindikaattorit 2013*. Selvityksiä ja ohjeita 52. Helsinki: Oikeusministeriö.

Deleuze, G. and Guattari, F. (1983) *Anti-Oedipus: Capitalism and Schizophrenia*. Minneapolis: Minnesota University Press.

Disch, L. (2011) Towards a Mobilization Conception of Democratic Representation. *American Political Science Review* 105(1), pp. 100–114.

Flyvbjerg, B. (1998) *Rationality and Power: Democracy in Practice*. Chicago: University of Chicago Press.

Gilbert, J. (2014) *Common Ground: Democracy and Collectivity in an Age of Individualism*. London: Pluto Press.

Griggs, S., Norval, A.J. and Wagenaar, H. (2014) *Practices of Freedom: Decentered Governance, Conflict and Democratic Participation*. New York and Cambridge: Cambridge University Press.

Healey, P. (2006) *Collaborative Planning: Shaping Places in Fragmented Societies*, 2nd ed. Basingstoke: Palgrave Macmillan.

Hernberg, H. (ed.) (2012) *Helsinki beyond Dreams: Actions towards a Creative and Sustainable Hometown*. Helsinki: Urban Dream Management.

Hillier, J. (2003) Agonizing over Consensus: Why Habermasian Ideals Cannot Be 'Real'. *Planning Theory* 2(1), pp. 37–59.

Jensen, C., Johansson, S. and Löfström, M. (2007) *Projektledning i offentlig miljö*. Malmö: Liber.

Kovách, I. and Kučerová, E. (2006) The Project Class in Central Europe: The Czech and Hungarian Cases. *Sociologia Ruralis* 46(1), pp. 3–21.

Kuokkanen, K. (2016) *Developing Participation through Projects? A Case Study from the Helsinki Metropolitan Area*. Faculty of Social Sciences Publications 6/2016. Helsinki: University of Helsinki.

Laclau, E. (1996) *Emancipation(s)*. London and New York: Verso.

Laclau, E. (2005) *On Populist Reason*. London and New York: Verso.

Laclau, E. and Mouffe, C. (1985) *Hegemony and Socialist Strategy: Towards Radically Democratic Politics*. London: Verso.

Larner, W. (2014) The Limits of Post-Politics: Rethinking Radical Social Enterprise. In J. Wilson and E. Swyngedouw (eds.) *The Post-Political and Its Discontents: Spaces of Depoliticisation, Spectres of Radical Politics*. Edinburgh: Edinburgh University Press, pp. 189–207.

Lebuhn, H. (2017, forthcoming) Shifting Struggles over Public Space and Public Goods in Berlin: Urban Activism between Protest and Participation. In J. Hou and S. Knierbein (eds.) *City Unsilenced: Public Space and Urban Resistance in the Age of Shrinking Democracy*. New York and London: Routledge.

Mouffe, C. (1993) *The Return of the Political*. London and New York: Verso.

Nonjon, M. (2012) De la 'militance' à la 'consultance': les bureaux d'études urbaines, acteurs et reflets de la 'procéduralisation' de la participation. *Revue Politiques et Management Public* 29(1), pp. 79–98.

Packendorff, J. (1995) Inquiring into the Temporary Organization: New Directions for Project Management Research. *Scandinavian Journal of Management* 11(4), pp. 319–333.

Paddison, R. (2009) Some Reflections on the Limitations to Public Participation in the Post-Political City. *L'espace Politique* 8(2). doi: 10.4000/espacepolitique. 1393.

Palonen, E. (2017) Radikaalidemokratiaa Helsingin Maunulassa. *Politiikasta*, 31 January 2017. Available at: http://politiikasta.fi/radikaalidemokratiaa-helsingin-maunulassa/ [Accessed 6 February 2017].

Papadopoulos, Y. and Warin, P. (2007) Are Innovative, Participatory and Deliberative Procedures in Policy Making Democratic and Effective? *European Journal of Political Research* 46, pp. 445–472.

Pinson, G. (2009) *Gouverner la ville par projet: Urbanisme et gouvernance des villes européennes*. Paris: Presses de Sciences Po.

Purcell, M. (2009) Resisting Neoliberalization: Communicative Planning or Counter-Hegemonic Movements? *Planning Theory* 8(2), pp. 140–165.

Sjöblom, S. (2011) Finland: The Limits of the Unitary Decentralized Model. In J. Loughlin, F. Hendriks and A. Lidström (eds.) *The Oxford Handbook of Local and Regional Democracy in Europe*. Oxford: Oxford University Press, pp. 241–260.

Sjöblom, J. (2014) *Lähidemokratiapilotti: Bacchilainen tapaustutkimus suoran osallistumisen kehittämisestä Arabian alueella Helsingissä*. Master's thesis in Social Policy, Helsinki: University of Helsinki [Online]. Available at: http://artova.fi/images/stories/Tutkimukset/Jonas-1204019191.pdf [Accessed 25 May 2016].

Sørensen, E. (2005) The Democratic Problems and Potentials of Network Governance. *European Political Science* 4(3), pp. 348–357.

Staffans, A. (2004) *Vaikuttavat asukkaat: Vuorovaikutus ja paikallinen tieto kaupunkisuunnittelun haasteina*. Yhdyskuntasuunnittelun tutkimus- ja koulutuskeskuksen julkaisuja A 29. Espoo: Yhdyskuntasuunnittelun tutkimus- ja koulutuskeskus, Teknillinen korkeakoulu.

Tranvik, T. and Selle, P. (2008) *Digital teknologi i sivilsamfunnet: Studier av fire frivillige organisasjoner*. Oslo: Unipub.

Tulikukka, P. (2012) Learning Peer-to-Peer Practices Step-by-Step: 3 Cases from Suburban Helsinki Neighbourhoods. In A. Botero, A. Gryf Paterson and J. Saad-Sulonen (eds.) *Towards Peer Production in Public Services: Cases from Finland*. Helsinki: Aalto University, pp. 76–88.

van de Wijdeven, T. and Hendriks, F. (2009) A Little Less Conversation, a Little More Action: Real-Life Expressions of Vital Citizenship in City Neighborhoods. In J.W. Duyvendak, F. Hendriks and M. van Niekerk (eds.) *City in Sight: Dutch Dealings with Urban Change*. Amsterdam: Amsterdam University Press, pp. 121–140.

Wilson, J. and Swyngedouw, E. (eds.) (2014a) *The Post-Political and Its Discontents: Spaces of Depoliticisation, Spectres of Radical Politics*. Edinburgh: Edinburgh University Press.

Wilson, J. and Swyngedouw, E. (2014b) Seeds of Dystopia: Post-Politics and the Return of the Political. In J. Wilson and E. Swyngedouw (eds.) *The Post-Political and Its Discontents: Spaces of Depoliticisation, Spectres of Radical Politics*. Edinburgh: Edinburgh University Press, pp. 1–22.

8 Urban Events Under the Post-Political Condition

(Im)Possibilities for Emancipation in a Small-Scale City of Switzerland

Monika Salzbrunn, Barbara Dellwo and Serjara Aleman

Introduction

Cities are spaces of imbrication of forms of belonging, constituting a platform for identification and for articulating world culture locally. Anne Raulin suggests that urban identity is confronted with new challenges by being "faced with the abstraction of national identities somehow outdated . . . , faced with a certain decline of class identities, faced with the distrust against ethnic and religious identities suspected of fundamentalism" (2001: 170). In this chapter, we investigate the urban event *La Grande Table* in order to show the actors' appropriation and redefinition of public space through the performance of multiple belongings. The highlighting of translocal and transnational ties during this event leads us to interrogate these practices as forms of emancipation and community building at the local scale under the post-political condition.

Urban events represent privileged entry points for researching processes of co-construction of social and political spaces. Indeed, events hold transformative power as they appear in a particular time-space, enabling the staging, negotiation and reconstruction of urban identities (Salzbrunn 2011b). *La Grande Table* in Morges constitutes an event displaying culinary specialties and multicultural folklore promoted under the label of "Morges World City: flavours from here and there" (CCSE 2014). The biannual celebration is organized by the city's Swiss-Foreigner Consultative Commission, following the integration policies of the public authorities, and provides a space for strategies of visibilization for different national communities represented in Morges. *La Grande Table* is organized in collaboration with the 'foreigners'[1] affected by these policies, and the event uses a participatory dimension.

Numerous studies have investigated processes of migrant settlement in Swiss metropolises by focusing on integration, political participation or social cohesion. Consequently, the urban environment is considered mere scenery for individuals to inscribe their presence upon. For several years, however, certain scholars have suggested that the city should also be considered a research object in its own right. While authors question the emancipatory potential and ambivalences of (urban) spaces, they also highlight actors' capacity to perform emancipatory acts despite hegemonic city planning practices.

Based on interviews and ethnographic observations carried out during and around *La Grande Table*,[2] we interrogate the way public space is thought, negotiated or consumed by its various actors—from organizers and crafts-people to performers and the public. We finally seek to understand if this event has emancipatory potential capable of changing power relations on a local level.

According to Wilson and Swyngedouw, "in post-politics, political con-tradictions are reduced to policy problems to be managed by experts and legitimated through participatory processes in which the scope of possible outcomes is narrowly defined in advance" (2015: 6). In this context, we ask to what extent *La Grande Table*, which symbolizes a participatory process aimed at facilitating foreigners' integration, is a mere expression of the post-political condition, or if it is actually repoliticized by its protagonists through the staging of (multiple) belongings as a practice of emancipation.

La Grande Table in Morges: Implementing Integration Policies in a Super-Diverse Town

Morges, a small town of 15,400 residents (Statistiques Vaud) in the Canton of Vaud, is part of the broader metropolitan region around Lake Geneva. Switzerland's official entry into the Schengen Agreement in 2008 as well as a liberal tax policy aimed at attracting multinational firms have led to a consid-erable diversification of the population in Morges. In 1974, about 24% of the city's population was of foreign nationality, but the number had climbed to 35.4% in 2014 (Statistiques Vaud). While immigration to the Swiss Confed-eration during the post-war boom years was predominantly characterized by male labour migration, comprised of mainly Italian and Spanish blue-collar workers, as well as German blue- and white-collar workers (Efionayi et al. 2005), family reunification policies in the 1970s contributed to the settlement of migrant populations (D'Amato 2008). The 1990s were characterized by the arrival of refugees fleeing conflict in former Yugoslavia and a decline of labour migration due to the economic crisis (*Ibid.*). At the same time, with the neolib-eral turn, selective immigration policies have increasingly aimed at attracting highly skilled professionals (Afonso 2006). In the Canton of Vaud, more than half of all newcomers are highly skilled migrants from EU (European Union) and EFTA (European Free Trade Association) countries (Statistique Vaud 2014). Meanwhile, matters of immigration have been growing increasingly tense as right-wing parties have put this theme at the centre of public debates since the 1960s, and the system of direct democracy has given them consider-able influence on immigration policymaking (Skenderovic 2007).

La Grande Table can be seen as a response to increasingly tense politiciza-tion of diversity (Vertovec 2007) by displaying multicultural folklore that promotes the consumption of cultural otherness through shared food, dance and clothing. The event is organized by the Swiss-Foreigner Consultative Commission of Morges, founded in 1981, which counts 22 members of Swiss and foreign nationality who, according to the Commission's website, constitute "representatives from the political class, professional and confessional milieus and associative and athletic spheres active in Morges" (http://ccse-morges.net/pages/qui.html [Accessed 4 October 2014]).

Chaired by Yves Paccaud, municipal councillor and member of the Socialist party, the Consultative Commission implements the recommendations on integration of the Federal Commission on Migration. One of its objectives is the "fostering of mutual recognition of all residents of the region of Morges, wherever they come from" (*Ibid.*). The Commission also seeks to "offer spaces and moments of conviviality" by organizing regular "cultural activities" such as "tropical nights" or "evenings of discovery" (*Ibid.*) featuring different countries for each event. Coordinated by a sub-commission comprised of a small group of active core members of the Consultative Commission, *La Grande Table* is the main event. Renato Santacruz is in charge of the artistic programme of the event, and he emphasizes that his engagement is not of a political nature as the Commission acts in a consultative capacity without exercising decision-making rights.

We consider that the Commission's approach holds a paternalistic dimension, not only because of the hegemonic conception of conviviality, but also because it holds a vision of integration inherited from the 1970s when integration was conceived in terms of assimilation into a purportedly homogenous national body. The shift towards the diversity paradigm (Salzbrunn 2014) means society is increasingly thought of as being intrinsically heterogeneous and that public policies should aim at promoting equality among residents regardless of their origins, gender or sexual orientation in order to favour social cohesion. Diversity policies refrain from the use of the term 'migration' and adopt a semantic shift towards 'cosmopolitanism'. Furthermore, despite the local authorities' awareness of the changes in migration patterns, the national integration policies still reproduce their own bias by almost exclusively addressing the low-skilled labour migrants from southern countries. The highly skilled professionals seem to not be framed as migrants and do therefore not face the same hegemonic injunction to integration (Faist 2013). This raises the question of the local potential for emancipation that is expressed symbolically and materially under these conditions.

We define an emancipatory process as one that occurs when actors are able to act outside of or redefine the categories they are assigned to. We will see that *La Grande Table* can be considered as a stage where multiple belongings are expressed and perceived, thereby offering a space for emancipatory action and incorporation processes (Salzbrunn 2011a). But how can the notion of cosmopolitanism allow us to rethink the emancipatory potential of displaying multiple belongings? Martha Nussbaum (1994: para IV), referring to Diogenes Laertius's story about the marriage between Crates and Hipparchia, states that "the life of the cosmopolitan, who puts right before country, and universal reason before the symbols of national belonging, need not be boring, flat, or lacking in love". However, from an emic point of view, *La Grande Table* is full of various signs of national belonging (like flags). Consequently, we explore the ways in which the appropriation of urban space by different groups of migrants as well as non-migrants can be read as a form of self-empowerment, despite of the paternalistic framing of the event.

Performing Multiple Belonging in Urban Public Space: The Use of Food, Dance and Clothes

The seventh edition of *La Grande Table* took place on a rainy Sunday in June 2014 on the main street of the pedestrian city centre framed by the temple of Morges on one end and the Château on its other. The official programme announced 40 food stands and cultural performances provided by nine sociocultural groups and associations, representing approximately 25 nationalities. Unlike the first edition of the event, where one long banquet-like table was set up in the middle of the street while all the food stands were lined up on one side of the road, the following editions have featured interspersed food stands and tables. Due to an electric overcharge caused by all the booths drawing from the same power line, the organizers were forced to rearrange the setting of public space. The original conception of the popular street event came from the adaptation of a Barcelonian version over a decade ago. Today, the appropriation of the city space by the vendors and sociocultural associations offering food and folklore influences the visitor's interpretation of space and precipitates the practice of grouping, which the original conception of the event sought to avoid.

The notion of conviviality is key and is used to advertise the event by highlighting the idea of an encounter and ideal interaction with the 'exotic other' through the shared consumption of food and folklore. Given that the aim of the event is to "facilitate the integration of migrant populations" (CCSE 2014: 3), *La Grande Table* incarnates the idea of incorporating foreign nationals through their normalization (Régnier 2006). The proposed consumption of an exoticized alterity seeks to encourage curiosity for the other, rather than its rejection, by offering an experience of the extraordinary through the transgression of food norms (*Ibid.*) for the specific time-space of the event. Indeed, the organizers emphasize that they wish to display a great variety of culinary specialties and folklore attractions. Thus, the most highly sought-after artists are those coming from the most faraway places, as Renato Santacruz explains (personal interview conducted by Aleman, 24 September 2014). For each edition, the organizers seek to display culinary and artistic exoticism. There are norms and discussions about which food stands may or may not be accepted in order to avoid repetition and the 'ordinary'. This year, for example, the organizers reduced the amount of

Asian food on offer, as it has become over-represented and is a type of cuisine already easily visible in public space, therefore reducing its exotic attraction, according to the coordinator (*Ibid.*).

Two associations are particularly visible during the event and provide folk dance, music and culinary specialties since its foundation. The *Cultural Association Teuta* from Lausanne attracts attention through their display of a national community by proudly presenting their national flag, tightly tucked to their food stand and regularly waved during parades. Performing 'traditional dances' from Kosovo and offering food such as *burek* and *qebapa*, *Teuta* have made themselves visible through their folkloric clothes and political symbolism as well as their relatively high number of members, who gather around their food stand and regularly parade up and down the street. Interestingly, no religious signs of belonging are visible, which stands in contrast with our observations the night before. After a long day of setting up tables and food stands for the following day, the Commission invited all volunteers to join them for some appetizers and wine. We observed that the Kosovarian volunteers didn't eat the appetizers made with pork; we attempted to address this apparent 'oversight', when they quietly shrugged: "They should know better, but perhaps it's best this way" (Kosovarian volunteer, personal communication, 28 June 2014). This episode is emblematic for the way groups and individuals with a Muslim background adopt invisibilization strategies specifically within the context of the Canton of Vaud. This observation of invisible religious signs of belonging, especially amongst Muslims from the Balkans, who are the largest group of Muslims in Switzerland, confirms previously published findings from our research project (see Salzbrunn 2016).

The *Folklore Group Coraçao do Minho* from Geneva is equally visible and performs multiple and transnational belonging. They represent a region of Northern Portugal and the Swiss Confederation by waving both national flags as well as the emblem of the association visibly during processions. These two associations are intentionally chosen to be part of the festivities time and again because, as Renato Santacruz explains (personal interview conducted by Aleman, 24 September 2014), they bring visitors from other parts of the country such as Geneva, Yverdon or sometimes even as far as Zurich with them. Thus, the Group *Coraçao do Minho* arrives with two coach buses full of members of the association but also of the Portuguese community, who tag along in hopes of being able to enjoy the music, sounds and flavours from their home country. These two groups not only reflect the population of the town, where Portuguese and Balkan nationals have a significant presence among foreign residents, but they are also considered an important pillar for the symbolic and economic effectiveness of the event.

Borce Tupanoski, of Macedonian origin and one of the youngest members of the Commission, also stresses how much he enjoys reviving flavours "from home" during the time-space of the event (personal communication, 29 June 2014). This tendency can be observed at several places such as the

Peruvian or Dominican booths. The *Macedonian Association Aleksandar Makedonski* from Yverdon set up their food stand right beside the stand of the Commission. Branislav Trajchevski, the president of the association, speaks with a heavy accent and a calm voice that doesn't conceal his enthusiasm when talking about his country of origin and the work of the association. Besides his involvement in the community, he is also a member of the Swiss-Foreigner Consultative Commission in Yverdon and thus takes part in numerous sociocultural events throughout the canton. The president states that the mission of his association not only consists in displaying Macedonian culture, preparing *cevapcici* and offering imported wine at *La Grande Table*. He also stresses his ambition to enable local Macedonian nationals to get to know their place of residence by organizing excursions to the Swiss countryside, when the association's small budget allows it, and by offering French and Macedonian language classes.

While dishes sold at numerous food stands run by associations evoke the image of a home-cooked meal, the six Southeast Asian and Indian food stands, which include Thai, Vietnamese, Japanese and Singaporean cuisine, are all run by professional restaurants. Here, no groups can be found gathering around the stands chatting, consuming or listening to music.

Figure 8.1 The Cultural Association *Teuta* performing 'traditional' dances and music from Kosovo, visibly displaying their national flag

Photograph by Barbara Dellwo, 2014

Figure 8.2 The Folklore Group *Coraçao do Minho* parading in folkloric costumes, holding the logo of the association featuring the Swiss and Portuguese national flags

Photograph by Serjara Aleman, 2014

Figure 8.3 Food stand of the Macedonian Association *Aleksandar Makedonski* displaying not only the Swiss and Macedonian national flags but also the flag of the canton Vaud, with its slogan '*Liberté et Patrie*' (Liberty and Patria)

Photograph by Serjara Aleman, 2014

Figure 8.4 Ly Thành Asian catering restaurant advertising professional menus
Photograph by Serjara Aleman 2014

By advertising their menus, the restaurants pursue a commercial strategy and display business logos rather than symbols of (national) belonging. In this case, the foreign nationals gain from cultural difference, positioning themselves in a market of ethnic consumption. This might be understood as appropriating the strategy of marketing urban diversity, implemented through local policies used to manage and capitalise on cultural difference. Thus, the restaurants contribute to the professionalization of the event. As the security and hygienic requirements (e.g. the installation of a refrigerator) expand, vendors' expenditures rise to fulfil them. Consequently, nonprofit associations and craftspeople have difficulties affording the costs of setting up a food stand and are therefore increasingly excluded from the event.

Urban Events as Spaces for Emancipation?

The approach that we propose accounts for the co-constructions of social spaces involving a multitude of actors, such as members of the city council, craftspeople, vendors, residents and visitors who, at the time of the event, rearrange the defined borders of identity and territory. Events are spaces of privileged observation to analyze social ties as the result of common actions of individuals in a social space (Salzbrunn 2010) as they manifest a form of social bond more or less ephemeral, as they crystallize the social (in)visibility of a cause (e.g. the national project of the Kosovarian association or the apparent transnational nationalism of the Macedonian association) or as an occasion whose social consequences can have a more or less important impact.

The multiplicity of actors needs to be taken into account in order to understand the multi-scalar dimension of *La Grande Table* and provide a situational analysis of each actor involved. This leads us to raise the question of the emancipatory potential of this event: What are the power dynamics at stake and which strategies are deployed by the different actors in order to gain agency and empower themselves?

La Grande Table pursues a double objective: first, to "facilitate the integration of the foreign population" (CCSE 2014: 3); second, to enhance the attractiveness of the city by promoting an image of openness in the sense of urban marketing of diversity. This double aim results in a variety of configurations during the event: sociocultural groups are present because their food is considered attractive, others because of their dance and folklore, others because their community is numerically important to include. Consequently, there are several Southeast Asian, Indian, Turkish, Syrian and Italian restaurants and catering services. These are already established businesses, occupying an ethnic niche and therefore attesting to their attractiveness. In the same way, there is a market for a specific kind of folklore performed at *La Grande Table*, such as Flamenco or belly dance. Other sociocultural groups and associations, whose cultural or culinary productions appear to be less popular, are nevertheless present due to other reasons: because of their numerical weight, e.g. the Portuguese, the largest foreign community in Morges, or because of their access to power positions, e.g. the Macedonians, who are numerically few but were invited by Borce, a member of the Commission. Likewise, there were a significant number of Latin American food stands despite the comparatively low population of those communities.

Consequently, we can think of these modes of (in)visibilization as strategies of empowerment through the acquisition or confirmation of certain types of capitals. As mentioned above, the Southeast Asian and Indian restaurants pursue a commercial strategy and confirm their economic capital, without seeking political and symbolic recognition as a foreign community. On the contrary, the Portuguese, Kosovarian and Macedonian associations use the event as a public arena to display their national flags or traditional dances and clothes to gain political recognition. By displaying foreign flags in the locality of Morges, they contribute to creating a transnational social space. The display of regional flags, such as the one of the canton Vaud, indicates their rooting in a local space which is connected to other localities and part of a translocal social space (Salzbrunn 2011a: 170). This practice is also demonstrated by the stand of the *Café Vaudois* which exclusively advertises Portuguese food products.

Visibilization can also lead to empowerment through the acquisition of the symbolic capital of being part of the locality of Morges. But interestingly, foreign nationals are perceived to be part of the locality and able to participate in the public display of a diverse local community by being on stage as an exotic other and highlighting alterity. Finally, these sociocultural associations are invited as representatives of their ethnic or national communities. While they gain symbolic capital within their respective communities by participating in the event, they are folklorized and exoticized, which encourages community building based on ethnic or cultural otherness.

Interestingly, the second most important foreign community in terms of numbers, the French, were visible neither in culinary nor in folkloric performances at *La Grande Table*. Likewise, we could observe the presence of several English-speaking and German visitors among the public at the event but no German, British or American food stand. This can be explained by the fact that they are solicited as consumers without having to empower themselves by making their presence visible. Also, the more recent and skilled migrants from EU and EFTA countries are not framed by the hegemonic discourse as 'migrants' aimed by the national integration policies. In addition to raising the question of why they are not exoticized and folklorized, this also highlights the implicit class-based distinction of integration policies, according to which the migrants that need to be integrated are the unskilled ones, located at the bottom of the social ladder (Dellwo in press).

While the Swiss-Foreigner Consultative Commission has no decision-making power in terms of local or national politics, the organizers of *La Grande Table* gain social and political recognition by their involvement in the planning and execution of a public event of local significance that increases the attractiveness of the town within the neoliberal scheme of global scaling of cities (Glick Schiller and Caglar 2011). Swiss organizers gain symbolic legitimacy by publicly shaking the mayor's hand during the event and being on familiar terms with local authorities. Through their involvement in the Commission, the foreign organizers are integrated into a political structure that enables them to express their opinion on local affairs concerning the foreign population even though they don't necessarily have the right to vote.[3] Moreover, the community-making effects of the event integrate them into the local social fabric and allow them to publicly perform their integration. Consequently, by participating in democratic processes and community building at a local level, the Swiss or foreign national organizers increase their 'capital of autochthony', conceived as the resources and powers that stem from their incorporation in localized networks of relationships (Renahy 2010: 9).

Swyngedouw, in his analysis of urban insurgencies, recalls that for Rancière, "democratising the polis is inaugurated when those who do not count stage the count, perform the process of being counted and thereby initiate a rupture in the order of things" (2015: 170). He thus insists on the disruptive nature of democratizing processes, because "a political space is a space of contestation" (2015: 178). In terms of political participation, the foreign protagonists of *La Grande Table* can be considered as aiming to count themselves by using a highly symbolic portion of the urban space to make themselves visible through the performance of their multiple and trans-local belongings. There is still a limit to the otherness they are expected to display during such an event, namely a consumable one: artistic folklore and food. The context of *La Grande Table* isn't the place to express dissent or make explicit claims, particularly very political ones such as claiming the right to vote, challenging the integration policy or contesting exoticization and consumption. The waving of the Kosovarian flag is perhaps the most political act we observed during the event, with the community claiming their right to display the symbol of their national identity even if Switzerland already recognized Kosovo as a sovereign and independent state in 2008. Hence, by acting consensually and conforming to the roles they are ascribed to by either themselves or others, *La Grande Table*'s protagonists would not be considered by Swyngedouw as challenging the established order.

Nevertheless, in our opinion, the emancipatory dimension of the practices we observed rather lies in the very structure of the event. Contrary to the political protests discussed by Swyngedouw, here the protagonists didn't spontaneously take to the streets but rather responded the Commission's invitation and participated in the organization of the event. Thus, it is not a bottom-up claim to "the right to the city" (Dikeç 2009: 83), but rather symbolizes the complex articulation of hegemonic policy-making through the federal integration policy, a participatory process through the organization of the event and the appropriation of urban public spaces by foreign communities. If the political is "the demand to be counted, named and recognised, theatrically and publicly staged by those 'who do not count', the inexistent" (Swyngedouw 2015: 174), then this goal is achieved by *La Grande Table*'s protagonists. They indeed use the time-space of the event to claim their belonging to the locality and act strategically to develop several forms of capital depending on their interests and positions. In addition, the ties that they create before and during the event foster their local recognition in the long term.

Finally, the concept of integration on which the event is based not only favours vertical assimilation but also creates spaces of encounter and participation, suggesting some degree of horizontality. Therefore, considering migrants as performers and hence highlighting their agency allows us to observe how they participate in broader community-making.

Conclusion

The multiplicity of actors and the variety of the groups' strategies forces us to adopt a nuanced and situated answer to the question of the emancipatory potential of this event. In fact, depending on their specific position in power relationships, social actors strategically chose to foster different forms of capital, but their room for manoeuvre is limited by the expectations of the

Commission and the roles they are assigned to. The event approach enabled us to seize how individuals take part in the city, how networks of sociability come to life, and how and under what circumstances these ties are (un)made, as we have mentioned in previous works (Salzbrunn 2004, 2010, 2011a, 2011b, 2016). This approach also allowed us to capture another form of discourse apart from the official and/or institutional and to compare different accounts of a shared experience.

We have shown to what extent different groups of migrants have acquired, alongside political actors, an important role in the ongoing rescaling process by appropriating and valorizing a locality since they have become 'scale-makers' and therefore contribute to shift power relations in cities in a context of neoliberal global restructuring processes (Glick Schiller and Caglar 2011: 10; Salzbrunn 2011a: 172). In this respect, they have participated in the reconfiguration of the socio-spatial order of the urban space through a reappropriation of an institutionally designed event. In addition, by attracting thousands of visitors and creating a sense of community (Salzbrunn and Sekine 2011) among the Morgian population, the protagonists of *La Grande Table* go far beyond the Commission's expectations of 'eating together in order to accept each other', by rendering the urban space more cosmopolitan and attractive even though the organizers control the visibilization of certain groups. However, under the post-political condition, these emancipation processes go along with the display of national or ethnic belonging. This essentializing way of showing cosmopolitanism differs from antique concepts to which researchers like Martha Nussbaum (1994) refer, inviting the consideration of right and universal reason before nation and national symbols of belonging. Hence, an open question remains: Can national symbols become less important than cosmopolitan ideals of a *vivre-ensemble* or do they coexist without contradictions? In the eyes of a range of actors with a migration background, pride in national belonging is compatible with a political, cosmopolitan engagement in a locality and therefore part of political participation and emancipation processes—but the passport and the right to vote still make an important difference between symbolic means of participation and equal rights. The Morgian population is not necessarily aware of the shifting political power relations since they attend the event as consumers of essentialized performances of alterity. Nevertheless, this aspect is not contradictory to the empowerment felt by the performing actors who maintain their translocal and transnational ties by staging their cultural differences. The active participants with a migration background are subject to both ascriptions of belonging to the imagined group of the 'exotic other' and to the legal definition of 'foreigner'. The participants' feelings of (non-)belonging are thereby configured by both urban policies and social ascriptions. Nevertheless, they remain actors for the entire event. Among and within the migrants' groups on display, the differences lie in the consciousness of each actor's agency, degree of emancipation and impact on urban rescaling processes.

Notes

1. It is a common term used to distinguish non-nationals in the Swiss legal context, where the procedure to obtain a passport is long and expensive, and can only be applied for after 12 years of permanent residence. As the *ius sanguinis* prevails, the naturalization is not automatic, and descendants of immigrants often don't have citizenship rights even if they were born in Switzerland. The term 'foreigner' holds a strong exclusionary dimension and reinforces an understanding of the nation as a homogeneous body.
2. These are part of the research project '(In)visible Islam in the city: material and immaterial expressions of Muslim practices within urban spaces in Switzerland', directed by Monika Salzbrunn and funded by the Swiss National Science Foundation. More information is available at www.unil.ch/issr/home/menuinst/recherches/religions-migration-diaspora/lislam-in-visible-en-ville.html
3. In the Canton of Vaud, foreign residents obtain the right to vote on a local level after ten years of registered residency, whereas citizenship can be applied for after twelve years.

References

Afonso, A. (2006) Les métamorphoses de l'étranger utile. Internationalisation et politique d'immigration dans la Suisse du tournant néolibéral. *A contrario* 4(1), pp. 99–116.

CCSE, Commission Consultative Suisses-Etrangers (2014) *La Grande Table Programme*. Ville de Morges: Commission Consultative Suisses-Etrangers.

D'Amato, G. (2008)Une revue historique et sociologique des migrations en Suisse. *Annuaire suisse de politique de développement* 27(2), pp. 169–187.

Dellwo, B. (in press) Les représentations de la mobilité au prisme de la culturalisation: pour une étude intersectionnelle des élites transnationales de culture musulmane à Genève. In N. Ortar, M. Salzbrunn and M. Stock (eds.) *Migrations, Circulations, Mobilité: Nouveaux enjeux épistémologiques et conceptuels à l'épreuve du terrain*. Aix-en-Provence: Presses Universitaires de Provence.

Dikeç, M. (2009) Justice and the Spatial Imagination. In P. Marcuse, J. Connolly, J. Novy, I. Olivo, C. Potter and J. Steil (eds.) *Searching for the Just City: Debates in Urban Theory and Practice*. Abingdon: Routledge, pp. 72–88.

Efionayi, D., Niederberger, J.M. and Wanner, P. (2005) Switzerland Faces Common European Challenges. *Migration Information Source*, 1 February [Online]. Available at: www.migrationpolicy.org/article/switzerland-faces-common-european-challenges [Accessed 18 June 2017].

Faist, T. (2013) The Mobility Turn: A New Paradigm for the Social Sciences? *Ethnic and Racial Studies* 36(11), pp. 1637–1646.

Glick Schiller, N. and Caglar, A. (eds.) (2011) *Locating Migration: Rescaling Cities and Migrants*. Ithaca: Cornell University Press.

Nussbaum, M. (1994) Patriotism and Cosmopolitanism. *The Boston Review*, 1 October [Online]. Available at: http://bostonreview.net/martha-nussbaum-patriotism-and-cosmopolitanism [Accessed 15 May 2017].

Raulin, A. (2001) *Anthropologie urbaine*. Paris: Armand Colin.

Régnier, F. (2006) Manger hors norme, respecter les norms. Le plaisir de l'exotisme culinaire. *Journal des anthropologues* 106–107, pp. 169–187.

Renahy, N. (2010) Classes populaires et capital d'autochtonie. Genèse et usages d'une notion. *Regards Sociologiques* 40, pp. 9–26.

Salzbrunn, M. (2004) The Occupation of Public Space through Religious and Political Events: How Senegalese Migrants became a Part of Harlem, New York. *Journal of Religion in Africa* 32(2), pp. 468–492.

Salzbrunn, M. (2010) Faire et défaire le voisinage: les fêtes de quartier comme reflet de relations sociales et culturelles. In J. Rainhorn and D. Terrier (eds.) *Etranges voisins. Altérité et relations de proximité dans la ville depuis le XVIIIe siècle.* Rennes: Presses Universitaires de Rennes, pp. 133–147.

Salzbrunn, M. (2011a) Rescaling Processes in Two 'Global' Cities: Festive Events as Pathways of Migrant Incorporation. In N. Glick Schiller and A. Caglar (eds.) *Locating Migration: Rescaling Cities and Migrants.* Ithaca: Cornell University Press, pp. 166–189.

Salzbrunn, M. (2011b) L'événement festif comme théâtre de conflits en zone urbaine: le carnaval des sans-papiers à Cologne. In M. Klinger and S. Schehr (eds.) *Lectures du conflit.* Strasbourg: Néothèque, pp. 111–126.

Salzbrunn, M. (2014) *Vielfalt/Diversität.* Bielefeld: Transcript Verlag.

Salzbrunn, M. (2016) When the Mosque Goes Beethoven: Expressing Religious Belongings through Music. *COMPASO: Journal of Comparative Research in Anthropology and Sociology* 7(1), pp. 59–74. Available at: http://compaso.eu/wpd/wp-content/uploads/2016/07/Compaso2016-71-Salzbrunn.pdf.

Salzbrunn, M. and Sekine, Y. (2011) *From Community to Commonality: Multiple Belonging and Street Phenomena in the Era of Reflexive Modernization.* Tokyo: Seijo University Press.

Skenderovic, D. (2007) Immigration and the Radical Right in Switzerland: Ideology, Discourse and Opportunities. *Patterns of Prejudice* 41(2), pp. 155–176.

Statistique Vaud (2014) Dix ans d'évolution de la population active vaudoise: la flexibilité gagne du terrain. In *Numerus Hors Série.* Lausanne: Statistique Vaud [Online]. Available at: www.scris.vd.ch/Data_Dir/ElementsDir/8003/2/F/Numerus-HS_vie-active.pdf [Accessed 13 February 2017].

Statistique Vaud, Atlas statistique du Canton de Vaud [Online]. Available at: www.cartostat.vd.ch [Accessed 14 February 2017].

Swyngedouw, E. (2015) Insurgent Architects, Radical Cities and the Promise of the Political. In J. Wilson and E. Swyngedouw (eds.) *The Post-Political and Its Discontents: Spaces of Depoliticisation, Spectres of Radical Politics.* Edinburgh: Edinburgh University Press, pp. 169–188.

Vertovec, S. (2007) Super-Diversity and Its Implications. *Ethnic and Racial Studies* 30(6), pp. 1024–1054.

Wilson, J. and Swyngedouw, E. (eds.) (2015) *The Post-Political and Its Discontents: Spaces of Depoliticisation, Spectres of Radical Politics.* Edinburgh: Edinburgh University Press.

9 Emancipatory Research in the Arts

Shift the City—the Temporary Lab of Non | Permanent Space

Amila Širbegović

Introduction

Shift the City—The Temporary Lab of Non | Permanent Space aims to inform emancipatory research in the arts through an exploratory approach originating from a research project on the interrelations between migration, city change and their visible manifestations in public spaces. It is an attempt to explore current connections and establish additional junctions between planners' professional practice and the everyday life in particular neighbourhoods in Vienna, Sarajevo and St. Louis. The social and physical spaces of these city parts have been selected for the influence of migrations and migrants' material practices on these spaces. Involved professional practices and connections between everyday life and planning have been explored, as well as made visible and accessible in an internet platform (www.shiftthecity. net). The approach has been concerned with two central research questions: (1) How can planners involved in areas characterized by migration participate in spaces of everyday culture without either victimizing or romanticizing their inhabitants? (2) How can transdisciplinary approaches help to simultaneously question and critically transform the role of researchers, and particularly planners, in the urban spaces shaped by migration?

Both migration and urban change are social phenomena characterized by complexity, ambivalence and juxtaposition. Thus, the first step in this project was to research the visibility of transnational identities in urban space, and the second step evolved from the transfer of knowledge gained through research practice into urban planning practices. In this chapter, I will first introduce the researched spaces of migration, as shaped by transnational and transcultural actions. The concept of transnationality refers to transnational mobility and transnational practices, which allow for construction of new identities and alternative forms of subject formation (Ong 2005), thus creating transnational space. These newly created identities evolve without dependence on political or even nation state borders and influence spaces of migration in selected neighbourhoods. Transculturality is a model of interweaving many different cultural practices, as opposed to the traditional model in which a society's cultures are clearly separated from one another (Welsch 2009). I explicate more on transnational spaces and transcultural practice, how these are influencing neighbourhood focus areas and why they should matter to the planners. Transcultural actions embedded in transnational space empower migrants to improve their lived spaces by using their skills, developing new ones and claiming their own space through self-determination. I will argue that there is a need for exploratory and new methods for engaging with the spaces shaped by migration, as both researcher and particularly as a planner, to avoid the mainstream participatory methods that often serve the institutional configurations to *pacify potential conflicts*, which frequently disregard, among others, migrants and their contributions to urban change. Spaces conditioned by migration and reshaped by migrants are often perceived as neglected, dysfunctional, criminal and in need of improvement. I will further explain how using mixing methods can develop approaches to alter this perception and make their potentialities visible for further research and planning. My research is situated within the context of the post-migratory society (Yildiz 2013), where, irrespective of national citizenship, migrants are recognized as equal contributors to urban spaces, in terms of structures and possibilities for the both newly and formerly arrived, in addition to their resources and networks. Instead of taking a punitive position by assuming some requisite amelioration of decay caused by migrants, I worked to discover structures and possibilities enabled by migrants' resources and networks. The empirical part will introduce the *Shift the City* project, beginning with how researchers approach the spaces of migration and simultaneously gain knowledge that is valuable for urban planning.

The Complexity of Spaces Shaped by Migration and Claimed by Migrants

The concept of transnationality addresses the ways of living of those who have experienced migration: It points to the places where they live, work, think and inhabit different countries and national spaces, using their transnationality to their benefit and countering the disadvantages that they experience in the countries to which, and from which, they migrate. Unlike the obsolete concept of living 'neither here nor there', the concept of transnationality understands the habitation of multiple national spaces, thereby creating various transnational spaces. These spaces are seen as "bottom up globalization" (Böse and Kogoj 2004), as "political demands to governments" (Bauböck 2012: 26), or as something that puts the power of national states into question (Ong 2005: 11). The debates about transnational spaces have hardly been acknowledged by planners. They often enter spaces of migration carrying their own bias, influenced by the nation state, which has an impact on their practice inside these spaces.

The concept of transcultural society (Welsch 1994) helps to provide a better understanding of coherence between migrants' practice and reshaping of urban spaces. Migrants often react to novel situations in their countries of arrival by relying on experiences from their country of origin. Migrants' practice can be culturally or individually shaped. Additionally, they adopt new practices in the country of arrival. The endurance of prior practices and iteration on adopted practices in a new culture embodies transcultural practice.

Whereas the interrelations between migration, transnational spaces, transcultural practice and the shaping of urban space are intensively researched in social science (e.g. Yildiz and Mattausch 2008; Hillmann 2011; Glick Schiller and Çağlar 2009, 2011), the transfer of transnational spaces and transcultural practices—and their impact on urban public space—into urban development and city planning are still lacking. Hillmann (2011) elaborates that the society still lacks information on migrants' contribution to the quality of life where they live. She sees the potential for urban planning in migration economics, because they provide urban life by embodying *difference* and *otherness*, which she argues is a core element of the urban (*Ibid.*). There is not only a gap in understanding the interactions of migration and cities but also regarding how deeply social research practices in planning understand migration (*Ibid.*). When it comes to relationships between social spaces of migration, migrants' informal practice and everyday culture and, in particular, their manifold relations to built spaces, urban planners are lacking experience, self-reflexivity and knowledge about different ways to engage with *difference* and *otherness*. Knowledge of these specific processes in urban spaces is important, because urban planners are able to strengthen these processes or weaken them, to support or destroy them, as they are formally reshaping the city through various processes of planning, thus spatializing political regulations and providing spatial opportunities to revisit regimes of political regulations.

Research into migration has taken various courses in past decades. Before discourse in migration economics research became actor-centred due to the individual resources of entrepreneurs coming to the fore (Schmiz 2011), it concentrated on migrants as disadvantaged and marginalized ethnic groups (*Ibid.*). The focus on entrepreneurship appreciated the active role of people with migration experience, but it overlooked numerous migrant actions. In the 1990s, a paradigmatic shift took place in migration research; there was a change in perspective linking the individual with structural circumstances (Light and Gold 2000; Kloostermann and Rath 2011). Schmiz (2011) broadened this perspective by using a transnational approach, which enhanced migration research not only regarding the structures and possibilities for migrants in the context of their host country, but also in terms of researching their resources and networks across political territories. However, planners' practice has not similarly developed and is still focused somewhere between perceiving spaces of migration as disadvantaged and seeing entrepreneurs as active contributors to public space, disregarding the existing resources and networks of many migrants. This is what Yildiz and Mattausch (2008) address when they seek to break the existing racist interpretation patterns and to acknowledge the contribution of migrants to urban spaces. It is about acknowledging and understanding migrants' actions in practice, their transnational identities and their impact on urban spaces, while simultaneously embedding them within planners' practice. This initial step might not automatically result in planning, designing and changing built spaces. Rather, it requires a community-focused and community-driven involvement of planners.

According to Swyngedouw (2015), the political is "the demand to be counted, named and recognised" and "the articulation of [a] voice that demands its place in the spaces of the police order" (Swyngedouw 2015: 174). The researched spaces in various cities have different political characteristics. Transcultural practices of migrants and their claim for the right to a transnational way of life can be identified as "the demand to be . . . recognized" (*Ibid.*: 174) and thus political. How can planners be involved in these spaces to support, rather than neglect, the political? Is planning a tool that could become politicized by supporting those (in this case, migrants inhabiting study areas) who demand to be "counted, named and recognised" (*Ibid.*: 174), and how does it need to be altered to reach that goal? The first step for planners to commit to a deeper understanding of the functionalities of spaces claimed by migrants is to recognize redesign of the urban spaces as "a democratic political field of disagreement" (*Ibid.*: 185). *Shift the City* has explored the means and paths that depart from established approaches planners were trained in. The project advocated new paths and different tools and methods as a prerequisite for different perspectives to be allowed into and heard within the planning discipline.

The Urge for New Methods

The selected researched sites were all impacted by migration and were selected because of adverse perspectives on the impacts of migrants:

- A neighbourhood perceived as criminal and dangerous surrounding Ottakringer Straße, Vienna (Austria), which is mostly populated by different generations of migrants from the former Yugoslavia (former *Gastarbeiter*,[1] children of former *Gastarbeiter*, refugees, students).
- A neighbourhood in the outskirts of the city, where a former separation line was during the 1990s' war in Bosnia and Herzegovina, Sarajevo, which was perceived as a dangerous China Town, mostly populated by Chinese migrants who had come to the Western Balkans in the late 90s.
- A formerly neglected neighbourhood around the Bevo area, South City, within the city borders of St. Louis (United States), which was perceived as prosperous, multi-ethnic and promising after being populated and renewed by Bosnian refugees in the 90s.

Each site is linked by having undergone significant urban renewal after settlement of migrants and refugees in the researched areas.

Outside perspectives on these sites differ enormously. A participatory method involving various persons, each with different interests, was required in order to research and analyze these spaces and to produce knowledge on how to alter and develop them. I needed to find a method to leave behind interpretations, such as planners' notions of disadvantaged spaces of migration (as advocated by Yildiz and Mattausch 2008). With the goal of acknowledging and appreciating the substantial contribution of migrants to the development of their lived spaces in particular and cities in general, a participatory action research approach was essential, as "a collaborative process of research, education and action" (Kindon et al. 2007: 9).

Participatory action research offers potential to both users and planners of urban spaces. Planners face at least two problems: (1) the planning discipline urges planners to act, change, design and rebuild spaces physically, rather than socially, through the concentration of their own practice on built spaces; and (2) there is a lack of transdisciplinary approaches in planning practice. Transdisciplinarity involves stepping out of the practice of one's field of expertise, appropriating different practices of other fields and implementing these for one's own planning practice.

By acknowledging the contribution of migrants, my aim was not to sustain perceived exoticism of multicultural spaces, but the opposite: I sought to sustain their everyday contribution to their lived environment and, finally, to society in general. By creating multifunctional spaces and sharing them with others in the neighbourhood; providing translations, information, advice and consulting for the newly arrived; and using local, translocal and transnational networks to establish their own economies, migrants make their neighbourhoods liveable through solidarity actions and networks. The following section outlines a suggestion on how to deal with the challenges of spaces shaped by migrants as planners in an emancipatory, transnational research praxis–led way.

Shift the City

Shift the City is a (1) research process which works with spaces shaped by migration and migrants. It is (2) an online platform, working to show that new spaces can be created, opened, shaped and, finally, claimed by many. As a (3) lab, it serves to develop and test context-specific methods. As (4) an explorative methodological approach, it shows the difficulties that occur when one is involved in the complexity of spaces of migration, characterized by transnational and transcultural practices. Generating visible research on-site creates possibilities for self-determined spaces claimed by migrants to become part of collective memories of imagining the city.

The aim of *Shift the City*'s approach is to provide legibility through visibility for the different dimensions of transnational spaces and transcultural practices, their impact on the researched city parts and, finally, their contribution to urbanity. This approach attempts to empower migrants by allowing them to claim space for themselves as any citizen is able to, through sharing their stories and experiences and thus becoming part of the narratives of urban spaces. On the other hand, it should encourage planners to participate actively in the spaces of migration. Planners who engage in these specific spaces can potentially achieve a better understanding of processes in urban spaces, in addition to the possible option of redesigning these spaces both with and for many, instead of just a few.

The research was performative and was conducted by using following tools:

- the method of walking interviews;
- recording the space;
- transferring videos and interviews into a web space;
- sharing access to this page as a tool.

These steps made the ongoing research accessible to everyone with internet access and created a new space for discussion. The walking interview was a tool with which to open the new and the (so far) unknown, but also the familiar. As I had been personally frustrated by *sitting interviews* and their unnatural situation for both interviewees and researchers, I started to develop the method of walking/migrating interviews, which additionally served as spatial interventions.

The method of walking interviews has a strong focus on the interrelation between built and social space(s) and the perception of different actors involved (inhabitants with and without migration experiences, politicians, artists, planners and other community members) in particular neighbourhoods, both shaped and changed by various migratory practices in the last 20 years. Simultaneously, these spaces are frequently perceived and represented as marginalized, poor and often criminal by the media, political rhetoric and planning practices. By walking alone at the beginning of my research and observing particular parts of Vienna, Sarajevo and St. Louis, it was hard to lose the biases of an outsider and become sufficiently comfortable in a local context to reveal the inner perspectives. By walking through the material arrangements of lived, perceived and conceived spaces (Lefebvre 2008 [1991/1974]) with residents, artists, activists, small business owners, local planners and involved researchers, it was possible to *capture* the specifications and characteristics of these complex spaces.

I used *mixing methods* (Mason 2006) by combining the method of walking interviews in connection with *strollology* (Burckhardt 2006) and *narrative urbanism* (Krasny 2008). Performative collective walking, as in strollology (Burckhardt 2006), seeks to make people's surroundings the context of research. This allows for the researcher to experience the appreciation,

narrative histories and everyday practices of inhabitants of particular neighbourhoods. Walking interviews are not confined to the everyday routes of
people and their lived social spaces. I invited them to show me places that
they considered special, different and important. In this way, I learned about
parts of their everyday practice and about their specific knowledge of the
locations—and thus a different understanding of space—that they had chosen to share with me.

Walking interviews include the natural situation of walking through the
city, which is an everyday practice, performed by every interviewee. Being
interviewed while walking reveals their own perceptions, feelings and imaginations (Kusenbach 2003), which they would not normally do in sitting
interview situations: "What makes the go-along technique unique is that eth-
nographers are able to observe their informants' spatial practices in situ while
accessing their experiences and interpretations at the same time" (*Ibid.*: 463).
Kusenbach talks of the sensitization of researchers using "go-along" methods
when witnessing "in situ the filtering and shaping of their subjects' perceptions" (*Ibid.*: 469). The researchers' "own perceptual presuppositions and
biases" are de-emphasized (*Ibid.*: 469). Reflecting upon my own positionality
as a researcher and how it changed when developing the interviews in the lab,
the walking interviews helped me to abolish my own prejudices about migratory spaces: as planner, as citizen, as inhabitant, as migrant and as visitor.

Mason (2006) points out that the use of *mixing methods* reveals how
"our ways of seeing, and framing questions, are strongly influenced by the
methods we have at our disposal, because the way we see shapes what we can
see, and what we think we can ask" (*Ibid.*: 13). Following Mason (2006), the
first step was to understand the interrelation of lived realities from a multi-
dimensional level. The interrelations between the micro- and macro-effects
were crucial for further research.

Krasny (2008) claims that *narrative urbanism* as urban research allows the
stories of the unheard and unseen to become privileged as a form of knowledge. Thus, talking about city space and sharing experiences and stories
of neighbourhoods creates a new situation in which the everyday practices
of local inhabitants, regardless of their national citizenship, visas and residential rights, legal or illegal status, are privileged as a form of knowledge
(*Ibid.*). Furthermore, various outer and inner perceptions appear when the
everyday practices of migrants in marginalized and stigmatized neighbourhoods receive special attention by walking through the city and sharing the
experiences of local actors.

Accompanying the interviewees created a change inside the familiar city
space. The change emerges through the translation from steps to words (cf.
Krasny 2008: 31), where one discovers not only persons telling their stories
and contributing information about spaces and everyday practices through
their biographies, but also the urban spaces themselves. The link to the city
and to people emerges through the figure of experience (cf. *Ibid.*). By walking

Figure 9.1 Video still from a performed walking interview on Ottakringer Straße
Source: Amila Širbegović, 2011

together, my perceptions continued to evolve as we moved through city space. This shared experience of walking is a certain type of 'reading' of the urban space but also an experience of collectively inhabiting the city (*Ibid.*). Krasny (2008) argues that narrative urbanism creates the potential for city planners to participate. What happens during walking interviews is that inhabitants allow planners and researchers to take part in their knowledge of the city. Thus, by shifting the perspective of who is listening to whom, the circumstances change (*Ibid.*: 38). Walking interviews transform us, as researchers, from outsiders to participants and involved actors.

The web portal provides visibility to the transformation taking place on site. This participatory platform is not solution-oriented but open to the processes and calls for the sharing of experiences and knowledge. I see my role as a researcher-and-planner aiming at mediating practices of sharing, participating and partaking. Multiple new experiences of different actors arose during the walking interviews: (1) personal experiences of the interviewees from the past, shared during walking interviews; (2) new experiences of the interviewees, which took place during the walking interviews; (3) my own experience as a researcher while walking with the interviewees and hearing their stories and experiences; and (4) the experiences of others, who were perceiving the walking interviews. According to Emmel and Clark (2009), walking interviews are well suited not only to researching the everyday practices and social spaces of residents' local and transnational networks, but also to an explorative journey to learn about different methods and to

Figure 9.2 Screen shot of the webpage Shift the City [www.shiftthecity.net]
Source: Amila Širbegović, 2014

comprehend the complexity of the situations, as suggested by Mason (2006) when using mixing methods.

The walking interviews involved an additional element by adding another actor, the video camera. The idea was to capture the inhabited space by collectively walking and trying out the transmission of shared experience in this specific space. Involving a camera began as an experiment to capture the walking interview. But given that a camera could disturb the interviews and their intimacy; I opted to film the space rather than the individual. This shift in focus appeared to make the camera less disturbing for the interviewees. The benefit of the camera was twofold. First, it allowed the documentation of spaces that are frequently in flux. Thus, the material can be used for further research of ephemeral spaces. For example, a simple store of everyday goods on Ottakringer Straße, which stands for transcultural praxis within migration economies, closed one year later after an interview was performed. Second, the material captured with the camera was used to share the information through the *Shift the City*'s web portal.

A second, successive translation into another form of knowledge took place by placing the results of empirical field research onto the website, *www.shiftthecity.net*. The '*Shift*' in *Shift the City* refers to the change of migration research in an urban context, as mentioned above, from either victimizing or criminalizing migrants to a post-migration discourse by documenting self-empowered migrant members of (urban) societies. Thus, *Shift the City* opened a new space that allowed a direct confrontation with migration and the city, where transnational identities, states of exception, visible phenomena of migration, emancipatory everyday practices and urbanism meet.

Five Principles

The questions of the research practices of particular urban social space(s), the translation of the findings back to the planning debate and the processes of planning appeared over and over again. The following principles developed by Novy and Habersack (2010) have supported the development of explorative research methodology. I amended the four aspects of the suggested principles for research into the social solidarity in the cities' research sites (*Ibid.*: 180) and introduced a fifth aspect:

(1) holistic research: "Overcoming Fragmentation";
(2) the interplay of different levels: "The City in the World";
(3) transdisciplinary research and acting: "Building Alliances of Knowledge";
(4) democracy and partaking: "One City for all—in its Diversity and Divergence";
(5) and the transgression of research knowledge (based on embedded and embodied walking interviews) into planning practice through *Shift the City*.

I used these principles as a guide to research the impact of migration and migrants' practices on the neighbourhoods in which I needed to research social space(s); before that, I had to learn how to approach them.

The first principle of holistic research was extremely important for researching the complex subject of migration. It is not about defining problems in terms of their professional solutions, but more about understanding and reviewing backgrounds of how particular urban areas work. This is relevant for planning practice, which is generally quite solution-oriented. What do diversity, identities, social solidarity and equality (Novy and Habersack 2010) mean in terms of urban space? Applying the principle of holistic research provided the basis for the post-migration context of my work.

The second principle of research of different levels and scales, global, European, national, transnational, regional and local is one of the core aspects of this work, whereas social realities are influenced by these various dynamics (*Ibid.*). For the purposes of this research, if one scale made difficulties visible, it didn't mean that these were produced on that same level. The impact on researched neighbourhoods by migrants as active actors, among other actors, becomes visible at the local level, but is usually a result of different global events, national preconditions and other supra-regional effects. The walking interviews established migrants as visible actors at the local level, but their practices, as revealed through the interviews, were global and transnational interventions.

The third principle of transdisciplinary research was crucial, because of the intention to transfer the research findings back to the planning practice. By emphasizing the transdisciplinary approach, I do not mean simply using tools and methods from other disciplines, but rather the intermingling of research and practice with tools from different disciplines, and beyond. It is the practical involvement on-site that creates the possibility for researchers and planners to develop new tools for the future, enabling them to participate in users' spaces.

The fourth principle, regarding democracy and partaking, is connected to the first principle of holistic research but also anchored to the post-migration discourse (Yildiz 2013), in which actors themselves define and rewrite their own migration history. The lack of partaking in society is one of the reasons for their actions, through the circumstances and marginalized situations in which they are forced to occupy spaces and to react in various and creative ways, which impacts neighbourhoods. This reaction to circumstances, created by claiming the space for themselves, can be seen as political, whereas transnational migration practices offer an alternative way to step out of existing structures and make themselves visible.

Starting from this point, and building on the four principles, I introduced the fifth principle: the transfer of transdisciplinary research knowledge into planning practice in order to foster processes of reciprocal learning and gaining knowledge (and again from planning practice into the research). The aim was to involve even more actors in order to produce a pool of collective scientific and practical knowledge by introducing the online lab platform for open discussion, which should provide not only a better understanding of social practice but also higher research quality by supplying the discipline with a deeper understanding of various perspectives and the experience and knowledge of everyday experts.

Emerging Spaces of Emancipation: Creativity—Practice—Knowledge

The developed method is one way to collectively explore the specific spaces of migration with the interviewees and simultaneously to make everyday practices visible to others while also supporting migrants in their endeavours. In addition to rethinking the spaces of migration within cities and their possible translations into urban development and planning, the methodological reflection presented in this chapter offers a discussion of how transdisciplinary approaches can help to question the role of the researcher and/or planner of such urban spaces. It also can help to define researchers' and planners' positionality when entering research fields, such as stigmatized sections of a city, in order to not run the risk of reproducing stigmatization.

The shared performance and research of filmed walking interviews, inner perspectives, spatial practices, personal biographies, social architecture(s) and social spaces are part of urban complexities. The individual and collective space are diverse, and it was therefore a challenge to capture and translate them. Researching spaces of migration inside their particular neighbourhoods regarding the suggested approach led to two main insights:

- marginalized actors and neglected knowledge do come into focus by using participatory research methods and thus become part of urban narrative; and
- spatial intervention through walking interviews makes social spaces visible, which was not considered before.

The perception of the interrelations of migration and urban space fluctuates, depending on who is the observer and whether the *observing* takes place inside or outside particular neighbourhoods; it is also important to consider the political situation and general acceptance of migrants in a region or country. Other places affect migrants' practices and their impact on researched neighbourhoods, especially the interviews frequently referred to in other countries or even other continents. The transnational connection takes place not only in the heads of people but also in their lives, as part of their acting; in this case, the interview situation enabled these connections to be expressed.

The presence of urban professionals within the interrelations of migration and urban change allowed for reflection on the positionality of urban professionals and how it can be shifted by walking interviews. These shifts in perspective can help enable abolishing our own prejudices about migratory spaces. Walking interviews have the potential to create a different understanding of planning, by allowing narrative to be seen as a critical source. For the planners involved in areas characterized by migration, the possibility of a new understanding of these spaces arises from the connection of single elements: walking, seeing, speaking out and listening. The challenge that remains is the transfer of this connection and the knowledge, whereas the lab is an attempt to capture and understand emerging spaces and emancipatory transnational and transcultural practice.

Note

1. The economic boom in the 1960 produced a need for workers in Germany and Austria. This need was supposed to be covered through *Gastarbeiter* (= guest workers) from countries with weaker economies, such as Yugoslavia or Turkey. Initial intention to replace the workers who were to return home with new ones changed through time. In the meantime, three generations of people have been affected by that migration. In the dominant public debates and in media in Austria, these people are still shown as objects of representation, while usually marginalized as subjects (Gürses et al. 2004).

References

Bauböck, R. (2012) Diaspora und transnationale Demokratie. In I. Charim and G. Auer Borea (eds.) *Lebensmodell Diaspora, Über moderne Nomaden*. Bielefeld: Transcript Verlag, pp. 19–33.

Böse, M. and Kogoj, C. (2004) Transnationale Medien und Kommunikation. In H. Gürses, C. Kogoj and S. Mattl (eds.) *Gastarbajteri, 40 Jahre Arbeitsmigration.* Wien: Mandelbaum Verlag, pp. 105–110.

Burckhardt, L. (2006) *Warum ist die Landschaft schön? Die Spaziergangswissenschaft* (ed. M. Ritter). Berlin: Martin Schmitz Verlag.

Emmel, N. and Clark, A. (2009) The Methods Used in Connected Lives: Investigating Networks, Neighbourhoods and Communities. *ESRC National Centre for Research Methods Working Paper Series* [Online]. Available at: eprints.ncrm.ac.uk/800/1/2009_connected_lives_methods_emmel_clark.pdf [Accessed 1 August 2015].

Glick Schiller, N. and Çağlar, A. (2009) Towards a Comparative Theory of Locality in Migration Studies: Migrants Incorporation and City Scale. *Journal of Ethnic and Migration Studies* 35(2), pp. 177–202.

Glick Schiller, N. and Çağlar, A. (eds.) (2011) *Locating Migration: Rescaling Cities and Migrants*. Ithaca: Cornell University Press.

Gürses, H., Kogoj, C. and Mattl, S. (eds.) (2004) *Gastarbajteri, 40 Jahre Arbeitsmigration*. Wien: Mandelbaum Verlag.

Hillmann, F. (2011) *Marginale Urbanität—Migrantisches Unternehmertum und Stadtentwicklung*. Bielefeld: Transcript Verlag.

Kindon, S., Pain, R. and Kesby, M. (2007) Participatory Action Research, Origins, Approaches and Methods. In S. Kindon, R. Pain and M. Kesby (eds.) *Participatory Action Research Approaches and Methods, Connecting people, Participation and Place*. Oxon, New York: Routledge, pp. 9–18.

Kloostermann, R. and Rath, J. (2011) Veränderte Konturen migrantischen Unternehmertum. In F. Hillmann (ed.) *Marginale Urbanität—Migrantisches Unternehmertum und Stadtentwicklung*. Bielefeld: Transcript Verlag, pp. 87–117.

Krasny, E. (2008) Narrativer Urbanismus oder die Kunst des City-Telling. In E. Krasny and I. Nierhaus (eds.) *Urbanografien*. Berlin: Dietrich Reimer Verlag, pp. 29–41.

Kusenbach, M. (2003) Street Phenomenology: The Go-Along as Ethnographic Research Tool. *Ethnography* 4(3), pp. 455–485.

Lefebvre, H. (2008 [1991/1974]) *The Production of Space*. Oxford: Blackwell.

Light, I. and Gold, S.J. (2000) *Ethnic Economies*. San Diego and London: University of California Press.

Mason, J. (2006) Mixing Methods in a Qualitatively Driven Way. *Qualitative Research* 6(1), pp. 9–25.

Novy, A. and Habersack, S. (2010) Wissensallianzen für eine Stadt für alle—in ihrer Verschiedenheit. *Dérive Zeitschrift für Stadtforschung* 40–41, pp. 178–183.

Ong, A. (2005) *Flexible Staatsbürgerschaften. Die kulturelle Logik von Transnationalität*. Frankfurt am Main: Suhrkamp Verlag.

Schmiz, A. (2011) Marginale Ökonomien—Vietnamesische GroßhändlerInnen in Berlin. In F. Hillmann (ed.) *Marginale Urbanität—Migrantisches Unternehmertum und Stadtentwicklun*. Bielefeld: Transcript Verlag, pp. 90–96.

Swyngedouw, E. (2015) Insurgent Architects, Radical Cities and the Promise of the Political. In J. Wilson and E. Swynhedouw (eds.) *The Post-Political and Its Disconnects, Spaces of Depoliticisation, Spectres of Radical Politics*. Edinburgh: Edinburgh University Press, pp. 169–188.

Welsch, W. (1994) Transkulturalität—die veränderte Verfassung heutiger Kulturen. *Via Regia—Blätter für internationale kulturelle Kommunikation* 20 [Online].

Available at: www.via-regia.org/bibliothek/pdf/heft20/welsch_transkulti.pdf [Accessed 25 May 2017].

Welsch, W. (2009) Was ist eigentlich Transkulturalität? In L. Darowska, T. Lüttenberg and C. Machold (eds.) *Hochschule als transkultureller Raum? Beiträge zur Kultur, Bildung und Differenz*. Bielefeld: Transcript Verlag, pp. 39–66.

Yildiz, E. (2013) Postmigrantische Urbanität: von der Heterotopie zur Transtopie. In B. Lange and G. Prasecn (eds.) *Ortsentwürfe: Urbanität im 21. Jahrhundert*. Berlin: Jovis Verlag, pp. 16–19.

Yildiz, E. and Mattausch, B. (eds.) (2008) *Urban Recycling. Migration als Großstadt-Ressource*. Basel: Birkhäuser Verlag.

Critical Emancipation.
On Romanticisms,
Agonism and Liberation

10 Alternative Participatory Planning Practices in the Global South

Learning From Co-Production Processes in Informal Communities

Vanessa Watson and Gilbert Siame

Introduction

Urban planning systems in many parts of the Global South are still strongly shaped by their colonial past, giving rise to laws and processes which adhere to ideals of highly regulated modernist cities but which result in the marginalization and exclusion of poor urban communities. In such contexts, consensus-seeking planning processes (should laws provide for them) are rarely successful given deep social divides and the complex nature of state-society relations. However, innovative ways have emerged in several places where poor communities engage with the state on planning issues. Co-production is one of these approaches, and the chapter explores a case study of this in Kampala (Uganda).

The chapter first explains the nature of planning and state-society relations in Kampala, and then an emergent form of engagement through a co-production process by focusing on three community strategies: self-enumeration and mapping, learning exchanges and savings groups. The chapter asks: Can co-production offer an alternative to 'mainstream' concepts of participatory planning? Central to co-production as a way of communities engaging with the state is an acknowledgement of societal divisions and conflict, but as the Kampala case shows, co-production efforts themselves cannot escape from such entrenched conflicts that are part of society in many parts of the world. Does co-production then have the potential to be sufficiently transformative to be considered as emancipatory, or even liberating? Or is it simply disciplining the poor to fit in with a state- and politically driven agenda?

Urban Planning in a (Post)Colonial Context: Kampala (Uganda)

Modernity and coloniality are relational and inseparably interlinked, and an understanding of modernity requires that its (ongoing) global project is considered; hence, "There is no modernity without coloniality" (Mignolo 2007: 476). Across large swathes of the Global South, colonized territories were drawn into the Western project of modernity, particularly in regards to the project's conceptions of economy, politics and knowledge-making. Urban planning, along with its institutional structures, hierarchical power relations, Cartesian concept of space and ideas about what constituted modern cities, was very much part of the colonial and modernizing project (Nunes Silva 2015; McAuslan 2003; Home 2014). But while the years since political independence have seen significant changes in these countries and their cities, the project of modernity has persisted, supported and taken forward by a national elite linked to global networks of power and money. This is very evident in urban planning, where national planning legislation in most African countries is imported as copies of the planning laws of colonizers, with little change up to the present time. The same can be said of 'master plans' which shape the growth and change of larger cities. While the plans themselves are revised on occasion, the top-down, state-directed and regulating approach to planning has persisted in most places (Berrisford 2011). While there may be a shift in the advanced economies of the West to post-modernism and to the post-political, aspirations of modernity persist in previously colonized territories, at least in terms of how present conditions and desired futures of cities are concerned.

Africa was colonized by different powers over time, and the effects of actual colonization and subsequent relationships with the metropole (coloniality) have been influenced by highly diverse contexts. The British Protectorate of Uganda (see Figure 10.1) was created in 1894 from two previously antagonistic kingdoms, the Buganda and the Bunyoro, creating political divisions from the start. Formal independence was gained in 1962. Planning in Uganda falls under inherited British planning law[1] in the form of the Town and Country Planning Act (1951; revised 1964) and the more recent Physical Planning Act (2010). The latter provides for public comment on new plans by publishing a notice in the *Government Gazette* inviting comment on draft plans lodged at a specified place. Collaborative or participatory planning processes have not found their way into Ugandan planning, which is still highly technocratic and centralized at the national and district government level, although 'permission to build' can be granted by the Kampala Municipality.[2] Essentially, the highly modernist form of planning which prevailed in the UK and other European countries in the post-war period still holds in Uganda and other colonized territories, even though it is wholly inappropriate for dealing with the very different dynamics and issues of these cities (see Home 2014; Nunes Silva 2015).

However, while such approaches to planning were introduced as part of the colonial project of control and have persisted over time, supported more recently by local elites who also find planning to be a useful tool to manage (or manipulate) the value and use of urban land, the implementation and effectiveness of these planning approaches has varied significantly. Goodfellow (2013: 91) argues that the particular "urban political bargaining environment" of a country or city strongly influences the way in which

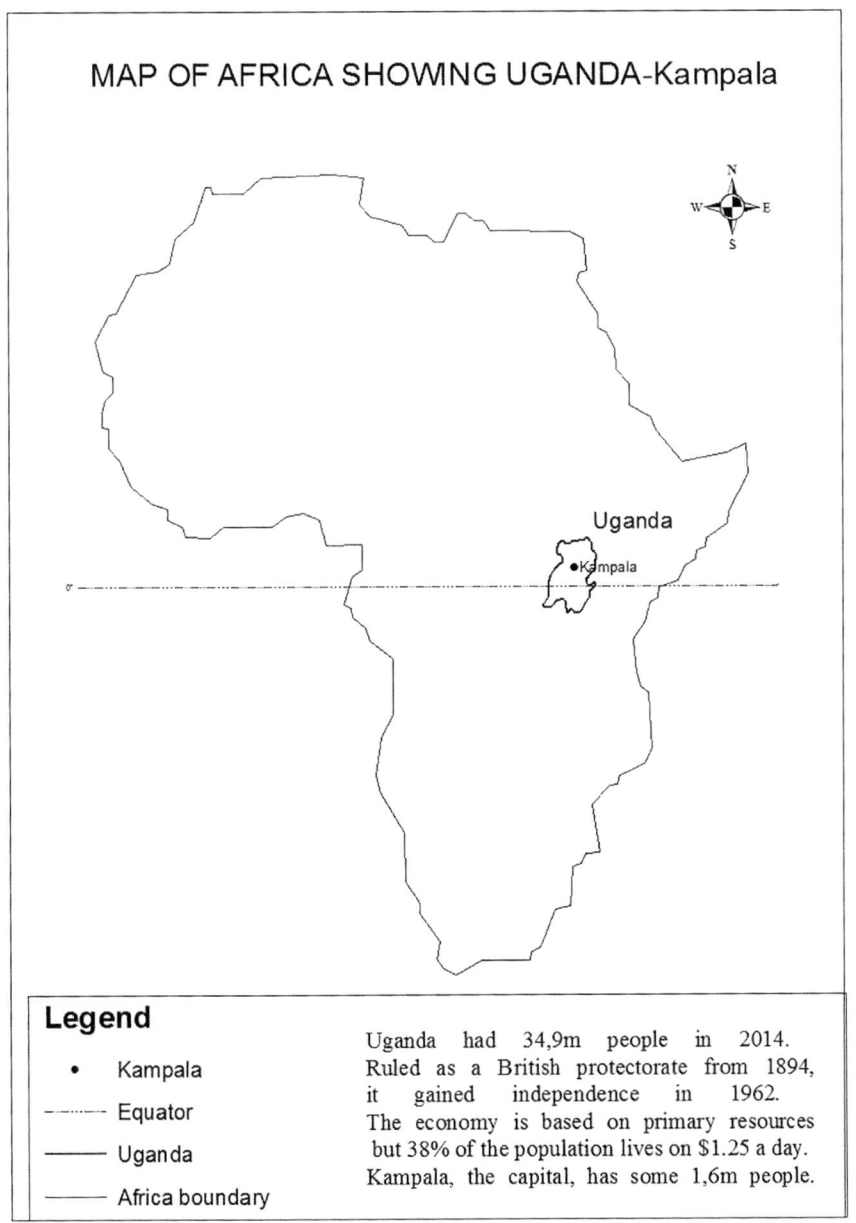

MAP OF AFRICA SHOWING UGANDA-Kampala

Uganda

•Kampala

0°

Legend

• Kampala

-------- Equator

———— Uganda

———— Africa boundary

Uganda had 34,9m people in 2014. Ruled as a British protectorate from 1894, it gained independence in 1962. The economy is based on primary resources but 38% of the population lives on $1.25 a day. Kampala, the capital, has some 1,6m people.

Figure 10.1 Map of Africa showing Uganda—Kampala

Source: David Namutoka, 2017

state actors implement policies and regulations, as well as how urban dwellers comply with them. He uses the cases of Kigali (Rwanda) and Kampala (Uganda) to show that, while the two countries have similar planning legislation, their planning systems are implemented in very different ways. Understanding the historically informed, city-level political economy in these two cities helps to explain this.

In Kampala, elite and popular groups that were negatively affected by planning could always find state agents to assist them in exchange for financial or electoral support. Political interference in planning decisions is described as 'a tradition' and hence planning rarely meets its own objectives. Goodfellow (2013) suggests the dominance of the political opposition party in Kampala plays a role here, with national government and ruling party actors keen to illustrate the opposition-run city council as corrupt and, at other times, keep political support for allowing lucrative land deals in violation of planning laws. Ruling party actors also find it expedient to appear to 'protect' the urban poor from local city planning initiatives which may threaten them, and hence buy political support. This creates a self-reinforcing dynamic of ineffective planning. The 2010 move by central government to make Kampala an entity of national government rather than a more autonomous local authority is probably related to efforts to control political opposition in the largest city.

In contrast, Kigali's unplanned urban development is viewed as a threat by governing elites, and there is consensus between national and local officials that implementing development controls matters, resulting in much higher levels of plan enforcement and urban resident compliance. Consequently, little popular resistance to planning has been allowed and informal settlements have been systematically removed to make way for the new (highly modernist) master plan of Kigali (Goodfellow 2013; Watson 2014a).

The contradiction between highly formalized and technocratic planning systems and their operation in practice is not unique to Kampala. As Myers (2011) suggests, African cities have long had dense social networks and informal institutions—essential strategies for survival and expanding livelihood options. But these stand apart from formal political and administrative institutions or are drawn into engagement with formal processes for purposes of patronage and clientelism. Robins et al. (2008) point out that civil society organizations do not automatically show characteristics of democratization which liberal democracy assumes to be the case. The decentralization and 'good governance' policy agenda has attempted to transplant institutions of Global North liberal democracy into very different social contexts, resulting in a major gap between actually occurring political practices and imported models of local governance and democracy. Older, but continually evolving, tactics and strategies involving the operationalizing of networks of power and influence are often a far more effective way for the poor to secure resources than the more abstract, less-known and less-reliable new institutions of local government. Although as Robins et al. (2008: 1079) suggest, "poor people tend to adopt plural strategies; they occupy multiple spaces and draw on multiple political identities, discourses and social relationships, often simultaneously". This has certainly been the case in Kampala.

This section sets the background for the innovative, and potentially emancipatory, co-production initiative in Kampala. It contrasts the modernist approach to planning which informed inherited planning in Uganda, and elsewhere, with a new approach introduced by an international NGO called Slum Dwellers International in the early 2000s. Possibly the highly complex, conflicted and informally networked way in which planning happens in Kampala opened the way for these innovative co-production processes. In a more autocratic, top-down and rule-bound system (such as Kigali), it is very unlikely that such a challenge would have been possible, suggesting that co-production may only have potential in societies where the state is relatively weak. Nonetheless, the question can be asked: Has the co-production process in Uganda been one of emancipation or liberation as well (to use the term Mignolo [2007] adopts from Enrique Dussel)? Mignolo (2007) argues that modernity includes the 'rational' concept of emancipation and belongs to the discourse of European enlightenment. Liberation, however, can only be achieved with decolonization of both the epistemology and political economy by social movements in previously colonized regions. He implies that emancipation is the project of Europe while liberation is the project of the colonies: They are located on different geo-political terrains.

Co-Production as an Innovative Pro-Poor Urban Upgrade Strategy: Kampala

Slum Dwellers International (SDI; www.sdinet.org), established in 1996, is a global network of community-based organizations of the urban poor with its origins in India and now has a presence in Africa, Asia and Latin America. It is made up of regional and national federations of urban poor movements and the NGOs that support them. SDI assists community-based organizations and their federations to engage with governments and national and international organizations around urban strategies which address urban land, shelter and service needs, and advocate shifting urban policy towards a more pro-poor stance. SDI promotes a set of grassroots practices, first tried in the context of urban India (see Arputham 2008), and has applied the practices globally through the work of the NGO. Practices include settlement self-enumeration and mapping, learning exchanges, community-based savings schemes and building relationships with city governments.

SDI's approach to negotiations between communities and governments on upgrade issues has been termed 'co-production' (Mitlin 2008; Watson 2014b). Mitlin (2008: 339) describes SDI's approach to co-production as a political strategy used by citizen groups and social movement organizations to "enable individual members and their associations to secure effective relations with state institutions that address both immediate basic needs and enable them to negotiate for greater benefits". SDI values collaborative relationships with government, but in practice these relationships can take on a combination of both conflict and collaboration, depending on the issues and strategies at hand (Bradlow 2013). Co-production is very different to current legal planning processes in Uganda, where there is still very little consultation with communities.

The immediate goal of co-production is to secure outcomes in terms of service and land delivery, but initiatives also aim to shift forms of democratic practice and power to create an alternative form of governmentality which both complies with and resists top-down rule. Appadurai (2001) calls this 'counter-governmentality'. Understanding the role of knowledge and power is central to these processes, and hence the need to exercise power through informal settlement self-enumerations, mapping and controlling the production and interpretation of this critical information. There is an awareness, drawing on Foucault, that power is embodied in development processes and in technologies of rule such as surveys and maps (Chatterji and Mehta 2007), and these must be appropriated by communities. These practices have shaped co-production in Kampala (Uganda).

In 2002, the Ugandan national minister of Housing and Urban Development approached SDI to request that they assist poor urban communities to engage in urban upgrade projects in partnership with the national government. This was an unusual move, as governments more frequently see SDI and their community mobilization tactics as a threat. However, national government possibly saw SDI involvement in community upgrade initiatives as a way of attracting votes and countering the dominance of the political opposition in Kampala.

The same year, an agreement was signed between the government and SDI for the NGO to initiate a co-production process involving information production on slums and implementation of infrastructural projects. It was agreed that the Kampala City Council (then under opposition party control) and the local council structures at the urban 'village' level would engage communities to plan for informal settlement upgrades. SDI helped establish the National Slum Dwellers Federation of Uganda (NSDFU)— a country-level NGO which co-ordinates committees and savings groups which operate at the community level. In December 2006, a technical arm of NSDFU called ACTogether[3] was formed, and a formal Partnership Agreement was signed by government, NSDFU and ACTogether. Over the next five years, community committees were established, local upgrade projects were initiated, co-production activities were scaled up to the national level and the scope of intervention was broadened beyond physical infrastructure to include income-generating activities. SDI presence in Uganda is ongoing with its programmes generally regarded as positive, especially in scaling co-production from the community to city level and in taking projects through to implementation.

Based on fieldwork,[4] the following sections explain first the aspects of co-production which have improved conditions of poor communities and second the divisions and conflicts which have also been part of the process.

How Co-Production Has Benefitted Communities in Kampala

SDI's invitation into Uganda by national government and the ruling political party was an important first step, even if potentially politically inspired. It did not prevent local community-based organizations that form the Federation, or NSDFU, and ACTogether as the technical arm of the NGO from working with the opposition-controlled municipal government of Kampala or the newer Kampala Capital City government as an entity of national government. These engagements have not been without problems.

The establishment of the NGO ACTogether in Kampala was of central importance. Being well staffed and funded, it could draw on experience and support from the long-established SDI global network. The established menu, termed 'rituals' of tactics and strategies which SDI employs in all locations, was implemented in Uganda and were generally effective. Community self-enumeration and mapping, carried out by the community members themselves and with NGO support, are always a first step. Community members develop their own household survey questionnaires and administer them, collecting information from each household.[5] They synthesize the information and tabulate it. Results show numbers of structures, their condition and the availability of toilets and water. Enumerations are a tactic used to reinforce and specify demands by poor communities and to increase their 'visibility' to the state. They create documented proof that communities exist as a collective and can speak back to government in its own language: that of numbers and maps. In some situations, the data is used to resist threatened evictions and relocations, or to negotiate with government for tenure and services. The process also aims to build community solidarity. The aim is to protect and improve the living environment for the urban poor (see Figures 10.2 and 10.3). A senior sociologist in the Ministry of Lands, Housing and Urban Development said:

> To create opportunity for joint slum interventions, enumerations became one of the key focus areas for the Partnership to build an informed grassroots movement that knows its responsibilities and rights, and can speak to power with confidence and engages with city development actors in a productive manner.
>
> (personal interview, 8 October 2015, Kampala)

In Uganda, one of the first steps in 2002 was for three parties to sign a Partnership Agreement: the state (national government), ACTogether and the Federation (NSDFU) representing communities. Conducting slum

Figure 10.2 Informal trading spaces in Kampala, Fieldwork
Source: Gilbert Siame, 2016

Figure 10.3 Housing conditions in informal settlements of Kampala, Fieldwork
Source: Gilbert Siame, 2016

enumerations and mapping was initiated in the name of the Partnership, and the Kampala City Council (KCC) assigned its Community Development Office and municipal staff to work with the Federation during enumerations. Slum enumerations have continued up to the present, spreading to other towns and cities in Uganda and upscaling from local community enumerations to the consolidation of information into citywide databases. Since 2002, and across Uganda, the Federation has conducted 245 settlement profiles and maps, 19 citywide profiles and 5 citywide enumerations (www. actogetherug.org).

A second important strategy to empower communities is called 'learning exchanges'. This involves groups of poor communities, and in Uganda government officials as well, moving between upgrade sites nationally or internationally to share knowledge and gains in savings, construction and engagement with authorities. They help indicate to authorities that the poor also travel and have international linkages, giving an element of authority and legitimation. The exchange also shows how the acquisition of knowledge by communities need not rely on texts and consultants, but can be gained from learning exchanges with communities in similar circumstances to see first-hand what they have built. The philosophy of experiential learning is a guiding principle where direct experience is the most effective way to gain knowledge.

In Kampala, there was strong reliance in the early days on the 'mature' Federations in Kenya and Tanzania, and 'learning exchange' visits were arranged to see co-production in action. Exchanges always included representatives from different state agencies, and they aimed to build rapport and solidify relationships with state officials, including top politicians. For example, in 2004, Federation leaders, an engineer from ACTogether, and an engineer and planner from KCC and the Ministry for Works went to Kenya and Tanzania to specifically learn about the use of alternative building technologies and apply them in the construction of the inaugural water and sanitation project. This visit was successful in changing state attitudes regarding the use of new building materials:

> After an exchange on alternative building materials, the Ministry for Works became one of the negotiators and advocates for KCC to allow the use of alternative building materials. ACTogether and the Federation used the exchange creatively to convince state technical staff to allow the use of construction technologies and materials produced by the Federation.
>
> (Structural engineer, ACTogether,
> personal interview, 8 February 2016, Kampala)

A third important strategy is the establishment of savings groups. Small-scale savings schemes are of central importance to community-based organizations and have ideological status (Appadurai 2001) in the sense that they embody a set of ideals and principles. They are an entry point for relationship building between individuals and groups, they express moral discipline in the organizations and a commitment to public good, and they highlight the role of women as primary savers. They also create a sense of community self-reliance and indicate to the state that poor communities can financially contribute to upgrade processes, even if amounts are small.

In Kampala, enumerations were a first step in community mobilization, followed immediately by the establishment of community savings groups. There are two forms of savings. One is 'daily savings' groups, introduced at the community level after 2002, each with a set of regulations and a constitution which follow an SDI template. The second is a national fund called the Ugandan Urban Poor Fund (or SUUBI) which helps to fund larger-scale and citywide infrastructure projects. Savings group members are expected to meet once a week and make a financial contribution of 100 Ugandan shillings[6] per day to SUUBI; there is no fixed contribution for the daily savings fund. A representative of SUUBI explained as follows:

> The Suubi fund is a national initiative managed by the National Federation Council on behalf of all the Federation members in Uganda. The Fund has helped the Partners to pull together large amount of resources that have later on been used to match external funds from government and donors for large scale communal and livelihood projects. The groups that are more active in the SUUBI Account easily compete for the funds from KCCA and ACTogether.
> (personal interview, 15 February 2016, Kampala)

Since its introduction, the SUUBI fund has been used as a lobbying strategy for increased pro-poor funding for projects at a citywide scale. Respondents argued that savings have made government re-profile the image of the people in slums and realize that they are not all lawbreakers and land encroachers, as was claimed in the past. As a result, ACTogether believes that the city government and the Ministry are now more willing to consider slum dwellers as essential partners in project and policy formulation initiatives. Another view could be that strategies such as enumerations and saving are supported by government, as it sees them as a way to 'tame' the poor and induce them to live in ways that are compatible with the modern state (Bayat 2010).

Today the Federation has over 400 community savings groups in six Ugandan cities, with women making up over 70% of the membership and tending to contribute more to the funds. At the national level, the Federation is sustained by women, as men are reportedly less committed to Federation rituals. Records reveal that proportionally, men are more dominant in applying for loans, demanding leadership positions and wanting to participate in international exchange activities. In one area, savings groups led by women are doing better and have less incidences of defaulting. Other savings groups led by men abused the funds and were consequently asked to step down so that the Federation in the area could recover and continue to grow.

A fourth important factor is the role of professionals in co-production, who are providing community support more than technical experts usually do. SDI makes use of architects and planners, located either within the NGO or in universities, but their involvement requires their need to recognize that the poor know best about how to survive in poverty. Professionals need to recognize their own biases and beliefs and reflect on their own positionality in relation to communities. Archer et al. (2012) suggest that the role of the 'community architect' should be to "provide the right guidance without controlling all the processes", should "ask the right questions" rather than provide all the answers, should assist the community in "finding answers for themselves", and should be able to bring together physical and social aspects of the process (*Ibid.*: 127). They need to play a teaching role, training communities to read maps and satellite pictures and to understand the financial aspects of upgrade. Their goal should be to set up a process that is sustainable without their continued intervention.

In Kampala, every effort has been made to employ professionals who understand their role in this way. Architects, planners and other professionals are employed by ACTogether, where they are expected to provide guidance in the design and execution of co-production projects in which the Federation has a leading role. They have built the capacity of the Federation in many technical aspects such as auditing, savings, project planning and design, construction, alternative construction materials, documentation and advice on how to build and sustain partnerships. They have also participated in training city officials and other partners on alternative ways of engaging with slums. Staff members from ACTogether are not allowed to make decisions without the approval and support of Federation counterparts.

In 2010, links were established with the University of Makerere School of Architecture and Planning (in Kampala) so that student studio-projects could happen in and with communities and students could learn directly how co-production works.[7] The director of the school was invited onto the board of ACTogether, and community-based student projects are ongoing.

Co-Production and Conflict Within and Between Communities and Government

Evidence suggests that in Uganda the approach to city and community improvement through co-production has been effective in bringing services to poor and informal communities as well as in fostering community organization in their engagement with the state. However, it is not surprising that this initiative has been unable to escape the deep conflicts which divide Ugandan society.

Some community groups have used political connections to secure their interests. Many leaders of the Federation are also members of the political ruling party and have used these links to influence co-production projects and processes through vote-banking and clientelism, with some Federation leaders actively promoting the ruling political party prior to elections in 2015. Landlords and vendors resisting the market upgrade project had links to the national ruling party and used these to safeguard their own interests. In another example, the KCC tried to use the Federation as a front when negotiating complex land deals with communities.

Research established that each group had lines of communication with different state actors and agencies and used these to protect their interests. Weaker groups, like women traders, networked amongst themselves to ensure there was a unified group in the Federation to counter the state-backed proposal for market upgrade. They feared this project could have adverse effects by introducing service charges and land rates and increasing evictions. Political leaders from the ruling party considered the various community groups as vote banks, especially in the wake of the 2015 general elections. These networks created fertile ground for clientelism and the politics of patronage to flourish.

Community mapping and enumeration reports were not always accepted by government as valid data, especially where they deviated from official statistics. The Federation and the Ministry officials disagreed on the sampling process for enumerations and on criteria defining inadequate housing. ACTogether and the Federation argued the need to count everybody and produce reports depicting what happens in the slums, but eventually they gave in to demands by the Ministry and KCC to include the Uganda National Bureau of Statistics as a participant during the enumerations and report writing. Sections of the community have sometimes seen enumerations as a threat. In the proposed market area, better-off landlords and vendors feared that enumerations could be used to take their land or impose business taxes, and the Federation has never been able to secure full community support.

The savings groups have also been a source of tension and division. Local savings groups have at times demanded more of a say in how the national SUUBI savings fund is managed and how the funds are distributed, as they want to see direct benefit from their contributions, or have demanded that saved funds stay at the local level. This has led to tension between the Federation and its technical arm, ACTogether. The state as well has made efforts to gain a more active controlling role in the national and community-based funds. Within local savings groups, there have been incidents of corruption and abuse of funds, with leaders sometimes attempting to use the funds for private interests.

Conclusion: Can Co-Production Be Considered Emancipatory or Even Liberating?

The co-production process in Uganda shows that this approach to state-society engagement in urban planning and development has, to a degree, empowered some communities, has established negotiating relations with various levels and departments of government, and is producing tangible positive outcomes for those involved. We argue that this approach has been able to achieve more than might have been the case with conventional approaches to participation involving collaborative and communicative planning (Robins et al. 2008; Watson 2002). The underlying assumptions of collaborative planning do not always hold in the Ugandan context, particularly state willingness to engage in democratic debate, community trust in state institutions, the ability of state-society engagement to overcome broader social and political conflicts and divisions, and stable civil society organizations with the capacity to both debate planning and project alternatives and to ensure implementation.

However, co-production has not been able to transform the modernist, and essentially colonial, planning laws and regulations which prevail, although their application and use is shaped and warped by what Robins et al. (2008) refer to as continually evolving tactics and strategies of society, operationalizing networks of power and influence. The new national planning law as well as the public consultation process in the new Kampala Master Plan, which involved merely asking for public comment on a document, are examples. Further, the co-production process itself has had challenges, conflicts and failures, and it is important not to be naively optimistic about any such engagement process in a context where conflict is a defining feature of broader society. Co-production processes were frequently ruptured and captured in Kampala through entrenched social dynamics, with local and global reach, which bedevil many other forms of governance. Colonial and modernist thinking still have a strong influence on planning and land development in Uganda, and there are many vested interests and established networks resisting change.

Co-production as a planning practice can deliver some community victories and should not be written off as a mere co-optive strategy on the part of the state. But in this context, and on its own, it is unlikely to be transformative in the sense used by Mignolo. Mignolo (2007: 454) calls for 'liberation', meaning a process of de-colonization 'of knowledge and being', a step beyond emancipation. Liberation is necessary, he argues, because the concept of emancipation does not question the logic of coloniality. Decolonization requires de-linking from the global reach of European modernity in the form of what he calls 'border thinking', which recognizes that the Western foundation of modernity and knowledge is both unavoidable and highly limited. But decolonization is not a project which can be taken on by one part of the world on its own: It must involve both the colonizer and the colonized and thus requires both emancipation and liberation. Border thinking then requires a challenge to dominant knowledge paradigms from critical perspectives informed by contexts outside of, and different to, those contexts which gave rise to the hegemony of Western thought.

Mignolo's (2007) position implies that planning practices supporting emancipation are not enough to achieve entrenched equitable planning and urban socio-spatial justice in regions experiencing coloniality. An intellectual de-linking from dominant paradigms of urban development and planning, both still strongly shaped by modernity, is an essential precondition for more liberatory planning practices. And while local initiatives such as co-production are important, also essential for deep urban change are liberatory shifts in the 'political bargaining environment', including the overcoming of corruption and patronage, at the national level and beyond.

Notes

1. The UK Town and Country Planning Act 1947.
2. The Kampala Capital City Act of 2010 removed its local government status and made Kampala an entity of national government, hence centralizing decision-making on the capital city.
3. www.actogetherug.org/ The NGO provides technical and financial assistance to NSDFU. Its staff and operations are funded by SDI.
4. Information on the case of Uganda is drawn from research conducted by co-author Gilbert Siame while working towards a PhD. The research involved visits to Kampala and interviews with community members, NGO associates and state participants in the co-production projects.
5. See Profile Enumeration Mapping: What and Why at www.actogetherug.org/index.php/features/profiling-enumeration-mapping/23-profiling-enumeration-mapping/76-what-and-why
6. 100 Ugandan shillings = US$.028. Average monthly household income in Kampala 2009/10 was 959,400 Ugandan shillings = US$268.73 (Uganda Bureau of Statistics, accessed 10 December 2016).
7. This was an initiative of the Association of African Planning Schools in partnership with SDI to improve planning education in Africa. See www.africanplanningschools.org.za

References

Appadurai, A. (2001) Deep Democracy: Urban Governmentality and the Horizon of Politics. *Environment and Urbanization* 13(2), pp. 23–43.

Archer, D., Luansang, C. and Boonmahathanakorn, S. (2012) Facilitating Community Mapping and Planning for Citywide Upgrading: The Role of Community Architects. *Environment and Urbanization* 24(2), pp. 115–129.

Arputham, J. (2008) Developing New Approaches for People-Centred Development. *Environment and Urbanization* 20(2), pp. 319–337.

Bayat, A. (2010) *Life as Politics: How Ordinary People Change the Middle East*. Amsterdam: Amsterdam University Press.

Berrisford, S. (2011) Why It Is Difficult to Change Urban Planning Laws in African Countries. *Urban Forum* 22(3), pp. 209–228.

Bradlow, B. (2013) *Quiet Conflict: Social Movements, Institutional Change, and Upgrading Informal Settlements in South Africa*. Master's thesis in City Planning,Cambridge, MA: Massachusetts Institute of Technology [Online]. Available at: https://dspace.mit.edu/handle/1721.1/80905 [Accessed 13 April 2017].

Chatterji, R. and Mehta, D. (2007) *Living with Violence: An Anthropology of Events and Everyday Life*. New Delhi and Abingdon: Routledge.

Goodfellow, T. (2013) Planning and Development Regulation Amid Rapid Urban Growth: Explaining Divergent Trajectories in Africa. *Geoforum* 48, pp. 83–93.

Home, R. (2014) Shaping Cities of the Global South: Legal Histories of Planning and Colonialism. In S. Parnell and S. Oldfield (eds.) *The Routledge Handbook on Cities of the Global South*. Abingdon and New York: Routledge, pp. 75–85.

McAuslan, P. (2003) *Bringing the Law Back in: Essays in Land, Law and Development*. Aldershot: Ashgate.

Mignolo, W. (2007) Delinking: The Rhetoric of Modernity, the Logic of Coloniality and the Grammar of De-Coloniality. *Cultural Studies* 21(2), pp. 449–514.

Mitlin, D. (2008) With and beyond the State—Coproduction as a Route to Political Influence, Power and Transformation for Grassroots Organizations. *Environment and Urbanization* 20(2), pp. 339–360.

Myers, G. (2011) *African Cities: Alternative Visions of Urban Theory and Practice*. London: Zed Press.

Nunes Silva, C. (2015) *Urban Planning in Sub-Saharan Africa: Colonial and Post-Colonial Planning Cultures*. New York and Abingdon: Routledge.

Robins, S., Cornwall, A. and Von Lieres, B. (2008) Rethinking 'Citizenship' in the Postcolony. *Third World Quarterly* 29(6), pp. 1069–1086.

Watson, V. (2002) The Usefulness of Normative Planning Theories in the Context of Sub-Saharan Africa. *Planning Theory* 1(1), pp. 27–52.

Watson, V. (2014a) African Urban Fantasies: Dreams or Nightmares? *Environment and Urbanization* 26(1), pp. 213–229.

Watson, V. (2014b) Co-Production and Collaboration in Planning: The Difference. *Planning Theory and Practice* 15(1), pp. 62–76.

11 Revitalizing the Yeldeğirmeni Neighbourhood in Istanbul

Towards an Emancipatory Urban Design in the Landscapes of Neoliberal Urbanism

Burcu Yigit Turan

Introduction: Cities as Spaces of Emancipation

According to the United Nations, which continues to view the world's rapid urbanization with both concern and hope, large parts of the world's urbanizing geographies currently lack the social, cultural, physical and natural systems and infrastructure that provide conditions for creating equality and progress (UN 2015). Neoliberalization, the hegemonic mode of operation in contemporary worldwide urbanization, has dismantled welfare systems and degenerated democracy (Harvey 2005; Brown 2015), producing cities of injustice, poverty, cultural and ecological homogenization and suppression (Brenner and Theodore 2002; Leitner et al. 2007; Harvey 2009). Protecting the benefits of capital has been continuously argued as the most important value for the general interest of society in decision-making processes, eliminating alternative voices and asserting a capital-centric hegemony over the meaning of public interest (Purcell 2009).

David Harvey (2012) argues that cities represent the frontline in struggles over urban resources and emancipatory utopian thinking and practices. Emancipation inhabits a dichotomy based on "a chasm between an emancipatory moment and the social order" (Laclau 1996: 1). From a spatial perspective, contemporary emancipatory struggles have mostly been associated with claiming the right to produce geographies with socioecological spatial qualities and relations in spaces of injustice enforced by the neoliberal hegemony (Swyngedouw 2011a). Yet the concept of emancipation has been charged with locally specific meanings according to characteristics of the oppression in different locations. As Laclau puts it, "emancipation is . . . liberation of something which precedes the liberating act" (1992: 1).

Accordingly, utopian thinking and practices in urban design have been searching for ways to engage with emancipatory battles in cities that are heavily embedded in neoliberal models of urban development. Moreover, they define different values of emancipation according to situated oppressive conditions particular to each location. Current utopian thinking and practices are interested in processes of social justice, democratic making of city spaces, social engagement, anonymity and a political stand in favour of the oppressed, as "opposed to the dead Utopianism of spatialized urban form" (Harvey 1996: 436). Designers are attempting to understand the richness of urban life, city spaces and the conditions and possibilities of bottom-up emergences, to better understand opportunities to fight against the current hegemony and to create alternative livelihoods.

This chapter aims to contribute to this argument with empirical findings obtained through a case study: The Yeldeğirmeni Neighbourhood Revitalisation Project (2010–2013). The research carried out explores urban design practices in engaging with emancipatory urban struggles in Istanbul against neoliberal urban development. The project was initiated by an alliance of the Foundation for Protecting and Introducing the Values of Environment and Culture (ÇEKÜL)[1] and the district municipality, which is governed by the CHP (Republican People's Party), an opponent to the AKP (Justice and Development Party), the ruling party. The project sought to identify an alternative to top-down gentrification based on a participatory model embracing local dwellers' social and spatial production. In particular, it gained autonomous characteristics colliding with socio-spatial practices realized by 'Yeldeğirmeni Solidarity', which was inspired by the Gezi Park movement in Istanbul.

Through this case study, the chapter attempts to provide perspectives on the following questions: How do different urban designers position themselves in relation to oppressive conditions emerging with neoliberal urbanism? How are urban landscapes formed in neoliberal urbanism? What do emancipation and emancipatory practice mean for urban design in this context? These questions were analyzed using outcomes derived from the empirical material and by relating back to the theoretical approaches outlined before. The case study utilized field visits, observations, in-depth interviews with primary actors and analyses of planning reports, documents and materials on media, and was carried out between 2013 and 2015.

Locating Urban Design in a Landscape of Neoliberal Urbanism

Waldheim (2016: 88) asserts,

> landscape is a medium structurally related to transformations in the spatial manifestation of particular economic orders. Rather than the autonomous expression of cultural forces, or stylistic concerns of taste culture, landscape urbanist practices emerged directly in response to structural transformations in the industrial economy of urbanism.

Despite minor differences at the local landscape level, the reconfiguration of landscapes through neoliberal hegemonies still retains particular patterns reported repeatedly by different researchers all over the world (e.g. Bartu Candan and Kolluoğlu 2008; He and Wu 2009; Brenner 2016; Mayer et al. 2016; Lees et al. 2016).

Neil Smith's (2002) account of gentrification in neoliberal cities at the beginning of this century is still valid in many places. Smith (2002: 443) described urban landscapes as the product of "third-wave gentrification that has evolved into a vehicle for transforming whole areas into new landscape complexes". Such 'landscape complexes', which include recreation, consumption, production, pleasure and housing, grab a part of the urban fabric and create enclaves produced through top-down planning and design mechanisms based on a *tabula rasa* approach that does not recognize the social, physical and ecological context of the place. Eventually, the city can be defined as a 'fragmented metropolis', or a series of fragments (Shane 2011). Many of these 'landscape complexes' or 'fragments' are the product of urban design, and urban design thus becomes the "art of the enclave" (Shane 2011: 25). In such a context, criticism has emerged regarding the role of urban design in the larger social, ecological and political context. Many scholars argue that urban design has become a depoliticized, conformist practice and the tool for production of 'landscape complexes' or 'fragments', and ultimately for reproduction of oppressive conditions in cities in the absence of democratic politics of city-making (Low 2006; Sorkin 2009; Madanipour 2010; Cuthbert 2011; Robles-Duran 2014; Boano and Talocci 2014; Mitrasinovic 2016).

There have also been different attempts to comprehend the critical landscapes of modern cities and to articulate alternative urban design practices searching for means to repoliticize city-making. Increasingly influenced by different strands of thoughts, ideas and practices from critical studies in the humanities, the arts and social sciences, these practices represent a "nonconformist minority in urban design, architecture, and planning" (Goonewardena 2011: 97). These perspectives argue that urban disciplines must liberate themselves from the predominance of market-oriented practices to enable a diversity of spaces, human subjectivities and histories to emerge within everyday life and mitigate capitalistic oppression (*Ibid.*: 97–99). This minority in urban design, mobilized by critical theory, thus has been in search of new perspectives, tactics, instruments, methodologies and knowledge that stress issues of urban pluralism, justice, democracy and rights (Fezer 2010; Swyngedouw 2011b; Cruz 2016; Mitrasinovic 2016).

Istanbul's Topographies as a Context for Counter-Urban Design Practice

Contemporary Istanbul has created unique examples of urban design projects developed through Turkey's own neoliberal mode of urbanism (İslam 2010). In response, counter-practices to that model and its particular projects have also emerged (Yigit-Turan 2012). Istanbul, a megalopolis of around 15 million people, became symbolic of the ruling AKP party's globalization ambitions immediately after they were elected in 2002 (Aksoy 2008). The city proposed massive construction projects and reurbanization to attract investors. Gentrification became an implicit suggestion and incentive through rhetoric of city marketing, branding or resilience, accompanied by the building of highways, luxury spaces of consumption, office spaces and gated communities (Bartu-Candan and Kolluoğlu 2008; Enlil 2011). Consequently, land rent began to rise dramatically and public land became the object of privatization (Balaban 2010). Large-scale urban construction and transportation projects started to emerge all over the city beginning in 2005, following newly introduced laws that empowered metropolitan municipal authorities to implement large-scale urban transformation projects (Bartu-Candan and Kolluoğlu 2008). These projects were enabled by the metropolitan municipalities through closed competitions, to which only invited international star architects were granted access. After the competition concluded, some information about the project would be published in the news under the heading *star architect x will design y*, alongside shiny, hyperreal architectural images embedded in the real view. Some of the projects were *Istanbul Seaport* by 5+Design (2006), *Küçükçekmece Internal-External Sand Zone Urban Renewal Project* by Ken Yeang (2006), *Kartal Urban Transformation Project* by Zaha Hadid (2006, see Figure 11.1), *New Istanbul* by a team from University of Michigan in the Master of Urban Design Program led by Prof. Dr. Roy Strickland (2007–2009), *Yenikapı Transfer Point and Archaeo-Park* by Eisenmann Architects/Aytaç Mimarlık (2008) and *Biocity Project* by a consortium consisting of Silvia Gmür Reto Gmür Architekten, DS Mimarlık, HAS Mimarlık, Tabanlıoğlu Architects, Rafael de La-Hoz, Avcı Architects and Saunders Architecture (2011), among many others.[2] After 2010, projects produced by municipal or national offices were allowed. These projects can be considered direct spatial translations of neoliberal, authoritarian and conservative ideologies of the government with their substandard design qualities, whose spatial solutions, sensibilities to ecological and social characteristics of place, aesthetics, visual representations, materials and top-down social processes all demonstrate a

Figure 11.1 Zaha Hadid Architects' master plan for Kartal-Pendik Area, Istanbul
Source: Zaha Hadid Architects, 2006

willingness to place consumption and profit over democracy and vitality. For instance, *Taksim Square and Environs Project* was developed in such a top-down mechanism with low design qualities in 2011. At the residential level, on the other hand, TOKI (Mass Housing Administration) was to become the key player in urban regeneration and consequently in social displacement (Türkün 2011) by changing the layout of housing projects by applying the same housing models repeatedly in different parts of Istanbul and across Turkey (Luth and Bedir 2013).

The large-scale urban design projects and large- or small-scale housing projects in Istanbul constitute the aforementioned 'landscape complexes'. Despite their locational differences or diversity in sizes and complexity, in most of the projects the decisions were top-down and displaced local populations, particularly low-income groups, towards peripheral locations that fragmented prior social relationships (see also Keyder 2005; Kurtuluş 2005; Pınarcıoğlu and Işık 2009; Türkün 2011). This shift in urban design practice did not recognize the local culture and nature, as these were erased from the land through massive operations: open spaces, recreational areas and eventually natural assets were converted for commercial purposes, such as hotels, restaurants, shopping centres, office spaces and luxury housing. The scale of this economically motivated reconfiguration resulted in the newly produced landscapes having limited to no relation to the existing urban fabric. Many open spaces, for instance, were covered with new private park spaces strictly managed by private companies; the urban landscape was further fragmented through an explosion of gated private housing projects (Islam 2010). New highway construction further divided the city and individual car ownership was encouraged and would eventually become necessary due to a lack of efficient public transportation and pedestrian-friendly connections. The image and identity developed by designers and developers were based on a design style mixing conservative values with consumerism. The loss of public transportation infrastructure and pedestrian mobility, combined with high operating costs of new buildings and the embrace of capitalistic individualism created deep divides in Istanbul. The loss of connectivity and public space due to new building masses and circulation patterns implicated brand new urban morphology that did not equitably include all residents. Despite the violence and division wrought by these reconfigurations, the city's dramatic new landscapes seek to position Istanbul as capital of neoconservative Turkey and as a city in global competition. In this way, urban design is stripped of its social, political and ecological context by means of topographical alterations, while systematically displacing the urban poor from the centre to the urban periphery. Topographical alterations have played a major role in unleashing a cascade of effects through social, political, economic and ecological systems. Demolishing existing buildings and structures, stripping vegetation and converting land to commercial plots all collectively represent the vast reconfiguration of terrain. Thousands of trucks carried the soil including debris, dead plants and objects from previous residents to peripheries. These 'landscape complexes', strictly tied to the capitalist and conservative system, were clear manifestations of loss of public space, fragmentation and segregation and of divesting people from any right to freely imagine, make, access or practise urban landscapes. In this context, definitions of emancipation and forms of critical and activist practices in the realm of urban design in Istanbul began to take on their own characteristics to combat these 'landscape complexes', which facilitate injustices and top-down imposition of monolithic culture and nature.

Architects and planners in Istanbul went to historical neighbourhoods facing demolition, such as Sulukule, recognizing their histories and identities that were aimed to be erased with new developments. They organized and attended many events and prepared a participatory project in 2008 as an alternative to the municipal approach. A group of local architects, who defined their role as 'medium' and 'catalyzer', opposed official planned changes by the municipality to develop a historic agricultural garden in the Kuzguncuk neighbourhood. They also organized cultural events and developed an alternative project for Bostan, another historic garden area, while involving neighbourhood residents (Dündaralp, personal interview, 25 June 2012, Kuzguncuk, Istanbul). As with designers' resistance to the government's project for Taksim Square and Gezi Park in 2011, architects and planners became involved in establishing a platform to raise public awareness, organized academic conferences, wrote for the popular media, took legal action to defeat the proposed projects, produced alternative projects, opened fake competitions in order to underline the grotesqueness of the government's project strategies, organized artistic and cultural events to enhance the use and conception of the park, marched, camped and were taken into custody shoulder to shoulder with others during the protests that aimed at protecting public space. Designers' activism spread into other places. The perspectives and practices derived from these acts of protest over a decade succeeded in infiltrating an official project, Yeldeğirmeni Neighbourhood Revitalisation Project in Kadıköy (2010–2013). It constitutes a relatively coherent case highlighting the characteristics of counter-urban design and the role of designers in search of emancipation in Istanbul.

Yeldeğirmeni Neighbourhood Revitalisation Project

> Because they have not left us any space in the city; because there are no more places where we can breathe; because there are no areas where we can express ourselves, or because we cannot find the real tranquillity. From now on we take the initiative.
>
> (a young man from Yeldeğirmeni Solidarity in video documentation by Pınar 2013)

Embracing a variety of diverse bottom-up placemaking movements as an official and systematic project, Yeldeğirmeni Neighbourhood Revitalisation

Project in Kadıköy (Figure 11.2) (2010–2013) was created by a district municipality that belonged to the opposition party CHP and ÇEKÜL. ÇEKÜL is an NGO trying to preserve cultural heritage and to combat the increasing lack of public space and social infrastructure. Aimed at protecting a densely built neighbourhood in decay, the district municipality and ÇEKÜL worked to prevent gentrification processes and the subsequent destruction of the historic urban fabric and further displacement of vulnerable parts of the population.[3] The project aimed "to protect the neighbourhood identity and relationships", "to protect small shops and businesses" and "to renovate the historical heritage and to create public space" (ÇEKÜL 2014: 38), while facilitating a comprehensive participatory action research-based urban design process to revitalize the neighbourhood.

Yeldeğirmeni Neighbourhood Revitalisation Project started with sociospatial research to understand the urban context of the neighbourhood through its relationalities, values, histories, everyday practices and cultures. This research addressed the area's plural heritages, including Jewish and Orthodox Christian minorities and contemporary ethnic, cultural and ideological diversity. It mapped the architectural heritage, local memories and histories of the neighbourhood, and everyday culture and social and spatial potentials to create public space. The research methods were based on spatial analysis, defining the heritage sites, abandoned sites and potential open spaces, and ethnographic studies including in-depth interviews with dwellers, participatory action research, community meetings, discussions and observations. The findings were shared with the inhabitants in both physical and virtual community spaces. The research process brought inhabitants from

Figure 11.2 Location of Yeldeğirmeni Neighbourhood in Kadıköy, Istanbul

Source: Burcu Yigit Turan, 2017

different backgrounds together to create public spaces themselves, thus fostering a positive politics of difference and encounter and emerging tolerance.

The project involved many social programmes: establishment of a voluntary centre, a research centre for children, a child protection and mental health centre and a cultural centre; as well as cultural events, a participatory park, a square and courtyard design and implementation, and a mural arts festival inviting foreign artists to paint the building facades at chosen strategic locations. Fundamental intervention in the urban fabric and housing stock was not the intention, except in establishing a community centre, restoration of a few public historical buildings and renewing street infrastructure for enhancing pedestrian flow. Rather, the project initiated actions through bottom-up initiatives by revealing the potential of open spaces (Figure 11.3). Revealing the potential of novel democratic practices motivated questioning the ownership status of public space and motivated public campaigns to convert parking lots or abandoned spaces into public parks through reaching out to the owners of the properties. In many cases, the spatial interventions occurred in a bottom-up way, or horizontally with collaborations between ÇEKÜL and other groups or individuals. Furthermore, a three-year participatory process that aimed to involve and empower individuals and groups gained particular momentum with the Gezi Park movement in 2013. Yeldeğirmeni Solidarity, which was set up by neighbourhood dwellers who attended the Taksim Gezi Park protests and encamped in Gezi, was established at that time as a

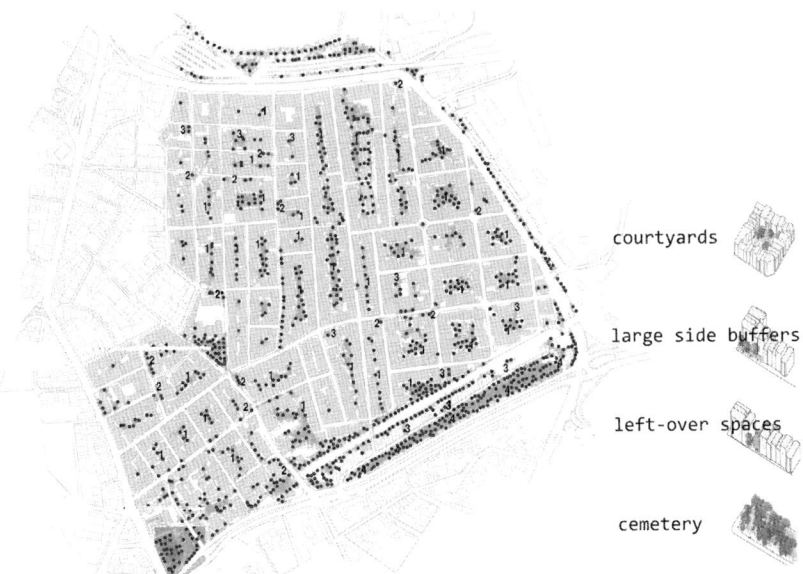

Figure 11.3 A mapping of open/green spaces in the neighbourhood

Source: ÇEKÜL (2014) (translated and amended by Burcu Yigit Turan)

collective and was to become very influential in placemaking practices. 'Gezi soul', which seeks emancipation through space (see video documentation by Tosun 2013), came to the neighbourhood and was embraced by the project.

During the project period, abandoned courtyards were transformed into allotment gardens through a collaboration between *Yeryüzü* (Earth) Foundation and local dwellers. An abandoned corner between buildings was converted into a public square and included a design addressing the neighbourhood's past as windmill hub with an installation entitled '*ben bir gün mutlaka . . .*' ('Surely one day . . .') on the wall of one of the surrounding buildings. This was created by the graphic designer Zeynep Gürcan, who is associated with TAK (Tasarım Araştırma Katılım/Design Research Participation)[4] (Figure 11.4). With *Mural-ist Wall Art Festival*, different artists from all over the world painted the facades of buildings adjacent to left-over spaces to create potential 'urban niches' (Figure 11.5) (Alp Arısoy, architect, personal interview, 8 May 2015, Istanbul). A neighbourhood park was constructed following the initiative of Yeldeğirmeni Solidarity and dedicated to Ali Ismail Korkmaz.[5] In addition, a building was occupied by Yeldeğirmeni Solidarity and converted into the 'Don Quixote Social Centre' (Figure 11.6), which facilitates art and cultural activities in order to collectively imagine and demonstrate that "a life outside the system can exist and is possible" (a young woman from Yeldeğirmeni Solidarity in video documentation by Pınar 2013). Finally, a civil initiative called 'Zumbara Assemblage' organized

Figure 11.4 View from the public square at the intersection of Karakolhane, Halitağa and Misak-I Milli Streets, with a design by local sculptor, Bülent Çınar, that addresses the neighbourhood's past as the land of windmills, and the installation '*ben bir gün mutlaka . . .*' by graphic designer Zeynep Gürcan, associated with the TAK square of wishes, on the wall of a neighbouring building

Source: Naz Beykan, 2013

Figure 11.5 Illustration of a future possibility in one of the 'urban niches' emerging
with wall art

Source: ÇEKÜL (2014)

Figure 11.6 View of the internal spaces of the building, which was occupied by
Yeldeğirmeni Solidarity and converted into the 'Don Quixote Social
Centre'

Source: Naz Beykan, 2013

festivals, concerts, charity bazaars and film screenings in the streets, in order to disseminate the idea of a barter economy.

Designers, artists and local people pursued the design of abandoned buildings, parks and squares together. These sites became public spaces for interaction, alternative uses, new social relations and everyday practices and consequently expanded the local imaginaries of an alternative future and alternative making of a city.

During the implementation of Yeldeğirmeni project, coordinating architect Alp Arısoy moved to the neighbourhood to live. He believes that through all the participatory research and design processes and shared social events and practices, he became one of them. He was invited to weddings and funerals and informed by the people about any news in the neighbourhood. He particularly emphasizes the pedagogic and communicative requirements of managing such a process as a 'social worker': collecting deep information about people's history, feelings, everyday practices and memories, and how they are connected with certain spaces and spatialities; hearing dissent and keeping relationships with different groups; and enacting and seeding hopes and power in people's minds to empower them to become agents of transformation. Consequently, the project transformed the identity, roles and skills of the designer. In the case of the Yeldeğirmeni Project, Arısoy considers himself a 'social worker', a self-depiction expressed with modesty, rather than an activist within the borders of the project. He thereby positions himself as one who tends to be closer to the decision-makers in order to have some influence for the public good in the middle of different camps in general.

A variety of processes has characterized counter-hegemonic approaches in contemporary Istanbul. Different groups have taken different positions regarding spatial characteristics, social and political message and aesthetics of programmed and spontaneous urban design or art. Younger generations and artists have become very politicized and active about creating space, while more conservative groups have become unhappy and angry about the developments. This atmosphere has generated an arena for political groups to become more visible and collide with each other, sometimes resulting in violent outbreaks. On 17 February 2015, journalist Nuh Köklü was murdered by a shopkeeper for playing snowball with a group of people from Yeldeğirmeni Solidarity Group. According to the Yeldeğirmeni Solidarity Group, this was "a hate murder and the outcome of the hate towards a cheerful group of women and men playing snowball" in a public space ("Journalist Nuh Köklü Murdered" 2015).

The Yeldeğirmeni revitalization project's overall aim was to protect the neighbourhood from massive displacement and rupture of social relationships. It succeeded in this despite the slow creep of gentrification. Property prices rose, unwillingly supported by all the social and cultural capital invested by counter-hegemonic groups who occupied and intervened in public space. The neighbourhood has become more attractive for foreigners, artists, design professionals and students, and eventually for people who are looking for culturally vibrant atmospheres. Many residents from different social and cultural profiles have come together to search for solutions to make the area affordable and collectively practice the negotiation and solidarity fomented by the project. Throughout the project, the Yeldeğirmeni community realized and learned that they can imagine and practise an alternative world. With its possibilities and paradoxes articulated with the hegemonic system, the Yeldeğirmeni community is engaging in an important experiment to find cracks in Istanbul's neoliberal hegemony to challenge the conventional descriptions of urban design and the roles of urban designers.

Conclusions

The Yeldeğirmeni Neighbourhood Revitalisation Project positioned itself against the *tabula rasa* approach used in the production of gentrified 'landscape complexes' by Istanbul's hegemonic neoliberal model of urban development. The authentic emancipatory characteristics and richness of utopian imaginaries and practices produced during the project are generated by both recognition of local landscapes and possible social and cultural engagements with it, as well as bottom-up insurgencies that tackle conservative, consumerist and oppressive conditions in local, national and global contexts. The project conserved the historic urban landscape fabric and also explored possibilities for left-over spaces as commons through different placemaking tactics. Contrary to landscapes of neoliberal urbanism, the semiotic and material content of landscapes evolved and maintained by local sources seeks to empower local vitality and cultural resources and minimize territorial reconfiguration to benefit neoliberal urban models. It reclaims peoples' right to the city.

The project recognized the historical, social, cultural and ecological aspects of place through research and identified features that could be used to graft future possibilities. In this context, urban design emancipated itself from mainstream top-down practices. The ability to reveal the phenomenalities of place was realized through transgressing theoretical realms, methodologies and pedagogies of different fields and disciplines, including the critical and projective perspectives.

Urban designers thereby emancipated themselves from a passive, conformist commitment to the production of spaces and landscapes of the economic *zeitgeist* through this critical exploration of urban possibilities, enabling social practices other than practices that neoliberal urbanism imposes. Direct contact with the richness of everyday life, nature, and human subjectivities and histories resulted in an exploration that is active and propositional rather than passive and reactive. The richness and spontaneity of life brought by such an urban design that embraces the local underlines the limitation of top-down urban design practice itself. It demonstrates how urban spaces lose democratic vitality when urban design is envisioned as a monist practice performed by technocratic and bureaucratic elites.

The unpredictable nature of bottom-up emergences generated by 'right to the city' movements breaks from the monist and monolithic system and enriches place with autonomous, open-ended spatial possibilities, particularly when urban design embraces and nurtures them. Purcell (2009: 141) suggests that democratic resistance to neoliberalism might only be possible through joining together elements of radical, participatory and revolutionary democracy with the 'right to the city' movements.

Regarding this hypothesis, the Yeldeğirmeni Neighbourhood Revitalisation Project embraces bottom-up movements through placemaking in a participatory process. Furthermore, it legitimizes them by collaborating with state/municipal institutions and actors. The project coordinator effectively recognized the diversity of political camps and risks of taking a side and consciously positioned himself as a creative medium between the camps. He therefore acts in the space between 'emancipatory moments' and 'social orders' (Laclau 1996), attempting to transform those emancipatory moments into new and ever-changing social orders. Thus, bottom-up emergences could be protected against marginalization and repression, and they could preserve belief in the possibility of another possible world in these hard times.

Notes

1. The Foundation for the Protection and Promotion of the Environment and Cultural Heritage (ÇEKÜL) identifies itself as a heritage NGO in Turkey that strives to foster and build a nationwide awareness and network for the preservation of the urban and rural, and the built and natural environment. For more information see www.cekulvakfi.org.tr/we-exist-through-nature-and-culture
2. Istanbul Independent Architects' Association (SMD) has been compiling and publicizing extensive data on megaprojects in Istanbul through an online interactive map. It is accessible on http://en.megaprojeleristanbul.com
3. The neighbourhood's name comes from windmills dating back to the 15th century. It experienced lively cosmopolitan times in the 19th century as a refuge for ethnic and religious minorities during the Ottoman Empire and Early Republican Period and gained its physically and culturally dense urban fabric at that period, attracting low-income groups, university students, migrants and artists (ÇEKÜL 2014).
4. See more about TAK on http://takortak.org/what-is-tak.html
5. Ali Ismail Korkmaz was a 19-year-old university student who was murdered by opposition groups and police during events in Eskisehir supporting the Taksim-Gezi Park protests. For more information see Uras (2014).

References

Aksoy, A. (2008) Istanbul's Choice. *Third Text* 22(1), pp. 71–83.

Balaban, U. (2010) The Enclosure of Urban Space and Consolidation of the Capitalist Land Regime in Turkish Cities. *Urban Studies* 48(10), pp. 2162–2179.

Bartu-Candan, A. and Kolluoğlu, B. (2008) Emerging Spaces of Neo-Liberalism: A Gated Town and a Public Housing Project in Istanbul. *New Perspectives on Turkey* 39, pp. 46–74.

Boano, C. and Talocci, G. (2014) Fences and Profanations: Questioning the Sacredness of Urban Design. *Journal of Urban Design* 19(5), pp. 700–721.

Brenner, N. (2016) The Hinterland, Urbanized? *Architectural Design* 86(4), pp. 118–127.

Brenner, N. and Theodore, N. (2002) Cities and the Geographies of 'Actually Exist-ing Neoliberalism'. In N. Brenner and N. Theodore (eds.) *Spaces of Neoliberalism: Urban Restructuring in North America and Western Europe*. Oxford: Blackwell, pp. 1–32.

Brown, W. (2015) *Undoing the Demos: Neoliberalism's Stealth Revolution*. New York: Zone Books.

ÇEKÜL (2014) *Yeldeğirmeni Deneyimi: Kentsel Yenilemeye Farklı Bir Yaklaşım* [Yeldeğirmeni Experience: A Different Approach to Urban Renewal]. Istanbul: ÇEKÜL Foundation Publications.

Cruz, T. (2016) Where Is Our Civic Imagination? In M. Mitrasinovic (ed.) *Concurrent Urbanities: Designing Infrastructures of Inclusion*. New York and London: Routledge, pp. 9–23.

Cuthbert, A. (2011) Urban Design and Spatial Political Economy. In T. Banerjee and A. Loukaitou-Sideris (eds.) *Companion to Urban Design*. Abingdon, Oxon: Rout-ledge, pp. 84–96.

Enlil, Z.M. (2011) The Neoliberal Agenda and the Changing Urban Form of Istan-bul. *International Planning Studies* 16(1), pp. 5–25.

Fezer, J. (2010) Design for a Post-Neoliberal City. *E-Flux Journal* 17.

Goonewardena, K. (2011) Critical Urbanism: Space, Design Revolution. In T. Baner-jee and A. Loukaitou-Sidaris (eds.) *Companion to Urban Design*. Abingdon, Oxon: Routledge, pp. 97–108.

Harvey, D. (1996) *Justice, Nature and the Geography of Difference*. Cambridge, MA: Blackwell.

Harvey, D. (2005) *A Brief History of Neoliberalism*. Oxford: Oxford University Press.

Harvey, D. (2009) *Social Justice and the City*. Athens, GA: Georgia University Press.

Harvey, D. (2012) *Rebel Cities: From the Right to the City to the Urban Revolution*. New York and London: Verso.

He, S. and Wu, F. (2009) China's Emerging Neoliberal Urbanism: Perspectives from Urban Redevelopment. *Antipode* 41(2), pp. 282–304.

Islam, T. (2010) Current Urban Discourse, Urban Transformation and Gentrification in Istanbul. *Architectural Design* 80(1), pp. 58–63.

'Journalist Nuh Köklü Murdered for Playing Snowball' (2015) *Agos*, 18 February [Online]. Available at: www.agos.com.tr/en/article/10618/journalist-nuh-koklu-murdered-for-playing-snowball [Accessed 7 July 2017].

Keyder, Ç. (2005) Globalization and Social Exclusion in Istanbul. *International Jour-nal of Urban and Regional Research* 29(1), pp. 124–134.

Kurtuluş, H. (ed.) (2005) *Istanbul'da Kentsel Ayrışma—Mekânsal Dönüşümde Farklı Boyutlar* [Urban Fragmentation in Istanbul: Different Dimensions in Spatial Transformations]. Istanbul: Bağlam Publications.

Laclau, E. (1992) Beyond Emancipation. *Development and Change* 23(3), pp. 121–137.

Laclau, E. (1996) *Emancipation(s)*. New York: Verso.

Lees, L., Shin, H. and Lopez-Morales, E. (eds.) (2016) *Planetary Gentrification*. Cambridge: Polity Press.

Leitner, H., Peck, J. and Sheppard, E. (eds.) (2007) *Contesting Neoliberalism: Urban Frontiers*. New York: Guilford Press.

Low, S. (2006) The Erosion of Public Space and the Public Realm: Paranoia, Surveil-lance and Privatization in New York City. *City and Society* 18(1), pp. 43–49.

Luth, C. and Bedir, M. (2013) *Agoraphobia Investigating Turkey's Urban Transformation* [Video file]. Available at: https://vimeo.com/118539061 [Accessed 9 January 2017].

Madanipour, A. (2010) *Whose Public Space? International Case Studies in Urban Design and Development*. Abingdon, Oxon: Routledge.

Mayer, M., Thörn, C. and Thörn, H. (eds.) (2016) *Urban Uprising: Challenging Neoliberal Urbanism in Europe*. Basingstoke: Palgrave Macmillan.

Mitrasinovic, M. (ed.) (2016) *Concurrent Urbanities: Designing Infrastructures of Inclusion*. New York and London: Routledge.

Pınar, F. (2013) *Türkiye'deki İlk İşgal Evi—Yeldeğirmeni Kadıköy Donkişot Sosyal Merkezi* [The First Squatted House in Turkey—Yeldeğirmeni Kadıköy Don Kişot Social Centre] [Video file]. Available at: www.youtube.com/watch?v=Lrl3ySaXq_o [Accessed 16 December 2016].

Pınarcıoğlu, M.M. and Işık, O. (2009) Segregation in Istanbul: Patterns and Processes. *Tijdschrift voor economische en sociale geografie* 100(4), pp. 469–484.

Purcell, M. (2009) Resisting Neoliberalization: Communicative Planning or Counter-Hegemonic Movements? *Planning Theory* 8(2), pp. 140–165.

Robles-Duran, M. (2014) The Haunting Presence of Urban Vampires. *Harvard Design Magazine* 37 [Online]. Available at: www.harvarddesignmagazine.org/issues/37/the-haunting-presence-of-urban-vampires [Accessed 2 May 2017].

Shane, D.G. (2011) *Urban Design since 1945: A Global Perspective*. West Sussex: John Wiley & Sons.

Smith, N. (2002) New Globalism, New Urbanism: Gentrification as Global Urban Strategy. *Antipode* 34(3), pp. 427–450.

Sorkin, M. (2009) The End(s) of Urban Design. In A. Krieger and W.S. Saunders (eds.) *Urban Design*. Minneapolis: University of Minnesota Press, pp. 155–182.

Swyngedouw, E. (2011a) Interrogating Post-Democratization: Reclaiming Egalitarian Political Spaces. *Political Geography* 30(7), pp. 370–380.

Swyngedouw, E. (2011b) *Designing the Post-Political City and the Insurgent Polis (Civic City Cahier 5)*. London: Bedford Press.

Tosun, H. (2013) *'Gezi olmasaydı burası olmazdı' . . . Don Kişot Evi İşgal Eylemi Büyüyor . . .* ['Here Would Not Exist, If Gezi Did Not Happen' . . . Don Kişot House Occupation Action Is Expanding] [Video file]. Available at: www.youtube.com/watch?v=mSdYVoKfYI8 [Accessed 16 December 2016].

Türkün, A. (2011) Urban Regeneration and Hegemonic Power Relationships. *International Planning Studies* 16(1), pp. 61–72.

UN (2015) World Urbanization Prospects: The 2014 Revision [Online]. Available at: http://esa.un.org/unpd/wup/FinalReport/WUP2014-Report.pdf [Accessed 7 July 2017].

Uras, U. (2014) The Killing of Ali Ismail Korkmaz. *Al Jazeera*, 7 February [Online]. Available at: www.aljazeera.com/indepth/features/2014/02/killing-ali-ismail-korkmaz-20142681450320113.html [Accessed 7 July 2017].

Waldheim, C. (2016) *Landscape as Urbanism: A General Theory*. New Jersey: Princeton University Press.

Yigit-Turan, B. (2012) *Dönüşen İstanbul'un Yeni Peyzajlarında Tasarımın Politik Ekolojisi* [Political Ecology of Design in the New Landscapes of Transforming Istanbul]. *Mimarlık* [*Architecture*] Dosya 28 *Kentsel Dönüşüm Özel Sayısı* (Dossier 28 Special Issue: Urban Transformation), pp. 113–119.

12 Conflict vs. Consensus

An Emancipatory Understanding of Planning in a Pluralist Society

Angelika Gabauer

Introduction

This chapter delivers a critical review of emancipatory contents in approaches subsumed under the paradigm of communicative planning. It draws on current scientific discourses and already articulated critique of communicative planning theories, thus particularly reflecting on aspects of dialogue, participation, consensus building and conflict resolution that lie at the heart of this strand of planning theory. It further employs theories of radical democracy to systematize somewhat abstract and vague conceptualizations of emancipation in order to infer an emancipatory understanding of planning. It is argued that the implementation of participatory instruments that pursues the ideal of democratizing planning procedures does not necessarily deliver on the postulated goal of creating more democratic planning practices. In fact, the opening up of planning procedures through involving different stakeholders may contribute to consolidating existing power relations. This paradox inherent in communicative planning renders emancipatory planning practices an impossible pursuit. Therefore, (1) communicative planning procedures are discussed in the context of current restructuring processes under way in European cities and brought into dialectics with (2) the theoretical planning discourse. Chantal Mouffe's notion of radical democracy serves to critically substantiate this discussion. (3) Taking off from Jean Hillier's *agonistic planning* approach and reflecting on Mouffe's theory of *agonistic pluralism*, possibilities for an emancipatory understanding of planning will be developed as an alternative to its predominant notion as a set of consensus-building procedures. Finally, (4) conceptualizations of emancipation within planning are systematized to address (5) the question of how truly emancipatory planning might be enabled.

Communicative Planning Procedures in the Context of Current Governance Strategies

The trend to implement participatory elements in urban planning procedures is embedded in current debates about institutional restructuring processes of European cities. While the state and public authorities still have a "propensity to structure the institutional framework of political exchanges between local actors, they have simultaneously created the conditions for opening urban institutions up to actors from civil society and have, therefore, worked hard toward redefining public policies in the cities" (Jouve 2005: 286). With the aim of making urban planning 'more dialogic', different stakeholders are to be involved in planning processes. What is often referred to as the shift from 'government' to 'governance' (Swyngedouw 2005) is the opening up of governmental processes, which were previously carried out almost exclusively by state institutions, to include as well actors from the private market and civil society organizations. However, an involvement of broader societal actors in urban planning by means of horizontal and socially innovative participatory processes does not necessarily result in more democratic planning procedures. On the contrary, such strategies may even further strengthen hegemonic positions of certain actors, as participatory practices tend to provide space to actors who have traditionally exerted influence on planning procedures, such as investors or real estate owners. Consequently, the private market sector in particular greatly benefits from this type of arrangements as it gains opportunity for more direct action in political decision-making while positions of many other groups can be simultaneously weakened. In accordance, Swyngedouw (2005) identifies such "horizontally organised stakeholder arrangements of governance that appear to empower civil society in the face of an apparently overcrowded and 'excessive' state", as a "Trojan Horse that diffuses and consolidates the 'market' as the principal institutional form" (*Ibid.*: 2003). The effects of such restructuring processes on political participation and democracy as a whole are often discussed in media or public discourses with terms such as 'democratic deficit', 'depoliticization', 'post-democracy', 'post-political' and 'post-politics'. These notions generally refer to the "erosion of democracy and the weakening of the public sphere, as a consensual mode of governance has colonised, if not sutured, political space" (Wilson and Swyngedouw 2015: 5).

In order to understand the whole extent of the two-sided relationship between seemingly empowering participatory processes and democratic planning, an outline of selected planning theory discourses will follow. Participatory planning instruments, which are mostly horizontally organized and follow the principle of stakeholder involvement, are within planning theory summarized under the paradigm of *communicative planning*[1] (cf. Healey 1992; Innes 2004). Seeing how this body of thought is mainly influenced by Jürgen Habermas's (1984) theory of communicative action, it largely revolves around consensus building procedures.

Communicative Planning Theory and Consensus-Building Procedures

The so-called 'positivism dispute' between the protagonists of the scientific theory of critical rationalism and the critical theorists of the Frankfurt

School in the 1960s inspired a growing critique of the predominant positivist paradigm of the planning discipline, thus giving rise to the 'communicative turn' (Healey 1992) in planning theories of the 1980s. The prevailing trust in naturalism and positivism has been superseded by "approaches that contextualise theories and disciplines in larger social and historical contexts" (Allmendinger 2002: 7). Habermas's theory of communicative action is considered as a "principal theoretical resource used in developing communicative planning theory" (Harris 2002: 25). Although the communicative planning approach has been widely accepted as the most important approach within international planning discourses (cf. Allmendinger 2002: 15–16), it has also been subject to substantial critique (e.g. Fainstein 2000; Hillier 2003).

Formulating a general critique of communicative planning approaches is beyond the scope of this chapter. Rather, its focus is placed on aspects of participation, consensus formation, conflict resolution and conflict prevention, which are discussed in terms of their democratic substance and emancipatory content. Even though communicative planning provides a critical take on power structures and a normative approach to developing 'more democratic' planning practices (Harris 2002: 34, referring to Healey 1997a: 72), it is precisely in these aspects that its weakness can be identified. As Fainstein (2000) states,

> its vulnerability lies in a tendency to substitute moral exhortation for analysis. Although their roots . . . are in critical theory, once the communicative theorists move away from critique and present a manual for action, their thought loses its edge.
>
> *(Ibid.: 455)*

The concept of consensus building is central to Habermas's theory of communicative action: "It is the actors themselves who seek consensus and measure it against truth, rightness, and sincerity" (Habermas 1984: 100). Accordingly, the shift "from competitive interest bargaining towards collaborative consensus-building" (Healey 1997b: 30) has become a core aspect of communicative planning. Consensus building is considered to carry a transformative potential by opening up new perspectives and approaches to solutions. Common interests, shared meanings and values are believed to build up through a dialogue and exchange of ideas developed on principles such as information transfer and transparency, equal voting rights, active listening, respect for other participants or a culture of sincere discussion. "Through participants' thinking and acting together, they may transform their ideas, values of what is important to them, their ways of working and organizing" (Hillier 2002: 116). For this reason, planning procedures entailing discussions and criticism should be made accessible to different civil society actors, with the aim of balancing interests and building political consensus. This is how planning projects are also believed to acquire better protection and legitimation. Planners are given a key position in the procedure. Their role is to mediate between the various stakeholders. Referring to Habermas's idea of communicative rationality, Innes (2004) argues that in planning practice "[t]he technology is . . . very well developed on how to create undistorted communications or ideal speech conditions" (*Ibid.*: 11). Unequal power relations "around the table" can, according to her, "largely be equalized with skillful management of dialogue, shared information, and education of the stakeholders" (*Ibid.*: 12) (Figure 12.1). Well-trained and self-reflective planners can create such an ideal situation. This assumption is based on the reasoning that power-neutral and undistorted speech acts are attainable. In such a planning situation, different actors (would) participate equally in decision-making processes independently of their social positions, and (would) discuss and negotiate topics without the bias of hierarchy. However, as Purcell (2009) states, "speech acts cannot be neutral and undistorted; they must necessarily contain distortion in order to be intelligible" (*Ibid.*: 150). Language is not a power-free medium. Speech acts are always traversed and distorted by the speaker, and thus by his or her (power) position. "Scrutiny of efforts to base planning on dialogue reveals serious problems of implementation and the continued dominance of the already powerful" (Fainstein 2000: 458). For example, in the planning setting certain persons take the role of experts, thus their statements are interpreted not as personal opinions but rather as 'neutral' knowledge about a situation. In a decision-making

Figure 12.1 Photograph illustrating participatory planning situation 'around the table'
Source: Vienna City Administration, MA21 Department, Christian Fürthner, 2015

process, the statements of so-called experts are assessed differently from, for example, those of interested citizens. A condition can never be created in which all stakeholders participate as equal members, since a person's statement is always evaluated by the listeners in the context of his or her role, which he or she is assigned or attributed to in a particular situation. This role or position of individual participants is at hand even before they express themselves verbally, which in turn leads to the weakening or strengthening of the respective groups or persons and their concerns. Moreover, persons who are, due to their profession, often involved in planning situations are familiar with certain codes of behaviour, at both verbal and nonverbal levels. Thus, they are generally better able to negotiate their positions than those who are unaccustomed to such procedures.

Although Innes (2004) postulates the possibility of a power-neutral negotiation, she nevertheless acknowledges that "[c]onsensus building is not, in any case, the place for redistributing power" (*Ibid.*: 12). This argument is a contradiction in terms, since planning procedures cannot be seen independently of their context. Rather, such an assumption inevitably fosters and consolidates existing power structures. How targets are formulated, which frameworks and participatory instruments are used, and which actors are defined as 'holding a stake' and thus are involved in a certain planning process, reflect (political) decisions resulting from specific social power structures. Conceiving of planning targets and methods as detached from their sociopolitical context veers out power structures. Proclaiming the possibility of achieving a rational consensus in a power-free negotiation space thus leads to a strengthening of the already powerful. Consequently, consensus building easily becomes an instrument of legitimizing existing configurations of power rather than empowering different societal groups.

Agonistic Planning Approach

Unlike Innes, Hillier (2003) emphasizes that "in the reality of practice, many planning strategies and/or disputes about development applications do not end in harmonious consensus" (*Ibid.*: 38), thus leaving "the ideals of communicative rationality and consensus-formation . . . rarely achieved" (*Ibid.*: 41). Furthermore, as Gunder (2003) argues,

> Habermas's communicative theory predicated on the 'ideal speech situation' is but a fantasy used to negate the potential terror of the 'oppressive mute presence' of the Other in a position of authority, because it is predicated on a metaphysical hope that universal equality is attainable in setting a universal public interest.
>
> (*Ibid.*: 245, referring to Žižek 1992: 104)

Hillier (2003) pleads for "dislodging an endorsement of the centrality of rational consensus, replacing it with a consideration of agonistic pluralism"

(*Ibid.*: 39). She develops an 'agonistic planning' approach that is strongly influenced by Mouffe's theory of radical democracy. Hillier's critique of consensus formation refers to Mouffe insofar as such an understanding is based on the possibility of constituting a harmonious and consensual coexistence, thus ignoring the existence of conflicts for which there are no rational solutions. Such an assumption disregards that the social world is permeated with antagonisms and conflicts which can never be (completely) overcome. To not acknowledge them leads to a degradation of democracy. The assumed capacity of deliberative approaches to establish a rational consensus by eliminating power structures ignores the fact that power is constitutive of social relations and cannot be resolved. Following Foucault (1978: 93–96), power is not (only) something which affects us as a form of authority per se. Rather, it means to understand power as a network extending through all of society. Power is omnipresent and is exerted from countless points in the play of unequal and mobile relations, beyond typically narrow and commonly understood dimensions of acquiring, taking away, sharing, preserving or losing. Power is thus immanent in all social conditions. This also means that forms of resistance "can only exist in the strategic field of power relations" (*Ibid.*: 96). Therefore, the central question of democratic politics must not be, Mouffe (2013) argues, how power structures can be eliminated, but rather how power can be used and transformed in support of democratic values.

Instead of the model of deliberative democracy, Mouffe calls for an 'agonistic pluralism', thereby advocating the recognition of the pluralist nature of social reality, which means that a final and absolute reconciliation of all views, opinions and conceptions is never possible. The distinction between 'politics' and 'the political' is central in her approach. 'The political' refers to this dimension of antagonism, which can take many forms and can emerge in diverse social relations: "It is a dimension that can never be eradicated" (*Ibid.*: 2). The political is thus the perpetually conflicting condition of the social world, which cannot be overcome by any rational solution-finding strategies. On the other hand, 'politics' "indicates the ensemble of practices, discourses and institutions which seek to establish a certain order and organize human coexistence in conditions that are always potentially conflictual because they are affected by the dimension of 'the political'" (*Ibid.* 2009: 101). The goal of democratic politics must be to transform antagonism into what Mouffe calls 'agonism', where a relationship between adversaries arises replacing the antagonistic friend/enemy opposition. Those 'friendly enemies' "are friends because they share a common symbolic space but also enemies because they want to organize this common symbolic space in a different way" (*Ibid.*: 13). Adversaries agree on the 'ethico-political' principles of liberal democracy, such as equality, the recognition of the rule of law, popular sovereignty and respect for human rights, but they differ in terms of their concrete meaning, structure and implementation (*Ibid.*: 102).

This means that pluralist democracies indeed demand a certain amount of consensus, but "since those ethico-political principles can only exist through many different and conflicting interpretations, such a consensus is bound to be a 'conflictual consensus'" (*Ibid.*: 103). What is central to Mouffe's approach and what distinguishes her position from deliberative models is that negotiations and conflicts about those different oppositions are not subjected to rationality, because passions, values and attitudes are not disregarded, but rather acknowledged as part of pluralist democracies. An agonistic approach also recognizes every consensus as a temporary manifestation of power structures, which therefore always entails forms of exclusion (*Ibid.*: 104). However, Mouffe argues, reflecting the impossibility of establishing a consensus without exclusion, thus being aware of the elusiveness of achieving a well-ordered, fully achieved democratic society at any time, means to acknowledge the ever-present temptation existing in democratic societies and forces us to continually keep democratic contestation alive (*Ibid.*: 105).

In respect of planning, this approach recognizes insurmountable conflicts, which will always be associated with the use of public spaces, large-scale projects, organization of traffic or changes in land use, but seeks to synergistically preserve difference instead of obscuring it under the cover of a rational consensus or a 'universal general interest'. Thus, following a democratic understanding, planning procedures should be characterized by the thematization and reflection on these plural conflict lines instead of merely striving after consensus through conflict avoidance. Such planning actually provides space and opportunities for conflicts, accepting the risk of ultimately failing to reach an agreement. This does not mean that planning processes should not be designed as solution-oriented. The attempt to reach compromise must remain at the forefront, but not under the premise of a consensus based on rational 'value-neutral' justifications. As Hillier (2002) puts it, planning practices

> should recognise the inherent undecidability of decisions and accept unresolvable differences of values and opinion without passing moral judgement on them. There should be freedom of dissent as well as of agreement. Where consensus cannot be achieved through negotiation, bargaining or transactions may take place to reach compromise agreements.
>
> (*Ibid.*: 132)

Consequently, following an agonistic planning approach, consensus-driven resolutions under the veil of rationality or morality are disregarded in favour of respectfully allowing multiple possibilities to coexist. Such an understanding is inherent to the regardful concurrence of insurmountable opposites and conflict lines that shape a space of a 'conflictual consensus' (Figure 12.2).

Communicative Planning Approach	**Agonistic Planning Approach**
Habermas' Theory of Communicative Action	Mouffe's Theory of Agonistic Pluralism
Possibility of eliminating power structures and creating power-free negotiations through establishing undistorted communications or ideal speech conditions	Power is constitutive of social relations and cannot be resolved but can be transformed in support of democratic planning
Rational consensus: collaborative consensus building based on rationality	Conflictual consensus: seeking for compromises without disregarding passions, values, attitudes and recognizing every consensus as temporary stabilization of power
Emphasis on conflict avoidance	Focus on providing opportunities for respectful conflicts
Rational solution-finding strategies	Reflection of plural conflict lines and acceptance of unresolvable disagreements

Figure 12.2 Scheme comparing communicative planning and agonistic planning approaches

Source: Angelika Gabauer, 2017

The Relationship Between Emancipation and Democracy

Emancipation is understood here as a form of self-empowerment that everyone has the right and ability to exercise. Thus, emancipation encompasses two dimensions, *empowerment from* as well as *empowerment to*. A radical understanding of democracy makes it possible to theorize emancipation and to make deductions for emancipatory action.

The term democracy dates back to ancient Greece. It is composed of the two words, *demos* and *kratos*, and is commonly translated as *the power of the people*. However, modern democracy, as we know it, "is only one variant of the sharing of political power connoted by the venerable Greek term" (Brown 2011: 45). Political power in the understanding of ancient Greece refers to "the empowered or ruling body" (Ober 2008: 3), which is expressed by the three core concepts monarchia, oligarchia and demokratia. As shown by Ober, only the last concept is not about numbers: "The term *demos* refers to a collective body" (*Ibid.*: 4, original emphasis). The second component *kratos*, which is translated as power, means in its original form, the ability to do something: "*kratos* . . . becomes power in the sense of strength, enablement, or 'capacity to do things'" (*Ibid.*: 6, original emphasis). Contrary to current interpretations, the initial meaning of democracy does not refer to a quantitative majority, but it expresses the power of everyone—i.e. everyone has the right to govern just as everyone is governed. The power of the demos does not provide an answer to the question of *how many*, rather:

> *Demokratia* is not just 'the power of the *demos*' in the sense 'the superior or monopolistic power of the *demos* relative to other potential

power-holders in the state.' Rather it means, more capaciously, 'the empowered *demos*'—it is the regime in which the *demos* gains a collective capacity to effect change in the public realm. And so it is not just a matter of *control* of a public realm but the collective *strength* and *ability* to act within that realm and, indeed, to reconstitute the public realm through action.

(Ibid.: 7, original emphasis)

Democracy is the ability to do something and must therefore be understood as a capacity to act. "It is . . . one of potentiality or enablement: the capacity of ordinary people to discover modes of action for realizing common concerns" (Ross 2011: 89). Such an understanding of democracy, which refers to a collective capacity for action, rejects the idea of dividing the demos into a group that possesses the ability to act and one that does not, and thus must be governed. Therefore, it can clearly not provide legitimization for the rule *over* others by virtue of special aptitude or the like; rather, it presupposes an equality of all. Thus, following Rancière, democracy is the embodiment of the principle of equality, wherein equality is not seen as "a utopian longing nor a sociologically verifiable condition", but as "an ontological given, which is affirmed and given content precisely through its performative staging and enacting" (Wilson and Swyngedouw 2015: 12, referring to Rancière 1999).

This conceptual-historical perspective on the meaning of democracy illustrates its inscribed emancipatory substance in the sense of *everyone's capacity to act*. Current debates about democratic deficit, the crisis of representative democracy and demands for 'real democracy' mirror a substantial shrinking of precisely this emancipatory content of democracy. Mouffe's (2009) concept of the 'democratic paradox' offers an analytical framework to grasp current developments of de-democratization, the erosion of democracy, the rising dissatisfaction and decreasing identification with representative-democratic institutions. Through outlining an idea-historical conception of 'Western' democracies, she argues that their origin is based on a contradiction that cannot be overcome. She employs the concept of the 'democratic paradox' (Figure 12.3) to point to the intrinsic tension of two traditions anchored in liberal democracy; the liberal and the democratic one. These traditions are based on different principles: liberalism on liberty and democracy on equality.

On the one side we have the liberal tradition constituted by the rule of law, the defence of human rights and the respect of individual liberty; on the other the democratic tradition whose main ideas are those of equality, identity between governing and governed and popular sovereignty.

(Ibid.: 2–3)

The two traditions are not compatible with each other, and nor is there a necessary relationship between them. However, as Mouffe argues, the paradox of liberal democracy cannot be abolished, but, on the contrary, must be

The Democratic Paradox by Chantal Mouffe

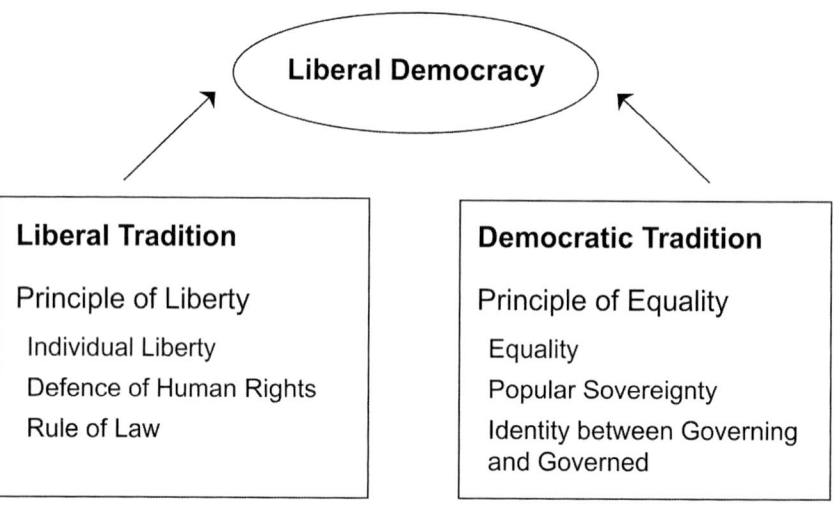

Figure 12.3 Scheme illustrating Mouffe's notion of the 'democratic paradox'
Source: Angelika Gabauer, 2017

acknowledged. She is particularly critical of theoretical endeavours to reconcile the democratic and liberal tradition. Mouffe considers this an impossible undertaking because

> [o]nly by coming to terms with its paradoxical nature will we be in a position to envisage modern democratic politics in an adequate manner, not as the search for an inaccessible consensus . . . but as an 'agonistic confrontation' between conflicting interpretations of the constitutive liberal-democratic values.
>
> *(Ibid.: 8–9)*

From Mouffe's perspective, in neoliberal hegemony, the liberal tradition of democracy has become superior, which means that it undermines the democratic principles of equality, popular sovereignty and identity between governing and governed in favour of liberal principles of individual freedom, the rule of law and the defence of human rights. However, the liberal idea is not capable of grasping the pluralist realities of the social world, instead it misjudges conflicts, eclipses them and transforms them into mere "competition of interests" (*Ibid.*: 111) that can be negotiated. The "liberal perspective . . . envisages democracy as a competition among elites, making adversary forces invisible and reducing politics to an exchange of arguments and the negotiation of compromises" (*Ibid.*: 111). Such a notion is accompanied by the conception of a democratic society, which functions as a dialogue and implies the absence of social inequalities and power relations. Yet, Mouffe reminds:

> Completely missing from such an approach is 'the political' in its dimension of power, antagonism and relationships of forces. What 'political liberalism' is at pains to eliminate is the element of 'undecidability' which is present in human relations. It offers us a picture of a well-ordered society as one from which—through rational agreement on justice—antagonism, violence, power and repression have disappeared.
> (*Ibid.*: 31)

However, as can be seen in many cities, 'the political' cannot be extinguished; space emptied of agonist political disagreement and pacified through liberal consensus has increasingly been taken over by identity politics, fundamentalisms and outbreaks of violent ethnic conflicts. Models of democracy that put rationality at the core of their approaches, as Mouffe aptly points out, ignore "a central element which is the crucial role played by passions and affects in securing allegiance to democratic values" (*Ibid.*: 95). The postulated capacity of deliberative models to eliminate power structures and establish a rational consensus ignores the fact that power is constitutive of social relations and can therefore not be removed. Furthermore, privileging rationality implies a certain conception of the subject, namely, one which sees individuals as prior to society, bearers of 'natural' rights who are able to act in an autonomous, rational way. "[T]hey are abstracted from social and power relations, language, culture and the whole set of practices that make agency possible" (*Ibid.*). Passions, as Mouffe states, "are erased from the realm of politics, which is reduced to a neutral field of competing interests" (*Ibid.*: 31). On the contrary, in Mouffe's understanding of democracy as agonistic pluralism, passions are not excluded from the public sphere to render a rational consensus possible, but become rather constructively mobilized around democratic objectives. "A well-functioning democracy calls for a vibrant clash of democratic political positions. . . . Too much emphasis on consensus and the refusal of confrontation lead to apathy and disaffection with political participation" (*Ibid.*: 104). The recognition of passions as part of the public realm also rethinks the understanding of democratic participation; it puts the emphasis on forms of practice rather than on argumentation. This means that planning procedures that pursue an emancipatory-participatory claim need to adopt an action-oriented approach that focuses on common practices and actions. Instead of the premises of rationality based on argumentation, the focus is on shared attitudes that are developed through joint action:

> we are led to acknowledge that democracy does not require a theory of truth and notions like unconditionality and universal validity but a

manifold of practices and pragmatic moves aiming at persuading people to broaden the range of their commitments to others, to build a more inclusive community.

(*Ibid.*: 65–66)

Conclusion

Comprehending planning as "a field where interests and social groups meet and clash under conditions created by the interaction of multiple forces" (Melucci 1996: 92) underlines its immanent conflicts as part of the sociopolitical sphere. This chapter has outlined that planning processes tackling this dimension of conflict by building on the logic of the rational argument and employing discursive conflict avoidance strategies (directed at consensus building) make emancipatory moments *a priori* impossible. An opening up of planning processes to a broader involvement of stakeholders thus not necessarily results in their democratization. On the contrary, they might consolidate existing power structures. Substantiated by considerations of radical democracy, it was argued that the goal of eliminating the conflict dimension of social reality through rational consensus formation is not worth pursuing. A more fruitful approach towards creating emancipatory dimensions of planning is to acknowledge the antagonisms and power structures that are inherent in all social spheres. An emancipatory understanding of planning is based on the democratic principle of equality "in the sense of . . . the power of those who have no special entitlement to exercise power" (Rancière 2011: 79). Conceiving of democracy as a collective capacity to act enables the notion of emancipation as self-empowerment. It presupposes a type of equality that capacitates action as a response to everyday concerns and the needs of every 'average person'. An emancipatory understanding therefore also requires the recognition of conflict and division as constitutive elements of pluralist societies in which a myriad of interests, needs, values and attitudes are not always compatible.

> Since we cannot eliminate antagonism, we need to domesticate it to a condition of agonism in which passion is mobilised constructively (rather than destructively) towards the promotion of democratic decisions that are partly consensual, but which also respectfully accept unresolvable disagreements.
>
> (Hillier 2003: 42)

At the level of planning practice, this means that compromises and arrangements between divergent positions are not to be derived through the logic of a rational consensus, but rather by means of building up of mutual understanding at the level of acting together. This would imply shifting the focus from the discursive level of traditional participatory planning instruments such as negotiations 'around the table', panel discussions or information events (Figure 12.4) to one centred on action by using methods that actively engage people with one another (Figure 12.5). It is of central importance that

Figure 12.4 Photograph showing a discussion event hosted for citizens as part of an urban planning project

Source: Plansinn, 2016

Figure 12.5 Photograph illustrating action-based planning

Source: Hannah Hentschel, 2016

such action moments are embedded within everyday life practices and reflect the different living realities of participants.

The actual democratization of planning procedures and realization of emancipatory potentials within them cannot be achieved solely through the involvement of different stakeholders while decision-making processes remain non-transparent for most affected populations. Swyngedouw (2005) illustrates that current participatory governance processes are characterized by a lack of democratic legitimacy:

> The status, inclusion or exclusion, legitimacy, system of representation, scale of operation and internal or external accountability of such groups or individuals often take place in non-transparent, *ad hoc* and context-dependent ways and differ greatly from those associated with pluralist democratic rules and codes.
>
> (*Ibid.*: 1999, original emphasis)

Knierbein's (2015) critique of the prevailing affirmative governance model is concerned with the "diffusion of economic thinking into planning and the dominance of business-related topics in the agendas of universities teaching planning" (*Ibid.*: 54). She points to the conceptual use of target groups as a "transfer of categories from the field of business economics into empirical sociology" (*Ibid.*: 53). Moreover, the concept of a target group is accompanied by a fuzzy idea of representation, which is characterized by not only frequently non-transparent and arbitrary invitation procedures, but also a lack of attention given to the obligations of the representatives towards those who are supposed to be represented. This leads to "more autocratic, non-transparent systems of governance that—as institutions—wield considerable power and, thus, assign considerable, albeit internally uneven power, to those who are entitled . . . to participate" (Swyngedouw 2005: 2000).

The central prerequisite is therefore ensuring real transparency of planning procedures. This means that decisions throughout the entire process, from its inception through its design, the involvement and exclusion of actors and its closing must be democratically decided on established and publicly accountable rules. Planning decisions should be "embodied in an institutional setting which offers all actors a real possibility of participating in planning policy decision-making and which recognises the ultimate non-consensual undecidability of decisions and hence makes it possible to disagree" (Hillier 2002: 130). Thus, the most essential aspect for an emancipatory understanding of planning requires recognizing that no planning situation can be created free of power relations. Instead of striving for this unattainable ideal, it is crucial for an emancipatory planning approach to recognize power as aporia of the social world.

In planning practice, therefore, it is important to raise the sensitivity of planners and, in particular, to address those groups of persons who are exposed to structural discrimination, disadvantages or individual impairments. Following Hillier (2002), "planners should be aware of the existence of intractable opposition and resistance as well as searching for agreement" (*Ibid*.: 133). There will hardly ever be a situation in which all affected people are satisfied with planning outcomes; however, it should be at the heart of planners to realize situations in which the marginalized will not be worse off. Finally, the unattainability of the absolute ideal of emancipatory planning must always be acknowledged, precisely because in the necessity of permanent contestations and reflections lies its emancipatory content.

Note

1. Terms like 'cooperative planning', 'collaborative planning' or 'deliberative planning' mostly refer to similar ideas and conceptions. For a detailed discussion of different approaches subsumed under this paradigm, see Allmendinger (2002).

References

Allmendinger, P. (2002) The Post-Positivist Landscape of Planning Theory. In P. Allmendinger and M. Tewdwr-Jones (eds.) *Planning Futures: New Directions for Planning Theory*. London: Routledge, pp. 3–17.

Brown, W. (2011) We Are All Democrats Now . . . In G. Agamben, A. Badiou, D. Bensaïd, W. Brown, J.L. Nancy, J. Rancière, K. Ross and S. Žižek (eds.) *Democracy in What State?* New York: Columbia University Press, pp. 44–57.

Fainstein, S. (2000) New Directions in Planning Theory. *Urban Affairs Review* 35(4), pp. 451–478.

Foucault, M. (1978) *The History of Sexuality, Volume 1: An Introduction*. New York: Pantheon Books.

Gunder, M. (2003) Passionate Planning for the Others' Desire: An Agonistic Response to the Dark Side of Planning. *Progress in Planning* 60(3), pp. 235–319.

Habermas, J. (1984 [1981]) *The Theory of Communicative Action: Reason and the Rationalization of Society*. Boston: Beacon Press.

Harris, N. (2002) Collaborative Planning: From Theoretical Foundations to Practice Forms. In P. Allmendinger and M. Tewdwr-Jones (eds.) *Planning Futures: New Directions for Planning Theory*. London: Routledge, pp. 21–43.

Healey, P. (1992) Planning through Debate: The Communicative Turn in Planning Theory. *Town Planning Review* 63(2), pp. 143–162.

Healey, P. (1997a) Situating Communicative Practices: Moving Beyond Urban Political Economy. *Planning Theory* 17, pp. 65–82.

Healey, P. (1997b) *Collaborative Planning: Shaping Places in Fragmented Societies*. Basingstoke: Macmillan.

Hillier, J. (2002) Direct Action and Agonism in Democratic Planning Practice. In P. Allmendinger and M. Tewdwr-Jones (eds.) *Planning Futures: New Directions for Planning Theory*. London: Routledge, pp. 110–135.

Hillier, J. (2003) Agon'izing over Consensus: Why Habermasian Ideals Cannot Be 'Real'. *Planning Theory* 2(1), pp. 37–59.

Innes, J.E. (2004) Consensus Building: Clarifications for the Critics. *Planning Theory* 3(1), pp. 5–20.

Jouve, B. (2005) From Government to Urban Governance in Western Europe: A Critical Analysis. *Public Administration and Development* 25(4), pp. 285–294.

Knierbein, S. (2015) Zielgruppen in der räumlichen Planung: Ein Zwischenruf. In S. Huning, T. Kuder and H. Nuissl (eds.) *Stadtentwicklung, Planungstheorie und Planungsgeschichte auf dem Prüfstand: Herausforderungen für Forschung und Lehre. Sonderausgabe der Planungsrundschau*. Berlin: Planungsrundschau, pp. 51–66.

Melucci, A. (1996) *Challenging Codes: Collective Action in the Information Age*. Cambridge: Cambridge University Press.

Mouffe, C. (2009) *The Democratic Paradox*. London: Verso.

Mouffe, C. (2013) *Agonistics: Thinking the World Politically*. London: Verso.

Ober, J. (2008) The Original Meaning of 'Democracy': Capacity to Do Things, Not Majority Rule. *Constellations* 15(1), pp. 3–9.

Purcell, M. (2009) Resisting Neoliberalization: Communicate Planning or Counter-Hegemonic Movements? *Planning Theory* 8(2), pp. 140–165.

Rancière, J. (1999) *Disagreement: Politics and Philosophy*. Minneapolis: University of Minnesota Press.

Rancière, J. (2011) Democracies against Democracy: An Interview with Eric Hazan. In G. Agamben, A. Badiou, D. Bensaïd, W. Brown, J.L. Nancy, J. Rancière, K. Ross and S. Žižek (eds.) *Democracy in What State?* New York: Columbia University Press, pp. 76–81.

Ross, K. (2011) Democracy for Sale. In G. Agamben, A. Badiou, D. Bensaïd, W. Brown, J.L. Nancy, J. Rancière, K. Ross and S. Žižek (eds.) *Democracy in What State?* New York: Columbia University Press, pp. 82–99.

Swyngedouw, E. (2005) Governance Innovation and the Citizen: The Janus Face of Governance-Beyond-the-State. *Urban Studies* 42(11), pp. 1991–2006.

Wilson, J. and Swyngedouw, E. (2015) Seeds of Dystopia: Post-Politics and the Return of the Political. In J. Wilson and E. Swyngedouw (eds.) *The Post-Political and Its Discontents: Spaces of Depoliticisation, Spectres of Radical Politics*. Edinburgh: Edinburgh University Press, pp. 1–22.

Žižek, S. (1992) *Enjoy Your Symptom!: Jacques Lacan in Hollywood and Out*. London: Routledge.

13 Public Space Activism in Unstable Contexts

Emancipation From Beirut's Postmemory

Christine Mady

Introduction

During conflicts such as wars, the rhythms of urban social practices are disrupted and the priority for security predominates. The primacy of security changes urban spaces from polyrhythmic to arrhythmic (Lefebvre 2004). Social relations and practices that generate heterogeneous public spaces seem to be eradicated not only by immediate conflicts but also by post-conflict narratives. This chapter investigates how public spaces become reconstituted within such contexts. In periods of stability, public spaces are enlivened through diverse publics' activities (Pask 2010). These spaces are avoided when political conflict and instability prevail, for instance during war. What happens when public spaces cease to provide opportunities for encounter and 'unplanned interaction' between disparate bodies and things (Amin 2012: 71; Watson 2006)? The answer is similar to Arendt's (1998 [1958]) analogy of people gathered around a table, who suddenly find themselves sitting without the table: "so that two persons sitting opposite each other were no longer separated but also would be entirely unrelated to each other by anything tangible" (Arendt 1998 [1958]: 53). The metaphor of resetting the table entails understanding the relation among these persons and the events linking them. Similarly, reinstating public spaces goes beyond the mere provision of the physical space. A suitable context to investigate this situation is Beirut, Lebanon, which has undergone conflict due to war and has witnessed ongoing instability.

This chapter focuses on public space activism, which in this case refers to "forging strategic linkages, mobilising people not otherwise connected with activism, and providing a more accessible and generalised language for advocacy and citizen engagement" (Pask 2010: 231). This understanding of people and their social practices is context specific (Knierbein 2015) and considers the meanings, qualities and values attached to spaces (Healey 2006: 128), prior to enabling the reinstatement of the spaces' social practices.

The chapter examines NAHNOO's work, an organization which succeeded in reopening Beirut's largest urban park, Horsh Beirut, after a closure of about 40 years since the civil war's outbreak in 1975. It argues that

NAHNOO contributed to the emancipation of Horsh (or forest) Beirut by dismantling postmemory, a term defined by Hirsch (2008) and explained later in the chapter, which is affecting people's socio-spatial practices and contributing to deepening war-generated divides. Since the civil war's end in 1989, Beirut still witnesses episodes of political instability, while remaining a lively city with various social practices forming its everyday life rhythm. NAHNOO's public space activism emerged within a context characterized by the dominance of politico-sectarian conflicts, a weak state and market-dominant development. This organization owes its ability to influence decision-making to its aversion to mainstream politico-sectarian affiliations and its concentration on building social cohesion, away from an entrepreneurial approach. These affiliations refer to differentiations amongst Christians and Muslims based on belonging to institutionalized politico-sectarian parties. The following sections present public spaces' role as media for encounter and social interaction, then explore memory and public space. The context of Beirut is introduced as background to NAHNOO's activism in reopening the forest. Horsh Beirut serves to demonstrate the relational approach to the reinstatement of public space in Beirut's fragmented society.

Conflict, Instability and Public Space Activism

Instability can lead to political action and also generate uncertainty about public spaces, providing fertile grounds for cultivating fear amongst people (Esposito De Vita 2014). Such tensions were witnessed in Istanbul, Brussels, Paris and Berlin after recent terror attacks and varying degrees of political instability. Unmitigated fear of public spaces could limit social practices to small communal spaces lacking in diversity, marking the end of public life (Watson 2006). This happened in Beirut, where during conflict and instability people became conditioned to frequenting secured spaces, such as controlled shopping centres, or remaining within socially homogeneous areas controlled by a political party (Khalaf 2002). Social interaction was confined to the familiar. Conflict and instability generate contexts of 'weak planning' (Andres 2013: 760) in states whose authorities are unable to provide secure public spaces; the spaces are either closed, inaccessible or controlled through surveillance. Market-led developers use political instability as a way to emphasize the space's exchange value over its use value, which often eradicates public space. Under such circumstances, third parties not affiliated with authorities or the market act to reinstate public spaces, focusing on shifting or de-commodifying them from an exchangeable resource to places with use value (Lefebvre 1991), often using media as a platform for such change. In unstable contexts, a relational perspective on public space is useful to understand this versatile role (Tornaghi and Knierbein 2015). Firstly, spatially reinstating the rhythm of everyday life within a specific spatio-temporal context to ensure the integrity of public space can be an important step in preserving social vitality (Knierbein 2015). Reestablishing such a rhythm becomes highly significant in socially challenged contexts within highly securitized environments. Secondly, public space could serve as a medium facilitating and enabling encounter, coexistence of difference and social interaction over time (*Ibid.*). In unstable contexts, 'the management of co-existence' in shared space requires an understanding of social relations and learning different ways of thinking and organizing (Healey 2006: 111), as well as an understanding of the range of everyday life practices. The latter requires a public platform to exchange 'local knowledge' openly, through the acknowledgement and acceptance of differences and their use to mobilize discussion into action (*Ibid.*: 129). Therefore, public spaces could be the medium for understanding social relations and the basis for establishing a social dynamic that is conducive to change. Moving from understanding to reinstating the use value of public spaces entails some form of individual or collective action for empowering people and 'de-alienating' public spaces (Knierbein 2015: 54).

As politics-related conflict leads to severing relations among people in shared spaces, empowering people in divided societies could begin by defining "how other people do things and what they are encouraged to value" (Healey 2006: 112). In divided societies, various social structures affect spatial practices (*Ibid.*), which could lead to differentiation, discrimination and exclusion. These divides could be entrenched over generations, affecting "ways of being, of giving meaning and value to things and relations, and in styles of expression" (*Ibid.*: 118–119). Conflict-generated modes of use and perceptions of people in public spaces need to be dismantled through action, by forging links in public spaces to those who are not kin or part of one's community (Healey 2006). One intangible consideration is the mnemonic role of public spaces as memory containers, and their meanings for different users. Elzanowski (2014) indicates how city planning and management authorities have the capacity to reconfigure public memory in such spaces. In addition to empowerment, public space activism in conflict situations could reinstate them in everyday life by seeking to liberate these spaces from post-memories (Hirsch 2008), which trap the spaces in between the past imbued with the war and the present.

Public Spaces as Mnemonic Tools

Before addressing postmemory, the role of memory is examined. The term memory refers to context-specific, previously acquired knowledge that is dynamic and represents many, often conflicting, voices (Larkin 2012). Memories are transferred, displaced and replaced in a process of embossing and/or forgetting experiences and practices within the framework of a construct (cultural, social, political, religious or other). Larkin (2012: 12) refers to this process as "colonising time" by selecting the timeline of events and places.

Memory dynamics are spatial, where experience in space-time provides the mnemonic tool for memory's images and sensations (Hebbert 2005). Over time, urban memories could undergo 'displacement' (Larkin 2012: 14) through the demolition, renaming, adaptive reuse or annihilation of spaces, which impact collective remembering, and forgetting.

> The shaping of space is an instrument for the shaping of memory. A shared space such as a street can be a locus of collective memory in a double sense. It can express group identity from above, through architectural order, monuments and symbols, commemorative sites, street names, civic spaces, and historic conservation; and it can express the accumulation of memories from below, through the physical and associative traces left by interweaving patterns of everyday life.
>
> (Hebbert 2005: 592)

Collective memories are formed through the experiences of different groups of people within urban spaces (Larkin 2012). Collective memory is historically and culturally framed yet transformed through 'narratives and commemorative practices' (Larkin 2012: 13). These narratives are often used to forge an identity, where "historic events, actors and interactions are woven into a unifying story, linking past to present and providing sequential progression, moral instruction and pointing towards a conclusive ending" (Larkin 2012: 16). Through urban social practices, spatial habits persisting over time are imprinted in individual and collective memories, similar to sporadic experiences that could leave traces or scars. Highmore (2002: 6) explains, in reference to Freud's *The Psychopathology of Everyday Life* (1901 [2001]), how the everyday holds beyond its 'actuality' a hidden layer that could be desire or fear, capable of disrupting everyday life and impacting people collectively. In prolonged conflict situations such as war, several generations are involved; their memories and postmemories might affect their spatial practices. While collective memories refer to past experiences of several people, postmemory according to Hirsch (2008) is an inherited form of memory that "forges both mnemonic bonds to the past . . . and repressive binds with the present" (Larkin 2012: 2), endangering the displacement of present-time stories by histories. Postmemory is "not personally experienced but socially felt" and is often used to affirm identities, traditions or even assert continuity (Larkin 2012: 10), for example war stories associated with specific spaces. For the post-war generation, postmemory narratives "risk having one's own stories and experiences displaced, even evacuated, by those of a previous generation" (Hirsch 2008: 107, cited in Larkin 2012: 2). Situating mnemonic public spaces between past and present by awakening collective memories and encouraging present-time practices could turn memory to a "vehicle of contestation of identity" with the potential for 'reconciliation' (Larkin 2012: 18). NAHNOO's attempt to address the latter is the starting point for investigating their public space activism. Mnemonic public spaces referring to collective memories could establish a shared sense of belonging, based on experiencing the space collectively rather than through inherited postmemory narratives trapped in assertive wartime divides, which leak into the present and affect everyday city life. For instance, the enclosure of the Horsh, physical barriers and shrapnel traces in the surroundings activate the postmemory of some publics, while suppressing the collective memories of the park before the war.

Beirut and the Lebanese Context

The 1975–1989 civil war[1] was characterized by social ruptures along politico-sectarian lines, which also led to Beirut's division into a prevailing Christian east and Muslim west. This demarcation began at Martyrs Square in the historical centre (BCD) and ran southward to Horsh Beirut (see Figure 13.1). Public spaces were annihilated and replaced by controlled militia spaces (Khalaf 2002) that were used by politico-sectarian communities. The eradication of pre-war public spaces[2] meant a total disruption of everyday city life (Mady 2012) and the dominance of splintered identities (Bollens 2012).

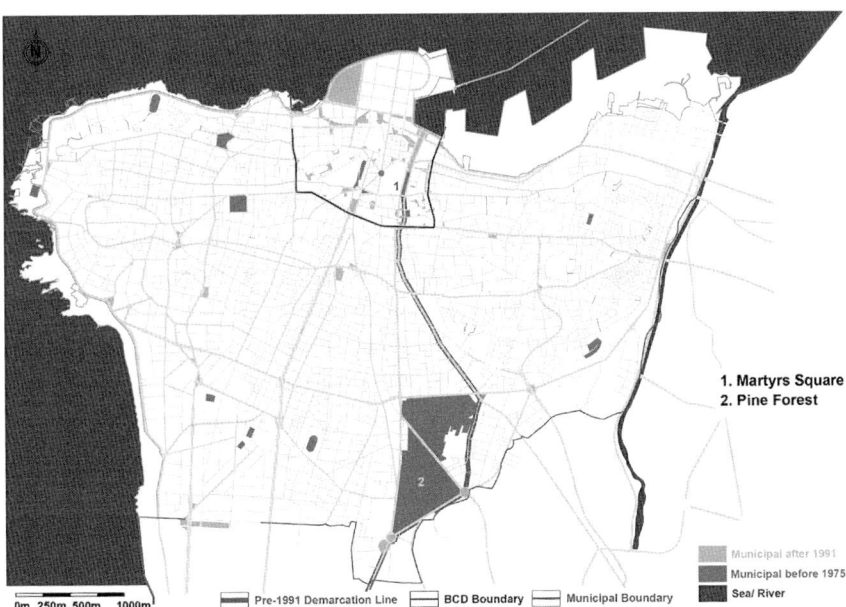

Figure 13.1 Map of Beirut indicating the reconstructed city centre BCD (Beirut Central District), the wartime demarcation line along Damascus Road, Martyrs Square and Horsh Beirut

Source: Christine Mady, 2010

The 1989 Taif Agreement signalled the war's end, and the process of unblocking streets and reconnecting the divided city began. The reopening of public spaces such as parks and squares took longer and was coupled with a high level of direct control mechanisms: complete closure, limited opening times, security patrols and CCTVs. Horsh Beirut and Martyrs Square (Khalaf 2006) remained as vacant spaces until 2005 and 2015 respectively, reminding inhabitants of the wartime divides and reflecting the post-war challenges of public space provision, which is "creating public space that is not coloured by sectarian and religious hues" (Bollens 2012: 190), or in Kabbani's (1998) terms, neutral spaces, not affiliated with political or sectarian belongings. The need in Beirut to be present in a specific location and liberated from the association to politico-sectarian belonging was imminent.

After the war, memories of wartime territorial divisions continued to affect public spaces along the demarcation line (Saksouk-Sasso 2015), often limiting their use. This was partly due to the prevailing situation with a weak state (Seidman 2012) confronted with the domination of politico-sectarian authorities within different regions of the city. Public spaces not within authorities' control were often secured by the state by limiting access to them or completely closing them, as in the case of the Horsh. In 2005, Beirut began to undergo heightened 'processes of securitisation' (Monroe 2011: 91) with some parts being fortified with defensive features. These spatial changes reconfigured how people used highly controlled public spaces and further led to the 'erosion of urban public space' (Seidman 2012: 8), creating public-less spaces (Yahya 2004), or spaces without users. Under these circumstances, people's needs for urban spaces and other facilities, including medical and educational, were often met by the politico-sectarian authorities (Myntti 2016) who also defined their territories within the city, thus establishing a sense of belonging to a community within a city rather than to the whole city (Seidman 2012). People of the post-war generations are cautious of these post-2005 multifaceted politico-sectarian, communal and mental divides, affecting which places they frequent and with whom they interact outside their communities (cf. Bou Akar 2012; Fawaz et al. 2009; Deeb and Harb 2013). These divides (Monroe 2011) are generating new spatial practices (Mady and Chettiparamab 2016) and are significantly defining the geography of public spaces in post-war Beirut. This situation, together with the increase in securitized consumer spaces (Fawaz et al. 2009), generated a mismatch between the municipally designated public-less spaces and those practised by people (Saksouk-Sasso 2015), such as Beirut's waterfront (or 'corniche') or empty lots frequented for public activities. In BCD and along the demarcation line, the memory narrative has focused on the mnemonic 'displacement' of the past (Larkin 2012) rather than facing or completely forgetting it (Yahya 2004). For young Lebanese, who according to Larkin (2012: 2) are "caught between the contradictory forces of collective memory and social forgetting", this approach meant a new construct of public spaces: knowing about the spaces' past without experiencing their traces.

NAHNOO and Public Spaces

In 2003, a group of students at the Lebanese University, the only public university, started a student club whose mission was to organize cultural activities that are non-religious and dissociated from local politics in a context with prevailing politico-sectarian belongings. Constant reference to 'us' as opposed to 'we' (war-inherited differentiations) dominated and led the students to select the name NAHNOO ('we' in Arabic), an inclusive 'we' that welcomes differences. Living through the series of crises in 2005 through 2007, when divisions within Lebanese society were exacerbated and an atmosphere of instability prevailed, NAHNOO founders who had graduated, defined their mission as promoting social cohesion. This decision stems from the founders' understanding that many problems originate from how the Lebanese have been "conditioned at our [their] homes to deal with differences". NAHNOO clearly state: "Our advocacy is not to let sects predominate" (Executive director at NAHNOO, personal interview, 12 July 2016). In 2009, NAHNOO registered as a non-profit association at the Ministry of Interior, and later in 2013, as an NGO, making it independent from the government. NAHNOO's mission statement is:

> NAHNOO is a non-sectarian and non-partisan youth-led organisation whose ambition is to build a socially cohesive society that is grounded in laws that protect individual differences of all types, and is supported by effective and transparent public institutions that reflect and realise the citizens' aspirations. It is a platform for self-development and civic engagement specialised in advocacy and participatory local governance.
>
> (Programmes manager at NAHNOO, personal interview, 19 July 2016)

NAHNOO's organization is horizontal, where members, volunteers and youth reorganize themselves for each project. NAHNOO collaborate with other initiatives[3] to raise awareness and engage people in an attempt to mitigate postmemory's effects of wartime divides (*Ibid.*). In promoting social cohesion, NAHNOO have established a portfolio of capacity-building projects, including life-skills, leadership, conflict resolution, advocacy training and awareness-raising on public space.

NAHNOO understood the need for meeting places and "the importance of public spaces to foster social cohesion. However, public spaces, public transport, all that connects people and allows for spontaneous interaction and encounter is missing in Beirut's post-war context" (Executive director at NAHNOO, personal interview, 12 July 2016). This is precisely why NAHNOO decided to "approach youth with familiar concepts to explain the importance of public space" (*Ibid.*). The founder uses the concept of the living room in the Lebanese dwelling to illustrate what its absence means for the family, and accordingly for the urban population. NAHNOO work to cultivate public space through participatory approaches as

> a 'living space', it is physical but also virtual, the online space, and the municipality, which should be open, inclusive and transparent . . . Public spaces gather people, have no stereotypes, allow people to accept each other, and provide for leisure activities and building creative activities.
> (*Ibid.*)

These views, which were informed by daily life and lectures from local experts in urban planning, are deeply similar to Watson's (2006) and Amin's (2012) understanding of public space. Moreover,

> public spaces are part of the collective memory of the city, Martyrs Square, Pine Forest, Ramlet el Bayda. They are a summary of the stories of the city and hence their importance . . . But Beirut's public spaces are empty, and therefore a reflection of its many problems: social, urban, and so on.
> (Executive director at NAHNOO,
> personal interview, 12 July 2016)

NAHNOO explain how neglected spaces are unattractive and acquire negative reputations, associations and memories. This reflects the NGO's understanding of the functional permutations of public spaces in cities undergoing instability. NAHNOO see public space as "an opportunity to decrease

Figure 13.2 NAHNOO's living room, which is used as a meeting and training space within their premises

Source: NAHNOO, 2015

conflicts, as the lack of public spaces cause conflict, when people do not have the chance to develop new types of relations with individuals outside their community" (*Ibid.*). This reflects their awareness that the reinstatement of public spaces starts with the understanding of people and the rebuilding of social relations away from consumer spaces targeting specific social segments.

Horsh Beirut

After the war and with the mnemonic displacement of the Horsh from people's everyday life, it is useful to understand the Horsh's history, which dates back to the 1600s, when Emir Fakhreddin Maan II requested its forestation. In the 1840s under Ottoman rule, the forest became public property and a buffer defining the extents for urban expansion. In 1942, the forest was protected by decree as a natural site, and in the 1960s it was fenced as a public park.[4] The spatial shrinking of the park through time resulted from using regulatory tools to carve out parts of it and circumscribe it with roads (Shayya 2010), a utilitarian approach to public spaces adopted by the Republic (Salam 1998). Following the 1975 war-division, these roads circumscribing Horsh Beirut (see Figure 13.1) demarcated a separation between the west, the east and a buffer area comprising military and official facilities. This situation contributed to the Horsh's annihilation, turning it into no-man's land. The pine trees were burnt down during the war, and afterwards a competition was launched in 1992 to redesign the Horsh. One of its parts referred to as the 'plaza' (Shayya 2010: 24) opened to the public in 1999, and the sports grounds opened in 2003, mainly used by residents in the politico-sectarian polarised immediate surroundings. The forested part was accessible only to foreigners through a permit granted by Beirut municipality and excluded the Lebanese. The justification for this decision was that the Lebanese would vandalize the trees, as they do not value nature, and would cause conflicts based on politico-sectarian disputes.[5] It was not until 2015 that the forest was opened on weekends to the Lebanese public following NAHNOO's activism.

To summarize, the Horsh was gradually transformed from a city-scale public space in the 1800s, to a gap in the city during the war, to a post-war 'neutral' island controlled by the municipality through security wardens, protecting it from the public, with only limited access to select visitors. It became an embedded demarcation area, traced through the tools of confining, enclosing and nurturing postmemories.

NAHNOO and the Emancipation of the Horsh

In light of this exclusionary management and the understanding of the need to free the forest from its imposed narrative, NAHNOO prepared an action plan mobilizing youth to collaborate with the municipality and Beirut's governor, to gradually implement the Horsh's complete reopening.

Based on public space research in Beirut and the identification of the pine forest as one of the few remaining natural open spaces, NAHNOO set the basis for their activism: "the Horsh is central, and should be returned to the city. It is the identity of the city . . . The cause [to act] was born" (Executive director at NAHNOO, personal interview, 12 July 2016). Moreover, what is socially important about this park is that it is surrounded by different communities 'in need of interaction': different politico-sectarian groups and socioeconomic levels, in need of a shared urban living room.

NAHNOO adopted a relational perspective to the park's emancipation by developing a platform for communication allowing people to further understand and share their aspirations for everyday needs. This NGO highlighted various perceptions of the forest:

- A natural space in the city
- Potential meeting place for various activities
- Spatial link within the city between peri-urban and suburban areas
- Mentally 'displaced', a park functioning as a buffer often considered as 'neutral' or 'polarized' in relation to the wartime demarcation line.

These perspectives indicate a relational perspective to the space, which is 'normalized' (Tornaghi 2015: 28), establishing a network among various actors and shared values.

NAHNOO's challenge was changing the status quo without creating other forms of exclusion. Their strategy was based on several tactics, including using popular language and social media, generating activities for different user groups, empowering people and organizing awareness campaigns.

Being a group of young university graduates with acquired public space expertise helped NAHNOO address people with the 'common person's language' through the broadly accessible means of social media (see Figure 13.3). In facing the obstacle of the government's negative outlook

Figure 13.3 'Our horsh, our stories' campaign leaflet to reinsert Horsh Beirut into its surrounding context by enabling dialogue across wartime divides

Source: NAHNOO, 2015

towards the public, this NGO empowered people by helping them understand their right to the pine forest and the beauty of this natural spot within Beirut's dense urban fabric. The use of both local and international media "meant everyone knew about the Horsh, in addition to the campaigns we did at schools and universities and the events we organised" (Programmes manager at NAHNOO, personal interview, 19 July 2016).

In generating activities for various users, holding workshops and conducting surveys, NAHNOO identified people's needs for public spaces around the forest. By 2013, "people started knowing about the Horsh and the municipality took the decision to open it" (*Ibid.*), but this did not materialize until 5 September 2015.

Between 5 September 2015 and 5 August 2016 when NAHNOO held a free concert in the park,

> official meetings with the municipality occurred to evaluate the opening but in most cases informal discussions with employees [occurred] to make sure all is well. We were regularly reminding the governor to open it daily, but did not put high pressure given that we felt confident that it was only a matter of a few weeks to months. Nothing particular happened, we consider the daily opening of the park a continuation of the gradual reopening.
>
> (*Ibid.*)

In June 2016, the Horsh started opening daily (see Figure 13.4).

From 2015 to 2016, NAHNOO observed that Horsh visitors came from a wider geographic area in contrast to its prior use by people from the immediate vicinity. Gradually people from different neighbourhoods in Beirut started visiting, and later people from the suburbs started coming, too. However, the gate along the park's southwest edge remained closed, excluding visitors from that neighbourhood resulting in the continuation of a wartime divide. Despite NAHNOO's notification, the municipality postponed opening this gate, stating that "it is hard to control the people going to that gate" (Programmes Manager at NAHNOO, personal communication, 13 February 2017).

When asked about people's reactions, one manager in the NGO responded: "People were ecstatic. Their reactions can be observed through Facebook. Of course, many also complain about the lack of maintenance, some littering, or that it is not dog-friendly" (*Ibid.*). NAHNOO try to establish attachment to the Horsh by engaging people through weekly volunteering: "People are 'live surveillance' and always inform us if something is happening in the park. They are our eye on the ground and they participate in the campaigns" (*Ibid.*).

NAHNOO continue to act as mediator between the public and municipality by partaking in the park's management committee created by Beirut's governor. They also act as the protector of public rights to the Horsh.

Figure 13.4 A poster by NAHNOO. The text reads: 'A musical celebration in Horsh Beirut' on reopening of Horsh Beirut following over 20 years of closure, NAHNOO invites you to a musical concert in Horsh Beirut to celebrate the opening of the park on Friday 5 August 2016 at 17.30. The concert programme: Ingrid Naccour – a group of English songs, the band Noul – Arabic songs, Mona Hallab accompanied by guitar: Baheej Jaroudi, the band 4 notes – Arabic jazz. Free entrance for all'

Source: NAHNOO, 2015

Over a five-year period, using various tactics presented in Table 13.1, this NGO managed to transform the Horsh from a sporadically inhabited site to one habitually involving diverse actors with panoply of activities.

Following this overview on the park's emancipation, two questions remain: Were NAHNOO's objectives met? Does this project serve as a pilot for public space emancipation in unstable contexts? First, NAHNOO state, "We had two objectives: open the park, and activate it" (Executive director at NAHNOO, personal interview, 12 July 2016). While the first goal was achieved after persevering for almost five years, the second objective is in progress. Activating the park means reintegrating it with its surroundings both physically and socially. Physical, logistic and political reasons distance NAHNOO from their second objective. Their executive director states, "We accomplished people's trust in NAHNOO, and became an example of how to do campaigns for public spaces . . . the Horsh was the template that NAHNOO used to initiate its different other campaigns" (*Ibid.*). One is their current activism along Beirut's waterfront. As a result, NAHNOO believe that they have built an NGO for the emancipation of public spaces.

Discussion and Conclusion

This chapter examined the struggle of reinstating public spaces in contexts of conflict and instability beyond their physical provision, through spatial practices, which enable social interaction and support social practices. The context of Beirut's intermittent instability embodied the challenge of reinstating 'neutral' public spaces that are inclusive within the context of politico-sectarian societal divides. In 2003, through the city's only public university, NAHNOO emerged to engage in public life and defined themselves as a non-sectarian entity and NGO focused on supporting social cohesion. NAHNOO developed a mechanism to reinstate public spaces within everyday urban life through an emancipatory approach mitigating the impact of postmemories.

The chapter focused on what must be learned, what links should be forged and what scales planning processes should address (Mady and Chettipa-ramab 2016) to reinstate public spaces. Similar to other conflict situations (Esposito De Vita 2014), the role of establishing a dialogue platform by building on collective memory to mitigate postmemory and reinstating physical and mental connections to marginalized spaces was examined through NAHNOO's campaigns. Through a relational perspective, NAHNOO emphasized understanding the role of public spaces, the people and their social practices. Communicating through popular language, NAHNOO managed to approach and engage people in organized activities, thus disconnecting them from the war-set structures of postmemory, which affect their current spatial practices. This was demonstrated in NAHNOO's activism for reopening Horsh Beirut and reinstating its use value as an urban interface.

Some limitations to this approach include the lack of documentation on the users after the reopening, which is one of NAHNOO's next tasks.

Table 13.1 Timeline of NAHNOO's activities related to the reopening of Horsh Beirut

End 2011	2012	2013	2014	2015	2016
Science days organized by NAHNOO	Public visits	NAHNOO appear on the media with the mayor, requesting a date to reopen the Horsh, but no date is specified	Horsh is still closed, campaign remobilization	Townhall meeting and discussion for reopening the Horsh without any clear dates	Daily reopening of the Horsh with limited access hours
NAHNOO school visits	Media mobilization	Municipality gives official decision on opening the Horsh in April	Picnic at the Horsh that was a media highlight, as municipality did not allow journalists to enter	Public statement for a partial reopening of the Horsh	August music festival to celebrate one year since the reopening of the Horsh
Media coverage	Townhall meeting	Meetings between NAHNOO and local authorities continue	Protests in front of the municipality demanding opening of the Horsh	Beirut's governor accepts to meet with NAHNOO for their plan on the partial reopening	NAHNOO stop construction of a hospital within the Horsh premises, which started in June by a municipal order
Presentations at universities by NAHNOO	Meetings with local authorities and municipality, submitting a plan for 'how to' reopen the Horsh	Other NAHNOO public space activism at Beirut's waterfront continue	Conference organized by NAHNOO on public spaces in crisis	Beirut's governor assigns a meeting with NAHNOO to discuss forming an executive committee for the reopening	

Documentary on Horsh, child visits and photography competition

Picnic action and its documentation

NAHNOO send a legal warning of lawsuit in case the Horsh is not reopened

Wigs protest to denounce discriminatory entry policy to the Horsh

Submitting a petition

June first reopening committee meeting, and governor fixing a date in July, delayed until August due to the solid waste management crisis

Municipality allows events inside the Horsh to take place

Townhall meeting and confrontation with the governor

NAHNOO study on legal status of public spaces in Lebanon is completed

September 5 partial opening of the Horsh only on Saturdays

Local authorities accept NAHNOO's proposal for a plan to reopen the Horsh

Regular meetings between the governor and the committee

Source: Christine Mady, 2016

Also, it is evident that one space does not solve the structural problem of politico-sectarian divides, though it appears to cause a ripple effect as more people seek to transcend divides and support social interaction. While this example is embedded in the specific context of Beirut, it demonstrates the possibility of emancipatory public space activism in unstable contexts.

Notes

1. For further information on the politico-sectarian divisions in Lebanon, refer to Hanf (1993), El-Khazen (2000) and Khalaf (2002).
2. Refer to Mady (2012) for a brief overview of Beirut's public spaces.
3. See http://youcitizen.org/events/52-our-horsh-our-stories regarding the identification of social practices around Horsh Beirut.
4. For further information on Horsh Beirut see Shayya (2010).
5. Refer to YouTube coverage of NAHNOO and Beirut's mayor (www.youtube.com/watch?v=FxmrU7jgQ00; www.youtube.com/watch?v=_dyEkA93AUs; www.youtube.com/watch?v=RJUltXkUfls), and stories related to this discrimination.

References

Amin, A. (2012) *Land of Strangers*. Cambridge: Polity.

Andres, L. (2013) Differential Spaces, Power Hierarchy and Collaborative Planning: A Critique of the Role of Temporary Uses in Shaping and Making Places. *Urban Studies* 50(4), pp. 759–775.

Arendt, H. (1998 [1958]) *The Human Condition*, 2nd ed. [first in 1958]. London and Chicago: The University of Chicago Press.

Bollens, S.A. (2012) *City and Soul in Divided Societies*. Oxfordshire, New York: Routledge.

Bou Akar, H. (2012) Contesting Beirut's Frontiers. *City and Society* 24(2), pp. 150–172.

Deeb, L. and Harb, M. (2013) *Leisurely Islam: Negotiating Geography and Morality in Shi'ite South Beirut*. Princeton, NJ and Oxford: Princeton University Press.

El-Khazen, F. (2000) *The Breakdown of the State in Lebanon*. Cambridge, MA: Harvard University Press.

Elzanowski, J. (2014) Memorials and Material Dislocation: The Politics of Public Space in Warsaw. In A. Madanipour, S. Knierbein and A. Degros (eds.) *Public Spaces and the Challenges of Urban Transformation in Europe*. Oxon: Routledge, pp. 88–102.

Esposito De Vita, G. (2014) Segregative Power of Violence in Belfast and Naples: Exploring the Role of Public Spaces Reconnecting Divided Societies. In A. Madanipour, S. Knierbein and A. Degros (eds.) *Public Spaces and the Challenges of Urban Transformation in Europe*. Oxon: Routledge, pp. 169–182.

Fawaz, M., Harb, M. and Gharbiyeh, A. (eds.) (2009) *Beirut: Mapping Security*. Stuttgart: Diwan.

Freud, S. (1901 [2001]) *The Psychopathology of Everyday Life* (Edited and translated by J. Strachey, A. Freud, A. Strachey and A. Tyson). London: Vintage, Hogarth Press and the Institute of Psycho-Analysis.

Hanf, T. (1993) *Coexistence in Wartime Lebanon: Decline of a State and Rise of a Nation*. London: Centre for Lebanese Studies in association with I. B. Tauris.

Healey, P. (2006) *Collaborative Planning: Shaping Places in Fragmented Societies*, 2nd ed. [first in 1997]. Basingstoke and New York: Palgrave McMillan.

Hebbert, M. (2005) The Street as Locus of Collective Memory. *Environment and Planning D* 23(4), pp. 581–596.

Highmore, B. (ed.) (2002) *The Everyday Life Reader*. London and New York: Routledge.

Hirsch, M. (2008) The Generation of Postmemory. *Poetics Today* 29(1), pp. 103–128.

Kabbani, O. (1998) Public Space as Infrastructure: The Case of Postwar Reconstruction of Beirut. In P. Rowe and H. Sarkis (eds.) *Projecting Beirut: Episodes in the Construction and Reconstruction of a Modern City*. Munich, London and New York: Prestel-Verlag, pp. 240–259.

Khalaf, S. (2002) *Civil and Uncivil Violence in Lebanon: A History of Internationalization of Communal Conflict*. New York: Columbia University Press.

Khalaf, S. (2006) *Heart of Beirut: Reclaiming the Bourj*. London: Palgrave Macmillan.

Knierbein, S. (2015) Public Space as Relational Counter Space: Scholarly Minefield or Epistemological Opportunity? In C. Tornaghi and S. Knierbein (eds.) *Public Space and Relational Perspectives: New Challenges for Architecture and Planning*. London and New York: Routledge, pp. 44–68.

Larkin, C. (2012) *Memory and Conflict in Lebanon: Remembering and Forgetting the Past*. Oxon, New York: Routledge.

Lefebvre, H. (1991) *The Production of Space* (Translated by D. Nicholson-Smith). Oxford: Blackwell.

Lefebvre, H. (2004) *Rhythmanalysis: Space, Time and Everyday Life*. London and New York: Continuum.

Mady, C. (2012) A Short Story of Beirut's Public Spaces. *Area* 120, pp. 36–37.

Mady, C. and Chettiparamab, A. (2016) Planning in the Face of 'Deep Divisions': A View from Beirut, Lebanon. *Planning Theory* (Advance online publication). doi: 10.1177/1473095216639087, pp. 1–23.

Monroe, K.V. (2011) Being Mobile in Beirut. *City and Society* 23(1), pp. 91–111.

Myntti, C. (2016) Civic Engagement in a Challenging Political Context: The Neighborhood Initiative at the American University of Beirut, Lebanon. *The Journal of General Education* 26(4), pp. 238–246.

Pask, A. (2010) Public Space Activism, Toronto and Vancouver. In J. Hou (ed.) *Insurgent Space: Guerrilla Urbanism and the Remaking of Contemporary Cities*. Oxon, New York: Routledge.

Saksouk-Sasso, A. (2015) Making Spaces for Communal Sovereignty: The Story of Beirut's Dalieh. *Arab Studies Journal* 23(1), pp. 296–318.

Salam, A. (1998) The Role of Government in Shaping the Built Environment. In P. Rowe and H. Sarkis (eds.) *Projecting Beirut: Episodes in the Construction and Reconstruction of a Modern City*. Munich, London and New York: Prestel, pp. 122–133.

Seidman, S. (2012) The Politics of Cosmopolitan Beirut from the Stranger to the Other. *Theory, Culture and Society* 29(2), pp. 3–36.

Shayya, F. (ed.) (2010) *At the Edge of the City: Reinhabiting Public Space toward the Recovery of Beirut's Horsh Al-Sanawbar*. Beirut: Discursive Formations.

Tornaghi, C. (2015) The Relational Ontology of Public Space and Action-Oriented Pedagogy in Action: Dilemmas of Professional Ethics and Social Justice.

In C. Tornaghi and S. Knierbein (eds.) *Public Space and Relational Perspectives: New Challenges for Architecture and Planning*. London and New York: Routledge, pp. 17–41.

Tornaghi, C. and Knierbein, S. (eds.) (2015) *Public Space and Relational Perspectives: New Challenges for Architecture and Planning*. London and New York: Routledge.

Watson, S. (2006) *City Publics: The (Dis)enchantments of Urban Encounters*. Oxon: Routledge.

Yahya, M. (2004) *Let the Dead Be Dead: Memory, Urban Narratives and the Post-Civil War Reconstitution of Beirut*. Centre of Contemporary Culture of Barcelona (CCCB) Conference: Urban Traumas. The City and Disasters, Barcelona: CCCB, 7–11 July.

Part IV

Active Emancipation.
On Influence, Recovery
and Hybrid Ownership

14 'The City Decides!'

Political Standstill and Social Movements in Post-Industrial Naples

Stefania Ragozino and Andrea Varriale

Introduction

Conflicts and power relations are constitutive elements of planning (Flyvbjerg 1998; Forester 1988). Therefore, a decisive factor for emancipation is who is included in the decision-making and the implementation processes, and how (Albrechts 2003). A short digression into grammar may help clarify this point. As a verb, 'emancipate' has a transitive (to emancipate somebody) and a reflexive form (to emancipate oneself from something). These two usages point at very different processes. The transitive and reflexive forms differ in directionality and agency. This tension of possessing or receiving the ability to 'emancipate' creates a tension that is also found in how the Italian planning approaches have dealt with issues of social welfare in the last decades. Italy's 'comprehensive' planning model (Benevolo 1974), which prevailed from the 1960s until the early 1980s, largely relied on the 'transitive' understanding of emancipation. Despite their explicitly progressive nature and their concern with the underprivileged, such planning policies embodied a typically top-down design, whereby beneficiaries remained on the receiving end of its measures (Esposito De Vita 2014).

Italy started veering from a command-and-control model to one based on 'governance' (Balducci 2000) in the early 1980s. Planning no longer took the form of a fixed, long-term *piano regolatore* (masterplan) produced by professionals. Rather, the plan became a matter of negotiation between public and private interests, had a more 'operative' nature and referred to shorter time frames for negotiations and policy reviews. Factors behind this change included a growing perception that traditional masterplans were too 'rigid' and that leaner tools were needed and a shift within the discipline towards abandoning the 'overly political' goals of spatial equity (Bianchetti 2011). Furthermore, the increased autonomy of cities and regional administrations put pressure on politicians to keep pace with urban change within their elected terms to ensure their ability to sell themselves as effective politicians (Servillo and Lingua 2014).

Critics warned that the pursuit of these goals might increase the ability of private individuals and small groups to shape planning at the expense of broader publics. Partially due to such concerns, cities like Naples continued to use traditional, 'armchair' approaches to planning. However, the choice of Naples should be understood through its post-war urbanization. Urban development has been dominated by real estate and developer interests, which has resulted in poorly controlled expansion of built environments (Pacione 1987; Allum 2003).

In this chapter, we analyze and elaborate on a complex case of post-industrial transformation in contemporary Naples and look at how informal, direct actions are intertwined with the actions of institutions. The regeneration of Bagnoli (1992–current) gathered the attention of several competing actors, due to its economic, political and social significance. These conflicts, we argue, provided fertile soil for potentially emancipatory practices to unfold. The case at hand condenses a set of environmental, cultural, economic, social and political issues, as well as conflicts between central and local institutions, between local institutions and local communities, and among locals. We discuss how emancipatory potentials are created and denied for the actors involved and for the broader public. In our interpretation, emancipation took place, to a certain extent, in instances where previously deprived groups managed to articulate their position and to have their voices heard (but not necessarily listened to). We conceptualize such outcomes as 'cognitive' and 'communicative' emancipation, respectively. Cases of actual, 'practiced' emancipation were few, did not last for very long and concerned marginal spaces.

In 2014, the national government stripped the city of its planning jurisdiction in Bagnoli and has taken over the urban transformation project. The encumbered legal process of remediation remains unfinished and has only intensified conflicts among different interests. This has caused the conflict to take an unusual configuration. Typically, institutional actors are aligned with or at least do not outwardly resist politics at the national level. However, the mayor has broken with national politics to side with local social movements. These movements were formed in the late 2000s and drew on previous political experiences. Since then, they have gathered the support of the mayor and portions of the local citizenry. This side draws on a repertoire of street protests, occupations, public assemblies and claims of embodying 'real', unfettered participation, as opposed to the government's 'undemocratic' plans to transform the area. On the other side are the national government, represented by its development agency, a group of local entrepreneurs, several civic associations and parts of the citizenry. Drawing on a vocabulary of effectiveness, competence and transparency, the national government has later introduced some elements of participatory planning. The relationship between the two sides is one of conflict. This 'tale of two participations' invites a number of empirical and theoretical questions. How did this configuration come about? How do the two sides differ in terms of representation, legitimacy and deliberative power afforded to participants? What happens when the grievances of social movements are openly endorsed by politicians? Would this be a case of 'transitive' emancipation of politicians bestowing their blessing on some social groups? Or are such forms of direct action and protests a sign of 'successful' self-emancipation?

This mixed-methods case study (Yin 2009) was developed along several steps. Firstly, we reconstructed the most salient physical, environmental and urban features of the area in a historical perspective. Secondly, we identified different layers of legislation, planning competences and planning measures in the area by collecting documents and information material and by attending both institutional and informal meetings. The fieldwork consisted of several field visits and direct observation in institutional and activist meetings and 22 in-depth, semi-structured interviews with local politicians, entrepreneurs, activists, professionals and former workers. The remainder of the chapter reviews extant theories of emancipation and presents the case of Bagnoli in terms of planning measures and informal initiatives. Later, we analyze the case with our definition of emancipation and conclude with some theoretical considerations.

Planning Emancipation: A Theoretical and an Empirical Riddle

Emancipation is often associated with approaches that, inspired by communicative action theory, attempt to build consensus among the different interests of a given arena. Prime examples are communicative and collaborative planning (Forester 1988; Healey 1997). Participation is deemed necessary not only for planners to acquire sufficient knowledge about the needs of the relevant communities, but also as a democratizing, progressive project in its own right. While marking a stark departure from older, 'armchair' planning, this approach has been criticized on both practical and theoretical grounds (see also chapter 12). To its critics, a wide gap separates actually existing, consensus-driven planning practices from its ideal, conflict-free model (Hillier 2002: 114). Participative practices may thus mask examples of choreographed participation, i.e. carefully orchestrated sequences of 'open' discussions with citizens who, despite their formally recognized right to participate (and sometimes vote), cannot actually deliberate, nor can they control what issues are brought up for debate. Unable to alter power relations between powerful actors and marginalized communities, participative practices may thus fail to lead to emancipation (Huxley 2000).

The second line of argument, articulated by the so-called second generation of post-positivist planning theorists, sees participatory planning as a theoretical non-starter (Fainstein 2000). Conflict should not be avoided or mitigated, since "suppressing conflict is suppressing freedom" (Flyvbjerg 1998: 209). Rather, conflicts should be allowed to unfold, for they carry the promise of actual change, i.e. a change in the distribution of power (Mouffe 2013). Others concur that "direct action" (Hillier 2002: 118ff) is an irreplaceable contribution to any political confrontation (Melucci 1996; Wilson and Swyngedouw 2014). The main criticism to this line of thought comes from a formal-egalitarian perspective: By relying on self-inclusion, it is argued, direct action risks replacing the unequal distribution of power with a new one (Hillier 2002: 119).

We do not seek to settle the debate from a normative point of view, but rather use it as an analytical framework to clarify some of the complexities of the case of Bagnoli. Hillier (2002), whose classification we draw upon, maps the debate on a two-dimensional graph, in which planning practices are plotted along two dimensions: the degree to which such processes are institutionalized or informal, and the degree of conflict or consensus they entail. In this chapter, emancipation is understood as a process in which groups and individuals are the protagonists of a set of practices of (potentially conflictual) self-inclusion, rather than the addressees of planners' benevolence. We understand emancipation as a transition through which a group of subaltern, marginalized or otherwise deprived people improves its ability to acquire knowledge (cognitive emancipation), articulate positions (communicative emancipation) and ultimately exert influence (practiced emancipation).

Planned Transformation in Bagnoli

By drawing on established and recent literature on the case (Andriello et al. 1991; Di Dato 2016), the following paragraph describes the evolution of Bagnoli as an industrial district and summarizes the main events surrounding its planned transformation after the shutdown of a factory. The former Italsider industrial site is located in the Bagnoli district and is part of the *Campi Flegrei* volcanic area. The area, called *Balneolis* (small baths) in Latin, was used by Roman aristocrats for its thermal sources, and later mainly for agriculture. In the late 18th century, however, Bagnoli became a popular beach resort, thanks also to a railway line that connected it to central Naples. Things changed at the turn of the century: Its proximity to the sea, good communication with the city centre and its level topography led to Bagnoli's hosting of Naples's earliest industrial facilities. This was part of the national government's strategy to finance and plan the industrialization of southern Italy. The first facilities for heavy industry, ranging from the production of concrete, asbestos, steel and other metals, were built in 1911. The entirety of the steelworks and most of the industrial area were owned by the Italian government through its national industrial complex (Institute for Industrial Reconstruction). Originally 220 ha wide, in the early 1960s the area was extended into the sea with a 21-ha artificial platform made of waste material and a 900-m pier to load and unload materials. The industries of Bagnoli employed 8800 workers at its peak in 1973.

Italian steel became less competitive and national and foreign demand for it decreased in the 1980s. Consequently, several Italian steelworks closed. The factory of Bagnoli was shut down in 1992, leaving the city in need of a plan to deal with 7 million cubic metres of built material, over 2100 unemployed workers and a large polluted area. The political debate on the future of Bagnoli had intensified by 1991, when a coalition of leftist and environmentalist politicians started opposing a proposed plan for Naples, called *NeoNapoli*, which had been initiated by a prominent centre-right politician and was based on high building density. The centrist city government collapsed under *Tangentopoli*, a nationwide corruption scandal, and the *NeoNapoli* plan was scrapped. A new city government, supported by parties that opposed *NeoNapoli*, started working on a new plan (technically, an amendment to the city's masterplan of 1972). This move intensified the political confrontation on the future of Bagnoli. Businesses favoured solutions focusing on a leisure harbour, residential facilities and tourism, whereas environmentalists wanted a large park, a free waterfront and low construction volumes and building density. The final version, approved in 1998, envisioned a large park, the remediation of the beach, a tourist port, public and private housing and a convention centre. The city also created an office to inform citizens about the implementation of the plan. In 1996, and based on Ministry guidelines, the Institute for Industrial Reconstruction (IRI) created *Bagnoli SpA*, a joint-stock company tasked to dismantle the factories and carry out the environmental reclamation. In 2001, the central government designated the former industrial site as a *Sito di Interesse Nazionale* (Area of National Interest), and subsequently included it in the national remediation plan.

In 2002, the city of Naples created a new joint-stock company, called *Bagnoli Futura*, to replace the government-owned *Bagnoli SpA* and take over responsibility for the transformation of Bagnoli. The property of the area was transferred from the Italian government to the city of Naples (in the form of the company *Bagnoli SpA*). The municipality of Naples owned the majority of the company's shares and controlled it politically. The company's main task was to complete soil remediation, build public infrastructure and services, and sell the land to private developers. Private companies would then build and resell the real estate. The actual soil remediation began in 2003. Nearly 87m€ and 277m€ were spent for the beach and the industrial area, respectively. In 2012, public prosecutors contested that, as of 2010, only 45% of the total remediation work had been completed (Di Dato 2016). In 2013, the court of Naples ordered that parts of the area be seized by the *Carabinieri*, and placed them under judicial custody.

This prevented *Bagnoli Futura* from working and selling the land. The company management was accused of having mixed the soil in order to lower pollution rates in some patches of land. The managing board of *Bagnoli Futura* was charged with fraud, environmental disaster and illegal disposal of waste. In May 2014, relations between the city administration and the industries deteriorated. The industries, indirectly owned by the government, requested *Bagnoli Futura* to complete the payment for the land the city had acquired in 2001. *Bagnoli Futura*'s inability to pay caused its immediate bankruptcy and ultimately stalled the transformation. Figures 14.1 and 14.2 depict the scenario starting from 2014.

In September 2014, the central government passed a decree titled *Sblocca Italia* (unlocking Italy), which implemented a set of urgent economic measures, including the transformation of Bagnoli. The government granted oversight of the soil remediation and of the implementation of the plan to *Invitalia*, its own development agency, and to a (yet-to-be-appointed) commissioner (Table 14.1).

Invitalia effectively replaced *Bagnoli Futura*, and thus the city administration, as the authority in charge of the transformation of Bagnoli. This stirred conflictual reactions from both the city administration and the social movements in Bagnoli, who feared that the bypassing of normal planning

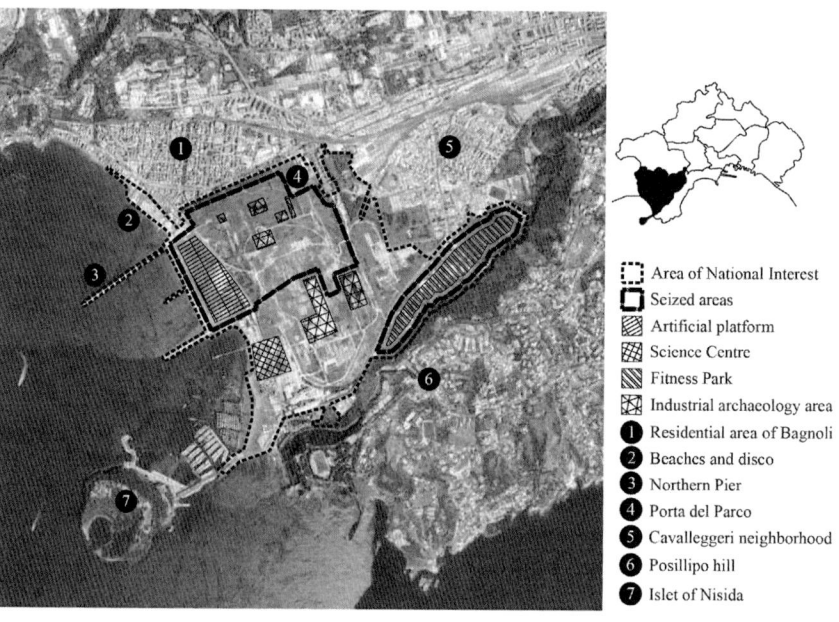

⬜ Area of National Interest
⬛ Seized areas
▨ Artificial platform
▨ Science Centre
▧ Fitness Park
▨ Industrial archaeology area
❶ Residential area of Bagnoli
❷ Beaches and disco
❸ Northern Pier
❹ Porta del Parco
❺ Cavalleggeri neighborhood
❻ Posillipo hill
❼ Islet of Nisida

Figure 14.1 Former industrial site of Bagnoli with the indication of the 10th District of Bagnoli-Fuorigrotta within the municipality of Naples

Source: Stefania Ragozino and Andrea Varriale, 2017

Figure 14.2 Aerial view of former industrial site of Bagnoli, seen from Posillipo
Source: Stefania Ragozino, 2016

Table 14.1 Changes in governance from 1996 until 2016

Name	Bagnoli SpA	Bagnoli Futura SpA	Invitalia SpA
Typology	Joint-stock company	Joint-stock company (Urban Renewal Agency)	Joint-stock company (National Investment Promotion Agency)
Owned by	National Government (Institute for Industrial Reconstruction—IRI)	City Council of Naples (90%), Campania Region (7.5%), Province of Naples (2.5%)	National Government (Ministry of the Economy)
Period of activity	1996–2002 (transformed in Bagnoli Futura)	2002–2014 (bankruptcy)	2014–current
Role and tasks	Dismantling of industrial facilities and environmental reclamation	Environmental reclamation, construction of public works infrastructure, sale of land to private investors	Environmental reclamation, planning, real estate development

Source: Stefania Ragozino and Andrea Varriale, 2017

procedures would pave the way for more speculative development of the area. In November 2014, also in response to such reaction, the national government amended the decree and created a steering committee in which the city could give (non-binding) recommendations to the commissioner's plan. The commissioner was only nominated in August 2015. The soil reclamation began in late 2016. In July 2017, to the surprise of many, the city administration signed an agreement with the national government for the reclamation and regeneration plan.

Beyond the Plan

Today's social movements are not the first form of extra-institutional social organization in Bagnoli. The works council of the factory was by far the most important group during the industrial phase. With a core membership of about 100 workers, their 'public assemblies' gathered up to 3500 participants from Bagnoli and beyond (Former worker and activist, personal interview, 27 September 2016, Naples). In the words of a prominent member of the works council, "a worker in Bagnoli's huge factory belonged to a respected group", but also "to the city" (*Ibid.*). In the late 1970s, the workers demonstrated to oppose the relocation of the factory. In the late 1980s, they mobilized to negotiate the shutdown with the city hall and, few years later, occupied the city hall to protest the factory's imminent closure. With early retirement schemes and the rehiring of some workers to undertake the remediation efforts, the works council disbanded in the early 1990s.

The enormous urban void soon attracted private actors. Shortly after the shutdown, a newly created foundation, called IDIS, bought a former chemical factory on the shoreline and created a for-profit organization based on research and communication of scientific knowledge, known as *Science Centre*. The city administration granted IDIS substantial public funds and an exception to its own plan, which foresaw the demolition of all buildings on the coastline. Other for-profit activities, including beach resorts and nightclubs, which lie outside of the industrial area but which have been reclaimed only partially, were licensed by the Port Authority to operate on the seafront. The most significant of these, called *Arenile*, hosts about 360,000 daytime visitors and half a million nighttime visitors per year.

Since the late 1980s, the transformation of Bagnoli captured the interest of architecture students and researchers at the University of Naples. Some of these, gathered in the *Political Collective* of the Faculty of Architecture, analyzed the amendment to the master plan, organized several thematic discussions and started a campaign to discuss the prospect of dismantling of the industrial buildings with experts and with the citizens of Bagnoli. The collective also organized a series of direct actions and protests to prevent their dismantlement. In 2002, it worked with local schools for an initiative called *Walk on the coastline*: Participants were asked to (try to) walk along the coastline, which was—and still is—interrupted by the above-mentioned private properties, gated public property and height differences. Along the walk, participants met three people: a waiter, a hotel owner and a fisherman. A single actor impersonated each role and narrated his (fictitious) daily life after the (imagined) transformation. Such initiatives were part of a larger set of cultural initiatives that blossomed in and about Bagnoli in those years.

In 2005, a group of activists and local citizens founded the *Assise di Bagnoli* (Assembly for Bagnoli) to host dialogues among professionals, researchers, political parties, environmental organizations, associations, former workers and citizens. The group aimed at fighting land speculation, which included demonstrating against the city hall's international call for projects for the area. By the end of the decade, the group had lost much of its attendees and was mostly comprised of a handful of experts and few local citizens. This was due to a variety of factors, including the death or illness of some of the most prominent activists, the social movements' shift of interests towards the garbage crisis and the downsizing of several environmental associations. The length of the transformation process and unclear information on its progress only exacerbated these difficulties (Activist of *Assise di Bagnoli*, personal interview, 9 September 2016, Naples). In 2012, other activists who were previously affiliated to the far-left party *Rifondazione Comunista* created the *Laboratorio Politico ISKRA*, a social movement characterized by a neo-Marxist position and a conflictual stance against institutions. In 2013, ISKRA occupied Villa Medusa, an abandoned community centre for elderly people in the northern coast of Bagnoli, outside of the industrial area. In the parlance of local social movements, the building was 'liberated' and 'given back to the community' in the form of a social club. Another collective, called *Bancarotta* (bankruptcy, or, more literally, 'broken bank') occupied the former bank of the steelworks. After being evicted, the collective relocated to an abandoned beach resort, called *Lido Pola*, south of the Science Centre. These collectives called upon other social movements in Naples to mobilize for a public, free beach in Bagnoli. They collected over 14,000 signatures, in a campaign called 'A beach for all'. In September 2012, the city hall stated its commitment to guaranteeing free access to the shore, i.e. for a beach without resorts. However, in 2015 the city government voted to extend the licenses of the beach resorts for another five-year term.

With the publication of the *Sblocca Italia* decree in 2014, the movements coalesced in opposition to the commissioner and *Invitalia*. This network, called *Bagnoli Libera* (Free Bagnoli), developed along a citywide network of social movements, called *Massa Critica: decide la città* (critical mass: the city decides). *Bagnoli Libera* organized several 'people's assemblies' (*assemblee popolari*) in Bagnoli's district council facilities. There, they discussed the transformation of the area and other local grievances, such as failures in transportation and healthcare facilities. In 2015, the group organized a symbolic and temporary trespassing of the seized industrial area. Their stance against the commissioner was seen favourably by the city government. In February of the same year, representatives of the city government participated in *Bagnoli Libera*'s people's assembly and drafted a new implementation plan for the transformation of Bagnoli. Meanwhile, *Invitalia* hired a firm to "understand the needs of the territory and to manage the moods of the community by monitoring the reactions to [our] actions on the ground" (Facilitator at *Invitalia*, personal interview, 29 September 2016, Naples). To do so, the cooperative invited a plurality of third-sector organizations in Bagnoli, including *Bagnoli Libera*. The latter declined, since it did not "recognize the Commissioner [as legitimate], and sees the [participation] process as top-down, and not definable as public participation" (Activist of *Assise di Bagnoli*, personal interview, 9 September 2016, Naples). Other groups, mostly third-sector organizations and small entrepreneurs, have instead participated. Some of those who participated actively support the appointment of a commissioner, which they regard as the only way to overcome a 20-year-long stall. In the words of a communication professional working with *Invitalia*, the participants were "critically observing, but open to dialogue" (Facilitator at *Invitalia*, personal interview, 29 September 2016, Naples).

The mayor of Naples, an independent leftist in power since 2011, was re-elected in June 2016. The simultaneous local elections for the district council of Bagnoli saw the victory of a former activist and environmental engineer affiliated with the mayor. The election of an anti-establishment candidate as head of the district council was remarkable, since Bagnoli has been a stronghold of traditional leftist parties (from the Communist Party to today's Democratic Party) for decades. In Figure 14.3, we distinguish between actors favouring and opposing the government commissioner. Figure 14.4 is a timeline of planned transformations and initiatives beyond the plan.

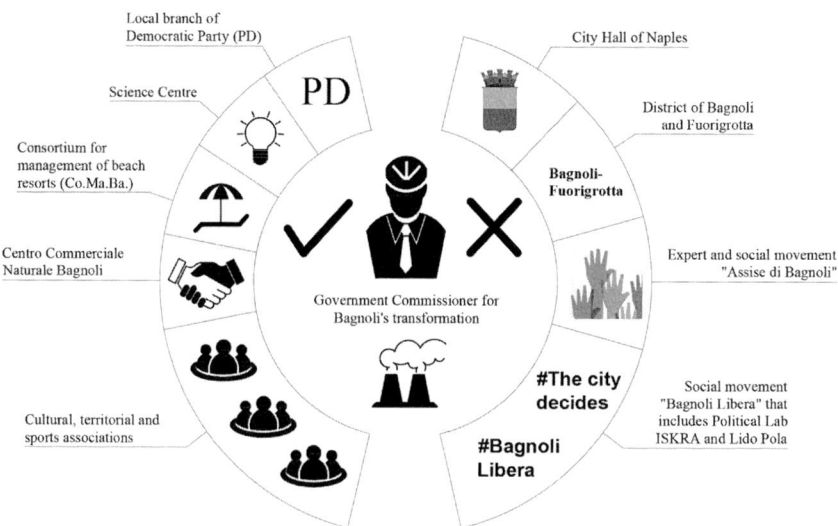

Figure 14.3 Actors favouring and opposing the government commissioner

Source: Stefania Ragozino and Andrea Varriale, 2017

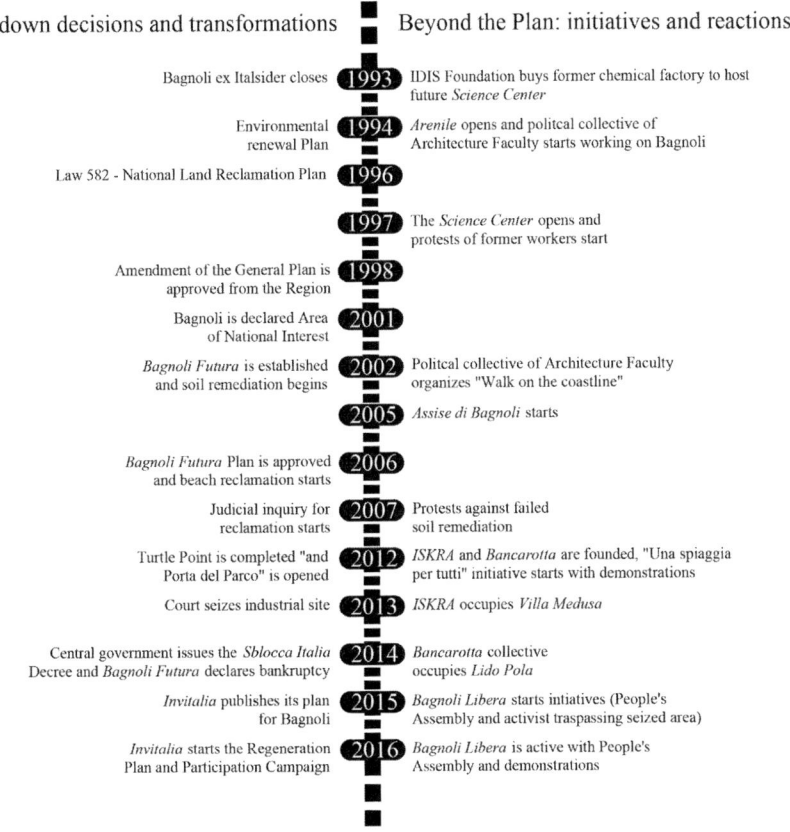

Top down decisions and transformations   Beyond the Plan: initiatives and reactions

Bagnoli ex Italsider closes	**1993**	IDIS Foundation buys former chemical factory to host future *Science Center*
Environmental renewal Plan	**1994**	*Arenile* opens and politcal collective of Architecture Faculty starts working on Bagnoli
Law 582 - National Land Reclamation Plan	**1996**	
	1997	The *Science Center* opens and protests of former workers start
Amendment of the General Plan is approved from the Region	**1998**	
Bagnoli is declared Area of National Interest	**2001**	
Bagnoli Futura is established and soil remediation begins	**2002**	Politcal collective of Architecture Faculty organizes "Walk on the coastline"
	2005	*Assise di Bagnoli* starts
Bagnoli Futura Plan is approved and beach reclamation starts	**2006**	
Judicial inquiry for reclamation starts	**2007**	Protests against failed soil remediation
Turtle Point is completed "and Porta del Parco" is opened	**2012**	*ISKRA* and *Bancarotta* are founded, "Una spiaggia per tutti" initiative starts with demonstrations
Court seizes industrial site	**2013**	*ISKRA* occupies *Villa Medusa*
Central government issues the *Sblocca Italia* Decree and *Bagnoli Futura* declares bankruptcy	**2014**	*Bancarotta* collective occupies *Lido Pola*
Invitalia publishes its plan for Bagnoli	**2015**	*Bagnoli Libera* starts intiatives (People's Assembly and activist traspassing seized area)
Invitalia starts the Regeneration Plan and Participation Campaign	**2016**	*Bagnoli Libera* is active with People's Assembly and demonstrations

Figure 14.4 Planned transformation and initiatives beyond the plan
Source: Stefania Ragozino and Andrea Varriale, 2017

Processing Emancipation in Bagnoli

While there have been instances in which planners and institutions have opened some channels with the population of Bagnoli (from the information office of 1998 to *Invitalia*'s 'participatory' meetings), the merely informative or at best the highly compartmentalized nature of these interactions puts them outside our definition of emancipation. Therefore, we shifted our focus to actions of more informal or non-institutional nature. Some of these include forms of informal dialogue within loose networks of actors that, after reaching a shared position, seek to have that position implemented within institutionalized planning (issue network). The campaign *Una spiaggia per tutti* (2011–2012) and the numerous discussions organized by the *Assise di Bagnoli* (2005–ongoing) seem to fall in this field. These two groups undertook initiatives aiming at promoting open access to physical and symbolic spaces by collecting signatures for a public beach and providing open space for discussion, respectively.

Other actions draw on a repertoire of conflict and contestation and are based on more radical claims for social justice. These, we argue, include the well-attended works councils in the 70s and 80s, recent occupations of social centres in the area and, most recently, the protests and mobilization organized by *Bagnoli Libera*, such as the trespassing of the industrial area and the occupation of the district's municipality building. The radical nature of such actions is also suggested by activists' refusal to participate in *Invitalia*'s meetings. We take this abundance of informal actions to signify that an emancipatory process has been under way in Bagnoli, at least in its cognitive and communicative dimensions. We now review the recent events in the light of the proposed definition of emancipation.

First, the mobilization has helped build a substantive body of knowledge, information material and forums for discussing the future of Bagnoli (cognitive emancipation). While, in earlier times, knowledge of the environmental, planning and economic issues at hand was confined to a handful of professionals and students who contributed their skills as volunteers, now this awareness has spread much wider. Importantly, this fluency in technical matters had made activists a tougher and more manipulation-proof interlocutor than, we would argue, the generic audience of participatory meetings would be. Second, participation and public interest has increased dramatically, as visible in the participation in open discussions, protests and occupations. More people are reached by the frequent and intensive information campaigns and through social networks. Partially thanks to the current administration's readiness to endorse their inputs, activists have also dramatically increased their political agency. They are able to elaborate and communicate their stance without the intermediation of political parties (also due to the withering away of far-left parties in the late 2000s). We interpret these developments as proxies that signal a process of 'communicative' emancipation. Such stances are also articulated in several conflictual (occupations, protests) and less conflictual actions (gatherings of signatures, assemblies in public spaces). This is not to say that institutional politics is altogether bypassed. As the recent election of a former activist in Bagnoli (and similar trajectories in other parts of Naples), activists in Naples showed little reticence towards entering institutionalized politics than was previously the case. In a more limited fashion, namely with regard to the peripheral position and small size of the occupied spaces or the temporality of the more symbolic occupations, the actions of the movements also achieved a practical dimension.

In order to dissect the 'practiced emancipation' further, we now look at how the cooperation between activists and the city government has evolved and introduce the main developments since 2016. Their cooperation may be seen as a precondition for activists to have their voices heard, and thus as a partial success. A pressing question here is whether this cooperation is a fortunate case of 'transmission' of wishes elaborated and expressed from below. This interpretation seems supported by the advantages that the movements receive from this alliance, in terms of legalization of occupation, increased visibility and various instances in which the mayor has absorbed proposals and inputs articulated by the movements. On the other hand, this cooperation can be read as a form of co-optation of the mayor at the expense of the movements, in a political climate in which new political formations, such as the one behind the mayor, draw legitimacy by contesting traditional parties and technocratic procedures. While the term co-optation conveys the image of one actor outwitting another to the latter's detriment, the configuration described above seems mutually beneficial. In the succinct formulation of a former activist: "co-optation is happening on both sides" (Former activist, personal interview, 6 September 2016, Naples). This may point to the ambiguous nature of potentially emancipatory processes. Two of the movements' main requests, namely that the government commissioner be withdrawn and that the decision-making process go back to its normal operation, have not been met. This is most likely due to the gap between the scale at which the movements can exert influence, namely the city, and the level at which such a decision can be taken, namely the national government. Being overwhelmingly rewarded by tokens such as solidarity from the city government or local laws with no direct impact, the actions of social movements, until that point in time, clearly fell short of accomplishing durable results with broader spatial implications. Until June 2017, it was not clear whether *Invitalia* would carry out the restoration of the coast (and thus remove the platform), as it had announced. The city administration officially protested at *Invitalia*'s ambiguity on the subject. In July 2017, however, the unexpected happened: the city signed an agreement with *Invitalia*. The agreement was drafted behind closed doors and with no public input or examination by the city council. Social movements, whom the city had pledged to work with, were also barred from reviewing the agreement. The plan foresees a building-free coast, the removal of the artificial platform, a public beach and, as compared to *Invitalia*'s original plan, a larger park and lower building density. Some activist groups—and the mayor—argue that their vociferous mobilization has forced the central government to reconsider some of its previous plans. In a recent interview, the mayor also suggested that the new national government has a "different attitude" than the one which had written the *Sblocca Italia* decree (Web TV Comune di Napoli 2017). But the new plan also raised substantial critiques. Most activists and other critics stress that the new plan does not specify the size of the public beach, prioritizes the construction of hotels on the non-contaminated soil and cautiously specifies that many elements of the plan are contingent on the available funds, which will be raised later as project bonds. Importantly, nearly all activist groups concur that despite the mayor's boastful support of their 'the city decides' slogan, there has been no participation whatsoever in the latter phases of the

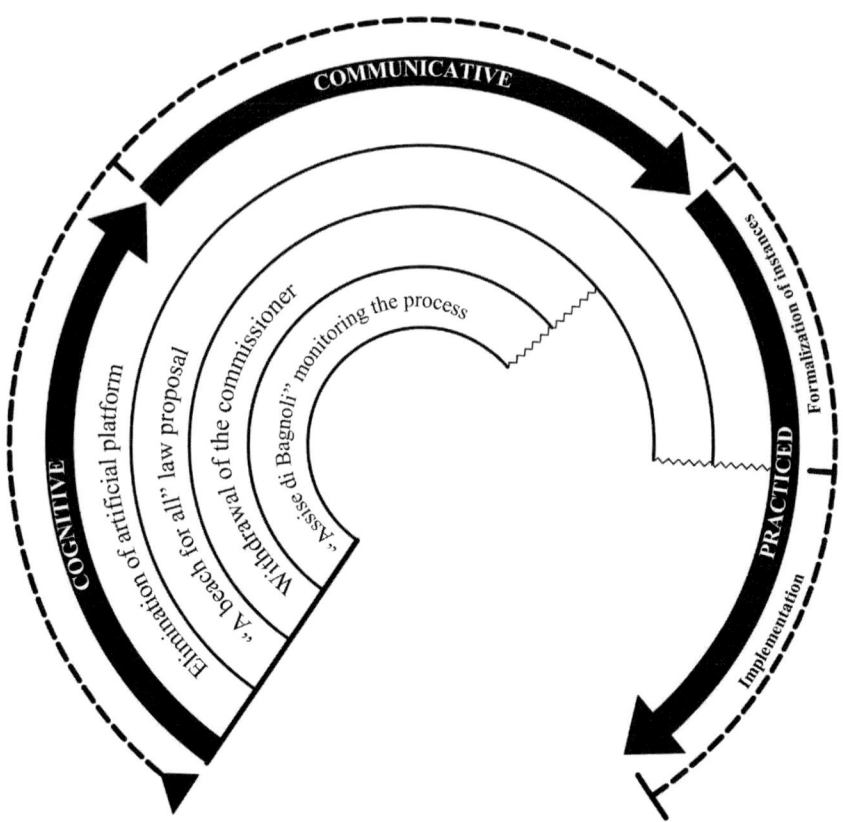

Figure 14.5 Levels of emancipation in Bagnoli
Source: Stefania Ragozino and Andrea Varriale, 2017

project. Highlighting the point, the *Assise di Bagnoli* has called on the mayor to have a citywide referendum about the plan. Due to a lack of transparency regarding the latest developments, it is difficult to say whether these changes are consequences of the earlier mobilizations. Figure 14.5 synthesizes our interpretation of the dimensions of emancipation reached through some of the initiatives presented above.

Conclusions

This chapter has sought to point out the theoretical, ethical and practical potentials and limitations of different ways to increase people's emancipation vis-à-vis spatial transformation. In this last section, we aim to draw insights from the case analyzed above and sketch a way to combine consensual and agonistic approaches to spatial transformations.

We begin with agreeing that one modality does not exclude the other, and that this binary thinking is contradicted by both theory and practice (Hillier 2002). Rather than an escape route to take when 'normal', formal procedures are unavailable, direct action is better understood as a normal feature of social and political life: the norm, rather than the exception. Tilly and Tarrow (2015) suggest that, in several critical junctures, direct action has been the only viable gate to institutionalized dialogue. Therefore, this dichotomy might better understood dialectically. This may not be an entirely new interpretation. Commenting on various grievance groups in the US, Cobb and Elder (1971: 903) noted that

> pre-political, or at least pre-decisional, processes are often of the most critical importance in determining which issues and alternatives are to be considered by the polity . . . What happens in the decision-making councils of the formal institutions of government may do little more than recognize, document, and legalize, if not legitimize, the momentary results of a continuing struggle.
>
> (*Ibid.*)

When placed in the realm of planning, we take this insight as an invitation to recognize direct action and its ability to introduce, or even force, certain discussions into the political debate. In view of the many limitations of institutionalized participation, allowing for this to happen seems a risk worth taking.

References

Albrechts, L. (2003) Planning and Power: Towards an Emancipatory Planning Approach. *Environment and Planning C* 21(6), pp. 905–924.

Allum, P. (2003) The Politics of Town Planning in Post-War Naples. *Journal of Modern Italian Studies* 8(4), pp. 500–527.

Andriello, V., Belli, A. and Lepore, D. (eds.) (1991) *Il luogo e la fabbrica. L'impianto siderurgico di Bagnoli e l'espansione occidentale di Napoli.* Napoli: Graphotonic.

Balducci, A. (2000) Le nuove politiche della governance urbana. *Territorio* 13.

Benevolo, L. (1974) *Le origini dell'urbanistica moderna.* Bari: Laterza.

Bianchetti, M.C. (2011) *Il Novecento è davvero finito: considerazioni sull'urbanistica.* Roma: Donzelli.

Cobb, R.W. and Elder, C.D. (1971) The Politics of Agenda-Building: An Alternative Perspective for Modern Democratic Theory. *The Journal of Politics* 33(4), pp. 892–915.

Di Dato, M. (2016) Sulla riqualificazione ambientale e urbanistica di Bagnoli. In L. Rossomando (ed.) *Lo stato della città. Napoli e la sua area metropolitana.* Napoli: Monitor edizioni, pp. 46–66.

Esposito De Vita, G. (2014) Segregative Power of Violence in Belfast and Naples: Exploring the Role of Public Spaces Reconnecting Divided Societies. In A. Madanipour, S. Knierbein and A. Degros (eds.) *Public Space and the Challenges of Urban Transformation in Europe*. London: Routledge, pp. 169–182.

Fainstein, S.S. (2000) New Directions in Planning Theory. *Urban Affairs Review* 35(4), pp. 451–478.

Flyvbjerg, B. (1998) *Rationality and Power: Democracy in Practice*. Chicago: University of Chicago Press.

Forester, J. (1988) *Planning in the Face of Power*. Oakland: University of California Press.

Healey, P. (1997) *Collaborative Planning: Shaping Places in Fragmented Societies*. Vancouver: UBC Press.

Hillier, J. (2002) Direct Action and Agonism in Democratic Planning Practice. In P. Allmendinger and M. Tewdwr-Jones (eds.) *Planning Futures: New Directions for Planning Theory*. London, New York: Routledge, pp. 110–135.

Huxley, M. (2000) The Limits to Communicative Planning. *Journal of Planning Education and Research* 19(4), pp. 369–377.

Melucci, A. (1996) *Challenging Codes: Collective Action in the Information Age*. Cambridge: Cambridge University Press.

Mouffe, C. (2013) *Agonistics: Thinking the World Politically*. London and New York: Verso Books.

Pacione, M. (1987) Socio-Spatial Development of the South Italian City: The Case of Naples. *Transactions of the Institute of British Geographers* 12(4), pp. 433–450.

Servillo, L. and Lingua, V. (2014) The Innovation of the Italian Planning System: Actors, Path Dependencies, Cultural Contradictions and a Missing Epilogue. *European Planning Studies* 22(2), pp. 400–417.

Tilly, C. and Tarrow, S.G. (2015) *Contentious Politics*. Oxford: Oxford University Press.

Web TV Comune di Napoli (2017) *Interview with L. De Magistris, Mayor of Naples*, 19 July [Video file] [Online]. Available at: www.youtube.com/watch?v=riYdscQxLSU [Accessed 15 September 2017].

Wilson, J. and Swyngedouw, E. (eds.) (2014) *The Post-Political and Its Discontents: Spaces of Depoliticisation, Spectres of Radical Politics*. Edinburgh: Edinburgh University Press.

Yin, R.K. (2009) *Case Study Research: Design and Methods*, 4th ed. Thousand Oaks: Sage Publications.

15 Emancipatory Practices of Self-Organized Workers in the Context of Neoliberal Policies

IMPA, the Case of a 'Recovered Factory' in Buenos Aires

Regina Vidosa and Paula Rosa

Introduction

The aim of this chapter is to analyze the experience of *Metallurgical and Plastic Industries of Argentina (IMPA)*, one of the first recovered factories in the city of Buenos Aires at the end of the 20th century. IMPA's transition reflects a deeper social process in which portions of society self-organize to generate new practices of solidarity for confronting the consequences of an economic depression whose complex roots can be linked to two decades of neoliberalization of economic and social policies.

The expression *recovered factories* is used to explain the action by which the workers of a factory that was near closure collectively decide to *occupy* the plant to avoid losing their jobs. In this way, they try to *recover* the factory activity through their own means. In many cases, the owners had already abandoned any attempt of reactivating the factory and some even dishonestly tried to file bankruptcy to avoid paying their debts. The proposal, especially promoted by workers who had no formal political participation, was to organize themselves, produce and administrate the factory autonomously, meaning without high-tier management. This means that professional administrative positions were kept only to a limited degree and without hierarchical roles previously attributed to them.

Workers' practices of occupying and recovering factories which are about to close can be interpreted through Laclau's (1996)[1] *emancipatory practices*, where political action gains visibility by showing what has been excluded from the established order. According to Laclau, there is always political action because every social order is incomplete, founded on a 'lack' and thus political action is needed to bring closure, even though this is always impossible. In this case, social exclusion is understood as the 'lack'. Politics exists because the production of the social order is a perpetual task and this opening would generate greater possibilities for the emergence of emancipatory struggles. Politics is an ontological category; there is politics because there is subversion and dislocation of the social (Muñoz 2006: 142).

In this way, emancipatory practices give way to politics by demonstrating how the antagonism of the contingencies of social order are overcome through the dislocation of power relationships (Laclau and Mouffe 2004). Specifically, the emancipatory practices of recovering factories in Argentina are closely connected to experiences which search for alternatives to the traditional forms of organization that are undergoing a *crisis of representation*. This can be seen in the widespread disrepute of political parties and syndicates whose performing as representatives of the society's interests is increasingly seen as inefficient. In the context of growing distrust towards institutional forms of organization and representation, the essential feature of *new* practices is that they emerge outside of the traditional political channels while revolving around unexpected, creative strategies, such as occupying a factory and reactivating it. We assert that this kind of experience can be interpreted from the perspective of *real democracy* explicated by Rancière (1996). From this point of view, the experiences could be understood as manifestations of political subjects in opposition to the empowerment of the police organization. In other words, they could be understood as practices that exercise politics outside the standards that have been embodied in the state or in the government. From this perspective, there is potential that the different collective experiences as emancipatory practices challenge the established routines of official politics and work towards producing a real democracy.

Our analysis makes use of the IMPA to dialectically connect insights into occupation and recovery of factories to the broader debates on emancipatory practices. The analysis is structured in three parts: (1) both occupation and recovery are related to the economic and political context in which they take place; (2) strategies of the workers are described where a central role is assigned to the body through horizontal decision-making, alliance with other social actors and openness to civil society as the legitimation of struggle; (3) finally, a reflection is made on the peculiarities which appear in the IMPA experience as an emancipatory practice.

Emergence of Recovered Factories

The dictatorship of 1970 changed the model of industrialized development in Argentina, increasing its specialization in raw materials, diminishing broader industrialization practices and returning in part to the agro-export model of the late 19th century. The Argentine economy was drawn into global economics through neoliberalization by positioning its role as a source of material resources. This model of development deepened during the 1980s and consolidated further in the early 1990s, departing from the structural reforms which—through the Washington Consensus—were advocated by the International Monetary Fund and the World Bank in the country (Bresser Pereira 1991; Duarte 2002). Argentina became entrenched as a source for material resource extraction for the benefit of an already globalized economy, instead of being more equitably integrated into the global economy. Measures such as macroeconomic stabilization have been implemented—forcing the reduction of public spending, through the economic liberalization of trade as well as inversion and expansion of the market forces within the domestic economy. Industrial and regional promotion of exportation were dismantled, and the prioritization of national products in state purchasing was undertaken. At the same time, state companies providing public services were privatized—consequently the state has lost the capacity of regulating prices that have a strong impact on the basic resources, such as electricity and gas prices. These transformations have coalesced with a series of structural reforms in the labour market. Because of the renegotiation of labour legislation, contract conditions were weakened, compensation prices were reduced, minimal wage negotiations became limited, and social benefits were diminished and the pension and health systems were privatized (Arceo et al. 2007; Andrenacci 2002). Finally, around the end of the 1990s, the effects of the structural reforms—strong tax pressure, constant rise of public services price, high interest rates, reduction of market stability due to unrestricted importation of products and a considerable contraction of the domestic consumption—created a recessive context for local industries. This was especially the case for small and medium-sized businesses, which compared to big industries often do not have sufficient capital to endure the crisis (Benito 2010). These political and economic shifts accelerated the deindustrialization process originally initiated by the military dictatorship in the mid-1970s.

Argentine society found itself facing extreme levels of poverty, high unemployment and precarious labour. Precarious work can be defined from a legal perspective as one without typical forms of full-time salaried employment or a contractual relationship for an indefinite period. These factors combined to create socioeconomic instability at the end of the 20th century manifesting in political discontent. Structural indicators comparing the period of economic liberalization and the preceding one show a significant fall in employment, from 37.1% of the population in the 1970s to 28.5% in 2001 (Arceo et al. 2007), as well as an excessive rise in poverty, from 2 million poor people in the country's overall population of 22 million in 1975 to 14 million in the overall population of 37 million in 2001. From the 15 million which show the population growth during the last quarter of the century, 12 million are under the poverty line (Lozano 2001: 3). In these circumstances, the economy starts showing signs of stagnation and conflict. At the end of 2001, these factors resulted in a financial and government crisis which led to a generalized questioning of the institutions of the neoliberal regime (Di Loreto et al. 2006).

Political mobilization became increasingly active after 2001. One could see people participating in assemblies in parks, organizing marches and occupations in streets and meeting with other workers. According to Rodríguez (2013: 2), the general mobilization during the period between 2000 and 2001 represents a generalized reaction in response to the model and its political class. Struggles gain significant importance and through them, new social movements emerge, which primarily show that there is a crisis of the traditional forms of participation, such as syndicates and political parties, exceeded by spontaneous actions of the population (*Ibid.*). A representative icon of this period is the *recovered factories* phenomenon. The phenomenon has gained a significant magnitude of people, to the point that, between 2000 and 2001, more than 150 factories of different kinds have been occupied and activated by their workers in Argentina.

The experience of recovered factories has provoked widespread and positive social valuation (Rebón et al. 2015: 175). This positive valuation emerges in spite of the disruptive and controversial character of the collective occupation and its consequent effect on private industrial properties. The legitimacy of this phenomenon in Argentina could be related with the historical path of the working class's struggles and some specific experiences of self-management in the country. Investigations like the one carried out by Rebón et al. (2015) link the legitimacy of the recovered factories to the positive value society places on work and, consequently, to the actions aimed at recovery. The authors recognize the importance of work culture in the Argentine society, because of the values of work as a form of social, material and symbolic reproduction. Thus, defending work in certain conditions can even—though it may cause strong social tension—weaken the social value of private ownership of the means of production (*Ibid.*: 175). The importance of the recovery of jobs can also be seen in the identity of the recovered factories, given the idea of an act of *recuperation* is recognized as defending the priority of jobs over any other claim.

The IMPA Experience

Located in Buenos Aires, the neighbourhood of Almagro (Figure 15.1), IMPA is one of the oldest and most important recovered company factories in the country. Nowadays, IMPA is known because it is the metallurgical company with the second-best billing in the country, processing and marketing aluminium in its smelting, lamination, extrusion and printing phases (Figure 15.2). With 174 metallurgical workers, IMPA produces collapsible containers, aluminium dispensable trays and paper foil. Aluminum processing in this factory includes the entire productive processes to create and transform aluminium paper into flexible containers. This factory, founded in 1918 with German capital, employed 500 workers at its peak in 1968. It was the first enterprise to produce aluminium, and the IMPA RR-11 aircraft was the first of a series of prototypes that would make IMPA the first private airplane factory in Argentina (Hernández 2013).

In 1997, the factory went bankrupt, leading to its closure. The factory's bankruptcy was brought on by dishonest practices, propelled by the complex economic context of the 1990s (Vázquez Blanco 2010).Facing numerous layoffs, and with many older workers knowing it would be difficult to get

Figure 15.1 Location of IMPA in Buenos Aires
Source: Regina Vidosa and Paula Rosa, 2017

Figure 15.2 Building of IMPA
Source: Noelia Pirsic, 2015

another job, the workers decided to organize themselves to articulate their claims to the right to work. The recovery of IMPA was the result of the organization of this factory's workers. They also had support for the occupation of the factory by workers from other metallurgical industries and with the legal and technical advice of the Union of Metallurgical Workers (UOM). The Union's Quilmes sector, which was one of the few that accompanied the process of corporate recovery, was a critical supporter (Vázquez Blanco 2010: 44).Thus, the workers retained a lawyer and occupied the factory. The factory was closed for four months, until May 1998, when about 60 workers took it over. Workers organized themselves to guard the building and sleep at the factory to avoid the robbery of machines.

Through these partnerships and support, the workers managed to organize themselves and remove the administration council, which was previously in charge of running the factory, and they created a new directive commission made up of workers. Among the measures, the directive commission decided that all the workers would be paid the same, no matter their position. They also formed work teams and substituted foremen for workshop coordinators, who distributed work duties (Hernández 2013). Initially, workers from other metallurgical industries came to help them, as well as small clients who trusted them and needed their services. The workers also went around the neighbourhood asking for money to eat and travel. Neighbours and local merchants helped with money but also with goods and food. This demonstrates the networks that workers were initially creating with the community. Some of the workers were part of the immediate or adjacent neighbourhoods, while others travelled long hours from further afield to get to work.

Workers ultimately managed to recover their source of work and made the factory productive again (Benito 2010). After the takeover, the administration council accepted the workers controlling the enterprise. At the beginning, 'being in charge of the company' was a great challenge. The cooperative's website (www.recuperadasdoc.com.ar) cites their president Campos, who wondered, what could they do? He remembers that they were told that they would not be able to run a company, that they would be there for a week or two and then they would have to go because they did not have the money to pay electricity and gas bills. However, as the president reaffirmed continuously, they wanted to stay in the factory.

IMPA workers indicated that several months went by before they could earn a salary, creating financial problems between workers and their families and partners. With few other viable models of recovered factories, sustained absence of workers from their home-life created both financial and social stress. Despite the initial achievements, fears of being forced to leave the factory—even though it was still occupied by workers—lingered for a long time. In part, this fear propelled a need for being more visible in the community and the neighbourhood.

The workers began to organize outside groups to enhance their visibility. They began allowing outside social groups created by university students, other activist groups and artists to hold political meetings within the factory. The combined efforts of outside groups and their presence in the factory broadened the cultural and educational possibilities for the factory's reestablishment and helped support the recovery process. Given that the recovery process was still incipient, the presence of a variety of groups allowed for simultaneous alternative proposals and uses of the space. By expanding possibilities for the site beyond monofunctional and corporate-driven productivity for aluminium, new possibilities for social and political activities could be realized, particularly because only around 33% of the 22,000-square-metre factory's area was initially used in the recovery process (Benito 2010). The extension of the factory created adequate space for the development of a variety of activities which required ample room for performance and acrobatics as well as for the organization of parties. These social events frequently invited the participation of the public as audience. As just one example, theatre plays started in an abandoned storeroom in the factory.

The recovered factory gained substantial visibility through these initiatives as a means of communication and engagement with the community. These activities attracted a diverse public, curious about the novel experiences made possible by the factory's recovery. Young people, professionals, students and especially artists were attracted by the experience that began in IMPA. In a very complex social context, the support given to the initiative was understood as a manifestation of solidarity. Various instances of precarity, either due to political or labour instabilities, manifested as a collective form of resistance through diverse uses of the factory. The respectful plurality of use amongst many different constituencies was indicative of IMPA and an emerging characteristic trait of Argentine resistance during the recovery period [1998–2000]. The collapse of large-scale industrial systems, made fragile by authoritarian rule and monofunctionalism, created an opportunity for more democratic, diverse and socially engaged possibilities. According to Benito (2010: 46), "a group of young people acted not only in the hope of a social change facing a critical situation, but also with the intention of aestheticizing a particular subjacent problem: the industrial system and its crisis".

The novelty of the IMPA recovery allowed for numerous publics to participate, which required defining what would be done about the plant and the activities over the long term. In this way, "an assembly space started to take form for the decision-making process in relation to the path the project would follow" (Benito 2010: 51). Both workers and artists agreed that the best way to join aluminum production and social/artistic functions was creating a cultural centre. In this way, cultural activities would have their own identity and specific regulations. This is how the *IMPA Cultural City Factory* emerged at the beginning of the 21st century. According to Vázquez Blanco (2010: 45) "this enterprise was pioneer when linking itself closely to the community, in return for the support it received through cultural and educational services". Up to that moment, there were no precedents in terms of a factory in which artists and workers could share the same space. It is worth pointing out that in other cosmopolitan cities where art is developed in non-conventional spaces, it frequently takes place in empty industry infrastructures, just as we have mentioned before, but not inhabited by workers trying to undertake a cooperative.

(Benito 2010: 52)

The need for agreements was related to various schedules and the noise of the machines, which created a challenge for events such as concerts. The cooperative's website (www.recuperadasdoc.com.ar) cites their president's anecdote that negotiations took time, eventually leading to all groups having lunch together like a big family. In 2000, one of the most well-known newspapers in the country published an article with the following title: 'A Factory Which Makes Magic'(Pacheco 2000). In this article, the factory scene is described in detail: "Very big rooms, machines, cement floor are the compulsory scenography" (Figure 15.3); and it goes on to discuss the theatre play that was carried out there: "for forty-five minutes, the theatre resources will turn this factory into an enormous box within which poetry and beauty are possible" (*Ibid.*).

The factory space housed a vast convergence of previously isolated use. While it is still running as an aluminium processor and marketer, the factory housed a museum about worker identity and a range of diverse activities

Figure 15.3 Opera at IMPA

Source: Noelia Pirsic, 2015

developed in self-managed ways by the artists (parties, festivals, theatre plays, concerts, film projections, debates and workshops on politics) and workshops (circus, theatre, serigraphy, musical instruments, singing) linked to the cultural centre. In 2001, the factory housed more than 30 workshops. The agreement with the workshops' teachers was that they could work there if they gave 30% of their earnings for the common fund, managed by the teachers, keeping 70% for themselves.

The continuity and strengthening of the cultural and educational activities in the factory plant created the first popular baccalaureate for young adults. In 2004, the baccalaureates initially had 140 participants studying under individuals older than 17. Some of the teachers also worked for the company and most students lived in nearby neighbourhoods (Vázquez Blanco 2010). Baccalaureates are public, free schools, where the course of study takes three years and official academic credits can be earned. These institutions were approved by the Government of the City of Buenos Aires, which also paid the teachers' salaries. The continued success of the baccalaureate led to the creation of the Workers University at IMPA, in 2010. The establishment of the Workers University received the necessary unanimous approval of the National Senate, unions and syndicates' leaders, members of social organizations, deputies, university deans and professors.

However, the struggle of recovery did not end there. Legal obtainment of the property by the workers was just beginning. In that process, IMPA workers met with other workers in similar situations, legislators and officials with whom they created laws, such as the expropriation of a factory in favour of workers. The creation of expropriation laws was critical, as IMPA was one of the first enterprises to promote and organize legal formalization of recovered factories. The IMPA community was one of the supporters of the National Movement of Recovered Companies (MNER)—an entity which would represent most of the factories in this situation.

During the process of occupation of factories there are different social actors, apart from the initial workers with a longer political trajectory. Lawyers, unionists and political activists are also involved in the process by contributing their technical and legal experience to factory recovery. For this reason, we consider "the recovery of factories as a strategy that does not come out spontaneously from the workers, but from the articulation of workers and other actors" (Rebón 2004: 67, cited in Vázquez Blanco 2010). Some of the recommendations given by legal and technical experts were related to gaining more unity and formalization. To attain this, the legal formation of workers' cooperatives is ideal because it is an association of people who have gathered freely to face their needs together in a democratic way, giving priority to keeping jobs and to improving their living conditions. The legal form of workers' cooperatives is critical to the success of the factory recovery process because it provides the possibility of being in charge of a factory, but without inheriting the unpaid debt from the managers.

Building social and legal legitimacies that allowed the long-term protection of jobs from legal and state counter-definitions was an early challenge for the workers. Recovered factories were given state subsidies to buy machines and/or raw materials and boxes of food. They received the subsidies so that the factories could continue their operation. Legal power allowed workers to safeguard the means of production until reforms to the Bankruptcy Law was approved in 2011. The changes have now allowed workers to oversee factories which have become cooperatives. It also allowed wage debts to be used for the purchase of the bankrupt company. Hence, during 2010 in Argentina, 63% of the factories have been expropriated[2] in favour of cooperatives, from which 19% have been a definite transference from the private property to the workers (Hernández 2013: 19).

However, this is not an automatic process, because it is not put into practice until there is a legal intervention in favour of the factory's workers. To be able to work, each cooperative within a process of recovery must have an *expropriation law*. This is not the same law for all cooperatives, but it must respond to each particular instance and to each cooperative's assets. In this sense, the process of recovery of a factory is not easy. It is fraught with judicial interventions, police violence, orders of eviction for charges of usurpation and a variety of challenges from the legal system. Therefore, recovery is a long process, in which the occupation of factories is essential to keep jobs. In consequence, one of the strategies for occupying and, later, to recovering factories is based on putting bodies into action. People cover machinery with their bodies and guard entrance doors, they block streets as a form of claim and organize assemblies to decide how to move forward. Workers must physically, politically and socially link to one another. Without putting bodies into action, the phenomenon of recovered factories could not exist.

Final Reflection

The IMPA experience can be interpreted as an *emancipatory practice*, because it contests the loss of workers' rights due to the implementation of neoliberal policies and it also challenges the established order through claims, alliances and the taking over of the factory. According to Rancière (1996), these actions can be understood as manifestations that actually exercise politics, given that they oppose the strengthening of the police order, which means they are organized outside the standards which have been corporatized in the state or government. In this way, facing the economic and political crisis of the neoliberal model, workers self-gather in spaces outside traditional institutional ways like syndicates or political parties. Even though the appropriation of the means of production by workers is a different practice from the traditional ones used by workers to mount pressure for changes, strikes were not eliminated, but there was a variation in the collective action and in the workers' traditional organizational field (Farinetti 1999). Even though a specific sector of the metallurgical syndicate supported the IMPA takeover, this situation is effectively an exception, as the syndicates are far from being the central actors in the process. It is estimated that in up to 62% of the cases, unions declared themselves as non-participants in recoveries (Rebón 2004: 68). To compensate for this lack of centralized support, the IMPA utilized a wide variety of actors and alliances as a strategy to gain legitimacy.

The sociopolitical network as well as the physical space was shared by metallurgical workers, artists and educators. The bodies that were in that space *produced* it in their particular ways. Some produced through the worker's body, which is used for production in the metallurgical industry, and others—the artists—produced through bodies representing fictional scenes within the factory place, which is as *real* a space of production as producing aluminium. The IMPA recovery involved not only physical, industrial production but also the artistic production of other possible realities. Both bodies and spaces are interlinked because both imaginations *live* within this space and *give it life* with their actions. As Benito points out, despite the integration that this space offered, living together "was not an easy task, because the worldviews were always different and in certain circumstances they resulted incompatibly" (Benito 2010: 51). At the beginning, it was like an "alien invasion" for some of the workers; however, for others it was a gratifying experience (*Ibid*: 52).

Bokser (2011) explains all the spaces in IMPA are full of stories of resistance and struggle, exceeding the initial recovery by the workers because they managed to bring together supposedly incompatible activities. According to the author,

> the circumstances and the form in which the workers developed collective actions have been a necessary condition for putting this project into practice: the collective devices and the form of inhabiting the factory after its recuperation have enabled the questioning of fragmentation and isolationism, characteristics of a neoliberal logic.
>
> (Bokser 2011: 2)

In relation to this, we agree with Lorey (2014) that these kinds of initiatives involve "more than imagining sociopolitical and economic alternatives. They were already practised in the assemblies and occupations of public and private spaces, in the conversations, debates and mobilization in the neighbourhoods" (*Ibid*.: 17). To strive for possibilities of horizontality and equality, the first step is ideally "listening, by being able to speak and letting others speak" ensuring that mutual respect can be realized (cf. *Ibid*.: 16–17). All this is also seen in the forms that production takes under the new modality. The great prominence that workers gain allows for new modes of production to be created. Without the presence of the previous hierarchy and owners, workers themselves gain prominence and influence of emancipatory productive possibilities, particularly diverse and multifunctional ones beyond the purely material. Old roles are reviewed and new ones are created as well, which brings tension into traditional areas. In this way, a new way of 'inhabiting' the factory is established (Bokser 2011).

However, a division of labour still existed across the production process, including the workers who performed operative tasks and other workers who were in charge of the coordination of the different areas of the production process. Both the noise and the physical challenges remained in the now-recovered factory. The difference lies in the fact that the loud noise implies the factory is active and there is work to be done—work that can be achieved in a more horizontal and community-driven way.

It is important to highlight the use of the body as one of the main tactics in this experience. In this sense, the spatial strategy *par excellence* in recovered factories is physically taking over the factory place. The plant is filled with bodies which stop state-sanctioned legal powers from approving the bankruptcy of the enterprise and the subsequent retaking of the site. They resist police violence during eviction attempts and even intercept the owners of the factory when they try to take and use the machinery. The occupation strategies and tactics bring into play both material and symbolic bodies, which dispute and create spaces (Moore 2013). Hence, if considered as spatial practice, they become emancipatory practices which can be recognized as the opening new forms of *making* politics. Moore (2013: 1) understands that "occupations differ from other forms of protest like marches and rallies primarily in their temporal and spatial persistence, and in this sense they allow for more of an explicit meditation on the role of the persisting, protesting body". The emancipatory practices take the form of spatial praxis in which the symbolic and material bodies take over and build embodied political spaces.

The experiences that develop skills for making decisions through deliberation are seen as a practice of Rancière's (1996) *real democracy*. IMPA workers, who were only used to doing manual tasks and obeying orders, started to participate in collective decisions, took part in the political discussions and assemblies, administrated the budget and subsidies, finished their studies and 'opened' the factory gates to the community and neighbourhood through meetings with different actors.

We could say that in the case of IMPA, in addition to Rancière (1996), the egalitarian principle that emerges is *democracy crystallized*. Understood as a disruptive and conflictive manifestation of the egalitarian principle, the collective production of democratic action displaces hierarchical distribution of established social places. The case of the IMPA shows how workers, accustomed to being the work force, organize themselves to distribute decisions, make shared proposals, start production and take on a new role: to become both employers and owners. In this way, they have legitimized themselves to organize and produce their own work. The disruptive nature of the IMPA is observed in workers assuming new positions and social functions. These new positions are not simply the reproduction of hierarchical systems but the attempt to democratically rearticulate the traditional functional logic the factory had. Workers no longer seek maximum benefit for the owner but work to achieve the collective well-being of all workers.

While the role of boss or leader may still be present, the new positions and relationships created by the workers are an attempt to change the logic of a traditionally functioning factory. IMPA factory recovery rejects maintaining the uneven distribution of benefit across a rigid hierarchy in favour of a horizontal engagement with material and social production that protects and celebrates the integrity of all participants.

Notes

1. All quotations in this chapter have been translated by the authors.
2. By expropriation, we refer to the process by which the public administration is dispossessing the owner of the ownership of the factory and transferring it to the workers of the factory who have organized under the cooperative figure.

References

Andrenacci, L. (2002) Algunas reflexiones en torno a la cuestión social y la asistencialización de la intervención social del Estado en la Argentina contemporánea. In L. Andrenacci (ed.) *Cuestión social y política social en el Gran Buenos Aires*. La Plata: Ediciones Al Margen—Universidad Nacional General Sarmiento, pp. 10–16.

Arceo, N., Monsalvo, A. and Wainer, A. (2007) Patrón de crecimiento y mercado de trabajo. *Realidad Económica* 226, pp. 9–24.

Benito, K. (2010) 'Piedra libre para todos los compañeros': análisis de la experiencia IMPA La Fábrica Ciudad Cultural. *Nómadas* 32, pp. 45–57.

Bokser, J. (2011) Teatristas trabajando: la experiencia IMPA. *La revista del* CCC 11.

Bresser Pereira, L. (1991) América Latina: ¿Consenso de Washington o crisis fiscal? *Pensamiento Iberoamericano* 19.

Di Loreto, M., García, L. and Slutzky, D. (2006) *Empresas recuperadas por los trabajadores. Situación actual y perspectivas*. Buenos Aires: Cuadernos del CEUR.

Duarte, M. (2002) El Consenso de Washington y su correlato en la Reforma del Estado en la Argentina: los efectos de la privatización. In M. Schorr, A. Castellani, M. Duarte and D. Debrott Sánchez (eds.) *Más allá del pensamiento único. Hacia una renovación de las ideas económicas en América Latina y el Caribe*. Buenos Aires: Clacso Libros, pp. 143–188.

Farinetti, M. (1999) ¿Qué queda del 'movimiento obrero'? Las formas del reclamo laboral en la nueva democracia argentina. *Trabajo y Sociedad* 1.

Hernández, M. (2013) *El movimiento de autogestión obrera en Argentina*. Buenos Aires: Topía.

Laclau, E. (1996) *Emancipación y diferencia*. Buenos Aires: Ariel.

Laclau, E. and Mouffe, C. (2004 [1985]) *Hegemony and Socialist Strategy*. Buenos Aires: Fondo de Cultura Económica.

Lorey, I. (2014) The 2011 Occupy Movements: Rancière and the Crisis of Democracy Theory. *Culture & Society* 31(7–8), pp. 43–65.

Lozano, C. (2001) Contexto económico y político en la protesta social de la Argentina contemporánea. *Observatorio Social para América Latina* 5, pp. 5–10.

Moore, S. (2013) Taking Up Space: Anthropology and Embodied Protest. *Radical Anthropology* 7, pp. 6–16.

Muñoz, M.A. (2006) Laclau and Rancière: Some Coordinates for the Interpretation of the Political. *Andamios* 2(4), pp. 119–144.

Pacheco, C. (2000) Una fábrica que produce magia. *La Nación*, 1 September. Available at: www.lanacion.com.ar/191142-una-fabrica-que-produce-magia [Accessed 2 May 2016].

Rancière, J. (1996) *El desacuerdo: política y filosofía.* Buenos Aires: Nueva Visión.

Rebón, J. (2004) *Desobedeciendo al desempleo. La experiencia de las empresas recuperadas.* Buenos Aires: PICASO/La Rosa Blindada.

Rebón, J., Kasparian, D. and Hernández, C. (2015) La economía moral del trabajo: La legitimidad social de las empresas recuperadas. *Trabajo y sociedad 25,* pp. 173–194.

Rodríguez, L.S. (2013) *Los movimientos sociales en la Argentina a partir de la década del 90.* Paper presented at XVIII Encuentro Nacional de Economía Política organized by Sociedad Brasilera de Economía Política.

Vázquez Blanco, J.M. (2010) *Empresas Recuperadas y Políticas Públicas En La Ciudad De Buenos Aires: Éxitos Y Fracasos.* Master's thesis in Public Administration, Buenos Aires: Facultad de Ciencias Económicas, Universidad de Buenos Aires.

16 Questioning Urban Commons
Challenges and Potentials in the Post-Democratic Era

Lukas Franta and Alexander Hamedinger

Setting the Context: Commons in the Neoliberal City?

In the course of the much-discussed shift from Fordism to post-Fordism (Amin 1994; Harvey 1989), cities are increasingly conceived of as sites of intensive economic, social and political restructuring. For some critical urban researchers, processes of neoliberalization can explain contemporary urban restructuring in different contexts (US; Western Europe; cf. Brenner and Theodore 2005; Hackworth 2007). Brenner and Theodore (2005: 103) argue that the consequences of neoliberal urbanization must be understood in their specific context, this "disjuncture" allows for the ideology's "specific pathways" of operation to be revealed which create the contested "uneven geographies of regulatory change". As a 'pure' form, neoliberalism does not exist; rather, it operates as a "process of market-driven social and spatial transformation" (*Ibid.*: 102) occurring in the context of specific forms of institutional and policy transformations. However, for a critical analysis of urban commons, the crucial characteristics of neoliberalization (Le Galès 2016; Harvey 2007) are that the market is seen as the best form of social and economic organization and that the state promotes market-driven urban policies (e.g. deregulation or privatization policies) and simultaneously embarks upon coercion and violence in an authoritarian manner to stabilize social and political order as well as upon more 'soft' policies, like seeing competition and the '*homo oeconomicus*' as universal norms disciplining individuals; this allows market actors to benefit from regulatory changes in terms of power relations (e.g. public-private partnerships) (Hackworth 2007). It is worth mentioning that neoliberalization remains a debated process with no fixed ends clearly demarcated. Questions persist on clear definitions (e.g. in contrast to liberalism; Le Galès 2016), on clear delineation from macro-developments (e.g. climate-change policies as another explanation for regulatory and institutional change in cities), on conceptual stretching and on converging or diverging development of cities worldwide (Brenner and Theodore 2010). However, an understanding of neoliberal urbanization helps to contextualize the potential, as well as the challenges, of urban commons.

The thinking behind radical democracy and some urban studies literature (Rancière 2008, 2014; Swyngedouw 2009, 2013) connects neoliberalism to losses in democratic quality and deficits in legitimation, hence neoliberalism is linked to post-democracy and the post-political. Swyngedouw (cf. 2013: 142) urges us to remember that the late capitalist political order of cities is based on the elimination of "contradiction", and hence the elimination of the "political". According to Purcell (2009), a main characteristic of this neoliberal order is that processes of political decision-making are consensus-oriented (see also Gabauer, this volume). Post-democracy furthers a consensual, technocratic and entrepreneurial form of urbanity, in which clearly identifiable social groups (with certain interests, goals, values, cultures) are connected or mediated between to reach a consensus.

Here we interpret urban commons as relational processes (not a product); as socio-spatial and sociopolitical practices of actors collectively producing and appropriating, maintaining, distributing and consuming certain urban resources. Commons are produced by actors with the aim to satisfy basic needs beyond state and market. The practice of commoning may have potential to emancipate various social groups from hegemonic neoliberal structures in the post-democratic city. We argue that only through interpreting urban commons as relational processes, as simultaneously spatial and political practices consciously countering neoliberalism, can their emancipatory potential can be unlocked. Emancipation (e.g. Laclau 2007) and the related approaches of 'emancipatory city' (e.g. Lees 2004) further help us to define urban commons in the context of the neoliberal city: emancipation means active political and social self-liberation from paternalistic and hegemonic structures and a democratization of social and political orders by citizens (e.g. through self-organization).[1]

The principal question of this paper is how urban commoning as a relational practice can unfold its emancipatory potential. Furthermore, we ask how urban commoning can cope with such challenges as instrumentalization by neoliberal rhetoric, as well as the risk of becoming socially exclusive through institutionalization and defining concepts of an 'us' versus a 'them'. The inspiring words of David Harvey on urban commons provide an important reference point: "Questions of the commons, we must conclude, are contradictory and therefore always contested. Behind these contestations lie conflicting social and political interests" (Harvey 2012: 71). We argue that the aforementioned understanding of urban commons enables not only grasping the relationship between the practices and policies of neoliberalization but also to discuss its relation to post-democracy, which is an inherent ingredient of neoliberalization, and urban commons.

We consider different approaches for defining urban commons by discussing relevant literature in the next section. Radical theories of democracy can help us understand the ambivalences of urban commoning, so we discuss it from the perspective of post-democratic reasoning. In the final section, we reflect on the relationship between urban commoning and the emancipatory processes.

Debates: Approaches to Urban Commons

In recent literature on urban commons,[2] the following core approaches can be identified:

- urban commons as an object
                 (in orthodox economic theory, commons are reduced
                     to a certain kind of good, i.e. a thing, leading to an
                 'ontologization' of the commons; see Helfrich 2012);

- urban commons as a practice to solve societal problems
                                    (Die Armutskonferenz 2013);

- urban commons as a governance mechanism
                                         (e.g. Ostrom 1994);

- commoning as a normative goal for transforming the organization of economy and society
                                           (Kratzwald 2015);

- commons as an analytical lens for understanding spatial counter-politics
                                    (Gibson-Graham et al. 2016).

Historically, commons are rooted in the 'Charter of the Forests' in the 13th century in England, regulating access rights for serfs to use the forest as a common resource for satisfying basic needs (e.g. firewood; Linebaugh 2008).

Within economic theory debates on commons (cf. Hardin 1968; Ostrom 1994), the work of Ostrom (1994) is a good starting point for discussions about governance mechanisms protecting shared, subtractive common-pool resources from overuse. Her approach focuses on self-organization as a governance mechanism and a policy goal on a small scale. She also analyzes the processes and structures behind organizing the access to and the use of the resources, which she finally formulated in design principles of 'common pool resources' (clear definition of users, collective choice arrangements, monitoring, conflict resolution mechanisms, definition of sanctions, etc.). According to Ostrom, to avoid the 'tragedy of the commons', forms of self-organization have some advantages over the state and the market, mainly because these are built on trust and reciprocity, which helps users to favour the 'common' and not the individual benefit. What emerges is that commons are seen as an object (e.g. water, land, firewood) with its own being, which is independent from its use by different actors, which is basically an ontological divide.

Kornberger and Borch (2015) allude to the work of Ostrom in trying to define 'urban' commons, while pointing to some serious shortcomings. Urban commons, according to them, are not to be interpreted as an object, but rather as a relational phenomenon (cf. *Ibid.* 2015: 7). The 'value' of commons in the city is strongly determined by density and relationality, meaning their value is determined by the activities of people, and urban commons are produced by consuming, using and appropriating: "Rather, usage and consumption practices are a constitutive part of the production of the urban commons" (*Ibid.*: 7). By this, the authors break away from the aforementioned ontological divide. More importantly, Kornberger and Borch (2015: 16) want to "downplay . . . the nostalgia often associated with the commons. . . . In other words, commons, and urban commons, are not just about opposing power and capitalism"; hence "all sorts of power and politics go into how commons are produced".

The relationship between the commons, commoning and space is another intensely debated topic involving the work of Ostrom. Moss (2014: 459–460) highlights deficits in research on the spatiality of commons. He stresses that most of this research interprets space as a natural, physical given (e.g. water), interprets space simply as the context of the development of institutional arrangements (mainly in Ostrom's work), or sees space as an exogenous phenomenon completely independent from agency. Moss argues that theories concerning space, place and scale in human geography have been developing over the years, and that new conceptualizations (e.g. the production of space by Lefebvre [1991] or the social construction of space by Löw [2001]) should be looked at by researchers interested in analyzing commons (cf. Moss 2014: 458). Taking into account a social constructivist and production approach to space avoids an 'essentialist' understanding of the commons. The relationship between governance mechanisms and space should be considered more clearly in future empirical research as commoning means producing space and, vice versa, spatial structures influence practices of commoning.

Dellenbaugh et al. (2015) interpret commons as an alternative model of economic and social organization—particularly attractive in the current context of severe austerity measures enforced in Europe. For them, commoning is not only about 'participatory self-governance', but also about reaching the goal of greater societal equity. Kip et al. (2015: 9) state: "It is also for this reason that we see alternative forms of commoning for health care, food, housing, or public spaces emerging most prominently in places devastated by austerity reforms." Kip et al. (2015) are not primarily interested in the resources shared themselves, but interpret urban commons as "collectively appropriating and regulating the shared concerns of the everyday" (*Ibid.*: 10). They share with Moss (2014) and Kornberger and Borch (2015) an interest in understanding the spatiality of the commons, particularly in defining the 'urban' in relation to the commons. The urban is understood as "a spatial organization of society" (Kip et al. 2015: 17) characterized by density and diversity of sociocultural structures. However, against a backdrop of increasingly differentiating urban societies and increasing socio-spatial mobilities, some ambivalences are mentioned: Kip et al. (2015) question whether commoning could also be a socially excluding practice. They conclude: "Urban commoners thus constantly need to negotiate and rearticulate the 'we'" (*Ibid.*: 18) and, moreover, the institutionalized inner and outer boundaries of the commons. These scholars see commons not as naturally given, because commons are produced through practices of actors with their specific perception and use of resources.

Exner and Kratzwald (2012) subscribe to this approach to commoning, interpreting commoning as a practice to solve societal problems beyond the state and the market, and believe in the transformative power of the commons. Helfrich and Bollier (2012) see commons as a way to build social capital and solidarity in society. Exner and Kratzwald (2012: 23) state that commons are social relations, created by commoners who want to collectively steward in order to satisfy basic social needs. According to Kratzwald (2015), commons consist of three elements: a resource (material or non-material), commoners using this resource, and processes and rules of negotiating the use and appropriation of the resources. Resources could entail renewable, non-renewable, natural, cultural or social objects, but a resource only becomes a commons when commoners decide to use it collectively. Kratzwald (2015) places the emerging discussion about urban commons in the context of the neoliberal city, and concedes that urban commons are interpreted differently by urban governments and marginalized social groups. For urban governments, urban commons are often welcomed mainly as a help to decentralize and outsource the provision of goods of collective consumption and to cushion fiscal constraints and outsource financial risks. Urban governments increasingly support the establishment of practices of commoning, e.g. by giving financial support or informing commoners about legal frameworks. Neoliberalism, with its salient features of privatization and marketization measures, increasingly deprives different social groups of basic rights by hampering access to services and basic human rights. For marginalized and politically active social groups, urban commons are seen as a way to reclaim the city, to realize the often formulated 'right to the city' (Lefebvre 1996) and to fulfil basic needs.

Exner and Kratzwald (2012) stress that commoning fundamentally differs from capitalist production. Ideally, commoning could be an emancipatory practice as it bypasses the narrow corsets defined by private property, competition, the market and scarcity. Historically, commons were starting points for resistance (e.g. against landowners) and thus bear the power of questioning power relations (Kratzwald 2015). Analyzing the potential of the commons requires taking hegemonic practices and power structures into account. Kratzwald (2015) also refers to the threats to commons from neoliberalism: "Commons are, even today, threatened by enclosure, destruction, criminalization, or appropriation within capitalist power structures" (*Ibid.*: 38). This is also underlined by Dawney et al. (2016), who see commons as spatial practices resisting privatization of resources through enclosure. They also emphasize the ethical aspects of commoning:

> The idea of the commons offers a romance, and through this romance, a way forward, a way to think out of the despondent political

narratives of ecological destruction, polarization and dispossession, and a counter-narrative to that of the inevitable and uncontrollable force of neoliberalism.

(Ibid.: 3)

This argument is strongly rooted in the work of David Harvey on urban commons and neoliberalism (2007, 2012). For Harvey (2012), capital accumulation involves a process in which resources such as land are increasingly incorporated and, thus, withdrawn from use for building social relations and for fulfilling basic needs. From a political-economic point of view, Harvey (2012) interprets commons "as an unstable and malleable social relation between particular self-defined social groups and those aspects of its actually existing or yet-to-be-created social and/or physical environment deemed crucial to its life and livelihood" (*Ibid.*: 73). He says that the relation between the resource and the commoners must be "collective and non-commodified" (*Ibid.*: 73), thus countering the logic of the market. He makes his position clear: "The political recognition that the commons can be produced, and used for social benefit becomes a framework for resisting capitalist power and rethinking the politics of an anti-capitalist tradition" (*Ibid.*: 87). Harvey is also ambivalent. He stresses that not all commons have open access, as setting the rules of commoning (e.g. who can take part?) implies defining a 'we' and a 'they'. Furthermore, he reminds us of the limits of horizontal coordination and the fact that decentralization and autonomy could be part of neoliberalization measures, too (Ostrom's polycentric governance). Capitalist urbanization has a tendency to not only destroy the city as a commons, but to simultaneously celebrate commons as a way to cut back state regulations. This way, commons can easily be incorporated into neoliberal market logic, e.g. community gardens utilized in market-led regeneration. Hardt and Negri (2009) consider how immaterial commons play an important role in capitalist accumulation, but point out that commons themselves can also accelerate capitalist production. In order to escape co-option through the market, Harvey suggests that commoners should steadfastly ensure their produced value remains under their control.

Harvey's contributions enable understanding urban commons as relational processes, as socio-spatial and sociopolitical practices, and this has implications for the theoretical conceptualization of space, and—inextricably linked—the meaning of political practice. Lefebvre's relational understanding of space based on the concept of the 'production of space' sets the ground for our further thinking. He considers everyday life and the 'political use of space': "It is the political use of space, however, that does the most to reinstate use value; it does this in terms of resources, spatial situations, and strategies" (Lefebvre 1991: 356). Practices of urban commoning have to be seen as political practices in which the use value of resources is put forward and strengthened.

Commons in Post-Democratic Societies: A Path to Emancipation

Urban commons are thus produced in a socio-spatial and sociopolitical practice and susceptible to struggles over resources, which themselves are rooted in societal power structures. In this way, urban commoning produces counter spaces where alternatives are imagined, invented or explored (Knierbein 2015). Here, the inherent 'political' of space emerges through 'individual acts of (re)appropriating, (re)politicising and de-alienating public space as counter space in everyday life' (Knierbein 2015: 54) for the practice of concrete social utopias.

Emancipation is understood as the process of overcoming a collective identity given by the police order, as a transgression of existing structures, norms or any socio-spatial arrangements (see Lees 2004) through encounters of difference in urban public space. While Lees's (2004) work is confined to analyzing processes of future emancipation, Lorey (2014) offers an account of present emancipatory processes, or 'presentist democracy', building on Rancière's theories of radical democracy. Besides authors such as Swyngedouw (2009, 2013) or Crouch (2008), Rancière's ideas on radical democracy (Rancière 2014; Badiou and Rancière 2010) are among the most widely discussed within post-democracy theory.

The work of Crouch, Swyngedouw and Rancière thus form the basis for the following analysis on the emancipatory potential of urban commoning in the post-democratic city. Post-democracy describes political practices based on consensus, objectivation and fixation of truth, but also on repression and social exclusion (Mullis and Schipper 2013: 84). In the words of Badiou and Rancière (2010): "Post-democracy best names itself consensual democracy" (*Ibid.*: 138, translated by authors). In post-democracy, everything can be seen and nothing new can emerge. Rancière asserts that the hegemonic model of neoliberalism and that of a market-driven society has been successful on its own terms, as it describes itself as a model without alternatives.

Rancière's concept integrates the socio-spatial order called 'the police', roughly equivalent to state and society, resistance against it, democracy and the politics of space, underscoring its usefulness in looking at a socio-spatial and sociopolitical practice as urban commoning. In Rancière's radical democracy (2014; Badiou and Rancière 2010), the 'police' plays a crucial role: it describes a socio-spatial order, allocating subjects their seemingly natural place in this spatial organization (see also Shields or van Wymeersch & Oosterlynck in this volume).

The practice of urban commoning, with its anti-economization, anti-financialization, anti-commodification principles and anti-capitalist attitude, stands clearly opposed to a capitalist 'police' order. An example of commoners' resistance was the passing of the 'Declaration of the Occupation of New York City' (New York City General Assembly 2011) in the first General Assembly of Occupy Wall Street in New York. The commons of the camp was symbolized by protesters referring to themselves as 'one people', and thus assuming an identity contrary to that allocated to them in the police order (Lorey 2014). In Rancière's framework (2014), the protesters/commoners can be interpreted as the 'unaccounted for', who are excluded from political decision-making in a certain order. Another aspect is important concerning counter-politics: the 'police' cannot precisely expect their form of emergence, i.e. which practices will be employed to form counter spaces. Commoners articulate their interests at a certain time and in a certain place, and disrupt the 'police' order to newly define the whole. These social groups reject status assigned to them by the 'police' and assume a new position in the social order through the practice of commoning via alternative modes of accumulation beyond the capitalist. This aligns with the definitions of urban commoning as an alternative to the neoliberal economy (see Harvey 2012; Kratzwald 2015; Dellenbaugh et al. 2015). Commoners construct a common space (Dikeç 2005: 178) in which perceived injustices can be questioned. A new socio-spatial and political order emerges through the practice of commoning—another 'partitioning of the sensible'—reminding us of Exner and Kratzwald's (2012) characterization of the emancipatory potential of urban commoning.

As the separation of the people from their assigned places is an act of politics (Rancière 2014), moments when commoners assume a new identity and place themselves outside the 'police' order are considered 'moments of democracy'. Again, Occupy Wall Street's declaration comes to mind, transgressing assigned positions in the police order.

While, as discussed, the practice of urban commoning certainly challenges the 'police' order, its status as separate from neoliberal forces is by no means clear cut or without ambivalence:

(1) Democratization, institutionalization and the relation to the 'police': Looking at Occupy Wall Street as an example of commons and emancipatory politics highlights the challenge for commoners to deal with existing institutions. In both Amsterdam and New York, Occupy protesters were under scrutiny from institutions, such as the city administrations that demanded permits for the operation of mobile toilets or electricity generators, and threatened with eviction (see Franta 2013). As soon as urban commoning is subjected to one of these institutional requirements and commoners accept these rules of the institutionalized game, the 'moment of democracy' has passed. Urban commoning then became part of the new 'police' order, an order that includes urban commoning in its institutional setup. Against this enclosure and from a relational perspective, commoning as a 'moment of democracy' is the constitution of the commoners as a group with simultaneous practices of consuming, using and appropriating (see Kornberger and Borch 2015) in an alternative mode of economic and social organization (see Dellenbaugh et al. 2015).

(2) Identity building: crucial for the construction of the socio-spatial and sociopolitical alternative is the moment of identification, in which the

commoners develop a new 'we'. However, an identity can only be formed in contrast with another identity. Laclau's observations (2007) on emancipatory politics points to this difficulty by discussing aspects to the inextricable entanglement between dominant structures and counter-politics. Urban commoning as an alternative form of organization only becomes meaningful when it is completely separate from the post-democratic, capitalist order. The meaning of post-democracy prescribes the content of its alternative politics. In the process of formulating alternative politics, urban commoners acknowledge the structures they want to counteract. Laclau describes the identity antagonism as follows: "I cannot assert a differential identity without distinguishing it from a context, and, in the process of making this distinction I am asserting the context at the same time" (Laclau 2007: 27).

(3) Co-optation: Assuming urban commoners want to change the post-democratic order through their actions and are aiming for a more egalitarian society, urban commoning faces another conundrum. If urban commoners succeed in changing the post-democratic order and a new phase of socio-political order emerges, the identity and the content of the urban commons will be affected: "I cannot destroy a context without destroying at the same time the identity of the particular subject who carries out the destruction" (Laclau 2007: 27). The re-articulation of the identity will be needed to retain the alternative content of urban commoning.

Positioned in the framework of radical democracy, however, urban commoning has a powerful potential for 'moments of democracy', for emancipation to assume a new position in sociopolitical structures.

Commons and Practices of Emancipation: Challenges and Potentials

Urban commoning as socio-spatial and sociopolitical practices has the potential to be emancipatory, particularly if emancipation is understood as self-liberation from hegemonic structures and self-empowerment. Urban commoning practices should rely on producing and maintaining use value as an alternative to the production of exchange value to fully unlock their potential. Commoning has the potential to offer emancipatory benefits through self-organization to alter patterns of allocation of and access to spaces and resources to foster equity in society. The identification process of 'we' and 'they' and the subsequent organization as a group of commoners encourages capacity building by internally structuring needs, aspirations and goals of commoning within their own self-governance framework. Commoning offers 'emancipation from' previously assigned positions in the social realm, and 'emancipation to' live a newly found identity, equipping individuals with collective strategies for self-liberation from previously assigned positions and structures in the sociopolitical and spatial order, which clearly shows the political use of space. Commoning may provide counter public spaces if such spaces are created by practising sociopolitical utopias of emancipation in the present urban environment.

Lorey and her notion of 'presentist democracy' are inspiring in the struggle against the aforementioned issues of co-optation, social exclusion and institutionalization. Presentist democracy is a 'political form that is practised in the situation of the assembly and in the organizing of the camps' (Lorey 2014: 18) and executed by a heterogeneous many. Here, the democratic moment lies in the context of a heterogeneous group organizing itself under the premise of horizontal equity and the rejection of hierarchy. Every time the heterogeneous many come together in this form, they challenge the police order, producing a counter space. This way, every general assembly is a 'moment of democracy'—the collective identity is reasserted through the coming together of the heterogeneous many.

Commons as the praxis of sociopolitical utopias and emergent counter public spaces are thus understood as sources of societal resistance, where alternatives to existing social, political and economic orders are developed and practised. Alternative politics and commoning are intrinsically linked, highlighting its potential as a locus of counter politics to the neoliberal order. One of the core characteristics of commons is the non-commodified and collective relationship between the resource and the commoners, a feature that clearly distinguishes commoning from neoliberal governance arrangements. As such, commoning is indeed an alternative to neoliberalism and can be a hotbed of resistance. Thus, commoning provides spaces important for the emergence of alternative socio-spatial and sociopolitical concepts as observed in insurgent movements, such as Occupy Wall Street, or even in a neighbourhood food co-op around the corner.

Notes

1. Another aspect, which is important but cannot be explored in this contribution, concerns the relation between citizenship and commoning. The ability to formulate collective aspirations, goals and needs through the practice of commoning affords a new form of citizenship, to develop the capacity to claim the 'right to have rights' (see Holston 2008), an important premise for politics in Rancière's understanding (Dikeç 2005) to emerge.
2. This chapter can only give an overview about prominent and important theoretical positions, as a precise discussion of the bulk of literature on (urban) commons recently developed would exceed the confines of this text (e.g. the city as commons from a legal perspective: Foster and Iaione 2016; the debate about urban commons in *Antipode*: Bunce 2015; Chatterton et al. 2012; Eizenberg 2011).

References

Amin, A. (ed.) (1994) *Post-Fordism: A Reader*. Oxford: Blackwell.
Badiou, A. and Rancière, J. (2010) *Politik der Wahrheit*. Wien: Verlag Turia+Kant.
Brenner, N. and Theodore, N. (2005) Neoliberalism and the Urban Condition. *City* 9(1), pp. 102–107.

Brenner, N. and Theodore, N. (2010) Variegated Neoliberalization: Geographies, Modalities, Pathways. *Global Networks* 10(2), pp. 182–222.

Bunce, S. (2015) Pursuing Urban Commons: Politics and Alliances in Community Land Trust Activism in East London. *Antipode* 48(1), pp. 134–150.

Chatterton, P., Featherstone, D. and Routledge, P. (2012) Articulating Climate Justice in Copenhagen: Antagonism, the Commons, and Solidarity. *Antipode* 45(3), pp. 602–620.

Crouch, C. (2008) *Postdemokratie*. Frankfurt am Main: Suhrkamp.

Dawney, L., Kirwan, S. and Brigstocke, J. (2016) Introduction: The Promise of the Commons. In S. Kirwan, L. Dawney and J. Brigstocke (eds.) *Space, Power and the Commons*. London: Routledge, p. 1.27.

Dellenbaugh, M., Kip, M., Bieniok, M., Müller, A.K. and Schwegmann, M. (eds.) (2015) *Urban Commons: Moving Beyond State and Market*. Basel: Birkhäuser.

Die Armutskonferenz (ed.) (2013) *Was allen gehört. Commons—Neue Perspektiven in der Armutsbekämpfung*. Wien: ÖGB Verlag.

Dikeç, M. (2005) Space, Politics, and the Political. *Environment and Planning D* 23(2), pp. 171–188.

Eizenberg, E. (2011) Actually Existing Commons: Three Moments of Space of Community Gardens in New York City. *Antipode* 44(3), pp. 764–782.

Exner, A. and Kratzwald, B. (2012) *Solidarische Ökonomie & Commons*. Wien: Mandelbaum Verlag.

Foster, S.R. and Iaione, C. (2016) The City as a Commons. *Yale Law & Policy Review* 34(2), pp. 281–349.

Franta, L. (2013) *The Geographies of Contentious Politics: The Role of Space in Occupy Wall Street*. Master's thesis in Urban Studies, Amsterdam: University of Amsterdam.

Gibson-Graham, J.K., Cameron, J. and Healy, S. (2016) Commoning as a Postcapitalist Politics. In A. Amin and P. Howell (eds.) *Releasing the Commons: Rethinking the Futures of the Commons*. London: Routledge, pp. 192–212.

Hackworth, J. (2007) *The Neoliberal City: Governance, Ideology, and Development in American Urbanism*. Ithaca: Cornell University Press.

Hardin, G. (1968) The Tragedy of the Commons. *Science* 162(3859), pp. 1243–1248.

Hardt, M. and Negri, A. (2009) *Commonwealth*. Cambridge: Harvard University Press.

Harvey, D. (1989) From Managerialism to Entrepreneurialism: Formation of Urban Governance in Late Capitalism. *Geografisker Annaler* 71B, pp. 3–17.

Harvey, D. (2007) *Kleine Geschichte des Neoliberalismus*. Zürich: Rotpunktverlag.

Harvey, D. (2012) *Rebel Cities: From the Right to the City to the Urban Revolution*. London: Verso.

Helfrich, S. (2012) Gemeingüter sind nicht, sie werden gemacht. In S. Helfrich and Heinrich-Böll-Stiftung (eds.) *Commons. Für eine neue Politik jenseits von Markt und Staat*. Bielefeld: Transcript Verlag, pp. 85–91.

Helfrich, S. and Bollier, D. (2012) Commons als transformative Kraft. Zur Einführung. In S. Helfrich and Heinrich-Böll-Stiftung (eds.) *Commmons. Für eine neue Politik jenseits von Markt und Staat*. Bielefeld: Transcript Verlag, pp. 15–23.

Holston, J. (2008) *Insurgent Citizenship: Disjunctions of Democracy and Modernity in Brazil*. Princeton: Princeton University Press.

Kip, M., Bieniok, M., Dellenbaugh, M., Müller, A.K. and Schwegmann, M. (2015) Seizing the (Every)day: Welcome to the Urban Commons! In M. Dellenbaugh,

M. Kip, M. Bieniok, A. Müller and M. Schwegmann (eds.) *Urban Commons: Moving Beyond State and Market*. Basel: Birkhäuser, pp. 9–25.

Knierbein, S. (2015) Public Space as Relational Counter Space: Scholarly Minefield or Epistemological Opportunity? In C. Tornaghi and S. Knierbein (eds.) *Public Space and Relational Perspectives: New Challenges for Architecture and Planning*. London: Routledge, pp. 42–63.

Kornberger, M. and Borch, C. (2015) Introduction: Urban Commons. In C. Borch and M. Kornberger (eds.) *Urban Commons: Rethinking the City*. London: Routledge, pp. 1–21.

Kratzwald, B. (2015) Urban Commons: Dissident Practices in Emancipatory Spaces. In M. Dellenbaugh, M. Kip, M. Bieniok, A. Müller and M. Schwegmann (eds.) *Urban Commons: Moving Beyond State and Market*. Basel: Birkhäuser, pp. 26–41.

Laclau, E. (2007) *Emancipation(s)*. London: Verso.

Lees, L. (ed.) (2004) *The Emancipatory City? Paradoxes and Possibilities*. London: Sage Publications.

Lefebvre, H. (1991) *The Production of Space*. Oxford: Blackwell.

Lefebvre, H. (1996) The Right to the City. In E. Kofman and E. Lebas (eds.) *Writings on Cities*. Cambridge: Wiley-Blackwell, pp. 147–159.

Le Galès, P. (2016) Neoliberalism and Urban Change: Stretching a Good Idea Too Far? *Territory, Politics, Governance* 4(2), pp. 154–172.

Linebaugh, P. (2008) *The Magna Carta Manifesto: Liberties and Commons for All*. Berkeley: University of California Press.

Lorey, I. (2014) The 2011 Occupy Movements: Rancière and the Crisis of Democracy. *Theory, Culture & Society* 31(7–8), pp. 43–65.

Löw, M. (2001) *Raumsoziologie*. Frankfurt am Main: Suhrkamp.

Moss, T. (2014) Spatiality of the Commons. *International Journal of the Commons* 8(2), pp. 457–471.

Mullis, D. and Schipper, S. (2013) Die postdemokratische Stadt zwischen Politisierung und Kontinuität. *Sub\urban—Zeitschrift für kritische Stadtforschung* 1(2), pp. 79–100.

New York City General Assembly (2011) *The Declaration of the Occupation of New York City*. New York: NYC General Assembly [Online]. Available at: http://occupywallstreet.net/policy/declaration-occupation-new-york-city [Accessed 14 June 2017].

Ostrom, E. (1994) *Governing the Commons: The Evolution of Institutions for Collective Action*. Cambridge: Cambridge University Press.

Purcell, M. (2009) Resisting Neoliberalization: Communicative Planning of Counter-Hegemonic Movements? *Planning Theory* 8(2), pp. 140–165.

Rancière, J. (2008) *Zehn Thesen zur Politik*. Zürich: Diaphanes.

Rancière, J. (2014) *Das Unvernehmen, 5. Auflage*. Frankfurt am Main: Suhrkamp.

Swyngedouw, E. (2009) The Antinomies of the Postpolitical City: In Search of a Democratic Politics of Environmental Production. *International Journal of Urban and Regional Studies* 33(3), pp. 601–620.

Swyngedouw, E. (2013) Die Post-Politische Stadt. *Suburban—Zeitschrift für kritische Stadtforschung* 1(2), pp. 141–158.

17 Hybridizing 'Ownership' of Public Space

Framings of Urban Emancipation in Crisis-Ridden Thessaloniki

Evangelia Athanassiou, Charis Christodoulou, Matina Kapsali and Maria Karagianni

Introduction

This chapter departs from the ongoing discussion on citizen participation in urban settings, examining such practices as hybridizing processes of public space ownership. During the recent, more-than-financial crisis in Greece, new modes of developing, managing and using public space emerged. Representing various degrees of 'publicness', these new modes correspond to a wide spectrum of public space ownership schemes, ranging from corporate management to citizen appropriation. Here, we seek to identify these new hybrid notions and forms of 'ownership' as they form in Thessaloniki's public spaces. We argue that, within the post-political city, the idea of 'ownership' is being hybridized through the actions of multiple agents, who embrace diversified narratives of participation and citizenship.

In doing so, we mobilize the concept of 'ownership' to examine whether it can act as a 'bridge' from property to emancipation in the production of public spaces. Hence, embracing a relational understanding of ownership, we refer to its hybridization as the blurring of the public/private divide when it comes to public space production. If emancipation should be understood as the "perpetual contestation of the alienating effects of contemporary neoliberalization" (Springer 2011: 525), are new hybrid forms of ownership contesting existing hegemonies? To what extent and in what ways are they contributing towards more participatory, representative, open, democratic urban politics? Does 'ownership' hybridization promote democratic change and emancipation, or does it form an intrinsic part of neoliberal governance within the post-political condition?

Public Space 'Ownership' and 'Emancipation'

The neoliberal "language of property" (Blomley 2004a: 614), as it unfolds through public space within post-political urban governance, is not solely expressed by the increasing influence of private interests on public property. This is undoubtedly a dominant and well-documented trend in different urban contexts, which reduces the role of the state in the management of public space through a variety of mechanisms (Miller 2007; De Magalhaes 2010). However, the shifting of our focus towards 'enacted ownership', as a material condition in public space, reveals different processes instigated both by local authorities and by citizens. New forms of 'ownership' emerge, beyond property rights, both in legal and in activist terms. In that, 'ownership' is not static but relational and cannot always be pigeonholed as either public or private.

Hence, in this chapter 'ownership' is not used interchangeably with the word 'property'. We use the term 'ownership' referring to all the sociopolitical attributes and relational conditions of the property that can be bestowed, attributed and/or managed through formal processes of planning and management and/or everyday action (e.g. materialized in terms of occupation or simply by everyday maintenance). By 'property', we refer to the material 'object' in its absolute title and legal rights as the notion in the Greek context derives from the civic Roman-Germanic law system (see also Van der Walt 2009: 29–39), as well as to the notion of the valued 'object' in the capitalist real-estate market. In the Greek context, property, whether private or public, is the rudiment of urban planning and urban space production. Thus, it constitutes a definitive part of long-standing spatial hegemony and control.

Public space, understood as relational and processual rather than fixed, is seen as a critical terrain in and through which 'emancipation' is performed. Emancipation, thus, is not understood as a utopian end-state but rather as the materialization of radical democratic politics in the here and now. "Politics", following Swyngedouw (2011: 7), "is an inherently public affair and unfolds in and through the transformation of space, both materially and symbolically". Within the context of this chapter, a praxis-oriented perspective of emancipation is emphasized. Emancipatory tactics have been enacted and embodied in urban public space as an outcry for radical democracy and closely intertwined with space in the production of concerns, raising desires, articulating needs and providing solutions to make the city a real political project. Democratic politics, in turn, are linked to *agonism* (Mouffe 2004: 124), which "refers to the idea that conflict cannot and should not be eradicated in democratic societies".

Urban Space Production in Greek Cities: Issues of Ownership and Authority

Originating from the Greek constitution, urban public space is ascribed to specified land within urban settings. It derives from plans which are developed through ad hoc long-term and solely state-driven processes. All types of public space—areas of common use such as roads, squares and parks and of public purpose uses such as schools, health and sports facilities—are generated through state-driven obligatory processes of distribution of private and public property. Urban public space is determined in statutory terms and is demarcated as residual to private landed property. Hence, it has, officially and almost solely, been developed by national and local authorities. At the same time, the significance of public property in attracting capital investment to promote development in Greece has been a focal point of discussion in dealing with the debt crisis. Since 2010, there have been continuing efforts towards 'minimizing' the state and promoting privatizations through successive 'Economic Adjustment Programs' (EAPs), orchestrated by the European Commission, the European Central Bank and the International Monetary Fund and imposed by Greek governments. This process of 'minimizing' the state was promoted by the introduction of an unprecedented amount of new legislation, through which public property has been introduced into the capitalist system of development as a "fictive individual" (Blomley 2004b: 7), a supposed private owner. Seen as a capital 'asset', it has been transferred to the Hellenic Republic Asset Development Fund to be sold to and developed by the private sector.

There has also been an overall urge of statutory (i.e. public agency) proprietors—municipalities included—to act as property managers. In fact, this process started long before the crisis. It is since the late 1990s that the management of numerous public/municipal services is being privatized or outsourced (Vitopoulou et al. 2015: 186). Nevertheless, public-private partnerships, introduced and strongly promoted by means of national legislation since the mid-2000s, never flourished. Public administration and the legal planning framework have largely operated beyond this and other similar policies. Thus, they are often hegemonically framed as a long-resisting "impediment" to large-scale capitalist urban development (*Ibid.*: 223–249).

Despite a series of steps taken to 'modernize' and simplify planning and development processes, there are areas in and around cities which are demarcated for public use, but their development status remains blurry in relation to planning attributes, responsible authority and property rights. Additionally, multiple authorities are enacted without being coordinated. This property fuzziness and entanglement of powers and jurisdictions on public space has often created delays in the implementation of public infrastructure projects and incited political clashes and citizen claims, which reflect conflicting interests in each case. In other words, it takes a very long time and political effort to institutionally facilitate (public or private) investment in public property. However, "institutions define not only constraints but also enablements" (Kazepov 2005: 32). This long-lasting inertia in some cases has provided an opportunity for contestations 'from below' to emerge, and in others has produced participatory infusions into official urban management (e.g. local authorities engaging with either citizens or private partners).

Corporate Management and Volunteering in Thessaloniki's Public Space

During the recent crisis, Thessaloniki's streets, sidewalks, squares and parks have become the theatre of urban poverty, neglect and lack of maintenance, but also of political insurgence and everyday collective and solidarity practices. Notwithstanding the shrinkage of economic resources, there has been increased activity by the current administration of the municipality aimed at enhancing, revitalizing or regulating the use of public space: architectural competitions, traffic calming, 'reclaiming' space for pedestrians, programming of events. With a few exceptions, these interventions are in the city centre and its most prominent part, the New Waterfront. We consider this increased activity part of the municipality's effort to internationalize the city and improve its image as a tourist destination. Adopting a branding identity, participating in international networks and hosting international events, as well as struggling for attractive, green, clean and safe public spaces, are all means towards the uncontested mandate of urban competitiveness.

The municipality's interest in public space is accompanied by discernible shifts on its management and regulation. During the last decade, a lively academic discussion, led by urban geographers, has been tracing developments signalling the privatization of public space in different contexts, identifying their agents and processes and discussing their repercussions on the 'publicness' of squares and streets (Langstaat and Van Melik 2013; Nemeth and Schmidt 2011). Outsourcing urban management services has become a common practice and is not particular to the management of public space (De Magalhaes 2010). During increasing urban neoliberalization processes, which were intensified during the recent crisis in Greece, municipalities surrender part of their responsibilities to the private sector. In Thessaloniki, the mechanisms through which the private sector is introduced to public space range from adopting trees or donating benches, urban equipment and whole playgrounds to sponsoring/co-organizing public events and taking over management, maintenance and redevelopment. These practices relativize the long-standing authority of municipalities and other public agents on publicly owned spaces, but do not transfer property. Instead, a new form of hybrid ownership is enacted that identifies public space as a value-producing terrain for the corporate sector. This process of hybridization of ownership materializes the local version of global trends, which point both towards privatization of public space and towards volunteering and participatory management. Such hybrid forms are legitimated on the grounds of lack of state funding and framed within the neoliberal mandate of reducing the state and the rhetoric of urban safety and attractiveness. Representative of this shift is that the mayor, Yannis Boutaris, has announced a "policy to seek private sponsoring for activities, for the common good" (Gerakaritou 2011, translated by authors).

Questioning this framing of 'common good' by the mayor, in what follows we examine four cases/spaces (Figure 17.1) where multiple stakeholders and citizen groups participated in the creation and/or management of public spaces. Empirical data was collected from published official documents and press releases, internet research and a limited number of interviews. Based on these, we attempt to map the agents, authorities, processes and tactics contributing to the creation of this new, hybrid and often conflictual public terrain.

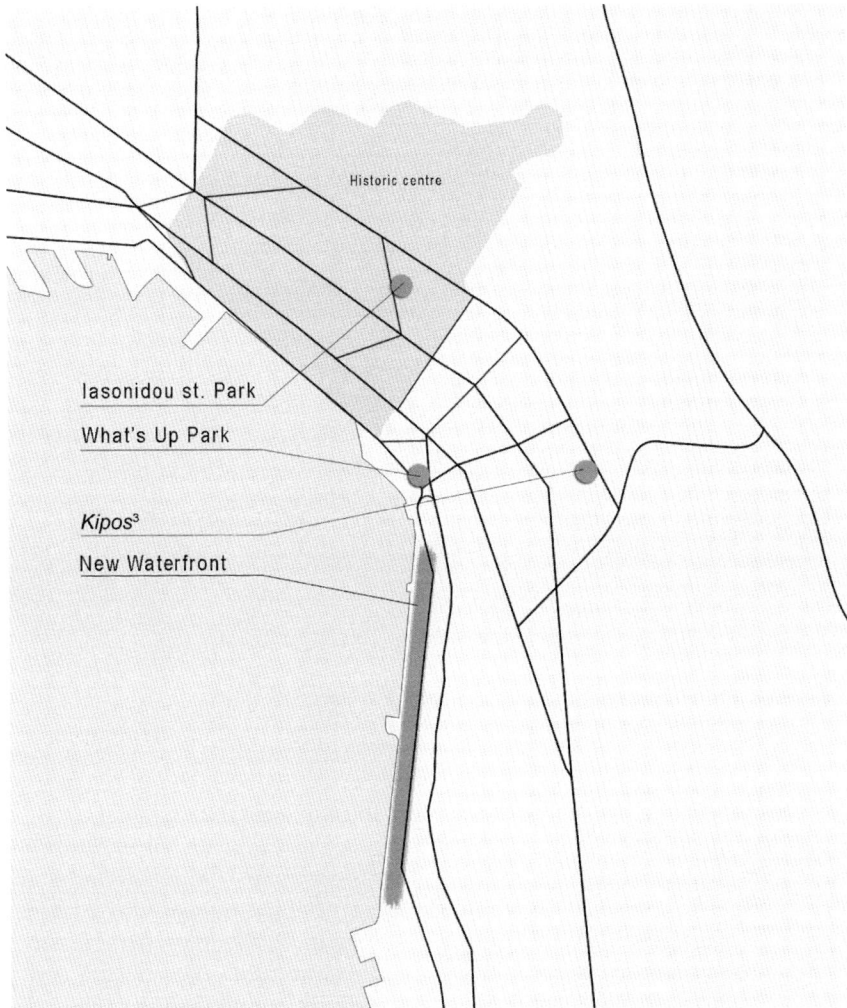

Figure 17.1 Map showing the location of the case studies in Thessaloniki
Source: Evangelia Athanassiou, Charis Christodoulou, Matina Kapsali and Maria Karagianni, 2017

What's Up Park is a telling example in this respect (Figure 17.2). The park was initiated and financed by the leading mobile telecommunications company in Greece. Before its redevelopment, the park was frequented by drug users and hence was considered a "phobic" place, as the vice mayor stated during our interview (25 May 2012, Thessaloniki Town Hall, personal interview). The municipality sought to cleanse it from those undesirable users by introducing new uses, rules and 24-hour surveillance. In this case,

Figure 17.2 Corporate promotion at *What's Up Park*
Source: Evangelia Athanassiou, 2011

redevelopment and private involvement in the management and maintenance of public space could be interpreted as an act of exclusion of undesirable users, promoting attractiveness and safety for 'citizens' (Mitchell and Staeheli 2006). The company withdrew its support before the two-year contract expired as the cost of maintenance was 'too high'. While the contract lasted, the company imposed its corporate image on the park, organized a series of events and used the park in its advertising campaign. In the municipality's hegemonic discourse, the park's temporary hybrid ownership 'reopened' public space to the 'citizens'. At the same time, though, it revealed public space as a new terrain of value production, as a space of continuous surveillance and ultimately as an active tool of exclusion, in this case of the park's previous users, who were mainly drug users.

The volunteering sector, in the form of community groups and individual volunteers, is also introduced to public space management and surveillance through formal contracts or informal collaborations with the local authority (Langstraat and Van Melik 2013; De Magalhaes 2010). The municipality increasingly engages 'active citizens' in the management or maintenance of public space through a rhetoric of 'empowerment' and 'citizenship'. Public space initiatives include co-organizing events, maintenance of urban equipment, environmental campaigns and more permanent arrangements such as the creation of a volunteer network. A campaign entitled 'I love my city—I adopt my neighbourhood' was also launched, encouraging citizens to engage in the management of 'their neighbourhood' and show their love to 'their city'. Thus, the idea of citizens 'taking ownership', and hence responsibility and pride over the city and its public spaces, was introduced.

The case of 'green space volunteers' is indicative. During his first term in office in 2010, the mayor of Thessaloniki made a call for 'green space volunteers', i.e. for "conscientious citizens who are interested in quality of life in the city" who would "adopt" a green space and take over its gardening and care (Municipality of Thessaloniki 2017). Also, volunteers would "protect urban furniture from destruction, vandalism, trespassing and unauthorized actions" (*Ibid.*). Beyond the intention to engage active citizens in the maintenance of public space, a different objective becomes evident. Namely, keeping public spaces 'clean and safe' for those who are defined as citizens, through surveillance and restrictions against other undesirable users (Mitchell and Staeheli 2006).

Strategies of 'Co-Ownership' in Thessaloniki Public Space

The processes analyzed in the previous section can be grouped together as a first wave of sporadic, rather unconnected top-down/official responses to the crisis, signalling the beginning of a process of hybridization of public space ownership. We identify a second wave of responses, which is based on Thessaloniki's Preliminary Resilience Assessment (PRA) (Office of Urban Resilience 2016), and forward a new institutional framing for this process, along with other concerted attempts.

Thessaloniki's participation in the '100 Resilient Cities' network is one among many similar networking initiatives taken by the city's central municipality, aiming at the city's internationalization. The network was initiated and funded by the Rockefeller Foundation. This project promotes 'resilience' (itself a blurry idea—see Davoudi 2012) in cities around the globe and offers funding for recruiting a 'chief resilience officer' and consultancy in each participating city. Additionally, the project is supported by a large network of corporate partners such as Microsoft, Nature Conservancy, Swiss Re and Veolia.

The PRA identifies "co-ownership of public space" as one of the five "discovery areas" that need to be addressed (Office of Urban Resilience 2016: 52–53). The report estimates that "considering the shortage of open spaces in Thessaloniki, the goal of successfully revitalising the existing ones rises as one of the top priorities for creating a more resilient city" (*Ibid.*: 52). Moreover, it recognizes "a great increase in community engagement and solidarity in times of crisis" and states that "the arising challenge is how the city could channel this valuable social capital into processes that will encourage the concept of shared ownership of public space to emerge" (*Ibid.*: 53). The concept of 'co-ownership' is framed as the management, maintenance and programming of spaces and not (yet) to changes in the property structure. It introduces new agents caring for or acting upon public space, i.e. performing a version of enacted ownership, specifically in the sense of stewardship or engagement. The possible agents are aptly called "stakeholders of a publicly owned area" and could be "a neighbourhood's committee, a local NGO, a school, a local initiative and so on" (*Ibid.*: 53).

In parallel to the municipality's practices, the urban dwellers' increased involvement in public space production and management leads to diverse forms of ownership. Here, we focus on three sites where four citizen-participation initiatives emerged during the last five years: the New Waterfront, an urban garden on Aghiou Dimitriou Street and a park on Iasonidou Street.

Citizens' Initiatives on the New Waterfront

One of the most prominent and advertised spaces in Thessaloniki is the recently revitalized New Waterfront, which is at the top of the municipality's agenda as well as a new terrain for citizens' initiatives of different kinds. The municipality has developed links with citizens' groups, granting them permission to organize events there, offering its support or co-organizing. However, not all urban dwellers are welcome in the newly regenerated waterfront. *Aganaktismeni* (the Greek *Indignados*), who camped there in 2011, were evicted by the police with the municipal authority's support, while political festivals, which used to take place there before the 'revitalization', stopped being licensed to use the space after that. Hence, the waterfront's 'revitalization' highly contributed to its depoliticization, as the space now seems to be designated only for those uses and users that fit into the aestheticized image promoted by the municipality.

Two of the most active citizens' initiatives in the city's waterfront are the *Los Lampicos* and the *Friends of the New Waterfront* (FNW). *Los Lampicos* (in Greek '*lampico*' means 'shiny clean'), founded in 2011, is a citizen initiative aimed at keeping the New Waterfront clean of garbage and graffiti. They frequently meet to clean the waterfront's urban equipment from what they deem as 'non-artistic graffiti', often with support from other volunteer groups (e.g. YMCA, private school groups). The *FNW* initiative has a more formal structure. It has a subscription cost for members, an administrative council and a constitution which determines its specific aims. Since its founding in 2013, the *FNW* have organized many cultural and educational events, including treasure hunting games, tree plantings, photography exhibitions and fashion show catwalks (Figure 17.3).

Both initiatives mark attempts of self-organized citizens to maintain, clean and promote the New Waterfront. As Nikiforidis—one of the architects who designed the New Waterfront and *FNW*'s leading figure—advocates, the motives for being a member of the *FNW* are a love for Thessaloniki and its public spaces and "a will to inhabit public space differently" (Zafeirakis 2014: para. 06, translated by authors). As *FNW* state on their Facebook page, "through research, cultural actions and activism, [they] aim to support

Figure 17.3 *FNW*-organized fashion catwalk at the *New Waterfront*, 2016
Source: Evangelia Athanassiou, 2016

a collective inhabiting of Thessaloniki's New Waterfront which constitutes an invaluable public space for the city's inhabitants and visitors" (FNW 2016). In line with this, Korikis of *Los Lampicos*, in a TV interview in 2014 to TV100, declared that volunteerism is the "utmost expression of democracy" (Korikis 2014). Indeed, Los Lampicos emphasize citizens' individual responsibility, as this constitutes, according to them, simultaneously a matter of 'civilization' and a way to promote the city's image. Curiously, they consider such actions one way out of the crisis and a generator of economic growth.

Although the New Waterfront is officially municipally managed, these two initiatives take up its ownership through their temporary spatial practices. *Los Lampicos* set 'cleanliness' and 'attractiveness' as their main purpose; while the *FNW* embrace a broader goal, focusing on maintenance, as well as on the intensive organizing of events. Most of these events take place in collaboration with the municipality and are backed by private sponsors. The New Waterfront is thus understood as a recreation space for the city's inhabitants and an attractive space contributing to the city's branding. Both groups present the waterfront as a space of empowerment, citizenship and civic pride. This is a shared vision of *Los Lampicos*, *FNW* and the municipality and there is no confrontation or conflict between them. Indeed, the PRA identifies volunteerism in the New Waterfront as a case of unofficial public space 'co-ownership' and a best practice (Office of Urban Resilience 2016: 53).

Kipos³—City as a Resource

Another initiative located at a public space in Thessaloniki emanated from an innovation funding call by the Angelopoulos-Clinton Foundation. The *Kipos³—City as a Resource* project, launched in 2014 on a municipally owned plot close to the city centre by two architects and one agriculturist, aims to promote "a new understanding . . . of dealing with urban unbuilt areas . . ., in particular with the 'public green'" (Gavrilidou et al. 2015: 78). It promotes the creation of a network of urban gardens that will contribute to "the transformation of unformed spaces and urban 'voids' into spots for communal gardening and activities, driving a broader impact on the Greek city's everyday life" (*Ibid.*: 72). The project was supported by the Schools of Architecture and Agriculture of the Aristotle University of Thessaloniki. Additionally, for its implementation a network of private sponsors, official institutions, experts and citizens participated in its different stages. This plot, officially designated for educational use, was opened as a public green space when the municipal gardening service that occupied it for years moved out. It was soon offered—without any property transfer or any other official process—to the organizers of *Kipos³*. As the project's creators stated during our interview, its uniqueness lies at their experimentation with a blend of "top-down and bottom-up dynamics, landscape design [and] the work of the experts with the shifting forces of communities" (Project co-ordinators, 14/05/2016, *Kipos³* project space, personal interview). The space, which is fenced, locked and hence inaccessible by passers-by when none of the gardeners or creators are present (Figure 17.4), was described during the interview as "shared" rather than public. While the organizers assert that access restriction to outsiders only aims to protect the garden, its symbolic and material connotations remain significant.

Iasonidou Street Park

Another manifestation of a different transformative intent emerged in an unused plot at the city centre, claimed as a small neighbourhood park by citizen groups and volunteers (*We Change the City* and *Friends of Green*) on the World Environment Day 2010. This initiative was supported by many public organizations, private stakeholders and volunteers pursuing an 'urban experiment' and seeking to change Thessaloniki 'from below' by crowdsourcing creativity and action on public space. Inspired by insurgent urban practices elsewhere, the whole endeavour was orchestrated by *Thessaloniki Allios* ('Thessaloniki otherwise'), an initiative put together by the local free press *Parallaxi*.

The transformation of the seemingly public unused plot on Iasonidou Street (Figure 17.5) into a new pocket-sized neighbourhood park was organized

Figure 17.4 Kipos³ fenced garden in 2017
Source: Matina Kapsali, 2017

Figure 17.5 Iasonidou Street Park in 2016, abandoned
Source: Charis Christodoulou, 2016

as an all-day event of volunteering work. Technical assistance was provided by an architectural practice, materials were donated by private companies and people from all around the city invested their labour on a single day to construct the park. However, after that day, the park was sparsely used, even by neighbourhood people. In 2011, during an international conference on public space, *Thessaloniki Allios* organized a second event to mobilize the neighbourhood people and encourage them to take over the park's mainte-nance and to use the space daily. Once more, volunteers from all around the city with municipal assistance cleaned the space, repaired the equipment and organized events. Some people were excited by the feeling of belonging and ownership that arose from actively claiming a public space for the neigh-bourhood and improving the urban environment. However, this instance of participation did not last and neither the nearby residents nor other urban dwellers used the park on a regular basis after the event. Eventually the park was stripped from its equipment and fenced by its legal owner, an act which demonstrated the private owner's absolute property rights. The absence of any reaction by the area's residents to the fencing of the space (Toulas 2013), combined with their lack of interest regarding the use of the park, could be the result of their limited participation and inclusion during the initial stages of the project.

Concluding Discussion

Swyngedouw (2007, 2009) writes that the pivotal terrain in and through which post-politicization unfolds is the urban arena. Nevertheless, post-politicization is not a global project that is transferred unchanged through time and space, but a dynamic process that operates in and through local urban spaces in distinct ways. The post-politics literature generally dismisses participation and volunteering enterprises as a trend entrenched within the mainstream politics of neoliberalism offering a lip service to urban emanci-pation. However, as Larner suggests, there is a need to "focus on the antago-nisms and heterogeneities that cut through neoliberal political projects", and "understand and work with the political possibilities of the current moment" (Larner 2015: 192–197). In this strand, we sought to contribute to the dis-cussion of urban mutations in the crisis-ridden European south and Greece in "inter-contextual" terms (Brenner and Schmid 2015: 163–165).

   In our analysis, we attempted to uncover the hybrid and sometimes con-flictual public terrain in Thessaloniki. As we documented, new agents are introduced in the management of public spaces and citizen groups and pri-vate actors reconsider their role as urban actors undertaking new or broader responsibilities and initiatives. Formal institutions, citizens' initiatives and private companies create complex networks of collaboration and produce new hybrid forms of public space ownership.

   Partnerships between different agents promote public space as a space of citizenship, engagement, empowerment and culture. Indeed, people are becoming involved in increasing numbers, 'taking ownership' of public space through temporary enterprises. A new terrain is unveiled as the hegemony of formal institutions and the constant threat of private interests on public space is relativized and new regimes are rehearsed. While there is no visible transfer of public space property yet, such enterprises of civic engagement and participation point towards the creation of a new paradigm which departs from the traditional model of municipally owned and managed public spaces towards an embodied kind of ownership. As this does not involve solely the private sector but also 'active' citizens, it may be thought to promote a more open and democratic management. Citizens are indeed actively engaged, and public spaces seem to be enlivened by the activities and presence of certain citizen groups. However, as shown in the previous section, this participation of citizens in public space often results in rather exclusionary or elitist practices.

Public space is central in the discourse and practices of the municipality, which embraces the dominant imaginary of attractiveness and safety for public spaces. The examined citizens' initiatives share these depoliticized imaginaries of public space. Without always building physical barriers and gates or clearly stating exclusionary rules of use, they favour certain activities in public space while deeming others 'undesirable'. Thus, they allude to tactics of surveillance introduced by Jane Jacobs (1961) with 'eyes upon the street' and clearly relate to crime prevention in Oscar Newman's 'defensible spaces' in the early 1970s (Newman, 1973).

In the period examined, public spaces were created through deeply consensus-driven processes (Swyngedouw 2007). Even in cases where antagonisms exist, they are only expressed as a competition among elite actors, away from everyday embodied intent. These actors set and operate within a context of opaque rules and procedures. Instead of agonistic debates, disputes over managerial, legal or administrative issues prevail. Post-democracy is, in the case of Thessaloniki, manifested in the form of consensual politics and thus loses its gravity. Indeed, initiatives presented in this chapter do not engage in oppositional campaigns or challenge private property. Instead, they form partnerships between different agents, ranging from the local authorities to private companies. Through these processes, a new order is created wherein urban inhabitants are separated in two categories: the 'responsible' ones, who are recognized by formal institutions and neoliberal governance regimes as 'stakeholders' and whose actions are legitimized, and the 'undesirable' or even dangerous ones, who disrupt the *proper(ty)* order of public space. A consensual arrangement is created in which "all those that are named and counted take part and participate within a given and generally accepted and shared/partitioned social and spatial distribution of things and people" (Swyngedouw 2011: 2).

Thus, while they place an emphasis on citizenship and perform hybrid forms of ownership, the initiatives studied in this chapter operate more as depoliticized underpinnings of the neoliberal politics of competitiveness, attractiveness and safety, rather than emancipatory practices. Previously monolithic bureaucratic and defensive understandings of public space have been destabilized and public space became unveiled as a space of active citizenship. The 'political possibility' of such processes of hybridization, however, is performed and lived when these processes move beyond hegemonic imaginaries, private property rights or exclusionary acts. As people in the city continuously rehearse ways of being-in-common, possibilities transcending the public/private binary may be reframed in an agonistic rather than a consensual way, planting the seeds of alternative and emancipatory urban futures.

References

Blomley, N.K. (2004a) Un-Real Estate Proprietary Space and Public Gardening. *Antipode* 36(4), pp. 614–641.

Blomley, N.K. (2004b) *Unsettling the City: Urban Land and the Politics of Property*. London: Routledge.

Brenner, N. and Schmid, C. (2015) Towards a New Epistemology of the Urban? *City* 19(2–3), pp. 151–182.

Davoudi, S. (2012) Resilience: A Bridging Concept of a Dead End? *Planning Theory and Practice* 13(2), pp. 299–333.

De Magalhaes, C. (2010) Public Space and the Contracting-Out of Publicness: A Framework for Analysis. *Journal of Urban Design* 15(4), pp. 559–574.

FNW (2016) Friends of the New Waterfront. *Facebook Post* [Online]. Available at: www.facebook.com/pg/filoineasparalias/about/?ref=page_internal [Accessed 27 November 2016].

Gavrilidou, E., Kleinmann, H., Oureilidou, E. and Zafeiropoulos, S.G.Z. (2015) Urban Agriculture in Thessaloniki: An Academic Project Meets Reality. *Ri-Vista* 13(2), pp. 60–85.

Gerakaritou, K. (2011) Πάρκο με extreme activities στο κέντρο της Θεσσαλονίκης [Extreme Activities Park in the Centre of Thessaloniki]. *Voria*, 26 September [Online]. Available at: www.voria.gr/article/parko-me-extreme-activities-sto-kentro-tis-thessalonikis [Accessed 26 June 2017].

Jacobs, J. (1961) *The Death and Life of Great American Cities*. New York: Vintage Books.

Kazepov, Y. (2005) Cities of Europe: Changing Contexts, Local Arrangements, and the Challenge to Urban Cohesion. In Y. Kazepov (ed.) *Cities of Europe: Changing Contexts, Local Arrangements, and the Challenge to Urban Cohesion*. Oxford: Blackwell, pp. 3–33.

Korikis, C. (2014) *Los Lampicos—As svisoume oles tis mountzoures apo ti nea paralia* [Los Lampicos: Let's Erase All the Scribbles from the New Waterfront]. *TV Interview to TV100* [Online]. Available at: www.youtube.com/watch?v=m7YUKoeoq5M [Accessed 26 June 2017].

Langstraat, F. and Van Melik, R. (2013) Challenging the End of Public Space: A Comparative Analysis of Publicness in British and Dutch Urban Spaces. *Journal of Urban Design* 18(3), pp. 429–448.

Larner, W. (2015) The Limits of Post-Politics: Rethinking Radical Social Enterprise. In J. Wilson and E. Swyngedouw (eds.) *The Post-Politics and Its Discontents:*

Spaces of Depoliticisation, Spectres of Radical Politics. Edinburgh: Edinburgh University Press, pp. 189–207.

Miller, K.F. (2007) *Designs of the Public: The Private Lives of New York's Public Spaces*. Minneapolis: University of Minnesota Press.

Mitchell, D. and Staeheli, L.A. (2006) Clean and Safe? Property Redevelopment, Public Space, and Homelessness in Downtown San Diego. In S. Low and N. Smith (eds.) *The Politics of Public Space*. New York: Routledge, pp. 105–123.

Mouffe, C. (2004) For an Agonistic Public Sphere. In L. Tønderand and L. Thomassen (eds.) *Radical Democracy: Politics between Abundance and Lack*. Manchester: Manchester University Press.

Municipality of Thessaloniki (2017) *Εθελοντές πρασίνου* [Green Volunteers] [Online]. Available at: www.thessaloniki.gr/ethelontes [Accessed 27 November 2013].

Nemeth, J. and Schmidt, S. (2011) The Privatization of Public Space: Modeling an Measuring Publicness. *Environment and Planning B: Planning and Design* 38(1), pp. 5–23.

Newman, O. (1973) *Defensible Spaces*. New York: Macmillan.

Office of Urban Resilience (2016) *Thessaloniki Preliminary Resilience Assessment 100 Resilient Cities*. Thessaloniki: The Office of Urban Resilience of the Metropolitan Development Agency of Thessaloniki.

Springer, S. (2011) Public Space as Emancipation: Meditations on Anarchism, Radical Democracy, Neoliberalism and Violence. *Antipode* 43(2), pp. 525–562.

Swyngedouw, E. (2007) The Post-Political City. In BAVO (ed.) *Urban Politics Now: Re-Imaging Democracy in the Neoliberal City*. Rotterdam: NAI Publishers, pp. 58–76.

Swyngedouw, E. (2009) The Antinomies of the Postpolitical City: In Search of a Democratic Politics of Environmental Production. *International Journal of Urban and Regional Research* 33(3), pp. 601–620.

Swyngedouw, E. (2011) Interrogating Post-Democratization: Reclaiming Egalitarian Political Spaces. *Political Geography* 30(7), pp. 370–380.

Toulas, G. (2013) Αξίζει τελικά να ονειρεύεσαι; [Is It Finally Worthwhile to Dream?]. *Parallaximag*, 24 January [Online]. Available at: http://parallaximag.gr/thessaloniki/thessaloniki-allios/axizi-telika-na-onirevese [Accessed 1 December 2016].

Van der Walt, A.J. (2009) *Property in the Margins*. Portland: Hart Publishing.

Vitopoulou, A., Gemenetzi, G., Yiannakou, A., Kafkalas, G. and Tassopoulou, A. (2015) *Βιώσιμες πόλεις. Προσαρμογή και ανθεκτικότητα σε περιόδους κρίσης* [Sustainable Cities: Adaptation and Resilience in Periods of Crisis]. Athens: NTUA-Kallipos.

Zafeirakis, K. (2014) 'Φίλοι της Νέας Παραλίας': Γιορτάζουν τον 1 χρόνο λειτουργίας της Νέας Παραλίας ['Friends of the New Waterfront': They Celebrate the 1 Year of Operation of the New Waterfront]. *The Huffington Post*, 5 December [Online]. Available at: www.huffingtonpost.gr/2014/12/05/filoi-neas-paralias-_n_6274748.html [Accessed 27 November 2016].

Conclusion

18 Public Space Unbound

Emancipatory Praxis and Lived Space

Tihomir Viderman and Sabine Knierbein

Gaining Emancipatory Ground

Moments of emancipation mark turning points in urban history. By unsettling urban routines, such moments introduce decisive changes to lived experience of space and time. Urban routines are imbued with the hope that the capacity of the human body to contest social constraints through improvisation and invention can transform modes of daily action. Emancipatory struggle had been endorsed during industrialization and related struggles of social reordering and restructuring, and it has again been evoked as global urbanization has gained momentum. This chapter draws conceptual connections between lived space and the praxis of radical democracy and thus includes into the analysis of socio-spatial relations notions of affect, passion and dissent alongside with reason, arguments and consent. In so doing, we establish analytical paths and methodologies for grasping emancipatory spatial praxis embedded in daily urban struggles, routines and experiences.

Contributions to this volume engage with emancipation beyond its modernist metanarrative in favour of both appreciation for and critical acclaim of emancipation as a key concept within post-foundational thought. Scholars analyzing the post-political condition of current liberal democracies have provided useful connections to possible conceptualizations of societal ordering within political theory. While most of the literature linking spatial praxis to emancipation tends to celebrate large-scale (revolutionary) acts, contributions to this volume draw attention to mo(ve)ments and places of change that sprout in cracks of structural power systems, often emerging from the messy minutiae of everyday life. By taking the critique of the capitalist production of space as a point of departure, we first delineate a somewhat paradoxical perseverance of the modernist conceptualizations of lived space as public space. Further, we argue that the productive critique of the post-political condition emerges in embodied space of engaged groups and individuals who in their emancipatory endeavours and encounters create very material (lived) places of capacity building. Based on the provided theoretical, empirical and methodological considerations, we sketch three main paths forward to work with emancipation:

Emancipation as Theme/Subject of Investigation

Post-foundational thinkers' claims for egalitarian difference in recognizing emancipation as an unequal struggle for equality have been somewhat anticipated by the more unorthodox Marxists claiming to combine an ethics of difference with the urge to unlock emancipation from the modernist fixation on progress:

> Insurgent democratic politics, . . . are radically anti-utopian; they are not about fighting for a utopian future, but are precisely about bringing into being, spatializing, what is already promised by the very principle upon which the political is constituted, i.e. equalitarian emancipation.
>
> (Swyngedouw 2015: 174)

Hence, emancipation has been reactivated in urban research and praxis as a call for the reinstatement of radical democracy, which "can be conceived as a basis for emancipation because it emphasizes non-violence and allows for dissent and difference. In contrast, overemphasizing consensus, coupled with aversion to confrontation 'engenders apathy and disaffection with political participation'" (Springer 2011: 531, referring to Mouffe 2004: 125). In this way, practical emancipation helps raise concerns, develop desires, articulate needs and provide solutions to make the city itself a real political project for social emancipation. A lack of egalitarian politics and social justice is thus the problem the concept of emancipation describes.

Emancipatory Urban Research, a Collective Project

Contributions to this volume have combined sociocultural analysis of the structural production of social inequalities with theoretical care for contextualizing emancipatory saying, seeing and doing. Tyler's (2015) reconceptualization of 'class' substantiates this approach as she (*Ibid.*: 1) examines the sociological practice of drawing conceptual lines between individuals and collectives by revisiting Bourdieu's (1984: 483) remark: "the fate of groups is bound up with the words that designate them". Through the contextualization of sociocultural aspects of class within broader political endeavours for societal change, Tyler articulates a critique against conceptualizations of class as an identity in favour of its radical understanding as a struggle against inequality. The lessons we can draw from this type of emancipatory advance to reveal gridlocked ways of thinking and doing social research is that the nature of the subjects we do research with needs to inform the nature of the research design: Therefore, research on urban emancipation ideally includes emancipatory ways of doing research, empowering oneself by the expanding methodological practices and perspectives of a researcher, but also creates opportunities for other researchers to participate and share the fruits of collective research efforts.

Emancipatory Placemaking: Embodied Space and Affective Encounters

Many contributors have recommended expanding urban and spatial analysis beyond rational discourse. However, an effort to involve theories on the body and affect into the conceptualization of emancipation is yet to be made, notwithstanding Lefebvre's (2014 [1947]) and Rancière's (2009) bodies of work that have already engaged theory production from and for the fields of arts, performance and dance. We argue that there is a need to establish connections between (1) an *emancipatory capacity to know* and (2) an *emancipatory power to act* which requires situating emancipatory praxis and thought within embodied space of everyday lives characterized by affective encounters, or, as Watson (2006) has it, by (dis)enchantments of urban encounters. The recognition of the spatial dimension of the political practice reveals emancipatory struggles as having path-dependency: Even though their universal demands might be articulated in the global realm, they have a place of origin in a specific everyday life setting and develop from and within the local space of bodies (Butler 2015), i.e. embodied space (Moore 2013). Uneven development and conditions of experienced social inequality, however, also mediate through bodies and embodied space.

On Ordinary, Practical, Critical and Active Emancipation

Having developed three recommendations for research on emancipation, in this section we discover how the empirical, methodological and conceptual ideas of the collected contributions have influenced our initial reading of emancipation. Four perspectives corresponding to the book sections help us synthesize the findings: *Emancipation is real*, *Emancipation is practised*, *Emancipation matters*, and *Emancipation is lived*.

Emancipation Is Real

The ideas of many planning theorists regarding emancipation echo the Habermasian ideal-speech situation, which has been conceived as a means of overcoming power relations through practising rational consensus (for a critique, see Gabauer, this volume). However, "instead of bringing about emancipation", such a proceeding "introduces a fundamental dependency into the logic of emancipation, since the one to be emancipated remains dependent upon the truth or knowledge revealed to [them] by the emancipator" (Biesta 2010: 40, referring to Rancière 2009). By articulating emancipation as real, we emphasize the existing plurality of knowledgeable embodied practices which enact change in everyday lives. Irrespective of their effectiveness in materializing their visionary projects, we argue that embodied practices carry the potential to unbound public space from modernist conceptualizations of emancipation as a (phantasmatic) promise of revolutionary change or a broad consensus: Insight into these practices offers a way to incorporate the experience and wisdom of everyday life into a conception of emancipation that combines reason and affect. Laclau (2007 [1996]), however, reminds that ambivalences regarding the modernist articulation of promises remain inscribed in emancipatory endeavours.

The book section on 'Everyday Emancipation' (Part I) has shed a light on territories in conflict and under post-political conditions, affected both within and beyond by the role of institutions. The effects of the political and the absence of democratic values accrue sedimentarily across the globe, manifesting as built structures producing *heterotopic counter sites* and *ambivalent utopian practices* between grand-scale projects and local dwellers' actions (chapter 2). Other conflictive sites require a *shift in attention within the post-political debate* to focus on the relations *between institutional politics and insurgent claims to the political* (chapter 3). Public policy and law can be creatively used to de-privatize land and properties in *territories challenged by Mafia rule and violence* (chapter 4). However, a more socio-theoretical approach suggests that the *focus on law in emancipation debates* needs to be overcome by *opening new emancipatory paths* gearing towards an *ethics of everyday encounters* (chapter 5).

The spatial dimension of emancipatory action cannot be separated from everyday life. By conceptualizing public space as a vision for and a practice of radical democracy, Springer (2011) made a valuable contribution towards establishing the relationship between emancipation and its spatial form. Public space is where agonism and antagonisms sediment as embodied and affective geographies: "It is in spaces of the public that the discovery of both power and demos is made, and it is in the contestation of public space that democracy lives" (*Ibid.*: 554). Both the notion of emancipation and public space, however, can be considered (part of the same) metanarrative (Lyotard 1980). We earnestly engaged with this criticism towards conceptualizing emancipation as an endlessly open pursuit unfolding through affective encounters and experiences. Accordingly, we argue that emancipatory struggle is enacted through ethical engagement with others, whether in conflict or 'getting along' (Shields, this volume), which creates a meaningful visible change for concerned publics in the present, sometimes in opposition to unmaterialized utopian fantasies. These struggles render everyday life political. Everyday life, in this sense, includes both design utopias and past pragmatisms of planning to display what society has desired and how it has desired, while simultaneously serving as both a motivation and medium for negotiating urban futures.

We pick up from here and engage with performative features of spatial(ized) emancipations as part of everyday lives, including notions of affect, passion and dissent. This allows us to conceptually detach emancipation from public space, which is charged with modernist, capitalist and colonialist underpinnings, and embed it in lived space, which is understood as an impetus, medium and objective of emancipatory struggles.

Emancipation Is Practiced

Practices of everyday life, regardless whether premediated or routinized, constitute political relations between subjects, or between subjects and things including nature, but also to oneself including the body, motivations and emotions (Reckwitz 2002: 259). While they might not make a 'politics of protest', they do constitute a "direct and disparate action" at places of everyday life "where various members of ethnic, racial, and religious groupings are conditioned to mix, mingle, undertake everyday encounters, and experience trust with one another" (Bayat 2013: 14). Their emancipatory capacity does not lie exclusively with the dimension of habituated encounters with others, but also in their role as unpremeditated tactical engagements in negotiating spatial appropriations and urban routines. Bayat's argument also points to a possible direction for discussing realities of lived space of concrete projects, which appear to be neither an ideal type of universal emancipatory struggle nor competition grounds of political and economic elites. In a broader understanding, such lived space is produced by a myriad of horizontally organized actors and collectives that equally rely upon theoretical and practice-based dimensions of inclusionary and involved practices. Involved learning about lived space does not only aim at attaining knowledge about a particular social space, but also at emancipating oneself through a responsive and reflexive interaction with research subjects to co-produce space.

A thriving scene of actors and performative practices, many of them rooted in design and planning disciplines, engages in creating potential situations of everyday emancipation for multiple city publics. These endeavours tend to be transdisciplinary and translocal in nature, thus changing notions of professional and experiential knowledge and practice. Planners and designers are confronted with the question of how their professional practice can make a difference. Situated learning about lived space as a practice of genuine and sensitive engagement with cultural and social difference may be one of the emancipatory means of overcoming one's prejudices, fears and mental barriers towards a particular social space and group.

Contributions included in Part II, 'Practical Emancipation', relativize the modern relations between professional knowledge and lay practices and explore how communities, their endeavours and concrete actions have considered the lives of residents, newcomers and communities across multiple scales and fields. These chapters systematically cover accounts spanning emancipatory action through *insurgencies challenging structures* and *power relations* (chapter 6); emancipatory planning through *participatory projects* (chapter 7); emancipatory practices through *multicultural events* (chapter 8); and *emancipatory tools of urban research praxis* (chapter 9), thus fostering transdisciplinary and translocal research and post-migrational perspectives.

In the collective production of knowledge, emancipation is understood as an endeavour that starts from oneself. Negotiating power and space inevitably means engaging with a plurality of social roles and identities. Our own emancipation should therefore not be considered of secondary importance. Self-reflection regarding representations, perceptions and prejudices of a particular social space or group plays a key role for an informed and more sensible action embedded in lived space. Johnson et al. (2004: 50f) emphasize: "Research is practice, or praxis in the strongest sense, aimed at social betterment or emancipation and seeking to overcome the splits between subjects and objects of research and between science and politics." While drawing reference to Gramsci's idea of the 'real philosopher', they stress that

> 'each one of us changes [themselves] . . . to the extent that [they] change and modify the complex relations of which [they are] the hub'. So that the 'real philosopher' (in the wider sense of knower) is the politically active person . . . who changes 'the ensemble of relations which each of us enter to take part in'.
>
> (Johnson et al. 2004: 50f, referring to Gramsci 1971: 351)

Emancipation Matters

In Gramsci's understanding of emancipation, "the struggle between ways of viewing reality is not a struggle between equals" and hence "emancipation in praxis needs to be preceded by ideational emancipation" (Bieler and Morton 2006: 78–79, referring to Gramsci). The ideational emancipation acts as a counter notion to oppressive practices and institutions of cultural hegemony, such as roles or classes, which are internalized as 'natural and right' by the broadest part of society. It concentrates on cultivating an alternative culture as the basis of an ideological resistance and the necessary means of persuading the oppressed and exploited to undertake a political action. In this sense,

> the first step in emancipating oneself from political and social slavery is freeing the mind . . . A new society cannot simply be constructed in practice. Rather, it must already be 'ideally active' in the minds of those fighting for change.
>
> (Gramsci 1985: 39, cited by Bieler and Morton 2006: 79)

Rancière's position is somewhat reminiscent of Gramsci's notion of time-space:

> Emancipation begins when we challenge the opposition between viewing and acting; when we understand that the self-evident facts that structure the relations between saying, seeing and doing themselves belong to the structure of domination. . . . It begins when we understand that viewing is also an action that confirms or transforms this distribution of positions. The spectator also acts.
>
> (Rancière 2009: 13)

At first sight, this perspective stands in a strong contrast with positions rooted in historical materialism, in which praxis is the main starting point for any theorization (Schmid 2005, referring to Lefebvre's oeuvre). Strict historical materialism risks flattening the necessitation of exploring possibilities embedded within difference more thoroughly. De Sousa Santos (2006: 53) argues for a necessity to construct emancipation starting from a new relation between respect for equality and the principle of recognizing difference. In this sense, a theoretical striving for equality needs to start from a recognition of difference, and thus dissent. Merrifield (2006: 114) adds that implementing the right to difference requires a "titanic combat between homogenizing powers and differential capacities". The 'right to difference', however, as Lefebvre warned, is very difficult to transform into formal demand, therefore rather than promoting yet another abstract right among others, it should be considered the source of them (*Ibid.*, referring to Lefebvre 1970: 45). At second sight, the politics of difference and a link to everyday life are immanent in the works of both Gramsci and Lefebvre, which enable crossovers between emancipatory thinking of unorthodox Marxist positions that rely on Lefebvre and emancipatory de- and reconstructions of post-Marxist thinkers drawing on Gramsci's work in political theory.

By putting the modern(ist) traditions in which Western planning and design professionals remain at the centre of radical critique, chapter authors in Part III, 'Critical Emancipation', decolonize and de-normalize action relating to oppression, injustice and social inequalities inherent in global urbanization processes. These contributions contrast the fast-growing number of consensus-oriented approaches and help to carve out multiple meanings and roles of lived space in times of resurging new authoritarianisms and post-sectarian divides and under post-war and postcolonial circumstances. Critique includes urban planning *emancipations from colonial pasts* through grassroots initiatives (chapter 10), urban design *emancipations from neoauthoritarian and neoconservative contexts* (chapter 11), an *emancipatory update of agonistic planning theory* including the acknowledgement of affect, passions and aporias in the social world (chapter 12), and *emancipations from traumatic and conflict-ridden pasts* in unstable geographical contexts (chapter 13).

Lefebvre and Gramsci both share a perspective on the enactment of emancipatory struggles, where even the smallest engagement or act of negotiating difference in everyday life institutes a certain dimension of emancipation. Emancipatory capacities of planning, however, cannot be unlocked by merely involving a growing number of stakeholders in communicative and collaborative procedures, which exclude affect and passion. Instead of retaining its domain to representations of space, planning must embrace lived space of a pluralist society of which dissent is part. Set against the perseverance of modernist planning to insert abstract planning institutions and instruments, such as hierarchical distribution or glossy hyperreal images of imagined urban environments, into lived space; critical design praxis thus involves multiple publics and supports the production of knowledge about space in a collectively shared manner, consequently fostering a positive politics of difference and encounter. Critical designers maintain relationships with diverse groups, hear dissent, give hope and provide means to publics to become active agents of their own urban transformation.

Emancipation Is Lived

Emancipatory struggles resonate with the Lefebvre's dialectics established in his *Critique of Everyday Life* (*Ibid.*: 2014): taken-for-granted, trivial and alienating practices of everyday life support hegemony of capitalist production of space, yet, everyday life moments also simultaneously carry a great potential of producing moments of possibility by continuously allowing revision of the boundaries between 'possible' and 'impossible'. In view of this dialectics, a critical insight into political, economic and social attempts to ground a social order uncovers an inherent tendency towards producing the 'other' while simultaneously reinforcing fears and suspicion of that 'other' within the hegemonic public.

Despite a plurality of participatory methodologies developed within the fields of planning and design to gain knowledge of people's struggles, needs and desires, they hardly ever reach members of publics who have very little power or capital. We argue that such endeavours are often ineffective not because of the lack of commitment on part of planning professionals, but because they are built on the post-political premise of public space, rather than on the promise of radical democratization that lived space entails. Where post-political accounts of public space have merely conceptualized public space as a container, the resurgence of lived space analysis focuses on a relational conception of space imbued with both power relations and moments of opportunity for escaping structural constraints. Lived space and everyday life have been scrutinized as sets of politically charged and "likely conflicting and unequal" social processes, practices and relations which both sediment within and are influenced by society's histories of struggles for concrete emancipatory projects (Massey 2005: 151–152, 181). The possibility of politics has thus been linked to "conceptualizing space as open, multiple and relational, unfinished and always becoming" (Massey 2005: 59). In addition to rational dimensions, this relational approach also involves a focus on bodies and affect and performative action, which have been included within urban research by feminist, queer and postcolonial studies.

Contributions from the book section 'Active Emancipation' (Part IV) have addressed this matter to discuss different forms of dealing with controversial aspects of individual, collective, public or hybrid ownership of and belonging to private areas, public space and urban commons, understood as counter sites of urban resistance and solidarity. The contributions include emancipatory practices in the field of *reclaiming abandoned industrial sites* (chapter 14), *emancipations of self-organizing workers* recovering production processes and *taking over the ownership of factories* in decline (chapter 15), *debates on urban commoning* under post-democratic conditions (chapter 16), and a *critical revision of the ambivalent notions of hybrid ownership in public space* in contexts of austerity (chapter 17).

Changes in the urban fabric reveal a tension between particular and universal interests, a tension which is best mirrored in the efforts of conceptualizing public space in capitalism. Equality in public space can never be achieved, as there is an inherent division already employed when defining public space. Following the reasoning of post-foundational thinkers, the need for constant and never-ending definition of who is part of a city and who is not, of who is heard in a city and who is not, of who is seen in a city and who is not, is an essential ingredient of defining and redefining publics. Any static articulation of what a public is or any attempt to socially ground its 'essence' therefore condemn it to failure. Radical democracy claims can only be achieved through lived spaces in their broadest sense and under constant negotiation of whose lived space is concerned. *Public Space Unbound*, therefore, is to be understood as an urgent need to raise a storm of conceptual critique against public space. For some, this storm will end in a reconceptualization of public space. For others—as shown in this volume—this storm will offer an invitation to dive beyond conceptions of public space which have historically been initiated with the rise of capitalist spatial separation (Lofland 2009 [1998]; Tornaghi and Knierbein 2015), and thus cannot be unbound from conflict-ridden pasts.

Emancipation Now!

Contributions to this volume have expanded the purview of the ethical dimensions of politics. We argue, by using Marchart's (2011) considerations of (doing) politics, that ethics is central to creating inclusive space for emancipation. In view of this perspective, any concerted effort, regardless of its scale or effectiveness, which is aimed at collectively producing knowledge, or engaging strategies and tactics in pursuit of meaningful change for concerned publics, constitutes an emancipatory struggle. Emancipated individuals and groups assume the social responsibility of their actions and take an active conscious role in transforming their lived space (Schmied-Kowarzik 1998). Virtues of solidarity with others, particularly with those who are not part of one's community, and respect of difference are intuitively recognized as key constituents of any such an ethical engagement. For the political project of emancipation, though, an ethical interaction with the Other primarily understands that "one's own political project should be open to heterogeneous demands" (Marchart 2011: 969). A democratic ethics inscribed in radical gestures nurtures a divergence and complexity of perspectives channelled into political agendas challenging exclusionary power structures. However, we also claim that political ethics and ethical encounters are not only crucial for defining what kind of urban futures we wish for ourselves, but also for imbuing everyday struggles with the necessary transformative hope. Here we refer to either individuals or collectives who, by creating affective bonds and solidarity linkages under the claim 'real democracy now', practice equality in a political present (presentist democracy, Lorey 2016). The focus on political ethics and affect in the research field allows

us to recognize emancipatory capacity in a plurality of struggles involving negotiations of difference and appropriations of space. Through our exploration of
post-foundational critique, we have joined with scholars rejecting the grand
modernist narrative of emancipation yet to come. Our rejection of this narrative
includes the recognition of the plurality of social foundations as always varied,
contingent and temporarily established (Marchart 2011: 966). The promise
of change can no longer be conceptualized of within a singular dialectics of
co-optation and revolution; rather, it must be sought in a multiplicity of hope-
filled political actions that range in scale from the small performative act to
the politics of grand revolutions. Spatial dimensions of emancipation entail
meaningful spaces of everyday encounters, affective interactions in lived space,
solidarity in struggles opposing capitalist urbanization and (political) passion
to engender structural transformation. Planners' and researchers' engagement
in the research field also has a capacity to tackle the silences and absences of
those whose voices are not heard and who may not have the requisite social,
cultural or economic capital to spatially exert power. Consequently, modes
of research may influence the possibility of passionate emancipatory struggle
against oppressive post-political governance regimes. Research approaches
must therefore expand both the subject of their practice as well as the narratives that construct and drive current prototypical methods and deliverables
of urban research. We conclude that public space must be unbound from its
modernist, colonialist and capitalist conceptualizations. This volume attempted
to deal with this needed reconceptualization, beyond the rational spatial order
of public-private divide, and in support of an inclusive lived space of everyday
emancipations with many facets and a broad range of possibilities.

Emancipation assumes political subjects whose claim for equality is firmly
rooted in an action of bodies and minds banded together, rather than a passive equal distribution managed by institutions or actors in power. Working
against rational promises of modern progress, contributions to this volume
have understood emancipation as now and real. In challenging utopian conceptualizations, this volume has articulated emancipation as a spatial praxis
and a vehicle of social critique which have been enacted and embodied in
urban lived space as an outcry for radical democracy. In this sense, non-
typical methods of inquiry are not just alternatives to predominant Western
modes of urban analysis but productive spaces of both urban research and
urban emancipation. Within the space of global urbanization, the notion
of emancipatory universality translates into "the prioritization of the lived
over the conceived", as well as transcending "compartmentalization between
thinking and acting, between theory and practice, life and thought—dissocia-
tion and sundering that spelled alienation and indifference" (Merrifield 2006:
115, referring to Lefebvre). Emancipation, hence, resonates with (the critique
of) lived space and starts from de-everydaying ordinary life:

> The question of 'making strange' or 'estrangement' is going to be a cru-
> cial tool for everyday life studies. . . . 'The theory of estrangement, which

always takes off from the numbness and familiarity of everyday life, must estrange us from the everyday.' . . . It is the everyday that receives our 'daily inattention' . . . and invites us to look elsewhere. It is to the everyday that we consign that which no longer holds our attention. Things become everyday by becoming invisible, unnoticed, part of the furniture. And if familiarity does not always breed contempt, it does encourage neglect.

(Highmore 2002: 21, citing Jameson 1998: 84)

Within this perspective, field work across a plurality of scales of lived space ranging from structural critique to mundane routines, is a key entry point to empirically track down contemporary emancipations, their ambivalences and spatial ramifications. In urban studies, emancipation has recently been coined as a conceptual framework for challenging a Western-centric bias prevailing in disciplines contributing to the study of urbanization. This critique invites perspectives and approaches which problematize inherited configurations of power within and pertaining to a particular research field, culture or place, thus expanding the dynamics and narratives produced within urbanism. Design and planning disciplines, involved professionals and engaged parts of publics, as well as their learning environments, carry a significant share of responsibility in urban restructuring and thus have more than one important role to play. Opportunities for emancipation exist across all scales and types of research, communities, populations and locations, particularly when their arrangement is uniquely responsive to the local conditions of everyday life and lived space while also producing linkages that cultivate mutual purpose and unity between those in dissent. Andy Merrifield (2006: 119) speaks to several such possibilities of these political roles, when affirming that:

we might start by emancipating ourselves and reclaiming our own work space, giving a nod to disruption rather than cooptation, to real difference rather than cowering conformity. Yet before imagination can seize power, some imagination is needed: imagination to free our minds and our bodies, to liberate our ideas, and to reclaim our society as a lived project . . . It's a project that can begin this afternoon.

(*Ibid.*)

References

Bayat, A. (2013 [2010]) *Life as Politics: How Ordinary People Change the Middle East*. Stanford, CA: Stanford Press.

Bieler, A. and Morton, A.D. (2006) *Images of Gramsci: Connections and Contentions in Political Theory and International Relations*. New York: Routledge.

Biesta, G. (2010) A New Logic of Emancipation: The Methodology of Jacques Rancière. *Educational Theory* 60(1), pp. 39–59.

Bourdieu, P. (1984) *Distinction: A Social Critique of the Judgement of Taste* (Translated by R. Nice). London: Routledge & Kegan Paul.

Butler, J. (2015) *Notes toward a Performative Theory of Assembly*. Cambridge: Harvard University Press.

De Sousa Santos, B. (2006) *Renovar la teoría crítica y reinventar la emancipación social*. Buenos Aires: Clacso Libros.

Gramsci, A. (1971) *Selections from the Prison Notebooks*. New York: International Publishers.

Gramsci, A. (1985) *Selections from Cultural Writings* (Edited by D. Forgacs and G. Nowell-Smith, translated by W. Boelhower). London: Lawrence and Wishart.

Highmore, B. (2002) *The Everyday Life Reader*. London: Routledge.

Jameson, F. (1998) *Brecht and Method*. London: Verso.

Johnson, R., Chambers, S., Raghuram, P. and Tincknell, E. (2004) *The Practice of Cultural Studies*. London: Sage Publications.

Laclau, E. (2007 [1996]) *Emancipation(s)*. London: Verso.

Lefebvre, H. (1970) *Le manifeste différentialiste*. Paris: Gallimard.

Lefebvre, H. (2014 [1947]) *The Critique of Everyday Life: The One Volume Edition*. London: Verso.

Lofland, L.H. (2009 [1998]) *The Public Realm: Exploring the Cities Quintessential Social Territory*. Brunswick: Aldine Transaction.

Lorey, I. (2016) Presentist Democracy: The Now-Time of Struggles. In A. Oberprantacher and A. Siclodi (eds.) *Subjectivation in Political Theory and Contemporary Practice*. London: Palgrave Macmillan, pp. 149–164.

Lyotard, J.F. (1980) *The Post-Modern Condition: A Report on Knowledge* (Translated by G. Bennington). Minneapolis: University of Minnesota Press.

Marchart, O. (2011) Democracy and Minimal Politics: The Political Difference and Its Consequences. *The South Atlantic Quarterly* 110(4), pp. 965–973.

Massey, D. (2005) *For Space*. Thousand Oaks: Sage Publications.

Merrifield, A. (2006) *Henri Lefebvre: A Critical Introduction*. New York: Routledge.

Moore, S. (2013) Taking Up Space: Anthropology and Embodied Protest. *Radical Anthropology* 7, pp. 6–16.

Mouffe, C. (2004) For an Agonistic Public Sphere. In L. Tønder and L. Thomassen (eds.) *Radical Democracy: Politics between Abundance and Lack*. Manchester: Manchester University Press, pp. 123–132.

Rancière, J. (2009) *The Emancipated Spectator*. London: Verso.

Reckwitz, A. (2002) Toward a Theory of Social Practices: A Development in Culturalist Theorizing. *European Journal of Social Theory* 5(2), pp. 243–263.

Schmid, C. (2005) *Stadt. Raum. Gesellschaft. Henri Lefebvre und die Theorie der Produktion des Raumes*. Stuttgart: Franz Steiner.

Schmied-Kowarzik, W. (1998) Karl Marx as a Philosopher of Human Emancipation. *Poznan Studies in the Philosophy of the Sciences and the Humanities* 60, pp. 355–368.

Springer, S. (2011) Public Space as Emancipation: Meditations on Anarchism, Radical Democracy, Neoliberalism and Violence. *Antipode* 43(2), pp. 525–562.

Swyngedouw, E. (2015) Insurgent Architects, Radical Cities and the Promise of the Political. In J. Wilson and E. Swyngedouw (eds.) *The Post-Political and Its Discontents*. Edinburgh: Edinburgh University Press, pp. 171–188.

Tornaghi, C. and Knierbein, S. (eds.) (2015) *Public Space and Relational Perspectives: New Challenges for Architecture and Planning*. New York: Routledge.

Tyler, I. (2015) Classificatory Struggles: Class, Culture and Inequality in Neoliberal Times. *The Sociological Review* 63(2), pp. 493–511.

Watson, S. (2006) *City Publics: The (Dis)enchantments of Urban Encounters*. New York: Routledge.

Index

Note: page numbers in *italic* type refer to Figures; those in **bold** type refer to Tables.